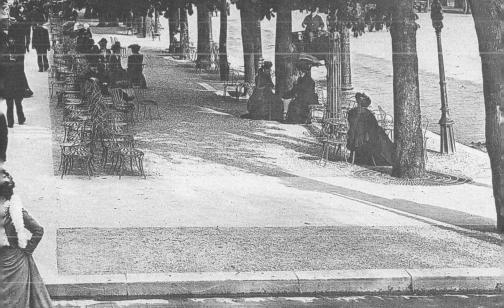

les Champs-Élysées

PARIS ON THE EVE

VINCENT CRONIN

PARIS
ON THE EVE
1900-1914

St. Martin's Press
New York

Library of Congress Cataloging-in-Publication Data

Cronin, Vincent.
    Paris on the eve, 1900–1914 / Vincent Cronin.
      p. cm.
    "A Thomas Dunne book."
    Includes bibliographical references and index.
    ISBN 0-312-04876-9
    1. Paris (France)—Intellectual life—20th century. 2. Arts—France—
Paris—History—20th century. 3. Intellectuals—France—
Paris—Biography. 4. World War, 1914–1918—France—Paris.
I. Title.
DC735.C76   1991
944'.360813—dc20   90-49008
                                                       CIP

First published in Great Britain by William Collins Sons and Company Limited.

First U.S. Edition: April 1991
10 9 8 7 6 5 4 3 2 1

for
Chantal

CONTENTS

ACKNOWLEDGEMENTS

Among friends who have been so kind as to help me with factual information or suggestions I particularly wish to thank the following: Basil Rooke-Ley, who has a flair for unearthing useful items in obscure corners of *The Times*, the *Independent* and the *Guardian*, and Nicolas de Schonen, who on my behalf combed files of French newspapers, examined the archives relating to Philippe Berthelot and Madame Cruppi, and copied family letters in the Delcassé files of the Archives du Ministère des Affaires Etrangères. I am also indebted to Julia Piasecka, who researched for me Péguy's *L'Argent* and *L'Argent suite*, and the abolition of theatre censorship, and to Olivier Michel of the Musée Maurice Denis, Saint Germain en Laye, who helped me with the Nabis and lent me his copy of a scarce biography of Gaston Gallimard.

In any non-fiction work structure and the elaboration of general themes owe much to an author's editor. For twenty years I have had the rare good fortune to be guided by one who is outstandingly perceptive and devoted. She has been too modest to allow me to thank her publicly before; now, at last, I should like to express my deep indebtedness to Elizabeth Walter for her help with this book and with its seven predecessors.

INTRODUCTION

France in 1900 was still a regional nation. The citizens of Bordeaux had different commercial interests from the citizens of Lyon or Marseille, and values too that were not quite the same. They operated their own Bourse, they published and read their own local newspapers, their intelligent young attended the local university. On Sundays in winter they went to watch bullfights. Though the Government publicly disapproved of England's war against the Boers, your fashionable Bordelais was pro-English, thanks to the long connection through the wine trade, and his stylish grey flannel suit would have been tailored in Savile Row. The Mediterranean, which was still Mare Nostrum to a Marseillais, meant as little to a Bordelais as did the German, Italian and Swiss banking links that provided a Lyonnais with the means to enjoy Lucullan meals. Paris, it is true, was *par excellence* the administrative and decision-making city, but remote, eight hours from Bordeaux by train.

This regionalism derived in part from history – Brittany accepted French rule as late as 1532, Nice only in 1860 – and, as in the United States, in part from geography. Paris is a city of the north-west, close to a vulnerable frontier; indeed Christianity, spreading from Rome up the river valleys, arrived there late, and the Archbishop of Lyon, on the Rhône, is still 'primate of the Gauls'.

Paris too was a region of France. The most populous,

13

the most influential, but still only a region. It is one of Europe's most ancient capitals, and with those two other Roman cities, London and Vienna, it has kept up a millennial rivalry and, sometimes, enmity. Partly because of that ancient lineage, partly because it could take justifiable pride in its immense contributions to civilization, nationalism was stronger here than in the provinces. Marseille, Bordeaux, Nantes felt the need to have friendly relations with neighbours or nearby overseas nations, but Paris wished to outdo, to excel, and, if necessary, to throw her weight about. In many ways Paris was more narrow-minded than the provincial cities, certainly more self-centred. It was of Parisians that an Englishman was thinking when he described France as the largest island in Europe.

French people of the provinces, by and large, are not show-offs. There are jewellers in Lyon, but no flashy jewellery shops such as those in Paris's rue de la Paix; they are installed in discreet first-floor offices without velvet showcases, for the Lyonnais are averse to displaying wealth or luxury, fearing to excite envy and, possibly, trade union claims. Your Parisian, by contrast, likes nothing better than to be envied, to be talked about.

In London Crown and Court set the tone. In Paris, no longer a royal city, the tone was set by higher civil servants, who in an age of short-lived governments possessed very considerable power, and by men, either intellectuals or business men, who had climbed or fought their way to the top. But the royal imprint lingered in a taste for aristocratic values and excellence of craftsmanship.

Your Parisian around 1900 might have been characterized by a tolerant Englishman as courageous, hardworking, with strong family loyalty, filled with a sense of his own importance, argumentative, touchy, given to

14

duelling. He prided himself on civilized living but probably did not own a comfortable armchair. Comfort did not interest him – he had so many more pressing matters in mind. Febrile? Perhaps, especially in politics where, then as now, his heart was on the left, his pocket-book on the right.

One other distinctive characteristic was noted by Rudyard Kipling in 1913: 'First to follow Truth and last to leave old truths behind.' There is a paradox here to be looked at later: how innovation arises from, and can best be nurtured by, a strong traditional inertia.

Englishmen tended to think of the city on the Seine as a place where intending artists – Wilson Steer, for instance, and Gwen John – went to learn how to paint or where discriminating music-lovers went to hear excellent organ recitals; where, too, a bachelor might spend a naughty weekend. Henry James viewed it as a literary meeting-place, where he could dine with Flaubert and converse with Turgenev – but he felt more at home in London, and Henry Adams was less drawn to Paris than to regional France – to Chartres and to Mont Saint-Michel. But to the educated men and women of eastern and south-eastern Europe Paris was all-in-all the city that provided books, plays, paintings, fashion, and to Paris many from these nations gravitated: Greeks like the symbolist poet Jean Moréas, Italians like d'Annunzio and Chirico, Rumanians like Proust's friends, the Bibesco brothers, and the actor Edouard de Max – the list could be extended. These adopted citizens enriched Paris with their talents and insights.

From the turn of the nineteenth century until the beginning of the European War in 1914 Paris was the scene of creative thinking and invention unusually rich in quantity and quality. Across a wide spectrum from physics to aviation, from literature to the newly developing cinema, the achievements were important and remain so.

Some of the creators, such as Proust, Picasso, Marie Curie have been the subject of detailed studies and monographs, as have some of the artistic influences such as the Ballets Russes. But the present work has two main aims. The first is to bring to life the creative achievements not in isolated compartments but as a whole. Almost every group of thinkers and creators influenced its neighbours. Either in practical terms or, just as important, in mood there was a continual knock-on effect. For example, France's remarkable development of the motor-car changed Proust's way of life in summer, allowing him to visit remote churches in Upper Normandy. This in turn led him to write influential newspaper articles in which he challenged the Government's plan to turn 'uneconomic' churches into museums or civic centres and in which he asserted the value of France's Christian heritage, a view which played its part in the movement of national revival.

The second aim is to present the period largely in terms of people. It concentrates on certain leading characters who, thanks to the survival of correspondence, of diaries or of memories by friends, happen to be knowable intimately. A considerable amount of the material, notably that relating to Gide, Proust, Romain Rolland and the Abbé Mugnier, confessor and friend to Paris's intellectuals, has only recently been published, and is here first used in an English book.

Also about the turn of the century Paris, as the seat of government, initiated a foreign policy more adventurous than the lie-low attitude of the thirty years after France's defeat by Prussia in 1870. This policy was not something separate from other fields of achievement. France as a republic was highly democratic, and an independent press of high quality – Paris had more newspapers than London, Berlin or New York – ensured that the views of her intelligentsia were widely read. Voltaire, Hugo and Lamartine had played an active role in the politics of the late eighteenth and early nineteenth centuries; the period 1900–14 saw other, lesser, but equally sincere writers influencing, or trying to influence, policy. Non-literary creative men too made their views known and were heeded. Debussy and Fauré, for example, were good friends of Georges Clemenceau, Prime Minister from 1906 to 1909. So the present book extends its panoramic view to include the remarkable dynamism in foreign policy. It tries to show how, in part, this was inseparable from the creative achievement.

Much that I have to say about Parisian attitudes to Germany is new and runs counter to traditional inter-pretations. Only when I had completed my research did I find that my views are close to those of some of the younger, more open-minded French historians, such as Joseph Caillaux's biographer, Jean-Claude Allain, who now accept that it takes two to make a quarrel.

One other aspect of the title calls for comment. The years 1880 to 1914 in Paris are sometimes termed the Belle Epoque. The term was not current at the time; it came into use only in the 1920s, mainly to indicate that France had then enjoyed peace and prosperity, and that Paris was the city *par excellence* where Frenchmen and foreigners spent money freely, dining out with their mistresses in expensive restaurants, watching theatre and operetta from boxes, spending on diamonds and clothes by Worth, and where even those less well-off, like the figures in Renoir's suburban Paris scenes, danced under the sky to an accordion.

It is true that those years were notable for their afflu-ence, but I believe that in nearly all important respects the period 1880–1914 is not homogeneous and falls into two distinct parts. Put in oversimplified terms, Parisians from 1880 to the end of the century went to parties in order to forget such matters as the defeat by Prussia, political scandals, the Dreyfus affair; from 1900 they went to parties to celebrate. The full extent of the difference is one of the themes of this book.

The precise dates I have chosen call for explanation. The turn of the century brought a change of mood, as it had done in 1800, first full year of the Consulate. It was specially marked in Paris, where in spring a great exhibition opened. The nature of that change of mood is the theme of Chapters One and Two. As for the closing date, the summer of 1914 ended, or profoundly modified, what had preceded it and so has become an accepted terminus.

Since the mood of Paris in the 1900s was not close to moods elsewhere, it may help the reader to acclimatize if note is made of two basic points of difference between the French capital and the great Anglo-Saxon cities.

First, the unusually high importance attached by people in general to the arts in the broadest sense of the term. In 1911 the *Mona Lisa* disappeared from its place in the Louvre. In the then current mood of hot-headed nationalism, some Paris newspapers claimed the Kaiser was behind the theft, which in fact had been perpetrated by an Italian nationalist, but when in the ensuing weeks and months an unknown Parisian placed a vase of fresh roses regularly before the empty space in the Louvre gallery where the *Mona Lisa* had hung, as at a shrine, the Paris press did not single out this gesture as unusual or extravagant. It was taken for granted that people should place an almost religious value on art and grieve greatly for a vanished masterpiece.

A second distinctive aspect of Paris at this period was an awareness of the presence of the dead; like the 'dead' masterpiece from the Louvre. The dead lived on in the names of Paris streets; on All Souls' Day Parisians thronged the cemeteries to lay wreaths of flowers on family graves. Gertrude Stein noticed 'the way they feel about the dead, it is so friendly so simply friendly and though inevitable not a sadness or though occurring not a shock. There is no difference between death and life in France and that too made it inevitable that they were the background of the twentieth century.' This attitude, which derives from, and is fostered by, the emphasis on history in French schools and analytical thinking, extended to the dead of Alsace-Lorraine, ceded to Germany after France's defeat, and was to play an essential role in the revival of nationalism. Prime Minister Raymond Poincaré had it in mind when he declared in a speech in Nancy in 1912: 'Like mankind, *la patrie* is composed more of the dead than of the living.'

But it is with the living we are concerned in the pages that follow. As far as possible I focus on men and women going about their work and pleasures, in the belief that in their lives we come most closely to see their period. Often I have to trace their emergence, butterfly-like; those I have chosen were artists in the widest sense, for artists' sensitive antennae detect early a new aspiration or dilemma, and by objectivizing it they bring it to others' awareness.

In concentrating on such innovators I am not forgetting what a protected and in some ways innocent world they lived in, one so far from ours that probably no artist today could accept their values or work from their assumptions. But this gives the period a certain poignancy, like watching tropical fish, brightly coloured as Dufy's flags, in the sunlit waters of a coral reef before it has begun to disintegrate.

* * *

The chief sources for the book are French newspapers, periodicals, 'little magazines', printed diaries, letters and memoirs, papers in private and public archives – all listed in Sources and Notes – and my conversations over a long period with Frenchmen and Frenchwomen who actually lived in Paris on the Eve. Aunts and great-aunts of my French wife who had known Paris when Debussy, Ravel and Satie were composing, when Braque, Matisse and Picasso were painting, told me of treasured memories: a Concert Colonne with Jacques Thibaud as violin soloist; a ball at a house in the Champs-Elysées, where the Lido now stands, with the young girls entering the names of partners in little ivory-backed dance books; a Friday lecture at the Collège de France by Henri Bergson, the small neat professor with his three-inch stiff collar fashioning phrases like a sculptor with his slim white hands. In the attic rooms of a Normandy house my children, looking for clothes to dress up in, would open a leather trunk, with covered top and canvas protective cover, and out would tumble lace ruffles, long silk evening gowns, dolls, pianola rolls and, too, packets of Russian bonds tied with ribbon which the family solicitor in 1900 had pronounced 'safe as the Pont Neuf'.

My father-in-law had known Paris before 1914 and he too told me stories of his youth. He served as an artillery subaltern on the Western Front for four years in 1914–18 and later, as mayor of his village, would preside at the annual ceremony of commemoration on 11 November in front of the war memorial. The ubiquitous war memorial – usually homely, seldom a work of art – stands as a memorial also to the period I have chosen, for that war, more than most wars, had come out of events within France; it was the other side of the same sequence. And this is the shape behind the pages that follow.

A word about the purchasing power of the franc. It remained constant between 1900 and 1910, then rose, but only slightly. Labour costs and food were much cheaper then than now, manufactured goods dearer. A haircut in 1900 cost 30 centimes, a Métro ticket first class 25 centimes, second class 15 centimes. A week's room and board in a modest Paris hotel cost 160 francs. Proust, however, spent nearly 500 francs a month on medicines, and in 1913 the Duc de Cossé-Brissac paid 30,000 francs for a Rochet-Schneider motor-car. Though no completely valid or exact correspondence can be made, roughly speaking a franc would have gone as far in Paris then as a pound sterling goes today in London or $1.65 in New York.

PARIS ON THE EVE

CHAPTER 1

A Bourgeois Civilization

O n New Year's Day 1900 a visitor to Paris would have found many of the landmarks familiar today: stone *quais* along the Seine, the towers of Notre-Dame, the Chambre des Députés with its pediment depicting Liberty and Public Order, the Invalides, with its chapel dome marking the tomb of Napoleon, the Eiffel Tower, the Place de la Concorde with its fountains and statues personifying provincial cities, the Opéra, the Louvre – the Ns carved on the outside effaced since the fall of Napoleon III – the bosky Champs-Elysées – flanked however with detached private houses – the Arc de Triomphe, but without its flame. In the tree-lined streets, many still cobbled, a few mainly electric motor-cars could be seen, but the traffic, much less of it than today, was mostly glossily varnished horse-drawn carriages and fiacres, and some buses and trams. The first Métro stations were visible, with wrought-iron *art nouveau* motifs, awaiting the opening in July of the first, west–east line, Porte Maillot to Porte de Vincennes.

A population of 2.7 million made Paris bigger than Berlin and New York, though smaller than London. On this first day of what many regarded as the new century, a Monday, not a public holiday, when the weather was mild with occasional showers, quite a few of the leisured would have gone for a stroll, window-shopping in the Boulevards, or, more quietly, in the Tuileries and Luxembourg Gardens.

Their appearance would have surprised a visitor from today's world. To start with, almost everyone wore a hat. The blue-denimed workman wore a cloth cap, artisans and shopkeepers bowlers, the liberal classes top hats. Even a schoolmaster would arrive in his lycée classroom wearing a top hat, while the British Ambassador, Sir Francis Bertie, though not a shining intelligence, was much respected for his gleaming, beautifully ironed topper.

Perhaps because the hat hid their short-cut hair, men made much of the hair on their faces. A large number wore beards. In ascending order of bushiness, there were goatee beards, Van Dyck beards, muttonchops, spade beards, and beaver beards, also called *à la Gauloise* or *à la rivière*, which might reach a width of eight inches and a length of twelve. Café waiters had recently gone on strike and won the right to wear a beard.

Those who did not choose to festoon their chin offered, most of them, a generous moustache. It might be thick and droopy, shaped like handlebars; thin, waxed and pointed; or limited to a bristly emphasis of the upper lip.

The Parisian man about town wore a tightly fitting black overcoat lined with black satin, a cut-away jacket, trousers with a crease down the front instead of, as ten years earlier, at the sides, a high stiff collar, a starched shirtfront and a foulard or tie held in place by a tiepin, over which might dangle a monocle. He wore gloves and possibly spats and carried a cane. By his correct turn-out he expressed his dignity and his readiness to defend it with sword or pistol in one of those duels that were a weekly occurrence.

If the Parisian gentleman's line was sleek and vertical, the Parisienne favoured the undulant. Her waist was narrow, her bosom and derrière were made prominent by means of a corset. The more of a lady she was, the more her body must be S-shaped. She wore her hair up, and a wide-brimmed hat profusely decorated with flowers or plumes. Under her coat she wore a boned, high-necked bodice, perhaps with a bolero or lace ruffle. The front of her skirt touched the ground, the back was four inches longer. She changed her dress more often than strictly necessary, on average five times a day. Parisian women felt the need for lots of pretty things, while smart clothes also fostered that mood of flirtation acknowledged to be a main ingredient in the charm of Paris.

In his Psychology Clinic a Paris doctor, Pierre Janet, had uncovered what he termed 'the unconscious'. If Janet's theory is applied here, the men, with their beards and moustaches, were emphasizing their virility, the ladies, with their full bosoms and luscious hats, their femininity. Their unconscious was saying in effect *Vive la différence*. Ladies accepted that they should please, be courted, be protected, knowing they had a free hand in running their home, making it a beautiful small counterpart of beautiful Paris, and bringing up their children, who lived with them and right through to their late teens attended day school. Parisian ladies certainly did not see themselves as hard done by. Indeed, both sexes relished their polarized roles and felt *bien dans leurs peaux* – at ease with themselves and with each other.

The core of Paris was the artisan class, living mainly east of the Place de la République. They manufactured the high-quality or luxury goods to be seen in the shops, and in one or two department stores on the Boulevards: furniture, leather goods, glass, jewellery, tailor-made clothes, foulards, harness, carriages and so on. They worked mainly in family units, the usual number being five or less. They prized their independence and were ready to work a twelve-hour day in order to keep it. Paris artisans voted then – they still do – for the Right and this, as we shall see, was to mark the city's political stance.

The employed working class ranged from drivers of buses and trams, street sweepers, restaurant and café waiters, to concierges, telephonists – Proust's 'invisible angels', a welcome new opening for women – and domestic servants, of whom in Paris there were 207,000, mainly recruited from poor regions such as Brittany and Auvergne. By 1914, what with more bathrooms, vacuum cleaners and central heating, that number was to drop slightly. As in other cities, their working day was shamefully long. But at least they were well fed and comparatively robust. There was none of the malnutrition which made England's poor less tall by five inches than her rich.

Romans had called their capital 'the city', implying that no other counted; well-to-do Parisian families, as though no other class and no other country counted, referred to themselves and their circle as *le monde*. It comprised the *noblesse*, senior civil servants, bankers, distinguished professional men, rising deputies and senators of proved worth, chairmen of those companies – few in number – that were turning to profit new inventions, such as rayon, and new resources, such as petroleum and liquid oxygen. They inhabited the west of Paris and, just south of the Seine, the Faubourg Saint-Germain.

There were fewer great fortunes here than in England: the Bastille had after all been stormed. No French family could emulate the Devonshires, who for weekends could lodge 470 people, including servants, under their roof at Chatsworth. On the last day of the old century the Duc de Chartres had held a shooting party, but the bag of 175 brace of pheasant was small compared to the thousand brace that might fall in one day at Sandringham. France nevertheless had enjoyed thirty years of peace and, just lately, prosperity, so there was plenty of money about. With France on the gold standard, no income tax, and inflation negligible, it was tempting to save, and many did. They invested their money for preference in Government bonds, French or foreign, for these were pretty safe and tax free, while interest on shares carried a 3% tax. This preference for bonds, like that for keeping a business small and family-sized, discouraged the growth of those large companies which were becoming the strength of England, Germany and the United States.

With Switzerland, France was one of the only two republics in Europe. And Frenchmen paid more than lip-service to the ideal of equality. The *noblesse* had less money and power than in England or Russia, the officer class almost none of the status it enjoyed in Germany. Indeed, perhaps the most distinctive aspect of Paris society was its permeability. Thanks to an excellent education system introduced in the 1880s, anyone of talent could rise to the top and a great many did. A network of scholarships gave poor boys a chance to reach the Ecole Normale, as prospective secondary school and university teachers, or to go through the long training to become lawyers. Since there are regional accents but no pronounced class accents in France, a rising man was not held back by his way of speaking.

Emile Loubet was the son of peasants in a poor region, the Drôme. He did well at school, studied law, became Mayor of Montélimar, married a tradesman's daughter, then entered national politics. A good committee man, at sixty he became Prime Minister. Now, eight years later, with his smiling open face, his reassuring white beaver beard and polished top hat, he was an esteemed President of the Republic – the first from the Left – and lived in the house called Elysium. His one foible was a wish to shine as a sportsman; at Rambouillet he would go duck-shooting but rare were the ducks Loubet laid low.

In every field there were similar self-made men. Jean Dupuy came from the Gironde where his father had had a small draper's shop and his mother was a foundling who never learned to read or write. The boy attended primary school, got coaching from the local curé and became office boy to a Blaye solicitor. He made the leap to Paris young, learned law the hard way in a bailiff's office, worked an eighteen-hour day, married the daughter of a Marais gilder and entered the Senate. Now he owned *Le Petit Parisien* newspaper and was Minister of Agriculture. The snobbishness of Proust's Guermantes applied only to a very few families, on the defensive because lacking the energy or freshness of thinking to move upwards. By and large Paris was considerably less snobbish than London, Berlin or New York.

Those Parisians who could afford it lived in detached private houses, preferably within walking distance of the two best clubs, the Jockey in Boulevard des Capucines and the Epatant in rue Royale. Parisians of the privileged class who without being very rich were well off lived in spacious balconied apartments, often in blocks built immediately after Prefect Haussmann had decreed, 'Let there be light.' Werner von Siemens's recent invention of the electric lift had reversed the traditional order of things by making the upper storeys the most sought-after, especially as noise in the streets began to increase with the motor-car. In contrast to London houses, with a stratified upstairs and downstairs, here everything was on a single floor: though the maid or maids slept in one or more attic bedrooms, they would spend all day in the apartment, an arrangement which, according to Mrs Gaskell, who knew it first hand, 'had the moral advantage of uniting mistresses and maids in a more complete family bond'.

Furnishings were chosen to express substance. Those of Madame Vasnier, a fashionable hostess, included heavy black lacquer rococo sofa and armchairs covered with embossed red velvet, brass North African tables, heroic bronzes, innumerable small but weighty, usually metallic, objects. Thick tasselled drapes were looped back from the windows, at dusk globe-shaded lamps were lit, in winter a coal-burning stove, though one literary hostess, Madame de Caillavet, preferred to shiver rather than install so drab-looking an article. Only in a few avant-garde apartments did one find the light woods, convolvulus lines and muted colours of the burgeoning style, *Art Nouveau*.

In a spacious apartment, furnished in the old style on the second floor of 9 Boulevard Malesherbes, lived Dr Adrien Proust and family, and on New Year's Day 1900 the doctor would have received as usual his copy of *Le Figaro*, a six-page daily, price 15 centimes, with a circulation of 30,000, whose assistant editor Gaston Calmette had two eminent doctor brothers and was showing interest in Marcel's articles about *le monde*.

Le Figaro carried mainly French news; of the nineteen Paris newspapers it has been calculated that they gave a meagre 1.8% of their space to happenings abroad. On the morning in question *Le Figaro* informed readers that coal was in short supply and its price rising because English supplies were going to the Royal Navy, an item clarified by Caran d'Ache's half-page cartoon 'New Year in Transvaal': crouching among rocks, John Bull turns to an officer in topee peering through a telescope: 'Anything on the way, General?' 'Yes, congratulations and good wishes, from the four corners of the world . . . for our enemy.'

Under Society News *Le Figaro*'s first entry informed readers that Prince and Princess Tenischeff had given a dinner for sixty-two guests in honour of the Russian commission to the forthcoming Exhibition. Under Motoring an item announced that the St Petersburg Cycling Club was soon to hold a 70 kilometre motor-car and motor-cycle race. Russia got more than its share of space in *Le Figaro*. For the past six years that country had been France's ally and many readers held high-yield Russian bonds.

One big difference between quality Paris newspapers like *Le Figaro* and, say, *The Times* of London, was that, bar an occasional communication correcting an error of fact, the former carried no letters to the Editor. Each Paris newspaper expressed forcefully the editor's point of view; he didn't want letters taking issue with him. The English notion of a spectrum of opinion, each containing part of the truth, and contributing perhaps to an eventual compromise – this was alien to Paris.

While Dr Proust read his newspaper over *café au lait* and warm croissants, his beautiful wife planned the day's menus with her cook. Madame Proust happened to be Jewish and this is perhaps the place to say that if there was any feeling in Paris against Jews it was so rare as to be negligible. We should not be misled by passages in her son's novel referring to a period before 1900. Now that the Dreyfus furore had died down, Paris had reverted to its former tolerance and its concomitant remarkable permeability. The city had 40,000 Jews and they were to be found at every level, so fully accepted that no one remarked on their Jewishness. Romain Rolland, Jacques Maritain and the high bourgeois novelist Paul Bourget married Jewish ladies; nowhere does Proust's correspondence show the slightest trace of unease at being half-Jewish; Madame de Caillavet was Jewish, as was Emma Debussy and the young composer Darius Milhaud, whom the poets Francis Jammes and Paul Claudel befriended and launched. We shall meet many more, especially in the theatre, so much a Jewish preserve that one Gentile playwright, initially unsuccessful, decided to take a Jewish name and thereafter prospered.

The Proust family cook, duly briefed, went out to buy the day's provisions. Each cook had her favourite shops, and her continuing patronage of them was rewarded by a 5 centimes in the franc commission. Some stern souls had declared this to be wrong, but in 1900 a committee presided over by the Archbishop of Paris ruled that it was not a sin.

Interspersed with the shops were cafés, whose owners were raising their shutters for another day's business, and here 1900 was to be a most important year. A daring young Finance Minister, Joseph Caillaux, increased the tax on alcoholic drinks and reduced the tax on beers and wines; what's more, Caillaux represented the Sarthe, not a wine-growing region! As a result French drinking habits speedily changed from absinthe, the fortified quinquina beverage that had destroyed many including Verlaine, to red or white wine or beer.

Léon Bloy, novelist and Catholic polemicist, noted in his diary, 'So ends . . . the painful and abject 19th century.' What did he mean? The 1880s and 1890s had indeed been a painful and depressing period: in the wake of the Prussian victory, civil war between the Paris Commune and Government troops had cost 100,000 lives, mourning for whom continued over the years; in the courtyard of the Ecole Militaire his superior officer had torn the epaulettes from a pallid Captain Dreyfus, while he cried, 'I am innocent'; a spate of anarchist bombings had killed innocent Parisians and culminated in a bomb being thrown actually in the Chamber of Deputies.

With the dawn of the new century, it looked as though the tide could be turning. The church built by public subscription to expiate the civil war killings, Sacré-Cœur, was completed in 1900; a year earlier President Loubet pardoned Alfred Dreyfus – though not before his Presidential top hat had been knocked off at the Auteuil races by an indignant nationalist; in 1894 bombings were at last halted by tougher laws and better security.

One man who felt definite optimism was Alfred Picard. Born in 1844 in Strasbourg, Picard was an engineer in the heroic mould of Isambard Kingdom Brunel: a specialist in railways and in everything relating to iron and steel, Picard had organized the successful 1889 Exhibition, and it might be thought that one such achievement would suffice for a lifetime. But Picard was a dynamo of energy with powerful connections. He had persuaded the Government and the Paris authorities to put up 20 million francs apiece so that he could organize, for spring 1900, the biggest international Exhibition ever to be held.

Some opposed this project on the grounds that Middle Eastern carpets would bring in the plague, or something as horrible, that prostitution would increase and the cost of living soar. But a much larger number approved it, for Parisians, as their interest in dress suggests, were temperamentally inclined to be exhibitionists.

So, on the afternoon of 1 January, quite a number of families walked down to the Seine to see whether the Exhibition buildings would be ready by opening day in April.

Builders were still riveting the iron frames of what were to be the Grand Palais (on top of which there was, as yet, no sign of Recipon's fine bronze group of prancing chariot horses) and the Petit Palais, but across the Seine the foreign pavilions were well advanced. They included a facsimile of part of the Kremlin, an English manor house, a Bulgarian cottage with a rose-water fountain, a German castle-cum-beer-garden, a small version of the US Capitol and a pinewood Danish-style house, which so took the fancy of Sir George Lewis, an English solicitor, that at the close of the Exhibition he was to buy it and re-erect it in Norfolk, screening it from the sea-wind with poplars and buckthorn.

'Paris is thick with dust,' grumbled Ambassador Paul Cambon that spring, 'nothing is ready.' Nevertheless on the day announced, 14 April, the Saturday before Easter, a smiling President Loubet made his entrance before 13,000 guests, while an orchestra played Massenet's *Solemn March*. The Exhibition, he said, 'surpasses infinitely the lustre of ordinary festivals', and he declared it open.

The President toured the main pavilions, headed by the spectacular Palace of Electricity, its façade in the shape of an open fan. On top, 120 feet up, in a chariot drawn by a horse and a dragon, backed by the thirty pointed rays of a star, stood the Fairy of Electricity. On Sundays and holidays the palace was illuminated by 5700 electric bulbs.

President Loubet went by river steamer to inaugurate a single-span bridge named after the late Tsar, Alexander III, and depicted on the pale blue Exhibition admission ticket. The bridge joined the Esplanade des Invalides to the Petit Palais and the main entrance gate: a triple archway surmounted by a cupola between two minaret-like towers and graced by the figure of a lady in evening gown personifying the City of Paris.

On Easter Tuesday the President was to honour the Russian pavilion with a long visit, receiving from the Russian Ambassador the insignia of the Order of St Andrew and a map of France in precious stones, the towns diamonds, the rivers platinum. Well might the young poet Pierre Louÿs write to his best friend, who happened to admire Rimsky-Korsakov:

> O Claude-Achille Debussy
> En quel endroit de notre sphère
> Criez-vous: Vive la Russy!
> Comme tout bon Français doit faire?

Among notable Parisians to visit the Exhibition was Madame Natanson. Born Misia Godebska to a mother who died in childbirth, she had grown up in Paris and married the owner of the excellent *Revue Blanche*, best of Paris's several dozen literary small magazines. Now aged twenty-eight, she was a good pianist and a discerning patron, helping among others Maurice Ravel, who dedicated *La Valse* to her. She was a close friend of Lautrec, who in allusion to her swift grace called her 'The Lark', and Renoir in seven different portraits had depicted her eager, wide-eyed cat face.

Misia brought to Paris a certain Slav abandon. She had a habit when alone of picking her teeth with scissors, and when she came to marry her very rich second husband, installed a piano in every room of her house, each right for a particular mood. She seldom got out of bed before noon yet usually managed to be at the centre of things.

Being adventurous, Misia Natanson headed for the Asiatic Russian display. Here she boarded the Trans-Siberian. The train did not move, but while she munched on zabuski and drank tea served by a moujik,

Misia delightedly watched a painted backcloth of Siberian snow, pinewoods and villages unroll. This little episode points to a wider truth: Parisians seldom went abroad, they expected the world to come to them.

Another visitor, Pierre Laborde, a university student from Bordeaux, wrote to a friend:

> You could say I've touched with my finger this delicious century that's just begun. I've danced all the dances of the world from the Pont des Invalides to the Pont de l'Alma, and travelled by 'moving carpet' from a Venetian palazzo to Washington's Capitol, from an Elizabethan manor [in fact Charles II] to a Byzantine church.
>
> I've drunk tokay, vodka, whisky, and milk from the udders of a Swiss cow ... I've become a satellite on the Big Wheel, chosen the house I'll share one day with an unknown beauty, built of Norwegian pine, with Regency furniture, drapes, windows and lamps by Gallé ...
>
> I've seen moving photographs and electrified dancing: cinematography and Loie Fuller [a red-headed free-style dancer] . . . Life on a screen . . . isn't yet art, but it will be. And on a glass floor when the lights change colour a woman becomes a flower, a butterfly, a storm, a flame from a brazier . . .
>
> Nothing annoys me? Oh yes . . . the Métro entrances, wrought-iron arabesques and flowers like Jane Avril's chignon and the hem of Sarah Bernhardt's skirts, pure 'spaghetti' style . . . And what annoyed me most was the opening of the painting exhibition. The academician, Gérôme [aged seventy-six], showed President Loubet round and at the entrance to

the Impressionists stuck out his arm. 'Stop,
Monsieur le Président. That way lies the dishonour of France.'

I went to let off steam in the Rat Mort café,
packed with nonconformists, when Toulouse-
Lautrec, who is tinier than ever now his
stumpy legs have gone limp, wearing a pince-
nez askew, shuffled in, singing a Bruant song
off-key. I told him how angry I was with
Gérôme, whereupon his pince-nez fell and
shuddered on its black cord. 'They are ten years
behind,' he said. 'They haven't yet understood
the Impressionists, whereas we've outgrown
them.'

According to its organizer, Picard, the Exhibition was
intended 'to reflect the bright genius of France, and to
show our fair country to be, today as yesterday, in the
very vanguard of Progress'; no one could touch a
Lorrainer for patriotism now that Lorraine was ceded
to Germany.

If part of the Exhibition was, as one might expect,
tinselly, there were in fact many solid wonders.
Cinéorama, for instance: cinema in the round realized
by ten synchronized projectors; the Rodin retrospective, mounted at the artist's expense, unfairly described
by Claudel as 'a banquet of breasts and buttocks'; the
Palace of Electricity after dark: so much concentrated
manmade light had not been seen before. In the Palace
of Horticulture, opened by Jean Dupuy, you could
savour the scents of new varieties of flowers. In the
Bulgarian pavilion you could taste a strange comestible
named yoghourt which, with suspicion or dry humour,
the British commissioners described as 'a mixture of
cheese and cream appreciated locally but requiring a
special palate to judge it'. In Loie Fuller's little theatre

you could watch the Japanese lady dancer Madame Sada Yacco kill her rival in love with an ivory hammer.

There were also fringe events. Madeleine Lemaire, a society flower-painter, was one of several to give a lavish costume ball, its theme the Exhibition. *Le Tout Paris* went, and one guest, attired as a maharajah complete with jewels, could claim to be *le Tout Europe.* This was Comte Robert de Montesquiou, poet, æsthete and man about town, who in *Qui êtes-vous?* described himself – correctly – as 'Related to most of the noble families of Europe'.

Centred on the Champ-de-Mars and Esplanade des Invalides, the Exhibition had, so to speak, colonies. At Vincennes you could see the leading makes of motorcar; also, hot air balloons and projects for flying machines. At La Croix Catalan you could watch the second Olympic Games; the Games had been founded by a young Saint-Cyr graduate, Baron Pierre de Coubertin, inspired by a study-tour of English public schools. Though they had not yet attained world fame, the Olympics unobtrusively ameliorated international relations. Frenchmen took most of the fencing medals, Americans the medals for athletics, Englishmen the tennis.

Finally, in the Congress Palace no less than 130 congresses met, proceedings being conducted in French, still the world's lingua franca. They included Congresses of Socialism, Peace, Fire-Fighting, Vegetarianism and Aviation. Perhaps the most important, in August, was the Congress of Philosophy. Here Bertrand Russell had a fruitful encounter with an Italian mathematician, Giuseppe Peano, after which the young Englishman hurried off to write *Principles of Mathematics*, in which he used Peano's notation to show that mathematics is in many respects an advanced form of logic.

Among the French speakers at that Congress were three philosophers of the front rank: Emile Boutroux, Maurice Blondel and Henri Bergson. The 'three B's' can be said to have contributed more than any other persons in the city to the tone underlying the Exhibition, and indeed to the tone of Paris in 1900. How this came about calls for a new chapter.

CHAPTER 2

A New Confidence

In order to begin to understand the values of intelligent young Parisians in 1900, one has to return briefly to the last years of the old century, and see how people, from about 1875, viewed the world and life.

Physicists were claiming to have got to the bedrock of matter in the tiny, solid atom, each with a measurable weight; biology, notably Spencer's version of Darwinism, saw man as a primate activated by glandular secretions, in principle predictable. Everything was subject to iron laws governing matter, so man had no free will, no soul. He became a point on the sociologists' graph, and Paris, in Zola's image, a huge stomach fed from the Halles, voided through vast sewers, through which it was fashionable for country cousins, up for a spree, to make guided tours. Dr Charcot, the nerve specialist, undertook to reproduce in his lab at the Salpetrière hospital most of the miracles of the Gospel. The thinking man's bedside book was Ernest Renan's *Vie de Jésus*, which in dulcet tones described Christ as a good man, but his supposed divinity a myth evolved by popular imagination.

This view made for pessimism, which was deepened by France's humiliating defeat at the hands of Prussia in 1870, followed by the loss of Alsace-Lorraine, then by the crash of the Union Générale Bank, entailing budget deficits and an industrial slump, and then by the Panama Canal Company scandal, when 104 Députés were found to have taken bribes.

Life as usual was mirrored in books and the theatre, where a tough, slice-of-life realism prevailed. Naturalism claimed to reveal the secrets society hid but more often gloried in sordidness. Joseph Pujol, *le Pétomane*, earned 2000 francs nightly from the rude noises most people try to hide, while the hefty singer Dufay at the Moulin Rouge cracked nuts between her breasts. A leading playwright, Henri Becque, offered as one of his recipes: 'If you want to keep your friends, avoid seeing them', and in *La Parisienne* (1885) depicted a scheming Clotilde pulling the wool over the eyes of an unsuccessful husband, an importunate ageing lover and a second lover as well. 'Women's chief gift,' declared the Goncourts, 'is for disguising their stupidity', while Maupassant in a succession of short stories portrayed them as compulsive deceivers.

That generation's mood of world-weary cynicism was personified by Anatole France. Aged fifty-six at the turn of the century, the Paris-born historical novelist and satirist had lampooned as penguins his fellow-Parisians, with their black frock coats, white shirts and inability to learn from experience, in his amusing *Penguin Island*; he lived at 5 Villa Said in the Avenue du Bois-de-Boulogne, surrounded by medieval stained glass, Gothic statues and an Eros from Alexandria, his usual dress a grey dressing-gown like a monk's habit and a red skullcap like a cardinal's, the idea being that the clergy had been superseded by enlightened men of letters. Divorced from his wife, Anatole France had a mistress, Léontine Arman de Caillavet, a very rich, bookish lady married to a jovial, intellectually inadequate yachtsman; it was she who made France write his daily stint, for he tended to laziness, and showed him off in her Friday salon before lesser writers like Loti and politicians including Jean Jaurès and Raymond Poincaré.

There the great man made the ironical or cynical

remarks expected of him: 'All the historical books which contain no lies are extremely tedious.' Shown a Roman cameo discovered by an antique collector and asked to say whose head he thought it was, France enquired coolly, 'Whose do you want it to be?' On a sightseeing tour of Lourdes with Léontine, after inspecting the crutches and ex-voto offerings left in gratitude for miraculous cures, France growled, 'I see no wooden legs.'

'The nineteenth century . . .' said Ernest Feydeau, novelist friend of the Goncourts, summing things up, 'deserves to be called the age of matter. Self-interest has replaced religious faith, love of beauty, of virtue, of an ideal.' Feydeau went on to ask, 'Can artists escape the mundane values of their century? Can they alone effect a reaction? Without the least fear of being contradicted by the facts we can answer, no.' And poor Feydeau was probably right. The new values had to be drawn initially from a deeper well: philosophy.

The oldest of the 'three B's' to address the Congress of Philosophy at the Exhibition was born near Paris in 1845. After attending the top university college, the Ecole Normale Supérieure, Emile Boutroux studied German philosophy at Heidelberg and at forty became a professor at the Sorbonne. A liberal practising Catholic, Boutroux sought to show the deficiencies of positivism by a critique of its method. He pointed out that the Greeks had distinguished between *dianoia*, which sees logical and mechanical connections, and *nous* which, according to Plato, separates or links things according to the 'Ideas' which represent the perfection towards which things are tending. The positivists saw only half the picture: *dianoia*; Boutroux proposed to bring back the other half: *nous*.

In making a consciously purposeful act, said Boutroux, a man uses *nous* to assess the value of options open to him. He chooses, and moves towards, a perfection. Perfections are graded and the ultimate perfection, 'the being whose creative action we feel deep within us, as we strive to get closer to him', Boutroux calls God.

In *The Contingency of the Laws of Nature* (1874) Boutroux declared that an individual's habits cannot be explained in terms of blind instincts, glands and nerves. Habits are formed by acts, acts by choices, choices by *nous*, touched sometimes by what Christians call grace. Boutroux was in effect re-asserting Blaise Pascal's claim that man's evaluative faculty – his heart – has reasons which the mind does not know, and in this seminal year, 1900, he published an important rehabilitation of France's foremost Christian thinker. A much-loved teacher, active in good causes, Boutroux influenced a generation of pupils, including Alphonse Darlu, who taught Marcel Proust philosophy at the Lycée Condorcet and co-founded the *Revue de Métaphysique et Morale*, the very title of which scandalized ageing materialists.

The second of our philosophers, Maurice Blondel, was born eighteen years after Boutroux in Dijon, but he made his home near Aix-en-Provence, where for thirty years he was professor of philosophy. Blondel was a country-lover, who in his garden grew 200 varieties of rose and collected butterflies, but no escapist. In 1893 he published his big, difficult book, *L'Action*. Blondel started from the premise that every rational being seeks to make, from the antitheses within him, a spiritual unity. He cannot achieve this, as positivists claim, by amassing facts and connecting them; he cannot achieve it just by speculation; he can achieve it only by action of a moral kind, for, says Blondel, all thinking is a beginning of action. Blondel is therefore a precursor of

Existentialism but actually goes further, declaring that the truly unifying end of action is the universal ground of every good, what he as a Christian calls God. 'The action that envelops and completes all others is to think truly about God.' It follows that Revelation is no longer superfluous but an essential element required by human reason if its aspirations are to be satisfied.

The third of the 'B's', Henri Bergson, had an unusual ancestry. His father was Mical Bergson of Warsaw. Poland, ruled by the Tsar of Russia, was not a happy country, and Mical Bergson moved to the free West, marrying Catherine Levison of Doncaster and taking a post in Paris as an organist. Here in 1859 his second son, Henri, was born. Four years later the Bergsons moved to Geneva – their address was Boulevard des Philosophes – and Bergson *père* taught piano at the Conservatory.

Bergson *père* was a modest man who never made much money from his serenades and songs, the best known of which was *Chanson de mai*. Catherine was a remarkably good person, 'almost a saint' according to Henri, who conversed with her in English.

Henri won a scholarship to the Lycée Condorcet and when his family moved to London remained in Paris, boarding at the Jewish Springler Institute. He scooped most of the prizes and went on to the Ecole Normale Supérieure, where one of his teachers was Boutroux. Slim, narrow-shouldered, in tightly fitting jacket, gentle in manner with a slight English accent, he was nicknamed 'Miss'. He graduated second and began a schoolteaching career, which was to lead him, at forty-one, to the Chair of Greek Philosophy in the prestigious Collège de France.

Bergson was a handsome man, with high protruding brow, brown hair already thinning, aquiline nose, bushy eyebrows and moustache, unforgettably piercing blue eyes. Perhaps because he was one of seven children he was more human than most of his profession. He was a good speaker, using long slim hands to shape his argument. He considered women to be as intelligent as men; this and his esteem for intuition made him popular with the fair sex: on Friday at 5.00 p.m. room 8 at the Collège de France was crowded not only with students but with society ladies.

Bergson possessed a gift, commoner in artists than in philosophers, for observing his own shades of feeling with precision, and this he brought to bear in his first book, *Essai sur les données immédiates de la conscience.* Bergson argues that because we talk more than we think and take more notice of the outside world than of our inner states, we mistakenly objectivize those inner states, quantify what are really qualities, and look for their causes outside ourselves. Science erects this mistaken tendency into a system. It projects feelings and inner states as separated entities in space graspable by intellect, whereas in fact they are unseparated, continuous and perceptible only by intuition. Furthermore, feelings and inner states occur in a temporal flux which Bergson calls duration, whereas the scientist, following from his original mistake of objectivizing them, claims they occur in time – that is, in mathematically measurable time, different from duration and, in Bergson's view, really a form of space.

By applying to the self and duration grids borrowed from the external quantitative world we have mistakenly come to believe that the former are ruled by scientific laws; in fact they are not; here in this continuously moving inner domain, at key moments, the master of the dance is free will.

In *Matter and Memory* (1896) Bergson defines more exactly the spiritual side of man. Its bases are the unconscious and memory. There are two kinds of memory: one comes into play when we recite a poem, the other when we evoke the various occasions when we read the poem while learning it. Recognition consists above all in knowing how to make use of the thing recognized. Thinking is never contemplation, it is invariably directed towards activity, towards survival.

A brain lesion, according to reductionist biology, should cripple mental activity, but Bergson points out that in cases of aphasia memory is not lost, only the bodily mechanism needed to express it. Man's memory is shown to be a central, perhaps *the* central, faculty of his soul, at work even in dreams – Bergson had read *The Interpretation of Dreams*, by Freud, who, like Bergson, had learned much from Charcot of Paris. Since in the course of being remembered each person's past is unique, it eludes the general causal pattern of scientific laws. Here then is further evidence that man is an autonomous spiritual being.

In 1900 Bergson published a book entitled *Laughter*, a newish topic for French philosophy. Bergson says laughter is often society's attempt to prevent the supple life of the spirit being dulled, stereotyped, made rigid by matter in the largest sense of the term. When an individual goes his own narrow way without troubling to get into touch with his fellows, matter has got the better of him, he becomes ridiculous and society tries to 'loosen him up' by laughing.

The tension between spirit and matter Bergson was to elaborate further in *L'Evolution Créatrice* (1907). Rejecting Darwinian natural selection, he developed Lamarck's view that nature is driven forward by an internal psychological principle, variously compared to a spray, a firework, a fountain, a geyser. The intelligent man should find fulfilment not, as Plato had said, in contemplating, but in actively participating in immanent creation, joining with others to shape and direct it.

This is close to Blondel's view that thinking is a beginning of action.

Bergson's arguments for the existence of an autonomous spirit, and those of Boutroux and Blondel, received unexpected support from science. That hard inflexible matter which had weighed men down – younger physicists were showing it to be supple, flexible, more like something mental than physical. In 1895 Röntgen's X-rays revealed the bones in a hand, while the following year Marconi sent a radio-wave message a distance of nine miles. Instead of mind being slave to matter, it now seemed sometimes to be the other way round. In 1900 Pierre Janet published cases of mental states so affecting the body as to induce partial paralysis, while Boutroux's brother-in-law, Nobel laureate Henri Poincaré, cousin of Raymond the politician, declared that mathematical solutions do not necessarily describe nature as it is, indeed they are selected by the subliminal self on the basis of elegance, that is, on æsthetic grounds.

After work Bergson took a tram to his modest home, with garden, in Auteuil, where he led a quiet life with his wife Louise, a cousin of Proust's mother, and their one child, Jeanne, who had the misfortune to be born deaf but was to find fulfilment as a sculptress and painter. In the summer he took them to his favourite Savoie, near Lake Geneva. He liked the silent cinema: he compared the process of thinking to the running of a film, and an idea to a frame taken from the film. He also liked the works of Rodin, and had a theory that *The Thinker* depicts primitive man struggling to arrive at the first glimmer of rational thought. He dressed soberly and was much amused when Jacques-Emile Blanche came to paint his portrait and insisted on posing him against books bound in green morocco wearing a bright blue tie to match his eyes and a yellow waistcoat.

Bergson was to lecture in England in 1911 and to receive an honorary doctorate from Oxford. Two years later he was to lecture at Columbia University, New York. But it was in Paris that his name became a household word. By teaching that there is a soul, and with what subtlety its workings have to be observed, Bergson influenced the poet Charles Péguy and the budding novelist Proust – though 'involuntary memory' appears to have been Proust's own discovery. By teaching that 'nothing in our past is lost, everything remains in the subconscious of memory', Bergson was to provide, unwittingly, a slogan for patriots. By teaching that any system to some degree falsifies the fluid reality of the spiritual life, he was to encourage Catholic Modernists in their attempt to down-grade dogma. By stressing, as Blondel had also done, that thought is fulfilled in action, he appealed to the young. 'Thanks to Bergson', said one of them, the essayist Henri Massis, 'our generation felt delivered from the idols of Spencerism and sociology, from the systematic negation and doctrinaire scepticism of the past.'

So a new mood of hope begins to emerge. Since spirit has been shown to exist, young people wish to discover their spiritual side and, having done so, fulfil its potential. Adventure is in the air, joy is just in being alive: *La Beauté de Vivre*, as Fernand Gregh entitles his first book of poems. Man feels himself to be free at the dawn of a new era. Anything is possible. After an age of absinthe begin the champagne years.

There was, however, one danger in Bergson's philosophy. It opened the door to subjectivism. Man felt inclined to attach value to the strength of his feelings about a particular action regardless of objective right and wrong. That way lay moral relativism. How to escape it? Only one in twenty-three Parisians practised the Catholic religion, the proportion being somewhat higher in the well-to-do parishes of St-Philippe-du-Roule and Ste-Clotilde, so quite a few sought to bind themselves by new, or seemingly new, moral, æsthetic or other imperatives. In the course of this book we shall meet quite a variety.

One form was a sort of Nature cult. The astronomer Camille Flammarion, for instance, believed industrialization was cutting off man from nature, dehumanizing him; he decided to reawaken cosmic awareness. On 21 June 1904 he entertained fellow-scientists, including Henri Poincaré, high up in the Tour Eiffel restaurant, 'a modern temple raised to the cult of nature', in order to salute the source of light and heat. When the sun reached the solstice, a cannon roared; then came a banquet, followed by speeches, poems and songs to 4.00 a.m. in praise of the sun.

A second form of search looked to spiritualism, and here our informant is the Abbé Mugnier, a witty priest of modest birth who had a way with writers – he converted Huysmans, author of *A Rebours*, a novel that exalted pagan hedonism – and with society ladies, to many of whom he was a father confessor. His kindly, craggy face could be seen at many a fashionable dinner table; detractors called him 'Little Brother of the Rich' but many esteemed his goodness and good sense.

On 23 January 1908 the Abbé Mugnier attended a séance in the house of Elisabeth Greffulhe, wife of banker Comte Greffulhe. The medium was Eusapia Paladino, daughter of a Neapolitan innkeeper. While Eusapia stood with her back to a curtain, guests, who included Madame de Caillavet and her cousin Comte Robert de Montesquiou, held hands in the dark round a big table. One guest saw a mandolin, Mugnier a hand. Suddenly the table rose in the air, then dropped noisily. New seating arrangements were tried, Mugnier next to Eusapia. Time seemed to pass very slowly; they were all urged to concentrate. Mugnier felt strong hands on his brow, on his shoulders, and thought they were making the sign of the cross. At last lamps were relit and as they began to disperse what guests remembered chiefly was Mugnier's quip: 'A hard night's Pentecost.'

The new mood of hope made itself felt also in politics. Of 585 Députés more than half sat on the Left, and from 1902 to 1912 France was to have a Radical government – that is, left of Centre – dedicated to improving conditions for workers. What the Noble Savage had been to Rousseau, the Good Worker now was to Radicals, and at the Exhibition you could see more than one Panathenæa of the proletariat. Sunday as a day of rest had been abolished by an anti-ecclesiastical ministry in the 1880s, but in 1906 a new law would re-establish if not Sunday at least one day a week as an obligatory period of rest for all.

The Radicals opposed the power of the Catholic Church – the reason why will emerge later. They wished to realize the French Revolution's dream of a disestablished Church, for France, they grumbled, 'is a Jesuit farm, like eighteenth-century Paraguay'. First, Prime Minister Emile Combes – a lapsed seminarist, 'Julian the Apostate' to the Right – would expel thousands of priests and nuns belonging to teaching orders, then hand over the administration of churches to the laity, and finally in 1905 abrogate Napoleon's Concordat. This was to cause resentment – the Sacred Heart convent in the Hôtel Biron turned into the workshop where Rodin sculpted nudes! – but in the long run it would be salutary, for by ending the Church's often misguided intervention in politics it released her energy for pastoral work. From this diaspora, incidentally, England gained, for Benedictines who emigrated to the Isle of Wight made Quarr Abbey a world centre of Gregorian chant.

While Radical ministries extended the social services, any gaps in them were readily filled by a growing number of charitable organizations. Catholics in 1901 founded L'Abri, under the presidency of Emile Boutroux, to provide lodgings for families evicted when the breadwinner fell ill and could not pay rent, while in 1900, at the cost of a million francs, the Comtesse de Castellane had inaugurated Galeries de la Charité, a cluster of shops selling donated foods for the relief of those in distress.

Again, if you happened to be passing through Paris's East End after working hours you might well encounter a group of well-dressed men making music. They were not buskers, there was no upturned hat on the pavement to solicit coins; these were distinguished virtuosi, eyes half-closed as they bent over their bows, bringing classical music to the poor in the form of a late Beethoven quartet. Further down the street, in a canteen not in use for meals, you might find a postman, a cabinet-maker, a street-cleaner and a seamstress seated at a trestle-table taking notes as Paul Painlevé, a Sorbonne don, explained, from chalk diagrams on a blackboard, the principles of aerodynamics.

These were two of several offerings by Paris People's University. Inspired by Tolstoy's later writings, academics and others sought, free of charge, to share their knowledge or skills with those who, for lack of a baccalauréat, could not attend the Sorbonne.

The politicians who worked, debated and intrigued in Paris paid little attention to the world outside France. They wanted peace to endure, but were not particularly active in working for it. It was assumed that Electricity and similar fairies of the scientific age would strengthen concord. The Exhibition too would help: a humanist art critic, Gustave Geffroy, hailed it as a 'coming together of races, a universal harmony. Let this new force,' he urged, 'champion the cause of art and ideas against the steel of cannon shells!'

This was not cant. France might be less populous than the United States and Russia but, as *Le Figaro* put it:

> What does it matter if France is no longer dominant in manpower, provided she continues to produce thinkers like Ampère and Pasteur. In future 'the Spirit will come down on the waters' and alone will reign.

The French word for Spirit – *Esprit* – has wider connotations than its English counterpart. It signifies the mind, it signifies inventive, creative and civilizing forces generally, it signifies the distilling of something heavy into something light and quintessential, it signifies wit, it signifies verve. The task of fostering *Esprit* in these forms had long been Paris's chosen role. For thirty years it had been interrupted by the positivists' denial of an autonomous human spirit, but at last philosophers and scientists working independently were reaffirming the soul's existence, the validity of the creative Spirit, and perhaps also the existence of a creator God. During the early years of the new century Paris would again address herself with a will to 'bringing the Spirit down on the waters' of the Seine.

In this she had two extra incentives: an unspoken wish to regild the city's blazon, tarnished in 1870, and, in response to the dawn of a new century, that mood, already touched on, of hope, *joie de vivre* and intellectual confidence.

In the admittedly limited context of the Exhibition, signs were encouraging. Clicking almost non-stop, turnstiles registered 39 million admissions, though quite a few got in without buying a 60-centime ticket, daughters of contractors considering it more amusing to borrow, and show at the gate, a token issued to one of the firm's workmen. Wine-bibbers had a field day tasting no less than 40,000 wines. Goodwill getting the better of thrift, the host country issued medals and mentions to more than half the 70,000 items examined. When it closed in the autumn, the Exhibition had registered a profit.

Out of that massive display-case the Spirit also came down on the waters. At her own theatre, named after herself, in Rostand's patriotic and moving verse play, *L'Aiglon*, Sarah Bernhardt was giving an inspired performance as Napoleon's young son. Debussy put the finishing touches to to *Pelléas et Mélisande* in preparation for its first performance. In a patched-up shed near the Ecole de Physique, Pierre and Marie Curie were working night and day to identify an extraordinary new element that glowed in the dark. In the Olympics rugby final France beat Germany, in Deauville that summer a French motor-car broke the world's speed record. And this was only a beginning.

CHAPTER 3

A New Vigour

On a summer afternoon in 1900 an observer of the Paris scene might have noticed a procession of men in black velvet suits with a double row of small buttons, and black tight-fitting knitted caps, women with a wide black ribbon tied in a big butterfly bow framing their cheeks, skirts of red bombasine braided with black velvet, silk aprons and silk shawls, carrying banners and flags draped in black crape. Singing patriotic songs, they marched to the Place de la Concorde, circled the fountains and halted before one of the stone female figures, where one of their number stepped forward and reverently laid in front of the figure a crown of roses and orchids. The tricolours were dipped in salute, followed by several minutes' silence. Speeches were then made, during which some of the listeners wept. Presently the procession moved off, singing *'Vous n'aurez pas l'Alsace et la Lorraine.'*

What was this all about? The female statue personified Strasbourg, the marchers consisted mainly of Alsace-Lorrainers living in Paris, headed by the municipal council of Strasbourg, and they had gathered, as they did every 14 July, to protest what seemed to them an injustice.

In the summer of 1870 Napoleon III had led French armies across the Rhine in order to try to prevent Prussia from unifying the German Empire. He suffered a crushing defeat, losing 150,000 men (against

Prussia's 28,000). Germany then annexed most of four prosperous French *départements*: Bas-Rhin, Haut-Rhin – traditionally known as Alsace; and Meurthe and Moselle – about half of what was traditionally known as Lorraine. The annexed land, in the shape of an inverted L, measured 150 kms north to south by 100 kilometres east to west at its widest. It was rich in forest, vineyards, iron, coal and manufacturing industry, and included two lovely cities, medieval Strasbourg and eighteenth-century Nancy. Most of the annexed population of 2.3 million were German-speaking but in their loyalties French. Alsace since 1681 and Lorraine since 1766 had been part of France and the educated classes looked to France for their values and fashions. This was even truer of mainly Catholic Lorraine than of Protestant Alsace.

Rather than fall under German rule 128,000 Alsace-Lorrainers emigrated, chiefly to other French regions. The rest stayed in what was thenceforth known as *Reichsland* – a state of the German Empire. They were not oppressed or discriminated against, but they enjoyed less free speech and fewer rights of public meeting than Frenchmen.

Germany argued that 85% of the annexed population was German-speaking, that for most of the period 870 to 1681 – or 1766 in the case of Lorraine – the area had belonged to German rulers and thereafter had served French kings, then governments of the French Revolution, to make war on the German Empire. The new arrangement, they claimed, merely safeguarded their vulnerable western frontier. Frenchmen, by contrast, abhorred the annexation and on schoolroom maps the lost territory was wreathed in black crape.

Parisians were peculiarly susceptible to matters of national honour. They did not think in terms of a war of revenge, but they did adopt towards Germany an atti-

tude of chilly rancour. No self-respecting Parisian hostess invited to her table a visiting German. Newspapers
rarely mentioned Germany. For long the Paris Opéra
had declined to produce works by Wagner. President
Loubet would no more have considered crossing the
threshold of the German Embassy than of referring, in a
speech, to God. If Zola's comparison of Paris to a giant
stomach be retained, this defeat weighed like un-
digested food and caused a distressing heartburn.

It was acerbated by awareness of Germany's industrial strength. In the Exhibition's German pavilion
stood a model of the *Deutschland*, which had crossed the
Atlantic in a record-breaking five days eight hours,
while the chief source of the electricity that ran the
Exhibition and lit it after dark was a giant 3000 h.p.
steam generator built by Siemens and Halske: one of
several signs that the fairy Electricity was perhaps
really a Rhinemaiden. Nettling too was Germany's
large population: 56 million and rising, compared to
France's 39 million, stationary.

If the statue symbolizing Strasbourg was important
to Parisians, still more so were two larger monuments.
In 1871 the Paris Commune had established itself on
the hill of Montmartre, defied the Government of
France, based then in Versailles, and wished to continue the war against Prussia. It had been a gallant
expression of patriotic fervour. But it had failed, disin-
tegrating into civil war in which 100,000 Frenchmen
had died. Now the church of Sacré-Cœur, with its large
white dome, crowned the hill of Montmartre, built by
public subscription to expiate the crimes on both sides
and which had reflected the political divisions that had
led to military defeat. The church was a plea for concord and political unity.

The other monument was the Arc de Triomphe, com-
memorating the Grande Armée's victories from Spain to

the outskirts of Moscow. Its huge bulk, decorated with Rude's impassioned bas-reliefs, dominated western Paris's twelve majestic avenues, and was a permanent call to Frenchmen to continue into the twentieth century the record of France's glory and her 'civilizing mission'.

It was under such signs as these that Frenchmen around 1900 addressed themselves to their country's position in the world. Rancour is a negative emotion and the French were becoming positive in their outlook. The tone of older boys' essays in the Paris lycées, the phrasing of toasts at Republican banquets, the increasing use of 'dignity' and 'decision' in editorials about foreign policy, an article in *Revue des Deux Mondes* by Ernest Lavisse of the Sorbonne, formerly tutor to Napoleon III's son, in which he adopted a lordly attitude to Europe – in dozens of small ways Frenchmen began to denote that the honour believed to have been lost thirty years before they would now like to redeem by some display of greatness. They certainly wanted peace – only peace could bring an improvement in workers' conditions and wages, a main plank in the Radicals' platform – but also they wanted to reassert the grandeur of France, as it had been, say, under the Sun King and Emperor Napoleon. It remains to be seen whether these goals were compatible.

It was in pursuit of both goals that France chose as the cornerstone of her foreign policy an alliance with Russia. First negotiated some years earlier, from 1898 onwards successive French ministries strengthened the alliance, which was a defensive pact 'for the maintenance of peace', obliging each country to give help to the other in the event of aggression by Germany or Austria. That Europe's leading republic should ally herself with the leading autocracy angered men of the far Left, but to most of Parisian middle- and upper-class society, as their newspapers make plain, it seemed a sensible arrangement, Russia's large population compensating for France's weakness in that respect.

In 1900 and the ensuing years things Russian became increasingly popular in France. Luminaries at the Sorbonne were reading Tolstoy or practising his theories. André Gide was enjoying, and learning from, Dostoievsky in a recent translation. Debussy was studying to good effect Rimsky-Korsakov and Moussorgsky. Restaurant Paillard packed its tables by offering *La sole à la Russe* and *La choucroute Impériale Russe au vin de champagne*. *Le Figaro* glowingly reported Tsar Nicholas's visit, and President Loubet's visit to the Russian capital, where it was said the staid Republican warmed to autocratic pomp and circumstance. In early 1901 the same newspaper reported delightedly that the French Government was sending to the Tsarina a tapestry depicting Vigée Lebrun's portrait of Marie Antoinette and her children: ominous gift. An article on another page complained that the French language was losing ground to German in the Russian Empire and urged the Alliance Française to start up more schools there with teaching in French: France's 'civilizing mission', but also perhaps petty jealousy.

Such was the background in 1900, when a Foreign Minister of exceptional single-mindedness began to re-think France's policy abroad. Théophile Delcassé came from Pamiers, at the foot of the Pyrenees. A bailiff's son, at the age of four Théophile lost his mother; the insecurity that resulted was sharpened when his father remarried and the new wife, who did not want Théophile at home, sent the boy away. Under his grandmother's roof the reject lived without a father or siblings but was made a fuss of by his grandmother. He grew up outwardly self-assertive, inwardly secretive and insecure.

When the Russians broke through French defences at Sedan, Delcassé was a nineteen-year-old undergraduate in Toulouse, hoping to become a playwright. Like many, including Bonaparte, bred in a frontier or marginal region, young Delcassé possessed a deep love of France; also perhaps he felt France to be his second mother. These feelings and the latent insecurity of his character made of the incursion a deep personal tragedy. According to his daughter, the defeat at Sedan was to shape his whole life. He saw it as a wrong done to France which true patriots must put right.

Léon Gambetta, another patriot from the south-west, but a self-assured extrovert, became a member of the Provisional Government formed after Napoleon III's fall. Gambetta's military ineptitude played a large part in France's final defeat; despite, or perhaps because of that, he refused to ratify the treaty surrendering Alsace and Lorraine. As Deputy for Paris's Twentieth Arrondissement, again and again Gambetta thundered out in the Chamber his chosen theme: France is still a great power, and the French are the only ones who seem to doubt it.

Delcassé made a hero of Gambetta. On leaving university, after failing to have a play accepted by the Comédie Française, he became a journalist on the newspaper Gambetta had founded, *La République Française.* For fifteen years Delcassé purveyed to French readers Gambetta's chosen theme. The ardent young journalist painted a grim picture of Europe and of the need for France to beware. 'War appears to us as a necessity,' he wrote. 'It is found everywhere in nature. For a long time it has been the normal state of Europe.' Germany in the modern sense had existed for less than fifty years yet had waged – and won – three wars. She could not and must not be trusted. Germany, declared Delcassé, was preparing a 'war of extermination'. When charged with being a chauvinist, Delcassé cheerfully agreed, saying he took the word as a compliment.

The Deputy for Foix having died, in 1889 Delcassé married the Deputy's rich widow and thus succeeded to the deceased man's bed and to his seat in the Assembly. This new recruit to Parliament had a thin voice and could speak only from a prepared script, but he impressed in three ways: by his industriousness – up at five, behind his desk at six – by his tenacity, and by his ardent patriotism.

Delcassé was known to favour the Russian alliance and to wish to work for France's grandeur. After a spell as Colonial Minister, in 1898 he was appointed Foreign Minister. Tenacious in this as in all else, he was to stay in that post an almost record seven years.

The new Minister was very small, dark-complexioned, with a large, smiling, full-lipped mouth, big, dark, intelligent, short-sighted eyes behind gold-rimmed spectacles, a thick, upturned nose, dark hair plastered over a flat cranium. He looked rather like a mole, and his methods were the mole's. Bypassing Cabinet colleagues and Quai d'Orsay officials, he chose to work directly with the President and with France's ambassadors. To Sir Edmund Monson, British Ambassador in Paris, he carried 'the practice of subterfuge to an extent which I have hardly ever met before in a Minister of Foreign Affairs'. And about no subject was Delcassé more secretive than Alsace-Lorraine. Here he applied Gambetta's motto: 'Think of it always, speak of it never.'

Delcassé, with Loubet's approval, began to tighten the Russian alliance. Delcassé went to St Petersburg and in accordance with his distrust of Germany altered the treaty's declared aim from 'maintenance of peace' to 'maintenance of the balance of power'. He arranged for Loubet to visit St Petersburg, and Tsar Nicholas Paris, and at other levels greatly improved relations. The little, busy, secretive man showed so much skill he began to be called 'the Gnome'.

Like other Frenchmen of his generation, the Gnome drew on the new mood of hope and confidence visible in the 1900 Exhibition, and his foreign policy became more adventurous. Not content to have one powerful ally, he sought a second.

France's relations with England were at this period strained. We have seen French opinion favouring the Boers; in 1900 it was so hostile that Queen Victoria cancelled her holiday in Hyères and went to Ireland, where she found the sky in more than one sense rather less blue. Moreover, the French were angry with Britain for having foiled, at Fashoda on the Nile, their ambitious plan to establish their African Empire on a new west–east axis; as a result of that failure Egypt, Napoleon's most admired overseas prize, had passed from French to English hegemony, though France's 'civilizing mission' still remained almost intact in law, language and schools.

Early in the new century two events happened which made Delcassé think relations with Britain could be improved. The Queen who had kept up a close friendship with Germany died and was succeeded by Edward VII, who ever since his visit to Empress Eugénie's court at fourteen had loved France, and one might add a number of French actresses. The following year saw peace with the Boers. These circumstances Delcassé quickly seized in order to make friendly overtures across the Channel.

*   *   *

Britain during the late nineteenth century had been powerful enough to hold aloof from the Continent. Her Empire, her navy, gave self-sufficiency. Then came the Boer War. In the first leader in *The Times* on 1 January 1900 the editor declared, with an almost audible sigh, that Britain's role in the coming century would be to hold on to her Empire. Heavy losses in South Africa showed that in this task she needed an ally.

Her first choice was Germany. But the Germans wanted a free hand abroad; they looked to the future, *their* future, not to a preservation of the status quo with Britain calling the shots, and they showed themselves cool towards Britain's signals.

For lack of a strong navy Spain in 1898 had lost Cuba and the Philippines – the latter territory being promptly bought by the United States; Germany, which possessed a few colonies and growing trade, notably in Latin America, determined not to suffer a similar fate. She began therefore to build up her navy. There seems no reason to doubt German assurances at this stage that her aim was to protect her investments and her businessmen, for commercial successes by a foreign nation often led to envy, trumped-up charges and imprisonment of European agents, and such incidents, as all the powers accepted, called for sending a gunboat or some larger naval vessel.

Britain, indeed, was so far in sympathy with this attitude that in the hope of drawing Germany into an alliance, she agreed to send the Royal Navy to join the German navy in a blockade of Venezuela, a country which had lately defaulted on loans. This was in 1902–3. The blockade failed at a practical level, while the growing strength of Germany's fleet began to disturb quite a few Englishmen. Rudyard Kipling, never averse to finding a secret enemy, wrote a much-noticed jingoist poem, 'The Rowers', denouncing this 'league anew / With the Goth and the Shameless Hun'.

This was the moment when Delcassé saw a chance for something big and radical. He would need support within France, and he found it. His fifteen years of articles followed by fifteen years of Assembly speeches urging France to be strong – these had won him followers. Prominent among them were the highly intelligent Cambon brothers. Both had held high positions in North Africa – Paul master-minded France's protectorate in Tunisia, Jules was Governor-General of Algeria – and retained links with Frenchmen in those countries. With deep-set eyes and tuft of beard Paul resembled a fox-terrier; he was forever fretting that Parisians lacked 'resonance' and would, unless kept up to the mark by men like himself and his brother, lapse into the decadence of late Rome or Byzantium. Paul served as Ambassador in London from 1898. Jules, two years his junior, with a pekinese cast of head, was a less forthright person than Paul. A specialist in bluff and ambiguous statements, he served as ambassador first in Madrid, then in Berlin, in both cities following Delcassé's anti-German line. Jules was known to Proust, who noted his 'cunning eyes . . . wrinkled and sly', and lampooned him as the self-important Monsieur de Norpois, behind his clichés a faceless person.

It was with Paul Cambon that Delcassé first began to work closely. He arranged for Cambon to propose an arrangement about North Africa to the British Foreign Secretary, Lord Lansdowne. Lansdowne was eager to find a friend and as a descendant of Talleyrand felt a personal sympathy with France. He showed interest. King Edward showed even more interest. Against the advice of his Cabinet, who believed it premature, he decided in May 1903 to pay a state visit to Paris.

Portly, smartly dressed, red carnation in his buttonhole, the sixty-two-year-old King possessed two useful gifts: he could speak fluent French and, with a kind word or a smile, he knew how to put people at ease. Arriving at the Bois de Boulogne station, he drove with President Loubet to the British Embassy. His aide, Charles Hardinge, followed in the second carriage with Delcassé: 'Although there were considerable crowds in the Champs-Elysées who cheered the King as he passed, I could not fail to notice that amongst them were small groups who shouted, "*Vivent les Boers!*" Naturally the King heard nothing, surrounded as was his carriage by the escort of cuirassiers with their clattering hoofs. I am sure Delcassé noticed it and hoped that I had not heard, for he was all the time trying to distract my attention by saying repeatedly, "*Quel enthousiasme!*" '

At the theatre that evening the King, walking in the foyer, recognized Jeanne Granier, a gifted actress. The King approached her and, having kissed her hand, said, 'Mademoiselle, I remember applauding you in London where you represented all the grace and spirit of France.' Those few words, spoken with feeling, spread through the theatre and when he returned to his box the audience rose to cheer the King.

Edward again showed his happy touch at the Hôtel de Ville. Replying to speeches by various Prefects, he said, 'I shall never forget my visit to your charming city, and I can assure you of my very great pleasure in returning to Paris, where I always feel as though I were at home.' These words, says Hardinge, 'produced an electric impression throughout Paris', and by the end of his three-day visit crowds were cheering him: '*Vive Edouard!*', '*Vive notre bon Teddy!*'

Well-pleased with the King's visit, Delcassé began to spell out some hard facts. The price of France's friendship would be this: in return for allowing England a free hand in Egypt (which England already had, *de facto*), France must be allowed by Britain a free hand in Morocco.

This proposal was in two ways astonishing. Morocco was a sovereign nation; by the Convention of Madrid, 1880, the Great Powers (including England, France and Germany) had guaranteed her independence and agreed that commerce with her should be open to all. Secondly, France already possessed the second largest colonial Empire: in Africa alone 11.5 million square kilometres, including Algeria and a protectorate in Tunisia, and could hardly claim the need for more, since unlike Germany, where the demand for *Lebensraum* was understandable, she had no superfluous population to develop fully even what she had.

Delcassé knew this, but he knew also that he held in his hand a number of strong cards. First, the French people were presently preoccupied with anti-clerical measures, so they had little time for foreign affairs, and this is reflected in parliamentary proceedings. In the Assembly – one blinks to read this – foreign affairs were discussed *once a year*, when the Quai d'Orsay budget was voted, while in the Senate five whole years passed without a serious debate on foreign policy. This would change after 1905, but until then the French were content to leave foreign policy to the President and the Gnome.

Delcassé's second advantage was support within the Quai d'Orsay from senior officials who wished to redeem France's honour by increasing her Empire; and his third, support from the most powerful Parliamentary pressure group, the French Africa Committee. This Committee received funds from leading banks (including Comte Greffulhe's), shipping companies, steel works, railway companies, Right-wing newspapers and 70,000 Alsace-Lorrainers who had settled in Algeria. It was headed by Eugène-Napoléon Etienne, deputy for Oran in Algeria, a burly, square-headed, very tough jingoist who had started as an executive in Algeria's railways and now, taking his second name seriously, saw himself called to promote France's grandeur.

Finally, Delcassé could count on sympathy from the literary avant-garde. André Gide and his circle, as we shall see, described their visits to Algeria in lyrical descriptive books and poems: they conjured up a Garden of Eden, where goatherds piped amid date orchards and orange groves. North Africa had become the fashion in Paris.

Delcassé sent his proposals to Paul Cambon, who placed them before Lansdowne. Now British policy at this time – we have Viscount Grey's word for it – aimed at preventing Germany getting ports in the colonial world. Morocco had both Mediterranean and Atlantic ports; though there was no sign that Germany was eyeing them acquisitively, Delcassé's proposals would nullify any such design in the future. Lansdowne showed interest, and it was Cambon who hesitated. He foresaw that Delcassé's plans would arouse German anger, and he urged Delcassé, before proceeding further, to negotiate directly with Chancellor Bülow.

Delcassé might have heeded Cambon but for the fact that Eugène-Napoléon Etienne had become president of the Assembly's Foreign Affairs Commission. According to Delcassé's private secretary, 'The support of Etienne and his group [the French Africa Committee] is indispensable for the survival of the Cabinet.' And Etienne opposed any deal with Germany.

Discussions in London continued and on 8 April 1904 Lansdowne signed an Anglo-French Convention. Morocco was kept in fairly good order by a Sultan but it suited the Powers to say that disorder reigned, hence Article 2 of the Convention stated:

The Government of the French Republic declare that they have no intention of altering the political status of Morocco. His Britannic Majesty's Government, for their part, recognize that it appertains to France more particularly as a Power whose dominions are conterminous for a great distance with those of Morocco, to preserve order in that country, and to provide assistance for the purpose of all administrative, economic, financial, and military reforms which it may require . . .

The phrases used were a recognized code for commercial domination to be followed by financial stranglehold, then by military domination.

It remains to be noted that the Anglo-French Convention was the only published written basis of the nexus of friendships which, encouraged by King Edward, and in France by Delcassé and all who felt rancour towards Germany, was now to develop between influential Englishmen and Frenchmen, and came to be termed the Entente Cordiale.

As well as the published Convention a *secret* agreement was signed between England and France. It said that should the Sultan cease to exercise authority over his country, that part of Morocco facing Gibraltar should go to Spain. But in the same year Delcassé safeguarded France's hegemony by negotiating a second *secret* treaty, this one with Spain, which stated that in the event of disorder France and Spain would partition Morocco, France to get four-fifths of it.

Delcassé now moved fast. On 12 June 1904 a consortium of eleven French banks arranged a loan of 62.5 million francs, at 5%, guaranteed by Moroccan customs duties, collection of which was to be supervised by French officials backed by the French legation. In December, ignoring Morocco's 'independence', he instructed France's resident in Fez, Saint-René Taillandier, to initiate police reforms, establish a French-dominated State Bank, construct roads and railways, spread the French language and settle claims for damages allegedly inflicted on Algerians by Moroccan raiders.

On 22 February 1905 in a speech to the assembly of Moroccan Notables Taillandier announced these 'reforms', adding that they had 'the assent of other foreign representatives in Tangier'.

Now this was untrue. Because Delcassé was secretive and anyway hated communicating directly with the Wilhelmstrasse, Germany had not been told, and Germany was a signatory to the Convention of Madrid, 1880, which, we have seen, guaranteed Morocco's political independence as well as equal commercial opportunities therein for all the Powers.

In spring 1905 the Emperor of Germany was cruising the Atlantic in his yacht *Hamburg*. Aged forty-six, he was a broad-shouldered, straight-backed man of medium height, with fair curly hair, prominent straight nose, blue eyes, resolute mouth surmounted by a moustache with waxed upturned ends. Because Prussia's social structure had military roots, he usually wore uniform. At first meeting he seemed stiff, but he would soon relax, talking fast in a pleasant, strong voice. He laughed easily and enjoyed telling funny stories, some lifted from *Punch*, including jokes about Irishmen complete with accent.

Wilhelm had studied law at Bonn, then joined a cavalry regiment. Despite a shrunken arm, he soon made

his name as an excellent horseman, shot and swords-
man. He had married a pious, plump, adoring lady who
had borne him one son and six daughters. With a nation
that wanted a ruler in the mould of a typical German
nobleman the Kaiser enjoyed wide popularity.

Wilhelm could tell you – and indeed did tell his uncle
Edward VII – about the comparative merits of petrol
and potato spirit for motor-car engines. He could identify every uniform and every decoration at a glance and
sketch their history. He knew about battleships and
even attempted to design one. He knew about ladies'
fashion and annually selected twelve hats as a birthday
present for his wife. He painted, he arranged ballets, he
designed a chapel for one of his castles, he took part in
archæological excavation in Corfu.

Wilhelm's salient characteristic was a love of the sea
and of ships. He was never happier than at the helm of
his racing yacht taking part in the Kiel Regatta. This
love of the sea is evident in his foreign policy. He
intended Germany to become a great world power
through hard work and commerce – and to protect its
power abroad with a strong navy. According to the
British Ambassador who knew him best, 'the Kaiser is
pacifically inclined and I think he would surprise a
great many people by his prudence and patience . . . It
would take a great deal to drive him into war and he
would require the whole nation behind him.'

'Full steam ahead' was one of Wilhelm's favourite
phrases. He himself was forever on the go, opening new
schools, technical colleges, hospitals, with patriotic
speeches which, to non-Germans, seemed conceited
and even offensive. For example, on New Year's Day
1900, he promised the rebirth of the navy so that
Germany might win 'the place which it has not yet
attained'.

Wilhelm fancied himself as a maker of foreign policy.

He felt sure that he personally could preserve the peace of Europe by working closely with his suave Chancellor, Bernhard von Bülow, and by charming his fellow-monarchs. Alas, Wilhelm II was too much the know-all to charm. He had the regrettable habit of hinting to others that they were less effective than he. This had already put Edward VII's back up, and would presently do as much to Nicholas II.

While the Kaiser was enjoying his spring cruise, von Bülow learned of Saint-René Taillandier's speech in Fez to the Moroccan Notables. Bülow knew of the Convention whereby France had been given a free hand by Britain and may also have had suspicions about the secret treaties. He was furious at Taillandier's unilateral proposals. To his Ambassador in London he wrote: 'Any man from whose pocket it is proposed to take money will defend himself to the extent of his capacities, whether five marks or five thousand. We possess economic interests in Morocco. That does not require proof. If, by our silence, we renounce them, we shall thus encourage the world, which is watching us, to adopt a similar lack of consideration to our detriment in other questions, perhaps more important.'

Bülow sent a message to the yacht *Hamburg*, requesting the Kaiser to land at Tangier, to ride to the German legation and to make a speech stating Germany's position: 'M. Delcassé,' he complained, 'has completely ignored us in this affair.'

Wilhelm liked making speeches – he delivered about fifty a year – but not being particularly interested in France or Morocco, at first he refused. But when Bülow explained the need for a firm stand, eventually Wilhelm agreed. Since the Moroccans tended to welcome visitors with rifle fire, he asked that his horse should be well exercised beforehand so that it would not be nervous.

On the morning of 31 March 1905 a stiff east wind made landing from the Imperial yacht impossible. In the afternoon the wind subsided, and Wilhelm went ashore. At the gold-braided bemedalled uniform his white Berber horse shied and bucked but was presently quieted. Followed by a score of riders, Wilhelm entered Tangier, greeted by rifle shots from the men and by flowers from women crowding the roof-tops. Arrived at the legation, he dismounted and received the Sultan's representatives. Then he made a speech. He had, he declared, 'great interest in the welfare and prosperity of the Moroccan Empire, he visited the Sultan as an independent ruler, and he hoped that under the Sultan's authority a free Morocco would be opened to the peaceful competition of all nations without monopoly or exclusion.' He was warmly applauded, then re-embarked. Hearing that all had gone off smoothly on what he regarded as a symbolically important occasion, Bülow shed tears of nervous relief.

Though it is hard now to see why, the Kaiser's landing and speech in Tangier caused a furore in London. *The Times* called the incident 'provocative' and said Germany intended to try to break up the Anglo-French entente by browbeating France. No one, even on the Left, said France had been provocative. Edward VII wrote to Lansdowne:

> The Tangier incident was the most mischievous and uncalled-for event which the German Emperor has ever been engaged in since he came to the throne. It was also a political fiasco ... He is no more or less than a political *enfant terrible* and one can have no faith in any of his assurances. His own pleasure seems to wish to set every country by the ears.

The King's displeasure was all the keener because the German Government had asked their friend, President Theodore Roosevelt – another irrepressibly active leader on the lines of Wilhelm – to sort out the Moroccan difficulty, and Roosevelt agreed to mediate between Germany and Britain. But on 19 May the President reported to Baron Sternburg that 'the British Government had given him to understand that it did not wish better relations with Germany', and that 'it had hinted broadly . . . that Great Britain could take care of her affairs alone'. He could not do more, he said, without exposing himself to an incivility.

How did Paris react to the Kaiser's surprise landing? Playing up the fact that Wilhelm had gone ashore wearing uniform, complete with sword and boots, the press presented the incident as yet another example of German sabre-rattling and an affront to France's civilizing mission to Africa. But the Prime Minister since January 1905, Maurice Rouvier, was a former banker who knew the importance for business of correct if not warm relations with Germany. Aged sixty-two, he felt no sympathy for his younger Foreign Minister's policy or for his secretive methods, though neither he nor his Cabinet knew the full extent of these, for – almost incredibly! – the secret treaties with England and Spain had not been divulged to them. Rouvier considered that the Convention with England should have been formally communicated to Germany, also the far-reaching 'reforms' announced by Taillandier. Rouvier pressed Delcassé to take the initiative with Germany, but the Foreign Minister refused.

It so happened that Delcassé had defended the Russian Government in its massacre of demonstrators on Bloody Sunday, 22 January 1905, and so lost the support of the Left wing of his party. On 19 April he was denounced in the Assembly for having neglected to consult Germany. He was pressed for further information on this subject but characteristically declined to give it.

On 1 May Edward VII, who happened to be paying another visit to Paris, gave strong support to Delcassé. The press had by now begun to feel that Delcassé had gone too far, and most editors came out against the King, complaining that he was trying to estrange France and Germany.

Meanwhile, the Sultan of Morocco, supported by Wilhelm and Bülow, proposed a conference. Delcassé opposed any conference. Then in late May Russia suffered her disastrous naval defeat by Japan and was obliged to sue for peace. Shocked by her supposedly strong ally's unexpectedly poor showing, the French Cabinet and public opinion became very uneasy. On 6 June at a Cabinet meeting, Russia's champion, Delcassé, got no support for his hostile attitude to Germany and to the idea of a conference, and was obliged to resign.

Both France and Germany prepared for a conference on Morocco, to be held in southern Spain. Wilhelm, by the fact of intervening personally in Tangier, had come to be involved directly with France and henceforth would play a leading role in defending against France what the Germans considered to be sacrosanct under the Convention of 1880: Moroccan independence and Germany's right to trade there as an equal.

But would the French, now that Delcassé had lost office, be ready to abandon an expansionist policy? That question turned on another. Were influential Frenchmen now ready to swallow their rancour about Alsace-Lorraine, to forget their schoolroom lesson that their neighbour was incorrigibly martial, and to work for détente?

The answers would depend on public opinion and this in turn on makers of opinion, who were not only, or even primarily, journalists and leader-writers. Creative Parisians generally – poets, novelists, playwrights, painters, choreographers, composers – were in this period reshaping people's imaginations and so helping to renew the values according to which attitudes generally and to foreign countries in particular, to peace and to war, came to be formed. The most influential among these creative people it is now time to begin to examine.

CHAPTER 4

A Quest for Sincerity: André Gide

I n a large canvas by a fashionable portraitist of the day five young men are shown in front of the Moorish Café at the Paris Exhibition. One is a doctor, another a lawyer, a third a landowner, all with literary tastes; the fourth is an Algerian in turban and jeballa, Athman by name. Dominating the group is a handsome man with a long face and long, drooping moustache. He is seated, wearing a black cloak and wide-brimmed felt hat, elbow supported on his thigh, between his fingers a cigarette. His name is André Gide, and the picture is entitled *André Gide and Friends*, for it was Gide who had shown his group the charms of North Africa, and he who found his guide and protégé Athman a job at the Algerian pavilion. Aged thirty-one, energetic, subtle, a fearless thinker, André Gide, critics predicted, might well become a great writer – once he had found himself. But that might not be easy, for his was a complex nature, stemming from an unusual background.

André Gide was the only child of Paul Gide, a professor of law, and Juliette, née Rondeaux, both devout Calvinists. Their house on a thousand-acre estate near Dieppe in Normandy was run with austere exactitude: floors polished like mirrors, furniture protected by dust covers, household expenses added up daily. But also there was much affection. Paul Gide, a sweet, sloping-shouldered scholar, called André *'mon petit ami'*, and was devoted to his wife, a big handsome woman with a deep voice. A Scottish governess was engaged, Anna Shackleton, of whom they were all very fond: from Anna André was fortunate enough to learn not only English and German but the piano – he became a pianist of almost concert-hall standard – and entomology, which gave him an understanding of the natural world to whose beauty he was early drawn.

When he was eleven André's father died and for the next few years he found himself in almost exclusively feminine company – his now rather masterful and intimidating mother, Anna Shackleton and his first cousin Madeleine Rondeaux, a pretty, exceptionally sweet girl, also a Calvinist, who nourished a finely grained inner life with books of devotion.

Madame Gide and her son moved to Paris, so that André could attend the Ecole Alsacienne (Paul had had links with Alsace). André began to show a gift for writing, and it was agreed that he should become a professional man of letters. He frequented literary salons, but the genres of the day – Symbolism, cynical realism and Satanism – held no appeal for one who believed in the existence of God and the soul and who aspired to deeper joys. A journey to North Africa had given him a taste for the desert – its immense space and sense of freedom – and his first, immature prose poetry had celebrated the joys to be found in this 'earthly paradise'.

When he was twenty-six Madame Gide died and André proposed marriage to Madeleine Rondeaux. They had grown up almost as brother and sister, they loved each other, but the love had almost no sexual basis, André's preference being for boys, and Madeleine's strict Calvinism having made her fearful of sex. There was the further fact that any children of the union between first cousins might easily be abnormal. On the understanding that theirs would be a *mariage blanc* André and Madeleine were married in 1895. In the five years since then the marriage had proved close and happy.

Gide and friends not only posed for their portraits at the Paris Exhibition, they explored it thoroughly, Gide being particularly receptive to foreign art. Himself the author of plays, he liked best the Japanese theatre and with typical zest went to see it six times.

Gide also began to plan a winter journey for himself, Madeleine, Athman and another friend depicted in the painting: Henri Ghéon. The only son of a domineering widowed mother, Ghéon practised medicine in the Norman town of Bray. He shared Gide's tastes for literature and boys.

In December 1900 the party of four set off by way of Marseille: Gide, very efficient, taking the lead; Madeleine pale, easily tired and quiet; Athman chattering in broken French; Ghéon, jolliness written all over his round, open, animated face, with red cheeks, white teeth and short dark beard. Since Ghéon had no money Gide paid for his ticket. Gide, though very well off, had been inculcated with Calvinist thrift and they all travelled second class.

They landed in Algiers and travelled south to Biskra, on the edge of the desert. Here they took rooms in the Hôtel Royal. Earlier in the year Madeleine had been knocked down by a motor-car in the Place de la Concorde: both arms had been broken and she was still not very strong. Madeleine would remain in Biskra, Gide decided, while the men entered the desert.

Two days south they reached the date-palm oasis of Touggourt. Gide dispatched a reassuring telegram but Madeleine felt frightened in her strange surroundings. 'Dearest, it is terrible being alone,' she wrote to André, 'worse than I thought. And only two days gone.' In a postscript she added: 'My dearest, my only love, come back, come back.'

Gide had no intention just yet of coming back. With Ghéon he explored the oasis, its walls built of pinkish clay, 'turned a little darker by the water, which the burning sun cracks, which hardens in the heat and softens with the first shower, so that it becomes a plastic soil that keeps the imprint of a bare foot'. Palm trees bending in a breeze, wood-pigeons, the notes of a flute: 'I walked on in a sort of ecstasy,' says Gide, 'of silent joy, of elation of the senses and the flesh.'

In Biskra Gide had read in the newspaper the news of Oscar Wilde's death. He had known the Irishman well in Paris after his gaol sentence and esteemed him as a wise, brave champion of sexual sincerity. He would have liked to have been one of the small group of mourners at Père-Lachaise. True, he had sometimes tired of Wilde sneeringly pitting pagan joys against the Christian ideal to the detriment of the latter; for Gide believed that the two could and should be squared.

In reaching that odd belief Gide had been helped by the writings of Friedrich Nietzsche. He had read only one book by Nietzsche, who died in 1900 – the philosophic poem *Also Sprach Zarathustra* – but he had seen reviews of others and picked up a number of Nietzsche's catch maxims. One maxim stated: 'What is best in us is that which sets us apart from others.' Now what set Gide apart was his pederasty. Could this be the best part of him?

In his sexual relations with boys Gide found more than physical satisfaction. He derived what he took to be spiritual joy from their good looks, their firm young tanned bodies, their spontaneity, their lack of *arrière pensée*. Calvinists viewed marriage as a sacrament, and Gide looked on his experiences with boys somewhat in that way. Since pederasty lifted his soul, it was, he decided, not something to be ashamed of but a way of experiencing, and praising, his Creator.

While Gide and Ghéon explored the oasis and wrote up their elation, Athman brought them meals from a hot-food stall and in the evening escorted them to 'interesting' cafés. Here they would chat up boys whose good looks caught their fancy and on the edge of the immense and to them mysterious desert indulge themselves to the full.

Ghéon took his pleasure greedily and gratefully, almost as though eating a delicious fruit. Gide, by contrast, observed his own subtle sensations. In the midst of pleasure he remained the writer, savouring new nuances, analysing them, relishing too the infringement of conventional taboos. He wanted to compare experiences with Ghéon, but the doctor declined. There were moments even when he turned away from Gide, shocked.

Ghéon had rejected the Catholicism taught him by a too-clinging mother and described himself as an agnostic. Yet he responded to sights in the oasis unnoted by Gide. He wrote a good poem about a small whitewashed domed building where a saintly teacher had retired to dwell in silence: 'With clean lines, abstract, blazingly white and, according to its occupant, "The thought with which he thinks God."' He noticed too a holy but slightly dotty hermit who wore up to thirty burnouses, and once a year peeled them off in order to shake out the accumulated vermin over a fire, then dance before the flames. The humble poor were always to touch Ghéon's heart.

So, for a week, the two young writers plunged themselves in pleasure. Gide was not unduly concerned about Madeleine. Pure and unworldly, she had no idea there was such a thing as pederasty and, in her hotel, was gravely reading the latest book on the spiritual life by a Dominican, Father Didon, breaking off at sunrise and sunset to climb the hotel minaret in order to share the beauty of the sky with her absent, adored André.

On Christmas Day, after a thirteen-hour muleback journey, Gide, Ghéon and Athman returned. Madeleine, overjoyed, told André how lonely she had been and how she had booked a seat on the post-coach to Touggourt, only to cancel it in the evening: it would have been expensive and might have displeased André. Indeed, it would have.

Leaving Athman in Algeria, the travellers sailed home. While Ghéon returned to his medical practice, Gide divided his time between his Normandy home, Cuverville, and Paris. He resumed correspondence with literary friends, notably Francis Jammes, who lived in the Pyrenees and was considered by Gide and Ghéon to be the best living poet. He played his favourite Schubert, invited neighbours for tennis, and Paris friends for the weekend. Ghéon would visit in his motor-car, which broke down so often they called it the 'antimobile' until a mechanic discovered that Ghéon had misaligned the batteries and was running it with current reversed.

Above all Gide enjoyed the quiet presence of Madeleine. 'Marriage for Gide,' says his secretary, 'was something *sacred*, freed of the troubles, the emotions (or tragedies) of carnal desire . . . In Madeleine's presence Gide became very simple, so far as he could be simple.'

About the closeness of the marriage, and Gide's protective affection there can be little doubt. One wedding anniversary Madeleine wrote to Gide: 'Twelve years ago today we entered the little *mairie* in Cuverville – and twelve years ago tomorrow the road to the church in Etretat seemed to me so short. Just as short and good have been these twelve years spent near you, my dar-

ling. The last year has always been the best. God grant
it may be so for the years he will still give us. I lay my
head on your shoulder and embrace you.'

Paris was becoming increasingly important to Gide.
There he met his many literary friends, and the editor
of *L'Ermitage*, which published his writing. There he
saw the latest plays and went to the salons. There too he
indulged his taste for boys, usually picking them up at
the Turkish Baths. Only Ghéon knew, and he could be
trusted.

Gide's visit to Algeria had crystallized the joys and
dilemmas of bisexuality. He believed that in his private
life he had solved the difficult matter of being a protective, loving, Platonic husband and also of satisfying his
sexual tastes. But this, he decided, was no longer
enough. He wished to do something neither Wilde nor
any writer since Roman days had done: describe in a
book the conflict of feeling within a bisexualist and, lest
he reveal his true nature to Madeleine, he must do so
cautiously.

Michel, the protagonist and narrator of Gide's novel,
The Immoralist, is an archæologist inclined, like his
father, to free-thinking but held back by a conscience
derived from a Calvinist mother. On a journey to North
Africa Michel falls ill with tuberculosis and is devot-
edly nursed by his wife Marceline. 'You *will* get well,'
Marceline assures him, but when she adds that she will
pray for him, Michel checks her – he does not wish to be
indebted to God.

Soon Michel is well enough to stroll in the oasis date
gardens. There he meets goatherds. He is attracted by
their healthy good looks, feels stronger in their presence and joins in their simple games. Marceline too
befriends some of these boys – the poorer ones for
whom she feels pity.

One of the boys, Michel notices, goes noiselessly up

to a table where Marceline has laid her sewing and a little pair of scissors beside it, seizes them furtively and in a flash engulfs them in the folds of his burnous. 'My heart beat quickly for a moment but neither reason nor reflection could arouse in me the smallest feeling of indignation. More than that! I could not manage to persuade myself that my reaction to the incident was anything but joy.'

Michel's Calvinism is evidently on the wane. He protects the boy by inventing a story to explain the disappearance of the scissors. His association with the good-looking boys makes him wish to develop his own body, for which formerly he felt a Calvinist shame. He sunbathes, does exercises, shaves off his scholar's beard and moustache. He sleeps with Marceline and makes her pregnant.

Michel, cured, returns to France with Marceline. There he comes under the influence of a shady but successful Nietzschean, who urges Michel to develop the most distinctive part of himself – the part society would disapprove of.

Marceline loses her child and falls ill with tuberculosis. Michel takes her south. In Rome he buys her a big bouquet of almond blossom but its scent is too strong for her and makes her dizzy. This irritates Michel. They continue south, to Algeria. Though he still loves her, Michel finds his sick wife a burden. At the end of each day he leaves her alone to haunt back-street cafés.

One night while Michel is with a prostitute, Marceline has a hæmorrhage. He returns too late to save her. After a period of shock he decides to settle in Algeria and takes up with a prostitute. This woman has a good-looking young brother. In the novel's last lines it is said that Michel is beginning to prefer the brother.

Zola in later life had been begged by an Italian to speak out in defence of sodomy (the word homosexuality had not yet been coined), and Zola, courageous and eminent though he was, had declined. Sodomy was in two ways a minefield. Forbidden by the Old Testament and New, by Catholics and Protestants, it was also believed to be a symptom of nervous degeneration, therefore hereditary. An avowed pederast in the family, and the rest of that family became virtually unmarriage-able – the sins of the father would be visited on the children . . . So around the subject a curtain of silence was drawn, and many considered it better so.

Gide dared to draw aside the curtain, cautiously it is true, because of Madeleine, but with such beauty and art that people who read the novel understood – and felt obliged to consider the plight of a man who is attracted to boys as well as to women.

Though it was denounced by many critics and by the Church, with *The Immoralist* Gide rescued the novel from late nineteenth-century cynicism and was duly hailed by the young. In answer to increasing claims from Paris in 1904 he decided to build a villa in Auteuil. Though not a beautiful building – Gide lacked visual taste – from 1905 the Villa Montmorency became Gide's Paris home for much of the year and an obligatory place of call for aspiring writers.

Gide's summons to French youth: 'Be honest with yourselves, however much society may disapprove,' did not go unchallenged. Paul Valéry lived in a Paris boarding-house, his library an open trunk, ruminating on a range of subjects from logic to music, on one wall a picture of a skeleton, to remind him to probe always to the bone. Valéry and Gide were friends – when Valéry married Gide stood witness – but Valéry felt uneasy that Gide should have chosen as a model of honesty Friedrich Nietzsche. Valéry saw Nietzsche as he really was, a weak man, imprisoned by females, wishing to be strong, now lashing out angrily, now flashing out ambiguous messages. When Gide claimed Nietzsche as a joyful champion of freedom, Valéry protested: 'You're in something of a hurry to give him unity. For me he is above all *contradictory*.' 'His big mistake,' continued Valéry, 'is to want to construct a philosophy of *violence* . . . Did you notice the marvellous prestidigitation that goes to make up the Superman? It allows him to be both optimistic and pessimistic . . . to be romantic and classical, etc. *ad libitum*.'

Then there were Nietzsche's last sad years, when he became mad and would eat only grass. Was that the right sort of man to be a model for Michel the Immoralist, and for young Frenchmen generally? To which Gide replied: 'Nietzsche gambles against himself, goes mad, but wins the game, precisely *because* he is mad.' Valéry, who couldn't stand the irrational, would have none of this, and so the two agreed to differ, Valéry opting for lucidity, Gide for sincerity, even if it meant paradox.

The second friend to take issue with Gide was Francis Jammes. A short, stocky bachelor with blue gimlet eyes and a square beard, Jammes grasped your arm at first meeting and by the end of it had made you his friend. He was fond of children, of animals, especially cats, and of fine cooking. Though he too had suffered from a dominating mother, he was heterosexual: he chased the pretty girls of Orthez, where he lived, and was known admiringly to Gide as the Faun. Jammes celebrated the beauty of nature in verse and, like Gide, considered the countryside an earthly paradise providing man with limitless joys of the flesh and the spirit. He had stayed in Gide's home, and Gide in his: the two were the best of friends.

In 1905 Jammes received a visit from a leading young Catholic writer, Paul Claudel. We shall get to know Claudel in the next chapter; for the present it is sufficient to say that he had written the first of his *Five Great Odes*, which drew from the beauty of nature and the wonders of the cosmos a conclusion quite different from that of Jammes and Gide: they were there not for man's pleasure but as evidence of God's power, intelligence and love.

In a series of letters Claudel had hinted that Jammes miscast himself as the Faun, with his tenderness for animals he was more akin to his namesake from Assisi. Jammes was already beginning to find Gide's philosophy of ever-renewed freedom too frenetic for a countryman, so Claudel's words fell on receptive ears. By the time of Claudel's arrival in Orthez from his consular post in China Jammes was ready. In July 1905 he was received back into the Catholic Church, Claudel standing beside him as witness. The two then went on a walking tour, Claudel in a tropical linen suit and panama hat, 'his tanned face setting off his charcoal-blue eyes in turn smiling, questioning, indignant', and Jammes even began looking round for a wife.

Jammes wrote to Gide telling him about this unexpected event and sending his latest book of poems, *L'Eglise habillée en feuilles*, in which the conversion is spelled out. One typical poem describes swallows shivering on telegraph wires, eager to be off for the warmth, making short sorties, then returning to the wires, longing for Africa without having seen it: '*C'est comme nous qui désirons le Ciel dans notre inquiétude.*'[1]

Gide was so moved by Jammes's book that on 29 November he could write to him: 'This evening I was already completely a Catholic.' Next day, at the home of Arthur Fontaine, a top civil servant specializing in workers' welfare and a patron of literature, Gide read Jammes's new poems aloud to a circle of Jammes's

---

[1] 'Just as we in our distress long for heaven.'

admirers, including Claudel. It was recognized as a key occasion in French literary history, almost a counterpart of Pascal's vision of God as fire one November night in 1654.

Five days later, lunching with Gide, Claudel developed Jammes's message by asserting that the real hero is not the man who goes to the limits of sincerity but the one who bears witness to the truth, that is, to Christ. 'For two years after my own conversion,' Claudel continued, 'I didn't write a word, I thought I must sacrifice art to religion ... I was saved when I understood that art and religion aren't meant to be in opposition. But they're not meant to merge either. They must, so to speak, remain at right angles, and their very struggle nurtures our life.'

Gide felt strongly drawn by some of Claudel's arguments, notably 'this absolute duty one has to be a saint', the sort of challenge that appealed to him. For six months he felt both attracted to, and repelled by, the authority that might lead to sanctity but would, as he saw it, stifle his originality as a writer. 'My temperament, most deplorably, revolts against any restraint, any rule that my mind would like to impose on it.' But also: 'My resolute paganism remains soaked in the tears Christ has shed.'

In May 1906 Gide made his choice. 'Yes, Claudel has been of great service to me,' he wrote to Jammes, 'but not in the way you imagine. My reaction against him has finally far exceeded his action on me, and it is for *that* that I am grateful to him . . .'

Gide made his meaning clear by publishing, in spring 1907, *The Return of the Prodigal Son*, an idiosyncratic amplification of Christ's parable. The Prodigal is a young man painfully aware that his home is not the whole universe. To remain within the limits of the home would be a form of laziness. So he leaves and begins to explore the world. Presently he returns – not because he is ashamed and sorry, but because he is hungry, tired, ill and discouraged.

On his return his father lectures him; then, in a tone like Claudel's, his elder brother: 'I am on the side of order; anything that holds out against order is the fruit or seed of pride.' 'Won't you allow me anything distinctive except failings?' asks the Prodigal, to which the elder brother replies: 'Call quality that which brings you back to order; the rest you must crush.'

His mother is afraid her youngest son intends to leave home and begs the Prodigal to stop him. The Prodigal speaks to the boy, explaining that he lacked courage to continue to the end his journey of discovery. But, undeterred, the boy says, 'You have opened the way for me, and your experience will give me courage.' He asks his brother to join him, but the Prodigal replies that he will stay at home and comfort their mother: 'You will be braver without me than with me.'

Gide's book was hailed by admirers. The creed of personal honesty, they claimed, had been strengthened by its implantation in a Protestant Christian context. But Claudel, to whom Gide sent a copy, had serious reservations: 'It is not laziness that leads to God. Terrible battles are required and a constant renewal of energy in order to regain and continue in one's faith. A Catholic's life is a continual scandal and contradiction. Every conversation, every book, every newspaper is the negation of all he believes and loves. He is quite alone with the word of God . . .'

Meanwhile, Gide participated to the full in Paris life. He attended the first performance of Strauss's *Salomé*, libretto by Wilde, and admired the character of Herod. He went to an exhibition of paintings by an acquaintance, Walter Sickert, and warmed to their 'defiant gloom'. He attended the dress rehearsal of *Monsieur*

Codomat, a comedy by Tristan Bernard, Paris's answer to Bernard Shaw, preceded, curiously, by a re-enactment of the volcanic eruption in Martinique which rather overdid the smoke. He was one of a lunch party at the Tour d'Argent in honour of Auguste Rodin, and when the sculptor modestly recalled how until his middle forties he had had to earn his bread turning out popular terracotta statuettes, Gide, whose readership was still small, felt sympathy. Calling at the Valérys', he met another grand old man, Edgar Degas, more obsti-nate and set in his opinions than ever, exaggerating his crustiness, and remarking, 'Art criticism! What non-sense! ... The Muses never talk among themselves; each one works in her domain; and when they aren't work-ing, they dance.' Degas then repeated twice, 'When they aren't working, they dance.'

In these and other activities Gide was on the hunt for sincerity, with one eye open for its opposite. He called on a young Jewish friend, the sociologist Léon Blum, who had written a book proposing that young un-married women should sleep around in order to gain the experience that would enable them to choose a satisfactory husband. Gide disagreed with Blum's view that happiness in the bedroom is the *summum bonum* but what disturbed him more was that Blum 'judges things and people according to his Socialist political opinions and not according to his taste. You can't be always quite sure that he likes everything he says he likes, but you can be sure that he thinks he likes it and knows why.'

One evening in Lent Gide went to Notre-Dame to hear a sermon by the eloquent Dominican, Father Janvier, listening to the end without being tired or bored, but noting this in his Journal: 'Subject of the sermon: Error – sins through ignorance. Necessity of informing oneself: that is, of learning to know *Truth*.

Ah, how beautiful! Let's rush out and imprison Galileo.'

Another day Gide went to the Institut de France to see Maurice Barrès, a leading nationalist Deputy, admired as a member of the Académie Française. As a young man Barrès had preached a cult of the ego, then switched to a cult of one's region and roots, expressing in his novels of Alsace-Lorraine an ardent nationalism. He was now fifty-five but looked younger and wore his bottle-green and gold uniform with style. 'How I like his thin face,' wrote Gide, 'his flattened-down hair, even his common vocabulary!' But when Barrès in his speech associated himself with Leconte de Lisle and Herédia (to whose seat he was succeeding), both of whom had conspicuously lacked roots, Gide winced at what he considered Barrès's sophistry.

One May evening Gide went to an auction at the Hôtel Drouot. André Lebey, a young poet, took a seat beside him and the two became so immersed in conversation Gide's attention wandered. He did notice a painting by Bonnard of a woman dressing; Bonnard was an acquaintance who had illustrated an edition of a satirical farce by Gide and the painting he felt he had seen somewhere before. As the bidding climbed to 460 francs, 'Suddenly I hear a voice shout "600!". In a daze I realize I am the one who shouted. With my eyes I implore a higher bid from the people around me – for I have no desire to own the painting – but none is forthcoming. I feel myself becoming purple and begin to sweat copiously. "It's stifling in here," I say to Lebey. We leave.' Gide recalled a similar experience once before. It surprised him that he should be capable of such occasional involuntary strayings and wondered what their relation was to the straight road of sincerity.

Believing that frequent uprooting enhances freshness and therefore sincerity, Gide travelled more often than most Parisians. Between 1906 and 1908 he visited the Toulouse region, Brittany – for a cycling holiday – Italy, Jersey, Oxford and Berlin. His companion-guide for two weeks in the German capital was a boring neo-Symbolist Christian painter, Maurice Denis; in his Journal Gide does not speak of Germans or indeed of the many excellent German paintings in the Berlin Museum; but he is much taken with the Italian Old Masters and with two works by the Dutch painter Dirk Bouts.

By and large in his Journal Gide writes about his work and what may feed it, about the character of his friends and of himself. He tends to highlight his weaknesses. For example, at an exhibition of paintings he meets Thadée Natanson – by now divorced from Misia – and, feeling under par, finds himself complaining that he is neglected by critics – though at heart he does not care about critics – and flattering Thadée with sugary compliments – 'the sort of things that, if written, I should cross out in shame'. That night he couldn't sleep, chewing over his bitterness like betel.

Turning to his correspondence, however, we find a less self-centred, more generous Gide. A gifted poet, Emmanuel Signoret, dies at twenty-eight: Gide goes to immense trouble not only to sponsor an edition of Signoret's poems but to try to obtain for his needy widow a tobacconist's agency, valuable in France where the sale of cigarettes is a state monopoly.

Again, Henri Ghéon is living beyond his means. He has few patients, continues to run his costly 'anti-mobile' and goes on frequent sprees in Paris. He has written an unpublishable novel and a play, *Le Pain*. In the hope that André Antoine will stage the play, Gide goes to see Thadée Natanson, and the Rumanian-born actor, Edouard de Max, both of whom have Antoine's ear. When the play is not accepted, Ghéon turns to painting. Again Gide helps by steering friends and critics to the still lifes when they were hung at the Salon des Indépendants. Two are sold, bringing Ghéon 550 francs, but the following year Ghéon sells nothing. Gide then tries to find Ghéon a Government sinecure. Having already loaned him 1000 francs, Gide makes him a second loan of 500. Ghéon could hardly have asked for a better friend.

Gide's marriage continued to be a source of calm and strength both to him and to Madeleine. Here too he was to prove of practical help. Madeleine's married sister Valentine, while undergoing treatment for tuberculosis in a Pau sanatorium, eloped with a fellow-patient and bore him an illegitimate child. Her husband died, then her lover – whom she had married *en deuxième noces*; in this series of dramas Gide gave his twice-widowed sister-in-law unstinting help and from 1907 he and Madeleine welcomed Valentine and her three children each summer to Cuverville.

As he entered his forties, physical pleasure with boys began to play less of a part in Gide's life and he became better placed to appreciate the unworldly, nun-like character of Madeleine and the beauty of their unusual marriage. Ever since writing *The Immoralist* he had felt the need to paint what he saw as the other half of a diptych – the sincerity of a woman who renounces physical love in the firm belief that it is inimical to the spiritual life. In 1908, after re-imbibing Calvinist principles from the pages of Pascal's more Jansenist writings, Gide completed his second novel, *Strait is the Gate*.

Jerome, an only child, grows up in a Calvinist home with his cousins. Alissa, two years his elder, is delicate, reflective and has a smile that is almost sad; Juliette, one year his junior, is strong and high-spirited.

The girls' Creole mother likes to lie on a chaise-longue, languidly reading poetry. She wears scent and –

rare for a country lady at the time – smokes. One day Jerome surprises her laughing and flirting with a young officer, as he lights her cigarette. Upstairs he finds Alissa in tears praying by her bedside – she too has noticed her mother flirting. Jerome kisses her and secretly resolves to devote his life to protecting this vulnerable girl 'from fear, from evil, from life'.

The girls' mother shocks everyone by eloping with her lover (Madeleine's mother had done the same in real life). The following Sunday the pastor preaches on the text, 'Strait is the Gate', deeply impressing Alissa.

Jerome grows up and, wanting sex, wishes to become engaged to Alissa, but she replies that they are happy enough already. Then Juliette proposes to marry Jerome, and Alissa offers to stand aside.

Juliette comes to see that Jerome doesn't love her and she marries another man. Again Jerome presses Alissa to become engaged but she prefers things as they are.

Jerome goes off to do his military service and corresponds with Alissa. Her letters become increasingly pious. In one she quotes Racine:

> *Malheureux l'homme qui fonde*
> *Sur les hommes son appui!*[1]

On his return Jerome goes to see Alissa. The meeting is unsatisfactory. They seem to love each other most when apart.

Time elapses. At a new meeting Jerome is disappointed to find that Alissa has removed photographs of Masaccio's paintings from her room which he had brought her from Florence and replaced her classic authors by little books of commonplace piety. She explains that she prefers them because they do not fall into the snare of fine language.

[1] Unhappy the man
Who looks for support to other men.

Alissa admits to Jerome that she feels happier with him than she thought it was possible to feel, but adds that they were not born for happiness. 'For what then?' 'For holiness.'

Again Jerome goes off. Presently he learns that Alissa's health is failing, then that she has died. Her Journal comes into his hands, and in it he is able to follow the stages of her withdrawal from him. Aware of Juliette's happiness in marriage, Alissa has written: 'O Lord! preserve me from a happiness to which I might too easily attain! Teach me to put off my happiness, to place it as far away from me as Thou art!' She longs to go to God, hand in hand with Jerome as with a brother. 'But no! The way Thou teachest, Lord, is a narrow way – so narrow that two cannot walk in it abreast.'

Alissa has bequeathed the Journal to Jerome, so that he 'may scale the heights of virtue'. Juliette has given birth to a daughter and named her Alissa; Jerome is invited to stand godfather. He accepts. He confides to Juliette that he won't marry, he intends to remain faithful to Alissa's idea of him.

Strait is the Gate is a novel of a young woman's attraction to, and fear of, sexual love, of the heroism she demands of herself and of the young man who wants to marry her. In the first respect it belongs with Tolstoy's *Family Happiness* among the supreme portrayals of a young woman in love. Though Claudel objected to Alissa going on and on about 'perfecting herself' – 'a very unChristian self-centredness' – the novel received high praise from Gide's circle of friends who read it in manuscript in 1908, a view the public would endorse when it appeared in book form some months later.

It so happened that in this same year, 1908, Gide found himself without a congenial periodical in which to place his work, both *L'Ermitage* and Thadée Natanson's *Revue Blanche* having folded. But he had gathered round him a group of like-minded friends and they decided to start a periodical of their own. Gide was the guiding spirit but, characteristically, he chose not to be the editor; there would be no editor, instead an editorial board of four friends, of which Gide was not one.

André Ruyters, aged thirty-two, was a Belgian writer of Symbolist stories and by profession a banker; Marcel Drouin, aged thirty-eight, Madeleine's somewhat lazy brother-in-law, was a professor of philosophy with special knowledge of Goethe and Kant; Jacques Copeau, aged twenty-nine, was a good mixer and popular with everyone; he supported his Danish-born wife and three children selling pictures in Georges Petit's gallery but his great passion was the serious theatre; Jean Schlumberger, aged thirty-one, a dapper bald man with a neat moustache, a descendant of Guizot and like Guizot a Protestant, was upright, scrupulously fair and wrote novels about duty triumphing over passion. He and his painter wife Suzanne were particularly fond of Madeleine Gide.

Copeau started things rolling by getting in touch with a young writer, Eugène Montfort, who had five years' experience of editing a periodical. Montfort suggested calling the new monthly *Revue Française*; when Copeau discovered that a periodical of that name had existed in the 1830s, they added the adjective *Nouvelle*. A trial number hastily put together by Montfort appeared on 15 November 1908. It included articles on Mallarmé and d'Annunzio which had not been seen by the editorial board, and which Gide considered trendy in the worst sense. Gide then decided to part company with Montfort. He and Schlumberger put up money for a new first issue, while Schlumberger's Paris apartment became the periodical's office.

The first number of the *Nouvelle Revue Française*, which appeared on 1 February 1909, contained the first chapter of *Strait is the Gate*, an article on Greece by Marcel Drouin, notices of a Seurat/Verhaeren exhibition and of Tristan Bernard's play *Le Poulailler*. Gide reviewed a first book of poems by a young admirer of Whitman, Valéry Larbaud, appreciating its sensuous insights into foreign countries, but reproving its occasional cynicism. A book about Jammes's feeling for nature was also reviewed.

Other early numbers published part of Rainer Maria Rilke's *The Notebooks of Malte Laurids Brigge*, poems and a play by Paul Claudel, two essays on religious faith by a young discovery of Claudel, Jacques Rivière, and two chapters of G. K. Chesterton's *Orthodoxy*, proposed and translated by Claudel, the sincerity of whose work and whose literary perceptiveness were much appreciated by the board.

What did the *Nouvelle Revue Française* stand for? In its first number it declared its intention of offering readers 'the most important of what is best'. 'We came together,' Schlumberger recalls, 'not around a programme; our programme was the expression of our shared views. We admired certain great writers . . . and principles that were moral rather than æsthetic.'

The *NRF* board rejected scepticism, which Gide declared 'is sometimes perhaps the beginning of wisdom, but is often the end of art'. They believed literature should concern itself primarily with moral sincerity: with man's aspirations and dilemmas, the interplay of spirit and flesh and the resultant unease – *inquiétude*, a key word for Gide.

In the year the *NRF* was launched and his novel *Strait is the Gate* hailed as a masterpiece, Gide – now recognized as France's best young serious writer – had to face an important new dilemma. France was pursuing an ambitious policy in the Mediterranean – later we shall see exactly how; this brought sabre-rattling from Germany, and in turn strengthened the hand of French nationalists. One such nationalist was Philippe Berthelot, chief implementer of France's hard-line foreign policy. Though not himself a writer, he had literary tastes and moved in literary circles. He was a cold, hard man. Of a bitter May Day strike he said, 'It exists only in the imagination of the frightened bourgeoisie.' The terrible San Francisco earthquake he described to Gide as 'an unimportant little event'. Germany he loathed, and all other countries he deemed inferior to France.

Berthelot, thought Gide, was a man of insufferable arrogance. But there was no denying the influence on writers of his hard-line chauvinism. Here Berthelot joined hands with Maurice Barrès, who held that literature is primarily about regional roots, about the dead and the sacred past. Around 1909–10 the nationalists' aim became specific: literature should make an assertion about territory, with an implicit plea for the recovery of Alsace-Lorraine. The shrilly nationalist League of Patriots, of which Barrès was to become President, and literary men who shared its views urged Gide and his editorial board to emphasize the *Française* in the title of their magazine, to make it committedly nationalist and patriotic.

Now for all his preoccupation with Parisian literary life, Gide was spiritually cosmopolitan. He often recalled his debt to Anna Shackleton, who had introduced him to English literature. He especially loved Elizabethan drama and for pleasure would read John Ford aloud, while with the guidance of Arnold Bennett, a frequent visitor to Paris, he kept abreast of new English books. He was an admirer of Goethe as well as of Nietzsche; he had written perceptively about

Dostoievsky. With such a range he was unlikely to welcome any view that limited literary excellence to France or called for flag-waving. Nor did he. To Barrès he made this reply: 'Born in Paris of a father from Uzès and a Norman mother, where, Monsieur Barrès, do you consider my roots to be? I have decided therefore to travel.' By 'travel' Gide meant that he would follow his personal tastes wherever they led. The call to patriotic literature he firmly rejected.

What then did the word *Française* in his periodical's title imply? Gide answered in effect that the *NRF* was championing classicism. By classicism he meant sincerity in a context of moderation, restraint and economy of form. Such qualities might be found in non-French works – the Japanese play performed by Sada Yacco had reminded Gide of Æschylus and he described it not as exotic but as classical; but Gide believed that the qualities were pre-eminent in French literature, from Racine to Baudelaire and even to Jammes. Gide claimed classicism as the most valuable feature of French civilization, the one that had to be defended at all costs if France were to remain true to herself.

No less than two hundred literary reviews appeared in France between 1900 and 1914. Many were ephemeral and chose to appear in December, so that a month later they could claim to be in their second year. Gide's *NRF* had a substance to it lacking in most, including its nearest rival, *Mercure de France*, whose values were merely æsthetic. Its championing of classicism in Gide's sense quickly won respect and a growing circulation.

Soon a young man with a flair for business and a taste for literature came to the office of the *NRF*. His name was Gaston Gallimard. His rich father had recently switched from collecting paintings to the much more costly habit of collecting pretty actresses, and young Gaston found himself obliged to make his own way.

After a short trial Gide appointed him administrator of the *NRF*.

As the review built up a stable of gifted young writers, it became desirable to extend into book publishing. Gaston Gallimard was given charge, guided by Gide and the editorial board, and the first titles appeared in 1912. Both the periodical and the publishing house were to flourish and to remain remarkably faithful to their origins, as well as to Gide's principle of total sincerity, books bearing Gallimard's imprint ranging for example from Saint-Exupéry's poetic accounts of pioneer aviation to the existentialist novels and plays of Camus and Sartre.

Meanwhile, counterpointing his work as editor and publisher, Gide continued his even more influential role as writer and exemplar for literary youth. In his Journal and letters, essays, reviews and novels he deepened and extended his quest for a sincerity that would do justice to his many-sidedness. His enemies naturally called it duplicity.

In 1908 Gide shaved off the attractive drooping moustache that is a feature of the 1900 portrait. It was unusual for a man not to sport facial hair, and Madeleine regretted his decision. But it was Gide's way of asserting, like Michel in *The Immoralist*, that he intended to live according to his own criteria.

'Be our conscience,' one of Gide's young friends had urged in the 'nineties, to which Gide had replied that he didn't believe in that kind of leadership. Nevertheless, without wishing it Gide had become if not quite the conscience at least a moral touchstone for many young Frenchmen. He claimed to be a Christian and to live according to the Gospel, but he kept free of dogma and Church. Though his sister-in-law Valentine became a Catholic in 1911 and Henri Ghéon, visiting Florence for the *NRF*, startled him by writing, eyes wet with tears, about his deep response to the Franciscan mood of Giotto's frescoes, Gide firmly resisted the 'cotton wool' of Catholicism, preferring his own interpretation of Christ's message.

During the decade since 1900 it would be fair to say that Gide did more than anyone to change the Paris literary scene, dragging it from the marshland of cynicism, lifting the curtain of silence about pederasty, recentring interest on man's soul and search for God, striving for a sincerity that would be fair to facets of the personality not previously discerned. Gide also rehabilitated freedom of will and asserted, with subtlety, the individual's duty, at no matter what cost in *inquiétude*, to free himself from unauthentic convention. From these freedoms, as we shall see, others – with very different messages – would profit.

CHAPTER 5

Redemptive Suffering: Paul Claudel

In contrast to the English who look to their living writers for entertainment, Parisians look to theirs for new ideas by which to live. Literature is at the very centre of life, rippling out to politics and to public opinion and its practitioners tend to see themselves as prophets. If we can bear with their earnestness – and in Claudel's case with his assertiveness – we may find the matters they deal with not only central to an understanding of their period but also of wider relevance.

Paul Claudel was born on 6 August 1868 in Villeneuve, in a part of Champagne he was to liken to the heath in *Wuthering Heights*. His father was one step up from the peasantry, a petty official in public administration, unremarkable save for a beard divided into two pendants like icicles. His mother came from a less humble milieu, being the daughter of a country doctor and niece of a curé. There were three children, Camille, Louise and Paul. All the family had violent tempers.

As a boy Paul Claudel enjoyed climbing trees. From the top, 'a spectator in the world's theatre', he liked to reflect on 'the relief and conformation of the earth, the disposition of its contours and its horizontal plan . . . missing nothing, neither the direction of the smoke, nor the quality of light and shade, the stage reached by work in the fields, the shots of the hunters'. His hero was Columbus, who had united separated lands, and he yearned for a connection among all things, a complete meaning.

The dominant figure in the quarrelsome Claudel cottáge was Camille. Four years older than Paul, she had a beautiful head, abundant auburn hair, big hazel eyes, a slim nose with a lift to it, sensuous lips, a proud expression tinged with scorn. Her appearance was made even more interesting by a slight limp. She intended to become a sculptress. Extremely strong-willed, she persuaded her mother to move with all three children to Paris, where they were later joined by Claudel *père*, who took a job in Rambouillet.

While Camille entered the Colarossi studio, Paul Claudel attended the lycée. Neither of his parents was religious, he had made his First Communion but by now had ceased to go to church. He therefore imbibed unquestioningly the materialism of what he later called the 'sad Eighties': 'Vice and virtue are by-products like vitriol and sugar' (Taine); 'Man is only an animated machine acting under the influence of heredity and environment' (Zola); 'as history the New Testament is unsatisfactory . . . and Jesus never claimed to be God' (Renan).

Claudel came first in oratory and received his prize from Renan, that 'secularized cathedral' as Daudet called him, together with a kiss on the brow. The point was pressed home by Camille, now a free-thinker: flourishing her copy of Renan's *Life of Jesus* in front of Paul, she would declare, 'Everything we were taught about religion is nonsense, here's the proof.' She encouraged the boy to be combative and made a bust of him as 'The Young Roman'. And she practised what she preached. A student of Auguste Rodin, she became the sculptor's mistress, accompanying him on a month's holiday to Touraine, where he sketched her clothed during the day and in the nude at night.

Paul Claudel entered law school. He had to earn a living but he wanted to be a writer. A peasant by birth and instinct, always close to the earth and harsh reality, he nevertheless felt in himself a lyrical vein. His first poem to survive, written at eighteen, is entitled 'For a Mass on a human scale', and describes a Christ in the style of Renan with soft hair, who tells those who have longed for his coming that he will love them like a bride, like a father, but that he is not God the Son.

Claudel frequented literary circles: Mallarmé's, where poets had to be hermetic and allusive, those of Montesquiou and Huysmans, where a poet was expected to dress like a dandy and to describe the exotic or decadent.

Claudel began to find himself dissatisfied. He still longed for 'complete meaning'. In his trouble he read *Les Illuminations*, a recently published kaleidoscopic, richly imaged prose-poem which Rimbaud had written from the hell of African gun-running. It is a cry half way between religious despair and hope, and Claudel was much moved by it.

Some months later, at Christmas 1886, Claudel went to Notre-Dame to hear Vespers in the belief that, treated with a condescending dilettantism, it might provide stimulus and copy for further verses. 'The Catholic religion still seemed to me a treasure-house of absurd stories. Its priests and faithful filled me with an aversion not far from disgust.'

Claudel stood near the second pillar at the entrance to the choir on the right of the sacristy listening to the boys' choir sing the *Magnificat*. As to an earlier Paul on the road to Damascus, an extraordinary thing happened: 'Suddenly my heart was touched, and I believed . . . with the force of my whole being . . . I was overcome with a sudden, overwhelming sense of the innocence and the eternal infancy of God.'

This 'revelation' as he termed it was 'not unmixed with fear and something very much resembling horror. For my philosophical opinions remained intact . . . Everything that was most repugnant to my opinions and tastes has turned out to be true.'

On his return to the family apartment Claudel picked up a copy of the Bible. French Catholics then did not own bibles, nor were they encouraged to read Scripture, let alone study it. This was a Protestant Bible given to Camille by a German student friend, and its presence at that moment was quite as providential as the events in Notre-Dame. Claudel's eye fell on lines in the apochryphal *Book of Wisdom* chiding men for failing to recognize the Creator in his works.

Claudel could not get the lines out of his mind, they were 'so sweet and so uncompromising'.

That was the beginning of a long study of the Bible, then of St Thomas Aquinas. Through them, and helped by Emile Boutroux's Sorbonne lectures rehabilitating the thought of Blaise Pascal, Claudel sought an intellectual justification for his new-found faith. Fearful of her scorn, he did not dare tell Camille – or his parents – that the 'young Roman' wished to become a 'young Roman Catholic'. Four years passed before he could bring himself to make his peace with the Church and tell his family.

Claudel sat the Foreign Office exams, came top of the list and at twenty-four took up the first of a series of consular posts abroad. A side of him liked files, archives, questionnaires, but he still hoped to be a writer. He might live much abroad but he saw himself primarily as a Parisian, spending most of every leave in Paris, keeping abreast of the latest literature and the best Paris periodicals, exchanging ideas and opinions on literary subjects with Parisians. He wrote to authors whose work pleased him, met them later in France and often became their friend. Among them were a gifted melancholic Jewish essayist, André Suarès, and Francis Jammes.

In January 1900, by way of the Holy Land – in Bethlehem he served Christmas Mass – Claudel returned on leave to Paris. He was aged thirty-one. He stayed with his sister Camille in a flat at 37 Quai d'Anjou, and there Francis Jammes called on him. Claudel's face, recalls Jammes, was 'unsmiling, rather full and pink, lit up by eyes that listen; in profile he looked like a bullock with a mesh of hair over his brow, a small moustache, a wide thin rather disdainful mouth, and a jaw that ruminated his thought in long soliloquies interrupted by pauses that left his listeners in suspense'.

The two young poets had exchanged a number of friendly letters but this was their first meeting. After shaking hands, Claudel said to his bearded visitor, 'Jammes, I've nothing to add to what I wrote. You know what I think of your friendship and your books.' This was meant kindly but Jammes felt rather put off by Claudel's brusque, staccato tone.

Jammes had brought Gide with him. Claudel had met Gide at Mallarmé's home, knew his books and commented on one of them: 'Your mind has no bias,' a criticism of which Gide would later remark: 'No praise could be higher.'

Jammes relates that Gide, in the florid style he then favoured, began questioning the young consul.

'Monsieur Paul Claudel, in China you have I believe many servants?'

'Far too many. Thirteen. One for my shoes, one for my shirts, one to serve at table, etc. . . . And I mustn't forget the one whose job it is to clean out the privy!'

'I don't want to pry, Monsieur Paul Claudel, but

103

there's a question that interests me greatly . . . That beautiful Catholic faith . . . that gift from heaven . . .'

'I owe it to Rimbaud. Before reading Rimbaud, I believed the world was a sort of threshing machine that science could dismantle at will.'

He said this incredibly fast, notes Jammes, like a child reciting the catechism, and as though it were unanswerable.

As for André Gide, his thoughts twisted and turned like Dr Faust's spaniel.

'Would it be indiscreet, Paul Claudel, to ask one more question? Your verse form, so distinctive . . .'

'Verse breathes in and breathes out. The poet has to find the turning-point, a very tricky business.'

'Dear Monsieur Claudel, dare I make a bold request? . . . I am much involved with a periodical, *L'Ermitage* . . . It would be truly a joy, a notable honour, ah! . . .'

'Of course. I have a play, *The Exchange*, which the *Revue de Paris* has just rejected, I don't know why.'

Without further fuss Claudel handed Gide the manuscript of this early unconvincing play, set in the United States, about an adultery leading to death, and Gide saw to it that it appeared in *L'Ermitage*.

Next day Claudel invited Jammes to lunch at a smart restaurant, Lapérouse. The other guest was Marcel Schwob, valetudinarian æsthete and student of slang who papered over the mirrors of his flat so as not to encounter his homely face. Claudel surprised them by arriving from the Quai d'Orsay in a top hat. Afterwards he handed each of them a signed copy of *Knowledge of the East*, beautiful poetic impressions of China. He was justifiably proud of the book and when it was published in April it soon made him famous among the discerning.

Camille had made a name too as a gifted lyric sculptor in the *art nouveau* style. *La Valse*, for instance, shows two dancers entwined, rising in a curve, flower-like from a block of bronze. She had also made a portrait bust of Rodin which the sculptor thought the best likeness of himself. But in her personal life Camille was unhappy. For many years Rodin had lived with a peasant woman, Rose Beuret, plain and uneducated, and had had a son by her. When Rodin showed signs of replacing her by Camille, Rose underwent, or claimed to undergo, heart attacks. Rodin delayed the break. For the moment the older mistress was winning.

Having given Camille what comfort he could, in August Claudel travelled to Solesmes for what he looked on as the momentous step of this inaugural year, 1900. There he began to write 'Ode to the Muses', intending it to be his last poem before he presented himself to the Benedictines as a candidate for the priesthood. For through his reading of the Bible and of Aquinas Claudel had come to the conclusion that man's highest function is to praise God through the Mass.

Something – we do not know what – went wrong at Solesmes; perhaps whoever interviewed Claudel raised objections. Anyway, the intending novice hurried off to the Benedictine monastery of Ligugé, near Poitiers. Here an understanding monk listened to the story of a consul-poet turned thirty who wished to serve God in a cloistered order. It did not take him long to see that this brilliant, combative, abrasive young man would not fit into community life and that he had better serve God in the world.

Claudel took it badly: 'I understood that God did not want me as his priest and was turning me back from his altars. It was a cruel moment.'

In October 1900 Claudel sailed on the *Ernest Simmons* to resume his post as consul in Foochow. At Réunion a Frenchman embarked – we know him only as Monsieur V. – with his very pretty wife and their four small sons.

The lady is known to us as R. She was Polish by birth and temperament: passionate, reckless, with a strong religious faith. Claudel came on her one day surrounded by some of the crew: she was teaching them to sing a racy song. There they were in mid-ocean, the fair-haired lady and the rough sailors, laughing as they chanted together what Claudel considered obscene verses.

He spoke to the lady afterwards, reprovingly, very much the would-be priest. The lady began to cry. They talked, confided, became friends. It appeared that her husband did not understand R., that he neglected her: a trite situation. One evening passengers played Hunt the Slipper, and Claudel was left with R.'s slipper. It seemed to him a sign.

At Foochow Claudel took up residence in the consulate. Monsieur V. installed his wife and children in a house in the European quarter, then set off on a business trip. In the aftermath of the Boxer Rebellion danger was in the air, the small French community were thrown on each other's company.

Though not a hedonist, Claudel was capable of very strong passion for a woman. He probably knew he was susceptible, like Camille, whose unhappy affair was a fresh memory and a warning. He certainly knew that in getting involved with R. he would be, in Catholic terms, committing grave sin. But stronger than these danger signals was the intensity of his love for R., and a sort of grudge against God for having turned him away.

Claudel and R. began an affair. Presently a child was born, Claudel being the father. On Claudel's side, the only one known to us, love filled his life:

Tu es droite comme une colonne! tu es claire comme le soleil levant!
Et où as-tu arraché sinon aux filières mêmes du soleil

d'un tour de ton cou ce grand lambeau jaune
De tes cheveux qui ont la matière d'un talent d'or?
Tu es fraîche comme une rose sous la rosée![1]

But Claudel knew his love to be selfish and, in the context of their religious beliefs, doomed.

We glimpsed Philippe Berthelot earlier as Delcassé's *éminence grise*; now he arrives in Foochow as a friend to Claudel. Son of the famous chemist, Marcellin Berthelot, Philippe had been brought up on the Left Bank amid the Sorbonne's positivists. As a young man he had sat at the feet of Renan and there imbibed agnosticism before moving on to atheism. He had literary tastes and could recite by heart Hugo's *La Légende des Siècles*; though not himself creative, he brought into the Foreign Service, and protected, writers as varied as Jean Giraudoux, Paul Morand and Aléxis Saint-Leger, future author of the lovely poem *Anabase*.

Now aged thirty-seven and head of the Quai d'Orsay's Far East Department, handsome, broad-shouldered, assured, rapid in his movements and incredibly efficient, Berthelot enjoyed getting a rise out of the touchy little poet-consul by denying the possibility of metaphysics. He scorned religion yet kept harking back to it. Once asked what he would do if he found himself suddenly penniless in New York, he replied coolly, 'Start a new religion.'

Arnold Bennett describes Berthelot 'clad in pale alpaca and yellow boots, and explaining the secret significance of Yellow Books, White Books, Orange

---

[1] You are straight as a column! You shine like the rising sun!
And that head of yellow hair, heavy as a gold talent,
Where did you wrest it if not, with a turn of your neck, from the pathways of the sun?
Your freshness is that of a rose with dewy petals.

Books, Blue Books'. But, noted Bennett, 'the ultimate issues were never touched on. I prefer his [Normandy-born] wife Hélène, who started her career on the streets and has slept with the whole group . . . She is nice but ignorant.'

Berthelot had a taste for erotica. In his *musée secret*, writes Bennett, 'what I chiefly noticed in several indecent prints was the exquisite drawing of the clitoris of prostitutes; realistic absolutely and yet beautiful. It was amusing how Madame Berthelot sent me and another man in to the *musée secret*, and left us there, and then asked our impressions.'

To this taste for erotica Berthelot added a fondness for Persian cats and for playing dominoes, 'the best game in the world'. Evening after evening he would play dominoes with Claudel and listen to him wax eloquent about the charms of R.

In Foochow and in Paris there were certainly calls for Claudel's dismissal from the Service. He was causing a great scandal. But the accused man had two points in his favour. An important part of any consul's job was to beat the Germans for large commercial contracts, and Claudel secured for French companies, against strong competition from Krupp's, the modernization of Foochow's arsenal and naval shipyard. Second, *Knowledge of the East* had shown Claudel to be a gifted writer. Berthelot prided himself on helping upcoming Chateaubriands and, whatever his faults, he was not a Puritan. By the end of his friend's visit to Foochow Claudel knew his job was safe, and in gratitude he would dedicate to Philippe and Hélène the play that grew out of his love-affair.

In August 1904 R. left Claudel and her husband: 'a horrible betrayal' was Claudel's self-righteous comment. In the following spring he obtained leave and followed her to Europe, accompanied, says one source, by

R.'s husband. Claudel eventually found R. in Holland – living with another man. She refused to rejoin Claudel. Their affair was at an end.

Claudel was deeply shaken, both in his love and in his considerable pride. In the weeks that followed he slowly took stock. He believed that the love-affair had been good in itself, he did not regret it, he saw himself as joined eternally to R. Nothing could ever approach that experience. But he believed firmly in marriage, as a social necessity and as a sacrament. He was thirty-six, time, he decided, to take a wife. He asked friends to make soundings.

While they did so, Claudel helped Jammes to become reconciled with the Church and tried to convert Gide – events already described. He also saw something of Camille, who had now been dropped by Rodin. Her looks fading, her limp more evident, she was a stricken spirit, finding it hard to make a living. Claudel felt pity and tried to help by publishing an appreciative article about her work.

A certain Reine Sainte-Marie-Perrin of Lyon was proposed as a suitable wife. She came from a strongly Catholic family – her father jointly designed the angel-festooned basilica at Lyon – but she was thin, gaunt, not robust, not pretty. At least on Claudel's side it would be a *mariage de raison*: he was now committed – and Camille's unhappiness reinforced the point – to a life of reason. On 15 March 1906 Claudel married Mademoiselle Sainte-Marie-Perrin and three days later they sailed for China.

Marriage was to give Claudel five children but never, as with R., complete joy of flesh and spirit. A New Year's resolution in his Journal for 1908 reads: 'Fight my wretched desire to look at, and read, indecent periodicals and books.' His consular work became a solace and increasingly he turned to the writing of poetry.

As a young man in Paris Claudel had moved in two poetic circles. One wished to convey the nuances of refined (often depraved) feelings; the other sought to attain the supposed inner meaning of things through hermetic allegory or incantation. In the light of his own poetic temperament, of his reading of the Bible, especially the Psalms, and of Aquinas, and of his life in unsophisticated provincial China, Claudel decided that neither approach was right for him. So he worked out his own rationale in a little book, *The Art of Poetry*.

Claudel starts from the view that things really exist, they are not mere constructs by the individual. But things are not self-sufficient. Each is interdependent on others and can be defined only in relation to the whole. What about man? He is set apart by his intelligence, but he too is interdependent on things. Socrates' (and Gide's) advice to man, 'Know yourself', is mistaken. The correct advice should be: 'Forget yourself.' Man should wonder that things exist at all and discover from them the spirit of God infusing them. The poet's function is to praise things in their entirety and thereby praise God.

Claudel put this theory into practice in *Five Great Odes*, written between 1905 and 1910. In the first, begun at Solesmes, he hails the nine Muses carved on a Roman sarcophagus, and envisages for himself a different poetic journey: not the return of Ulysses, nor the flight of Æneas from Troy, nor Dante's descent to the underworld, but travel across the earth in order to name things as God did on the days of Creation, thereby revealing an essence that may have been lost or hidden.

The second Ode, 'The Spirit of Water', is set in Peking. There, inland, the poet recalls the sea, symbol of his freedom. But freedom does not fully satisfy, he aspires to God. As he recalls his wrong-doing, the image of water reappears in the poet's tears of penitence:

> *J'ai voulu l'âme, la savoir, cette eau qui ne connaît*
> *point la mort! J'ai tenu entre mes bras l'astre*
> *humain!*
> *O amie, je ne suis pas un dieu,*
> *Et mon âme, je ne puis te la partager et tu ne peux me*
> *prendre et me contenir et me posséder.*[1]

The suggestion is that all carnal possession is incomplete in its scale and duration.

In the third Ode, 'Magnificat', the poet thanks God for delivering him from the idols of Justice, Progress, Divinity and Humanity. In lines that have been called smug Claudel writes: 'Do not cast me to perdition with the Voltaires and Renans, the Michelets and Hugos, and all the other infamous ones!' He thanks God for the gift of a daughter, whose fatherhood they share:

> *L'esprit de joie ne m'entre pas droit au corps*
> *Que lorsque parole fut adressée à Jean dans le désert ...*[2]

In the fourth Ode the poet resists the call of the Muse who is Grace. Instead of turning inwards to find his own unity in order to be able to unify what he describes, he reverts to the scene of his wrong-doing.

In the final Ode the poet heeds God's Grace. He agrees to close his soul to limitless yearnings, to set guard at its gates the four cardinal virtues, for only

---

[1] I wanted to possess and know a soul, water that is deathless.
I held in my arms a star in human form!
O woman, I am not a god,
And my soul I cannot share with you, nor can you take and contain and possess me.

[2] The spirit of joy enters my body no less
Than when the word came to John in the desert ...

so can he survey a world that is finite. In a new mood of confidence he exclaims: 'Hail, dawn of the century just begun!' and as at the opening of the first Ode turns to the past, this time to the dead, from whom we the living are not separated and whom we can help by our prayers.

Claudel's sequence marks a turning-point in French poetry, and perhaps he had to travel far to be so revolutionary compared with current offerings at home. They re-assert a realist ontology; they strike a note of joy in the wonder and variety of created things; they bring back God to the centre. They were at once recognized as a very important work and quickly began to influence contemporaries.

Claudel took a great liking to China and to his busy life there. We glimpse him on a hot summer's day, bare to the waist, blotting-paper round his chest to absorb perspiration, writing letters in Latin to the local Spanish-speaking bishop. He warms to the spontaneity and skills of the little artisans and traders, the all-importance of family and community life and, also, the pervading sense of the supernatural: tombs, temples, humble small sanctuaries under a tree where worship consisted of a stick of incense or a scrap of paper. He notes that whereas the letters of the Western alphabet are based on an upright line, the Chinese are based on the horizontal. 'A word exists through a succession of letters, a character through the proportion of its constituents . . . One can detect in the Chinese character a schematic being, a scriptural person, with its particular nature, modalities and . . . physiognomy. Hence the pious attitude of the Chinese toward calligraphy.'

Claudel too is not averse to Chinese male dominance. He notes down a local story entitled 'The Bell', which was later to influence him. The daughter of a bell-maker, seeing that her old father is unable to achieve the right alloy for his masterpiece, throws herself into the crucible, and so gives her soul to the bell.

Claudel struck people as very combative. He seemed to feel a need to contest and oppose, not only friends' opinions with which he disagreed, but untruth in general. He was a man of extremes: as Léon Daudet put it: 'With Claudel it is either noon or midnight, never four or five in the afternoon.'

Such a temperament is drawn to the theatre. As a student Claudel had enjoyed the Théâtre d'Art, run by Paul Fort, a flamboyant young man who wore a Rembrandt hat and cameo tie-pin, wrote ballads about his native Champagne and produced poetic drama: Shelley's *Cenci*, Marlowe's *Dr Faustus*, and the heart-plucking plays of Maurice Maeterlinck.

Claudel particularly liked Maeterlinck's *The Princess Maleine*. She is the innocent victim of a sensual murderous mother and a cowardly senile father. Its settings are unspecified: a 'corridor', a forest, a tower; war is declared, waged and won between two of its acts; rain, hail and lightning abound and it ends in suicide and murder. Though the plot is preposterous and the characters lack body, passion is poured out quite effectively.

Claudel had a shot at writing a verse play in this genre, but much more virile. *Tête d'Or* is the name of heroic adventurer in the mould of Alexander, who cold-bloodedly kills a King, assumes his throne and is defied by the King's daughter. He then makes war in Asia, is deserted by his army and wounded; as he lies dying he names the Princess his successor. But she too has been wounded and falls dead on his body.

Tête d'Or is a hymn to Claudel's love of life and hot ambition, counterpointed by his pre-conversion terror of death with nothing to follow. It is full of sometimes brilliant, sometimes preposterous images, but unstageable and Paul Fort declined to produce it. Claudel published it anonymously in 1900 and sent a copy to Maeterlinck, whose gentler nature was shaken by its rawness: 'I feel like a diver attacked by a shark.'

The next step in Claudel's theatrical development occurred when he received from their author copies of Gide's plays. After reading Nietzsche, Gide concluded that traditional Christian morality had been superseded as a basis for drama, and he had set himself to write plays in which the hero would disregard conventional good and evil and act from his own inner truth. This was what Philoctetes and Saul do in plays with those titles. *King Candaulus* goes further: the hero, a man generous to excess, wishes to share his wife with his friend Gyges. He persuades both his wife and Gyges to agree, then to his own surprise falls prey to jealousy, and the drama ends in bloodshed.

Gide was a novelist specializing in nuances, uncertainty and unusual motivation. To succeed as a playwright a writer had to be cast in the mould of Claudel and to share the deep, more commonplace emotions of one's audience. *King Candaulus*, produced in Paris and in Berlin, was received with jeers.

Claudel, however, learned from Gide's strange plays. He saw that timeless lyrical outpouring was insufficient: there had to be real-life people in a real-life context. And the Biblical characters of Saul and Candaulus directed Claudel's thoughts to the possibilities of Christian drama.

Whereas Gide believed the Christian to be a boring subject for drama, because stereotyped and predictable, Claudel thought just the opposite: 'By obliging us to examine our conscience daily, by arousing in us deep feelings of tenderness and affection, Christianity gives our inner life an elasticity, a richness, a delicacy sadly lacking in the most vaunted works of this lately ended nineteenth century . . . The Christian's soul is in effect the supreme battleground, with grace pitted against nature. And there is the larger dimension: a Christian knows that it is not he who is of ultimate importance but the purpose each of us has been created to attain and to proclaim.'

Strengthened by these convictions, in 1905 Claudel set himself to write a play in free verse about his love-affair with Madame R. The hero of *Partage de Midi – Sharing at Noon* – is a Chinese customs official, Mesa, who happens also to be a Catholic. After being turned down for the priesthood, while travelling back to the East, Mesa meets a married woman, Ysé de Ciz. They fall in love. In China Mesa sends Ysé's husband to a distant post in a notoriously unhealthy region: we recall David and Uzziah the Hittite. Mesa and Ysé enjoy a brief but intense period of joy, but Mesa, who had been unable to give himself entirely to God, is unable to conquer his selfishness and give himself entirely to Ysé. Ysé becomes pregnant by Mesa, but she decides to leave him for an old friend, Amalric, who, though dissolute, is more human, less rancorous and self-centred than Mesa.

Mesa encounters Ysé again; her husband has died, she is free to marry. He expects pardon and happiness. But Ysé does not utter a word. The town is under siege; only one travel permit is available. Amalric takes it and leaves with Ysé. Presently, however, she returns. The two lovers await death in the doomed town, the death that will punish Mesa's adultery and alone break his egoism, trusting, however, in the mercy of God who will, they hope, sanction their love in eternity.

By Claudel's friends *Sharing at Noon* was welcomed not only as a considerable verse play but as a turning-point in the contemporary theatre: in a modern setting a reawakening of the spirit of Racine. It is a truer, because less exaggerated work than the pagan love-death dear to Wagner and the Symbolists. While recognizing that even an adulterous affair can prepare us for the beatific vision, it accepts that in this life at least such a love is against the will of God.

A prominent Paris producer offered to stage *Sharing at Noon* but on the advice of his spiritual director, who thought it would be unfair to Madame R. and her children, Claudel sadly withheld permission. Its stage success, and admission to the repertory of the Comédie Française, would come later: for the present in book form it passed from hand to hand among the Paris cognoscenti.

For the theme of his next play, *The Hostage*, written in 1909, Claudel again chose self-sacrifice by a woman: at the time of the Revolution Pope Pius VII is sheltering in a royalist home: in order to save the Pope, at the urging of her curé, the lady of the house, though engaged to a royalist officer, agrees to marry her powerful enemy, the local Prefect. The play ends with the death of the lady and the royalist officer. Again, love and marriage are mutually exclusive. *The Hostage* was to be played three times to full houses at the Odéon in summer 1914, and performed the same year in London, with Sybil Thorndike in a production by Edith Craig.

After *The Hostage* Claudel began to rewrite a final version of a play he had been working on for seventeen years and which already existed in two earlier versions. Like some Symbolist plays Claudel had liked as a student, *The Tidings Given to Mary* is set in the Middle Ages, but Claudel makes the period authentic in its blend of hardship and faith. The leading character is a peasant girl, Violaine, life-loving, with a quick tongue in her pretty head, and the theme is set in a Prologue. Violaine meets a church architect, Pierre de Craon, who once tried to rape her. Pierre still loves her and tells her his spirit is eaten up, knowing she is to marry someone else. Violaine replies, 'If your spirit must be eaten up – let it be on a gold candelabrum like the Paschal Candle in the middle of the choir for the glory of the whole Church.' When she learns that Pierre has the beginnings of leprosy, quixotically she gives him a kiss.

Violaine contracts leprosy. Her sister Mara convinces Violaine's fiancé Jacques that Violaine has been unchaste with Pierre. Because of her leprosy Violaine has to leave her family and live as an outcast, while Mara marries Jacques and bears a child. All these trials Violaine accepts without bitterness.

Mara's baby dies, and she carries it to Violaine, who now has a reputation for holiness, begging her to restore it to life. Violaine holds the dead child to her breast beneath her garment and miraculously revives it to the accompaniment of the songs of angels.

Mara is jealous of her sister's holiness and tries to kill her by pushing her into a precipitous sandpit. There she is found by Pierre – cured now of his leprosy, and we are given to understand that this has followed from Violaine's uncomplaining acceptance of *her* leprosy. Pierre carries Violaine home. In her last minutes the two have time to experience a mystical love. Mara confesses her crime and Violaine dies amid general reconciliation.

The strength of Claudel's play lies in the convincingness of Violaine. As she becomes holier she grows more, not less, human, and artistically this was imperative, given the pervasiveness of the supernatural. By renouncing happiness and accepting her afflictions Violaine receives the power of spreading love around her; having kept her virginity she is granted the miracle of suckling and reviving a dead child; by accepting for her own body Pierre's leprosy she allows him to build new churches for France; and her reward at the moment of death is the sense of mystical union with Pierre.

Claudel's intention in this play is clarified by looking at the second of the earlier versions, entitled *La Jeune Fille Violaine*. Here there is no leprosy and Violaine's sacrifice is voluntary. Mara threatens to kill herself unless she marries Jacques, and she tells him that Violaine is secretly in love with Pierre. Violaine chooses to sacrifice her own happiness to Mara's, lets Jacques believe Pierre has seduced her, signs away her heritage, leaves home and soon becomes blind. The Violaine of this version has similarities with Alissa in *Strait is the Gate*. In choosing, for his definitive version, to shift the emphasis from Violaine as a person to the will of God made manifest in her, Claudel was putting into practice his stated belief that a Christian is interesting only in so far as he or she is passive rather than active.

In all three versions, and in its Paris production, which we shall come to presently, *The Tidings Given to Mary* was one of the most original works of our period. It broke with the accepted subjects of current drama: wife seeking a new lover, unscrupulous businessman seeking higher profits, clinging mother seeking to prevent a married daughter from emigrating. It broke with naturalistic dialogue. It broke with the never-never world of Symbolism. For the first time in living memory it asserted that self-sacrifice could be fruitful and even joyous. Above all, in an anti-clerical society, it affirmed the fact of God's grace at work in souls. Indeed, just as *Strait is the Gate* presented an extreme Calvinism, so *Tidings* depicted a harsher Catholicism than that of François de Sales and Thérèse of Lisieux.

The most gifted producer in Paris was Aurélien Lugné. The son of a bank clerk, tall, powerfully built, with commanding presence, he had founded the Théâtre l'Œuvre to perform avant-garde works, especially

Ibsen, and himself gave notable performances as Stockman, Solness and John Gabriel Borkmann. Lugné had a heavy head, which in repose hung down and sideways; this and his doomsday expression suggested Edgar Allan Poe's Raven; liking to mystify, early in his career Aurélien Lugné added Poe to his name.

In August 1912 Lugné-Poe came to an agreement with Claudel to stage *The Tidings Given to Mary*. He would play Violaine's father and he invited a Dutch-born actress, Marie Kalff, one of the earliest admirers of Claudel's plays, to take the role of Violaine, but before rehearsals began she developed tuberculosis and had to go to Davos for treatment; her place was taken by Madame Lara.

In October 1912 Claudel left Frankfurt, where he held the post of Consul General and came to Paris to meet Lugné-Poe. Forty-five years old, assured, on the road to becoming an Ambassador, Claudel had definite ideas about the staging of his play, and though Lugné-Poe had a reputation for terrorizing authors, the raven and the ox settled down to a fruitful collaboration. Lugné-Poe had chosen a small theatre at 56a rue Malakoff normally used for school plays, because it had an 'unpolluted' atmosphere. Its stage was only five metres wide. He entrusted the decor to Jean Variot, who had studied avant-garde theatre in Munich, and Claudel took Variot to his birthplace in Villeneuve so that he could get the feel of the region depicted in the play. Variot spent his tiny budget of 800 francs on grey bunting, a barn door, a chimneypiece, a silhouette of a town and a tree. He dressed Violaine in a nun's habit, complete with wimple, rope belt and crucifix; Claudel would have preferred a simple linen dress with, over it, a sort of cloth of gold dalmatic decorated with big flowers.

It was Lugné-Poe's idea to replace realistic speech

with formal intoning and to his cast he indicated the overall mood he wanted: innocence. In this framework Claudel was allowed to rehearse and, as he told Gide, he got a great deal of pleasure in securing the desired gestures and emphases.

The first performance took place on 21 December 1912. Hanging from the ceiling was a big bunch of mistletoe, sent by Claudel from Germany. The full house included Variot's friend, the composer Vincent d'Indy, who had done much to rehabilitate plainchant, Robert de Flers, dramatist and theatre critic of *Le Figaro*, and Jean Schlumberger of the *NRF*.

At first the audience seemed disconcerted, but gradually, says Lugné-Poe, they became 'gripped, carried away, enchanted'. At the end everyone from the old porter to the critics applauded loudly. Ghéon spoke for many in praising the dramatic power of Claudel's language: 'This tense, knotted style comes over better on the stage than in the text,' while Jean Laurec in *La Semaine Littéraire* wrote: 'The play is alive, its characters are consistent, scenically it is totally effective.'

Just three performances in the little theatre ensured the success of *Tidings*. As a young man Claudel had winced at sugary plaster statues of saints and the Sacred Heart, at superficial and inelegant Sunday sermons; now he had done what probably no other person could have done: made Catholicism artistically acceptable to the demanding intelligentsia of Paris.

In the next eighteen months *Tidings* was performed in several provincial cities and in Frankfurt, Strasbourg and Hellebrau. Lugné-Poe also staged *The Hostage* – this time Claudel was able to be present and was called to take a bow. Claudel's early *The Exchange* also saw the stage, its producer being an athletic young showman, Jacques Copeau, who with the help of Gaston Gallimard, Gide and the editorial board of the *NRF* had founded the experimental Théâtre du Vieux Colombier. Paris by now had two good avant-garde companies.

As these successes came his way Claudel had to face a real-life drama. His sister Camille was by now physically and mentally broken by her hopeless attachment to Rodin. On account of his numerous affairs, the ageing sculptor was depicted by caricaturists as 'The Sacred Goat': for Camille he no longer felt physical attraction, but he was sorry for her and offered her financial help. This, with characteristic hauteur, she declined. She was now living as a recluse in her shuttered ground-floor apartment and in her pain seems to have made her peace with religion, for to the walls of her room she had pinned the Stations of the Cross, cut with a pair of scissors from a newspaper. She did not go out, neglected her food and to dust and clean her apartment. It was beginning to be said by neighbours that poor Camille Claudel was well down the road to madness.

There were three subjects one did not mention in Paris: Germany and perversion we have noted; the third was madness. All were matters of great danger, for they were believed to threaten society. Madness – whatever its form – was reckoned to run in families.

Camille was not so unwell that she could not be looked after in a loving home, the home, say, of the brother to whom since childhood she had been so close. To Paul Claudel that was now certainly one of the options open. But already his position in the Foreign Service was shaky. First an adulterous liaison with a married foreigner; Catholic plays and poems that much displeased anti-clerical governments and senior civil servants; some of his reports from China so idiosyncratic they had been minuted: 'Mad'. If he tried to take into his home *en poste* – a home flying the tricolour – a sister whose behaviour gave every sign of being 'peculiar', Paul Claudel could say goodbye to any hope of advancement, might indeed be forced to resign. There was the further fact that he and Reine now had two sons and two daughters. With a weird aunt hovering around, gone altogether were their children's chances of making respectable marriages.

Claudel never put on paper the ordeal he went through in 1913, but it surely caused him intense anguish. He decided finally to put his sister away. He took Camille to Avignon and placed her in a home for the deranged. Camille hated the place, and for the rest of her long life was to write pitiful, perfectly coherent letters to Paul protesting her confinement. Like Violaine, she was obliged to suffer so that others could enjoy the fullness of life. But Camille's suffering was sent by man, and the episode serves to show that at least one area of Claudel's life remained untouched both by the ultra-intelligent quest for sincerity and by the softening touch of Grace.

The tragedy of Camille's breakdown was, in a serious way, to cast a shadow on Claudel's friendship with Gide. Gide had written a satirical novel, *The Vatican Cellars*, which supposes that the Pope is a prisoner held to ransom, while a pretender rules the Church. Among those involved is a Balkan adventurer with homosexual tastes and a Nietzschean creed, Lafcadio. Drawing on his strange experience in the auction room, Gide has Lafcadio perform a wholly unmotivated act by pushing from the carriage of a fast-moving train a fellow-traveller. Valéry had been correct in detecting violence in Nietzsche and its possible influence on Gide.

In 1913 Gide asked Claudel if he would allow him to use as an epigraph for this novel a couple of lines from *Tidings*: 'But what King are you talking about, and what

Pope? For there are two and we don't know which is the good one.' Since the novel derides the clergy, Gide's request was rather sly, but Claudel unwittingly agreed.

Prior to its appearance in the *NRF* Claudel received proofs. As he read them he came on a passage where Lafcadio recalls with pleasure certain homosexual experiences. Claudel was still under the shadow of Camille and convinced that her life had been ruined by unwise reading in her teens. Shocked, he dashed off a letter: 'In heaven's name, Gide, how have you brought yourself to write this passage? . . . Don't you realize the effect your books can have on unhappy young people? It pains me to speak to you like this, but I think I have to. Your sad friend, P. Claudel.'

Gide wrote back, demanding to know by what right Claudel took him to task. Claudel replied that he had acted first from friendship: by countenancing 'sodomy' Gide would be putting himself beyond the pale – 'Opinion in Paris is not so outspoken as in London, but it is more pitiless' – and also from a concern for consciences: 'Literature sometimes does a little good but, above all, it can do much harm.'

As Emerson had argued long and earnestly with Whitman to omit certain passages of *Leaves of Grass*, so Claudel, seconded by Jammes, argued with Gide. The novelist accused Claudel of being a hypocrite and was himself accused by Claudel of cynicism. Gide declined to remove the offending passage, but did agree to omit the epigraph.

This correspondence – among the most profound in French literature – brought to a head the main difference between the friends: Claudel accepting an authority outside himself, Gide declining to do so; as Claudel had written apropos *King Candaulus*: 'You yourself are plot, actor and theatre.' The conflict, as old as the Reformation, had a new actuality. For now that it was admitted that man possessed free will and a spiritual destiny, it became imperative to know according to what criteria he should build his life. If the conflict cast a long shadow over a friendship, it had the great merit of showing a parting of the ways. It offered young Frenchmen of a Christian cast of mind a real choice.

Many young men chose to follow Gide – he had the more engaging character and was a trail-blazer; a few rallied to Claudel. One was Jacques Rivière. Son of a professor of medicine in the Bordeaux region, as a boy he had been fascinated by railway lines, swerving, meandering, slithering along hills, yet finally reaching a destination, and in his life he was to show a similar sinuous, subtle but determined attitude. In appearance he was slim, with a long face, full sensuous lips, a straight look in his dark eyes. During military service he gave up Catholicism, priding himself on picking fights and stealing. He wrote an admiring letter about *Tête d'Or* to Claudel, not knowing he was a Catholic, and was advised by the dramatist to read Pascal and become a schoolmaster. In 1909 he married a young woman as sincere as he: Isabelle Fournier, sister of Alain-Fournier, the future novelist. The previous year Rivière had met Gide, warmed to his subtle mind and his honesty and in 1911 became secretary of the *NRF*.

Rivière wrote two beautifully argued articles for Gide's periodical on 'Sincerity to Oneself' and 'On Faith'. In the second he describes how he feels drawn to the doctrine of original sin but cannot find in himself a desire to condemn certain of his actions as bad: 'For every feeling arising in my soul fills me with too much wonder, interest and pleasure. I don't reflect on its quality or its worth.'

This was Rivière's position in December 1913, when with a friend from the same Bordeaux region, François Mauriac, he took a seat in the Salle Malakoff. Young

Mauriac had reacted against the bigoted Catholicism of his high bourgeoisie family and arrived in Paris wishing to shock. He mixed with dilettantes like Jean Cocteau and, possessed of a gift for irony, warmed to Gide's works in that vein. Then he fell under the charm of Claudel's work, rethought Catholicism, and on the night of 21 December attended the opening of *The Tidings Given to Mary*. Next day he wrote to Rivière:

> Before that miraculous last act it seems to me that you must surely understand what faith is and that nothing is doubtless further from it than that self-satisfaction in which you are dallying and which you describe with such exactitude. In reading your articles, I feel that two men are fighting in and for you. One is the Gide of *Nourritures Terrestres* [extolling the self and pagan pleasures], the other Claudel. You have heard their two voices. But you know that Violaine is right.

Four days later the secretary of the *NRF* proclaimed his return to the Church by receiving Holy Communion at Christmas Mass. One small event among many in a large city, it does point up two general truths: the French intelligentsia's need to see issues spelled out in literary terms, and the fact that Christianity, either in the form of Gide's Protestantism or Claudel's Catholicism, which the 1890s had pronounced dead, was in fact, yeast-like, still at work.

CHAPTER 6

Apotheosis through Art:
Marcel Proust

I n the summer of 1908 a well-to-do Parisian manufacturer of silk foulards named Camille Plantevignes rented for the month of August the Villa des
Cerises in the newly fashionable seaside resort of
Cabourg in Normandy. At three o'clock one afternoon
his only child, Marcel, aged nineteen, was sitting on a
sofa in the main hall of the Casino, looking anxiously
out at the sea and the sky. He had arranged to meet a girl
in the Golf Club if it was fine, and in the Casino if it was
raining. At present, as so often during a Norman summer, the weather was neither fine nor wet.

Opposite, on another sofa, sat a lady in her forties,
Vicomtesse d'Alton, wife of the president of the Golf
Club, with a gentleman who had recently arrived from
Paris and who usually appeared for a short while about
noon at the door looking on to the promenade, where he
became a centre of attention. In Cabourg people dressed
in light, casual clothes, but this gentleman wore a pearl-
grey overcoat, a suit of the same colour and a pearl-grey
bowler above a fringe of bluish-black hair that came
down almost to his eyebrows. He wore white kid gloves
with black stitching and pointed ankle-high boots with
buttons in the latest town fashion, and he spoke to
Madame d'Alton with one hand raised to his mouth, as
though to keep his words for her alone. As the conversation continued, he crossed his legs and it became apparent that his coat had purple satin lining.

The lady made a signal that Marcel Plantevignes should join her. In none too good a mood because of the uncertainty about his rendezvous, the young man crossed the room.

'Marcel,' she said, 'I want to introduce you to Monsieur Proust. Like all of us, he finds your name very French and very attractive. He's written some verses about it.' Proust bowed and offered the young man his hand, while Madame d'Alton held out a piece of paper.

The young man took the paper and ran his eye over the verses.

> *Si je m'appelais Plantevignes,*
> *J'aurais des pampres à mon balcon . . .*
> *Des raisins pleins des compotiers,*
> *Si je m'appelais Plantevignes.*[1]

'Monsieur,' said the young man, 'I've never much appreciated jokes about names. At school or in the Army, perhaps, but not elsewhere.'

Proust made a face, visibly rather piqued, and studied the young man with a mixture of surprise and interest. Quickly he took back the paper and said, 'You are right, Monsieur. It's ridiculous to joke about names.' He then tore up the verses.

While Marcel Plantevignes stood awkwardly in front of the sofa, the girl he was to meet arrived and they left together.

Two days later rain kept the holidaymakers indoors. Marcel Plantevignes was skimming through periodicals in the Casino reading-room when he heard sounds of argument in the bar; some Paris ladies were attacking Vigny, Lamartine and the Romantics generally. Marcel

---

[1] If Plantevignes were my name,
Vines would grace my balcony . . .
Grapes would heap my bowls
If my name were Plantevignes.

Plantevignes entered the bar and was asked by the ladies which side he backed.

'The Romantics of course!' Romanticism, he continued, could please or displease according to our taste, but it could not be said to mislead or to deform reality since reality is something we know in the most uncertain fashion only through our personal perceptions.

The argument became spirited; then one of the more outspoken of the ladies turned to a figure seated on a high stool at the corner of the bar: 'Proust, you decide.'

The elegant figure in grey pointed a finger at Marcel Plantevignes. 'This young man is right, and brilliantly so . . .'

A hubbub ensued, then the party broke up and the most smartly dressed of the ladies came to Plantevignes. 'My compliments!' she said somewhat crossly. 'From now on you'll probably be unapproachable . . . on a pinnacle.'

'But why, Madame?'

'Because the gentleman who's just publicly declared you to be right is Marcel Proust, *the* Proust, subtle man of letters, wit, intimate friend of Robert de Montesquiou and all the Paris ladies who have literary salons.' She pressed his hand and went out.

As Plantevignes made for the door, his path crossed Proust's; they walked through the drawing-room together and he thanked the older man for his support, adding that people sometimes criticized him for being 'steeped in Bergson', the leading champion of subjectivism.

'Steeped in Bergson! I'm delighted to hear it. Exactly what people said of me when I was your age!' Again he apologized for his verses; then, advancing and turning to face Plantevignes, he removed his hat with a flourish and made him a graceful half-bow. 'Yes, I'm very sorry indeed I displeased you. All the more since I'd heard much about you and had already decided to ask you to become one of my friends.'

Plantevignes was stupefied. He had heard that Proust went in for florid politenesses, but such deference from someone almost twenty years older than he was surely very strange? However, he took Proust at his word, begged him to replace his hat and accepted gratefully the offer of friendship. The other said that he hardly ever went out and received in his room at the top of the Grand Hôtel. He would expect Plantevignes that evening after dinner, at nine.

Promptly at nine, after his name had been checked against a list prepared daily by Proust, young Plantevignes was taken up in the lift and shown into Proust's room. At that meeting, to be followed by a second, by a third and many more, an observant young man came to know Proust in the year that was to mark a turning-point in his life and work.

What had induced a rich bachelor who did not swim or play golf to spend the summer alone in a Normandy resort hotel? First, the sea air he found good for his delicate health. Second, many Parisians had villas near by: he visited them and they came to him, sometimes for dinner. Third, he had at his disposal one of the new motor-cars. In this he visited the pretty countryside – he particularly liked the high ground between Trouville and Honfleur, where rhododendrons added colour to a sea view – and studied ecclesiastical architecture, not only Bayeux and Lisieux cathedrals but country churches hidden away – the very old revealed by the very modern.

During their talks that summer of 1908 Proust, aged thirty-seven, asked Plantevignes to tell him about his life in Paris, his reading, his ambitions. He seemed to see his visitor as the little Marcel he had once been, sensitive to nuances, 'but better behaved than I, and stronger'. On his side, Plantevignes found himself up against what he called the Proust mystery. Why did the writer cut himself off from the throng yet to anyone admitted to his room show the greatest kindness? Why did he break down in tears, saying he had one foot in the grave and was glad of it, and next day declare that he hoped to live long enough to complete the work he had in mind? Why did he speak longingly of noble families and another day say he preferred to chat with his cook rather than with a Duke? Why did he describe with pleasure the splendid parties he had been to, then advise Plantevignes to keep social life to a minimum? Why was he one moment laughing and cheerful, the next in the depth of sadness? Plantevignes mother believed he had proposed to a girl of noble birth and been turned down because he came from the bourgeoisie; Camille Plantevignes offered no theory, but said to his son, 'You always enjoyed splitting hairs in four; here's someone who shows how to split them in eight. So of course you're delighted.'

Before being resolved, the Proust mystery took an unexpected turn. Marcel Plantevignes was riding high on his new friendship. Only the Vicomte d'Alton, president of the Golf Club, went to Proust's room more often. Then, one afternoon about three, a page-boy from the Grand Hôtel called at the Villa des Cerises bearing a letter for Marcel in Proust's pointed hand.

'Monsieur,' it began, 'While you were showering on me marks of sincere friendship with a tenacity and insistence that sometimes disconcerted me, because I wondered whether one day they would not become abject, I was far from imagining that you were getting ready to stab me in the back.' Proust went on to say that Plantevignes had now ruined what might have been a beautiful friendship, and that he, Proust, felt no regrets at not having even said farewell.

Plantevignes could hardly believe his eyes. Shaken and completely at a loss, he hurried to the hotel. But there the lift boy refused to take him up, saying Proust had forbidden it.

Plantevignes then showed the letter to his parents. What could he have done, they asked sharply, and Plantevignes said he had no idea.

Plantevignes *père* then went to the hotel and twenty minutes later returned, arms raised in consternation. 'Proust wants to fight a duel with me!'

Proust, he said, had been stiff, dry and very angry. 'Since your son is under twenty-one, you will act on his behalf, and though I'm the injured party, I allow you to choose the weapons.'

But again, what on earth could young Plantevignes have done? The perplexed youth recalled recent events and could think of no word or action that might have provoked such anger.

While the unhappy young man was ordered to stay in his room, Plantevignes *père* set about finding seconds, and asked the Vicomte d'Alton to be one of them. Alton had heard about the affair and understood that Proust had chosen as *his* seconds a Prince and a Duke. Worse and worse! Alton then paid one more visit to Proust and at last learned what the offence was.

Plantevignes had been walking on the promenade when a lady he knew came up to him and spoke about Proust, saying that he had 'unusual morals'. Instead of denying this Plantevignes had said, 'I know, I know, Madame, what you're about to say, but for me that doesn't matter in the least . . . Excuse me, Madame, goodbye, I'm in a great hurry . . . !' Then he had beaten a retreat, and next day the lady had repeated the conversation to Proust.

Plantevignes had been wrong to beat a retreat. His parents said so, so did his friends. Proust having always behaved correctly with him, he ought to have protested. Plantevignes now admitted as much, but regret did not alter the fact of the impending duel. And why had the writer taken it so hard? Was this at the heart of the Proust mystery?

Proust was very susceptible to pretty women. Since boyhood, when he had played in the Tuileries with Antoinette Fauré, daughter of a future President, girls had excited his imagination and elicited his confidences. It was to an attractive girl, Marie de Chevilly, on a visit to Savoie, that he had first confided, as early as 1900, his ambition to write a book that would cost him much pain because it would mean describing and mixing with people he did not much care for. With Marie Nordlinger, an English enamellist working in Paris, 'fresh and graceful as a branch of hawthorn', he had read Ruskin in the original and explored some of the churches Ruskin loved. At present a young actress, Louisa de Mornand, was much in his thoughts. A brunette with big dark eyes and peroxided hair, she had been the mistress of one of his friends. She and Proust had exchanged affectionate letters, he had written her a poem, and among his possessions was a signed photograph to 'mon cher petit Marcel' – *petit* in the context being an intensification: 'to my dearest Marcel'. Before the death of his father in 1903 and his mother in 1905 Proust would have been unable to support a wife, but now he was rich and in a position to propose marriage. There were times when he thought he wished to do so and was looking for a possible young lady.

Proust was also easily attracted to charming young men. What he sought were good looks – especially big dark eyes, like those of Louisa – and intelligence and seriousness. His first friend, in college days, had been

Léon Daudet, son of the novelist Alphonse. Léon had been succeeded by Reynaldo Hahn, of German descent and a gifted composer of songs, who shared Proust's passion for poetry and keen interest in Paris society. The two had gone on holiday in Brittany when Proust was twenty-four; that holiday, and the friendship generally, became the subject of *Jean Santeuil*, an unconvincing narcissistic novel which had been rejected by a Paris publisher. Reynaldo Hahn, now a darling of the Paris salons, and perpetually hovering on the brink of marrying an actress, was still Proust's closest friend and in Paris called at his flat after a fashionable recital to give him the gossip.

These friendships both with young women and with young men were Platonic. Ardent in imagination, Proust was much less so in life. Answering one of those questionnaires which were then popular as a game, Proust, aged twenty, said his most marked characteristic was 'A craving to be loved, or, to be more precise, to be caressed and spoiled rather than to be admired', while the quality he would most like to possess would be a strong will. We know that as a creative artist Proust did possess an exceptionally strong will, so here he evidently had in mind the drive associated with virility. Ultra-sensitive, hair-splittingly subtle, Proust had been exceedingly close to his mother but held back from physical involvement with anyone else. His abnormality, if one insists on that word, was not that he was homosexual, but rather that he had a tendency to fear all sexual relations.

The explanation of Proust's extraordinary challenge to a duel, then, is that he wished to assert that he was not homosexual, that he possessed the normal man's feelings for women and that one day he might very well overcome his fear of sexual relations and take a wife. In this Proust may have been over-wishful, but he was not purposely deceiving himself or others.

The literary dandy's challenge of course plunged the Plantevignes into a frenzy of alarm. The scandal! The damage to business! The actual physical danger! And doubtless some obliging friend recalled that eleven years before a gossipy journalist, Jean Lorrain, had published insinuations about Proust's friendship with Léon Daudet, whereupon Proust had challenged Lorrain and the two had actually fought a duel, happily without harm to either.

It was decided that Plantevignes *père* would go to Proust's room on the top floor of the Grand Hôtel and attempt to explain to the offended man that his son's failure to protest was not ill-intentioned. This the maker of neck-ties duly did. Proust listened but gave no indication of withdrawing his challenge.

Hours passed; suspense grew. Then the elegant figure of Proust emerged from the Grand Hôtel. The Villa des Cerises stood just across the square. Nevertheless Proust got into a motor-car hired for the occasion and was driven round the square to the Villa des Cerises. Here he got out and delivered his card, on which he had written an acceptance of Plantevignes *père*'s apologies for his son. Relations were then formally resumed. The young man was again taken up in the lift after dinner to Proust's room; he apologized and was forgiven.

Before the reader loses patience with this self-important fop and skips to the next chapter, let us pause to look at his good side. To his mother he was a perfect son, affectionate, supportive, confiding, solicitous. 'I can't possibly tell you how much I wish you were here,' he wrote to her on a yachting holiday. 'There's the sea that you love so well, colours that would bewitch you, air that has nothing in common with that of the dining-room at home, a temperature that keeps everyone smothered in shawls . . . Having seen you tormented with the heat, always trying to escape it . . . I should so like to see you here admiring everything and breathing easily.' Ten months after his father's death: 'It seems to me that I think of you even more tenderly (though really it isn't possible) today, the 24th of September. Every time this day returns, all the thoughts we've accumulated since the very first day might be expected to make the time that's already passed by seem so terribly long. But our habit of incessantly thinking back to that day and to all the happiness that came before it . . . makes it seem, on the contrary, like yesterday . . . When, as we two are, people who are constantly linked by a kind of wireless telegraphy, it doesn't matter whether they're far or near, they're always in close communion, always side by side.' He had accompanied his mother to Evian when she went to treat incipient uræmia with the waters there, he was at her bedside when she died and heard her repeat her favourite exhortation to him as a schoolboy: 'If you're not a Roman, at least practise virtue.' She meant, specifically, courage.

Proust required courage in large quantities because for years he had been battling against asthma. He held himself like a guardsman, head back, bulging chest forward the better to inhale. Yet suddenly, often in the middle of the night, he would feel he was suffocating. Lips violet, perspiration on his brow and cheeks, he would stagger to the window and lean on the sill, bracing himself for the terrible struggle to take air into his lungs. If this was a slow and difficult task, even slower and more painful was the effort to expel his breath. The normal rate of twenty breaths a minute fell to ten, and this would continue for half an hour, perhaps a full hour. As the crisis eased, his mouth would fill with globules of saliva thickened with crystals of phosphate, and these he had to expectorate.

For some reason asthma was prevalent among

Parisians at this time: perhaps a combination of dust, pollen from the avenue trees and petrol fumes. In the first days of January 1900, for example, *Le Figaro* carried advertisements for no less than three anti-asthma medicines, including Exibard, 'an Abyssinian cure'. Proust used one of them – smoking Lepic cigarettes; he also inhaled fumigations of potassium or of datura, and dosed himself with syrup containing ether.

Asthmatics have weaknesses in the pulmonary and nervous systems, and these can be a consequence of breeding from refined stock. Though his paternal ancestors were mostly hardy and mediocre, on his mother's side Proust's immediate forebears included a president of the Paris Appeal Court, a barrister of brilliance, a Minister of Trade, a Navy Minister and a Minister of Justice. When we add that while love-marriages tend to bring in strength, marriages arranged at this level within smallish circles tend to refine intelligence and weaken physique, it may well be that both Proust's gifts and his disability had a common source.

Proust had to battle also against a consequence of asthma, insomnia. Though he took trional, seldom did he enjoy a full night's sleep. Only those who have suffered from sleeplessness can fully appreciate the strain it puts on the body and on the mind, which is obliged to fight for serenity against a continual feeling of oppression and sometimes of persecution, to conjure gentle manners out of the urge to retaliate against a seemingly hostile world. All things considered, it is wonderful that Proust managed to make, and keep in good repair, a dozen close friendships.

We can now perhaps better understand Proust's behaviour to Plantevignes, and why Plantevignes, glad to be forgiven, eagerly resumed his evening visits. There he noticed the writer's excellent memory: he would recite poem after poem by his favourites, Sully

Prudhomme, Musset and Baudelaire, many of them regrets for happier days. He noticed that one of Proust's favourite ideas was that the great moments of life often arise not from important events but from very small circumstances that set in motion associated ideas, and it is these that are infinitely rich and precious. Recalling later Proust's conversation in Cabourg, Plantevignes summed up its special quality in one of the novelist's own phrases: 'An hour is not just an hour: it is a vase filled with scents, sounds, plans, atmospheres.'

Proust questioned Plantevignes about the fashionable men and ladies who frequented the Golf Club and when the younger Marcel showed an interest in one of the ladies urged him to press his suit with vigour. He liked to give his friends pet names – Hahn became Bouls-ni-Bouls – and Plantevignes, still full of youthful illusions, Proust decided to call the Chevalier Fantaisie. Sometimes they went out to a local restaurant and ate langoustes – delicious, but it was their designation on the menu that Proust most savoured: *demoiselles de Cherbourg au feu éternel*, lobsters grilled on an open fire.

'Am I a novelist?' Proust asked himself in his notebook for 1908, and young Plantevignes might well have replied, 'No reason to think so.' Proust was known as a dilettante *Figaro* contributor, first about fashionable parties, more recently about religious art: he had made a well-argued plea for the retention of France's medieval churches as places of worship, many of which under a Government plan were to be turned into museums or halls. But Proust's question was not an idle one, nor induced by vanity, and to understand its importance for him we must glance at his education and the metamorphosis he underwent in his mid-twenties.

Proust had been brought up as a Catholic by his mother, though she herself, out of deference to her family, retained her Jewish faith. At the lycée he had imbibed the positivism of the day and became, as he put it, 'crazy about determinism'. Then, at seventeen, he began his year's philosophy course under Alphonse Darlu, a short, narrow-shouldered, exuberant Gascon, beard trimmed to a neat point, large ears, strong Bordeaux accent. At thirty-nine Darlu had thought himself out of the vogue cults of his day. He believed that philosophy should deal with metaphysics and morals and was soon to co-found an influential Review devoted to those topics. Darlu was not a Christian. He believed that while religion could help shape moral feelings, moral principles must be elicited from a study of metaphysics.

Proust quickly came to like and admire Darlu the man. After school he would be invited to Darlu's modest fifth-floor flat and continue till suppertime discussing questions raised in class. Once when Darlu fell ill Proust solicitously sent him up a jug of orangeade. 'Darlu taught me to think,' Proust later recalled.

By the end of his year Proust had rejected positivist materialism in favour of Darlu's view that mind orders the phenomena our senses perceive and seeks to discover within them a single 'divine' truth that may also become a foundation for moral choices.

At university Proust came under the spell of Emile Boutroux, the Catholic philosopher who, in a famous book, had shown scientific laws to be of limited, quantitative validity, in no way binding on man's spiritual self. In an essay on 'The Spirituality of the Soul' Proust defended the view of Plato as taught by Boutroux: that there exists a universal spiritual substance in which our individual thought participates.

By the age of twenty, to the question 'Who are your real-life heroes?' Proust replied, 'Monsieur Darlu, Monsieur Boutroux.' He meant that he believed in man's soul and free will, and was beginning to seek a metaphysic – it might be moral truth, it might be

Christianity, or it might be an absolute of a third kind.

The 'converted' Proust emerges in a letter to Reynaldo Hahn:

> Dinner yesterday at the Daudets, with my nice little [Léon], M. de Goncourt, Coppée, M. Philipe, M. Vacques. Sad to observe the frightful materialism, extraordinary from 'intellectuals'. They explain character and genius in terms of physical habits or race. Musset, Baudelaire, Verlaine explained by the different kind of alcoholic drinks they consumed.

Proust felt strongly enough about his new belief to criticize, in his earliest published article, 'The Irreligion of the State'. 'Surely, in the field of education,' he wrote, 'not to take sides on questions about God and the soul is a way – and the worst of ways – of taking sides. "We're content not to discuss these matters" is the stock phrase. But that in effect is Materialism.'

A year later, in his first published review – of a novel about the havoc wrought by a pretty widow on the lives of two young men – Proust felt able to speak up for like-minded friends:

> If the new generation differs from its predecessor and in a way goes beyond it, it is assuredly because we feel drawn to reflect calmly, to dream, to give due place to thinking, which materialists had banished from the universe and naturalists from art. These aspirations, perhaps vague but certainly strongly held, tend to give life a background, our destiny a meaning and a sanction to what we do.

With the new century Proust's aspirations became less vague. He came to know well several Paris sets and thought he saw why they behaved as they did. He reflected much on his happy childhood and on the mother whose love to him was the centre of his life. He pondered the nature of literature and of the creative process; from these and related activities he deduced certain general truths, one of which, or a combination of several, might, he believed, provide the metaphysic he was seeking.

He became aware also of his literary gifts. He felt an urge to match them to the discoveries he had been making by writing a metaphysical book that would offer the reader a spiritual Absolute. What part Christianity would play in the Absolute remained to be seen. The form of the work also still remained to be decided. Perhaps a novel, despite the failure of his first novel. Hence the entry in Proust's notebook of 1908: 'Am I a novelist?' The answer Proust gave to that question is not a simple Yes or No. It emerges from the writing programme he began in that same year to sketch.

Proust decided he would couch the metaphysic in the form of an essay about the nature of literature and, by extension, of life itself, illustrating it with a fictional episode of Paris society, '*Souvenir d'une matinée*'. In other words, he would write a composite book, not a novel, but it would be an ambitious work, offering the reader an original overall view of the meaning of life.

In September Proust said goodbye to young Plantevignes and went off by taxi, via the churches of the Seine valley, to the Hôtel des Réservoirs, Versailles. Georges de Lauris, a friend with literary tastes who resembled a sad sheepdog, had broken his leg and Proust, notably loyal in adversity, kept Georges company while he was laid up.

In early November Proust arrived home on the first floor of 102 Boulevard Haussmann. Here, looked after by a manservant and his cook wife, he worked very hard that winter and spring writing his composite book. He suffered much from asthma and kept in touch with friends mainly by letter. He did not forget Plantevignes, getting him admitted to the Polo Club, to which Proust belonged, and asking Plantevignes to try to get a job in his father's factory for a young man, down on his luck, whom Georges de Lauris had befriended during military service.

By August 1909 Proust had completed his composite book and submitted the manuscript to *Mercure de France*. They turned it down – one of the fortunate rejections in literary history, for it had the effect of obliging Proust to reconstruct the work in entirety.

On 20 August Proust left Paris for the Grand Hôtel, Cabourg, and there exchanged the traffic of Boulevard Haussmann and select little suppers at the Ritz for the ozone of the Channel and encounters with pretty girls bicycling on the promenade. He also began his most determined efforts so far to find a suitable young lady. The Vicomte d'Alton had two pretty daughters, Colette and Hélène: the Alton title was only Second Empire, so these girls were not socially out of reach and Proust saw much of them. Colette he particularly liked and he gave her a gold handbag from Cartier's.

But the girl who most took Proust's fancy was a tall summer visitor whom he first glimpsed wearing a black riding habit, holding a long whip as gracefully as a fan. She had, thought Proust, all the charm of a Watteau or Boldini. He would go to the promenade or Casino just to catch a glimpse of her, and one day he accompanied Plantevignes by taxi to watch her take tea at the 'Marie Antoinette' farmhouse restaurant. She had a somewhat sad expression, and Proust chose to believe that she belonged to the impoverished nobility.

'How pretty she must look on horseback,' said Proust, eyeing her with admiration. 'Women like that,' he continued pensively, 'deserve a rich protector.'

141

One evening shortly afterwards Proust confided to Plantevignes: 'How lovely it would be to have enough money and good health to ask for the hand of a girl like that in marriage – solely for her sake, for her happiness – if need be, even a *mariage blanc*. And once married, how one would love to say, "Don't bother about me, I've married you only to make you happy, by giving you my money, and to watch you live, as in a painting . . ." ' Excitedly Proust described her as a thoroughbred, hunting the boar, managing a choice salon. 'Ah, if only one could save such a girl and help her to fulfil her gifts! . . .'

As he broke off, Plantevignes glanced up at his friend and saw that he was in tears.

Meanwhile, that same summer of 1909, Proust decided to take the step over which he had so long hesitated, to assume that he *was* indeed a novelist and to reshape his material as a long first-person novel. At the purely narrative level it would tell of childhood joys, of puppy-love, of a troubled love-affair, ending with the death of the girl; it would describe various levels of Paris society, notably artists and the most distinguished *noblesse*. It would end with the main protagonists grown old. It would be a novel of remembrance, but unlike so much French literature ever since François Villon had wept for the snows of yesteryear, it would not be suffused with regret. It would be a novel describing joys, written in a mood of joy, as Proust had already made plain in a self-portrait:

> Drops of rain beginning to fall, a sunbeam reappearing were enough to recall rainy autumns, sunlit summers, whole stretches of his life, dark hours of his soul which then brightened and filled him with the elation of remembrance and poetry . . . He seemed to look straight at something he did not fully under-

142

stand. And in a series of strong, delicate movements, especially of the hands which clenched
as he raised his head, his whole body seemed to
imitate the efforts made by his mind. Then all
of a sudden he seemed full of joy and ready to
write.

The chapters Proust wrote that summer describe the
narrator's childhood in Combray, notably a country
walk with hawthorn in blossom. Proust's drafts have
survived. The first version is already so beautiful one
would judge it quite perfect, but Proust manages to
make it even better and then in a third version better
still. It is a rare and poignant example of genius at
painstaking work.

At the end of September Proust returned to Paris. In
November he asked Georges de Lauris to read his
Combray chapters. Lauris did so and was enthusiastic.
After his disappointment in August this was welcome
news, and probably in celebration Proust took three
boxes at the theatre to see Feydeau's new play about the
motor-racing world, *Le Circuit*; among those he invited
were Lauris and Plantevignes. Proust then went to
ground and gave himself totally to writing his novel.

Into his narrative Proust wove certain themes. One of
the most important is the strongly subjective nature of
our experience. To some degree this reflected Proust's
character – we have seen him fantasizing about the girl
in the riding-habit – but to a greater degree I believe it
grew out of the period. Röntgen's discovery of X-rays
had revealed under the visible flesh of a hand the bones
that really matter, the *inside* of things; doctors were
discovering that supposedly organic illnesses – asthma
in some cases, though not Proust's – are induced by

anxiety, and Bergson had shown that our notion of time is subjective. This view Proust carried very far. It is inaccurate to say of a girl: 'She was very sweet'; one can only say, 'I enjoyed kissing her.' Furthermore, the self is largely composed of desires that *change*: so that tomorrow my modified self may no longer enjoy kissing the girl.

A second theme in Proust's novel is that sexual desire of itself is neutral and it is our spiritual side that focuses it on a woman or a man. This too was in accord with the most advanced medical research – known to Proust, son and brother of doctors, though not to most Frenchmen. But Proust added a twist of his own. According to Plantevignes, in summer 1908 Proust watched two girls dancing very close in the Casino and wrote a description of the sexual pleasure they evidently derived which he read to his friend. Plantevignes protested. He knew the girls well, they were sporting types, and the pleasure they took was in graceful synchronized steps. To which Proust replied, 'You see them in terms of your style of dancing – the poetic style,' and he clung to his opinion. Plantevignes adds that Proust never lost an occasion of describing two girls enjoying each other's company as lesbians, and nothing would make him change. If genius contains at least one irrational element, this was Proust's, rather as the belief that the self-sacrificing role in life belongs primarily to women was the irrational element behind Claudel's plays.

A third theme in Proust's novel stems from events in the winter after he had started to write it. He was continuing, in Paris, his search for a suitable wife. He heard from a friend about a pretty girl of good family who was having a coming-out ball. Proust looked the family up in the *Bottin Mondain*, saw that they owned a historic château, and managed to get invited to the ball. He observed the girl, even spoke to her. But she seemed pleased with herself, fell short of his ideal – and he went home disillusioned.

Proust had often found reality failing to measure up to imagination. But, engaged on his novel and the self-analysis it demanded, he had to be honest about such incidents. Now or soon afterwards Proust admitted to himself that he would never marry, not because he preferred young men but because, through a combination of character and upbringing, he was powerless to engage in real-life love. There is every reason to believe Céleste Albaret, who cared for him in later life and knew him very well indeed, when she said that she didn't think Proust had ever been really in love.

Jottings in his notebooks show Proust trying to come to terms with this painful realization:

> Do not try to possess, because of [your] powerlessness to give pleasure and happiness.

> In the second part of the novel the girl loses her money; I will support her without trying to sleep with her, because of powerlessness to attain [that kind of] happiness.

And another entry reads:

> What is deep, what is inaccessible – this for us is the sole sign of value – and perhaps of a certain kind of joy.

This is important, for it anticipates one of the novel's main themes: unfulfilled desire is more satisfactory than possession.

Closely akin to the themes already noticed is the theme that involuntary memory allows us privileged access to our past. Here also Proust used the discoveries of his period as a basis for an original theory.

As a boy Marcel Proust heard the following story. In a

Paris hospital his father treated a case of pneumonia. The patient recovered and was about to be discharged when he announced that his coat was missing. He couldn't remember where he had left it and was too poor to afford a new one. The man was put under hypnosis and questioned, whereupon he said where he had left the coat. It was recovered and handed to him. 'Where did you find it?' the man asked in astonishment, oblivious of what he had said under hypnosis.

Proust was very interested in the working of that new convenience, the telephone, and more than once compared the electricity that powered it to the working of memory, both overcoming distance. By linking up to a system called Théâtrephone you could listen on your telephone to a performance at any state opera house or theatre. This system, which Proust subscribed to, may well have strengthened his view that memory not only overcomes distance but plugs us into an objective reservoir of beauty.

As he told Plantevignes, young Proust was 'steeped' in Bergson. He particularly warmed to Bergson's view that our personal awareness of time – duration – is different and independent from time as shown by the hands of a clock.

In the framework of these incidents and beliefs Proust noticed, and reflected upon, an unusual happening in his own life. During the latter part of 1908, probably in Versailles or Paris, he happened to step on some uneven paving-stones. Immediately he had the impression of being in the Baptistery of St Mark's, Venice, which he had visited eight years earlier, and where he had had a similar experience of walking on an uneven pavement. The sense of displacement was total and the pleasure afforded by it more intense than any everyday pleasure.

Proust concluded that there are two kinds of memory:

voluntary memory, which gives us a view of the past defaced by our intelligence and practical needs, and involuntary memory, which allows us to relive the past as it was and so gives us entry into a spiritual world, higher than the everyday world. Just as desire is better than possession, so the remembered past is better than the lived present. The word *Recherche* in the title of his novel connotes that, like a research scientist, the author intends to reveal the working of memory in its second form, supported by actual cases.

One important theme in Proust's novel – the last to be noticed here – receives no direct treatment yet permeates the whole, as it permeated the author's thinking. In 1914 Proust declared to his financial adviser, Lionel Hauser: 'If as you say I'm not a believing Christian, never for a single day has a preoccupation with religion been absent from my life,' and the truth of that is borne out by the stages of Proust the pilgrim's progress.

Until the age of thirty Proust held a strong residual Catholicism. On entering a church he would dip his fingers in holy water and make the sign of the cross with feeling, he had Masses said for friends who died. In 1900, when he became very fond of Gothic, he chose two guides: Emile Mâle, who shows how Christian iconography exactly illustrates Christian theology, and John Ruskin. In his earlier works Ruskin had written as a Victorian Christian, but in 1858 he was 'unconverted', as he puts it, from his parents' Evangelicalism and thereafter taught what may be called a milk-and-water view of Christian art, expressing it notably in *The Bible of Amiens*. This book for young people plays down the Cross and dogma generally: religion is held to consist in hope and faith.

Proust admired Ruskin and wished to share his

admiration by translating one of Ruskin's works. The work he chose was *The Bible of Amiens*. In the process of translating it quite a lot of Ruskin's view that Christianity is a matter of noble feelings and beautiful art rubbed off on Proust.

In 1904 Proust wrote his articles pleading for the retention of France's churches as places of worship. Here he uses some arguments from Ruskin but draws more tellingly on Mâle and, in one strong passage, his own Catholicism comes to the fore: 'When the sacrifice of the body and blood of Christ . . . will no longer be celebrated in our churches, there will no longer be life in them.'

In 1905 Proust's mother became aware that she was dying. 'My poor little canary,' she would say to Marcel, 'what will you do without me? But whatever you do, remain a Catholic.' When his mother did die, her admonition must surely have weighed heavily with the son who adored her. The hope of being reunited in heaven with those he loved: that, he told Georges de Lauris, would indeed be self-fulfilment. And in 1909, when he came to know Proust well, Plantevignes heard the writer more than once exclaim, when learning of a discreet act of kindness or generosity: 'Those are the things that will be placed to our credit.' Wrong-doing, significantly, is not mentioned, for Parisians of the period, Proust in particular, were conspicuously devoid of feelings of guilt.

When he began in summer 1909 to write his novel, Proust had no overall religious or anti-religious purpose. Into early chapters, to point out secular pleasures, he occasionally brings in religious metaphors, but since the Romantics this had been common enough, and Proust did it in everyday life, praising the poet Anna de Noailles as a new Blessed Virgin, though she was far from answering either term of the description.

In the first year of writing his novel Proust, we have seen, underwent the shock of recognizing that he was, and would remain for life, a prisoner of his own ultra-sensitivity, locked out forever from fulfilled love, and from marriage. Though Catholicism offers no promise of happiness here below, in his residual watered-down form of it Proust rather expected it to do so. He believed that the intense longing he had for complete love ought, in justice, to be met.

This terrible realization proved, I believe, a turning-point in Proust's religious attitude. That there could exist a loving God who would debar him from loving, this Proust could no longer accept. He let his residual Catholicism slip from him; he became an unbeliever.

In so far as his temperament allowed, Proust was very positive. He valued honour, family life, France, disliked violence, cynicism, bitterness. He was not the man either to nurse grievances or to attack a religion practised by his friends. As a novelist he had committed himself to celebrating life, to describing and analysing its joys, its achievements, its humorous contretemps. Again as a novelist, the admirer of Darlu and Boutroux sought a metaphysic, a Claudelian total view, yet Proust meant it when he told Hauser that he thought about religion daily.

What happened next has two stages. First Proust began to increase considerably the religious metaphors and similes applied to the high-points of everyday life. Proust's very first entry for his novel in his 1908 note-book is: 'An usher in the antechamber, on his shoulder a halberd . . . ' This he now changed to: 'An usher, dressed like an usher in church, in the antechamber, etc. . . .' Describing distant kin of a great family making an infrequent appearance at a social function, Proust wrote: 'they now rarely took part in the communion of high society, like nominal Catholics who go to the altar rails only once a year'. Madame de Cambremer Proust describes as dressing up for a visit in a cloak like a dalmatic, an ermine stole, a baroness's coronet on a chain like a pectoral cross; as she climbs into her carriage she raises her parasol crozier-fashion and sets off 'like an old bishop going to administer confirmation'. Numerous other examples could be cited: cumulatively they serve the purpose of blurring the distinction between what is sacred and what is profane.

As this happened, his novel grew and Proust's personal life contracted. In 1912 he had his walls lined with cork and wrote at night when the traffic was still. He who loved social life saw no one except, briefly, intimates like Hahn and Plantevignes. More and more the expanding book took over. And then the second stage of the change in its nature occurred. Proust began to apply religious imagery to the central themes and, more importantly, to the actual creative process. He slowly replaced the religion that had failed him with a secular religion, according to which the artist, priest-like, sacrifices himself in order to create a book so true, so beautiful it will transport the reader into a timeless mystical state.

By 1913, though parts of *Sodom and Gomorrah* remained to be written and only the structure of *Time Regained* had been committed to paper, Proust had substantially completed *A la Recherche du Temps Perdu*, thereby marrying the themes we have noticed to a narrative of flesh-and-blood characters.

In the first volume the narrator's childhood joys are depicted against the background of a love-affair between a society Parisian, Charles Swann, and a high-class cocotte. Swann marries the cocotte only to find that possession has extinguished his love.

In the next volume the narrator, now a young man, spends a summer at the seaside town of Balbec. His feeling of sexual longing passes from one to another of a group of pretty girls who ride bicycles along the promenade and finally focuses on one of them, Albertine. He discovers that Albertine is a lesbian and, in the hope of reforming her, shuts her up and spies on her. Eventually she runs away and dies in a riding accident.

The narrator seeks to assuage his grief by entering the world of high society. He finds endless delight in observing the complexities of the highly bred; even their pretences he comes to enjoy by dwelling on the humorous side. He encounters more and more inversion, so that by this stage of the novel everyone save the narrator seems to be homosexual. But inversion is found to provide the most convincing proof that mind or spirit (*l'esprit*) fashions each individual's world.

The narrator is saddened to see his friends ageing and some of them dying. But here as throughout disappointed hopes are not allowed the last word. For by analysing exactly how and why disillusion occurs the narrator achieves the joy of discovering a psychological truth. Proust not only wrote his novel in a joyful frame of mind, wherever possible he sought in human experience the substratum of joy, and this is borne out by the fact that 'regret' and its synonyms occur in the novel much less often than 'happiness' and its synonyms.

In involuntary memory the narrator finds a means of reliving the past with an intensity of joy unmatched by any real-life experience. He finds also a new vocation. He will write about the past from the insights of involuntary memory, create a world-in-words so beautiful as to be timeless, and so share with readers, present and future, the intensity of joy he has been privileged to know. His role becomes partly that of a god, who has ascended above the shortcomings of actual life, partly that of a bodhisattva, helping others to a similar apotheosis – not a moral apotheosis, but an æsthetic one with religious overtones.

Many scenes in Proust's novel throw light on life in Paris. The striving for excellence, and the appreciation of excellence, come out even in the sometimes absurd clannishness of Madame Verdurin. The belief that art is the absolute was widely held in Paris – though only Proust makes so much of its religious aspect. Then too we have a taste for dining at the Pré Catalan and for walking and driving in the Bois, a fondness for fancy-dress balls and, more generally, an interest in disguise, masks and pretence.

In two respects Proust's novel is untrue to Paris life as we find it in more reliable first-hand sources. First, the *noblesse* was by no means as witty as Proust depicts. The Comtesse de Pange's four-volume Memoirs are concerned largely with horseflesh, Boni de Castellane's reminiscences are a banal exercise in self-righteousness, while Madame de Caillavet's correspondence with Georg Brandes is wholly devoid of sparkle. It was the literary set that was witty, and the one amusing remark in Madame de Caillavet's salon was made by the wife of the humorous writer, Alphonse Allais: introduced to a lady with fourteen children, she remarked of her afterwards: 'That's not motherhood, it's spawning.' It was witticisms such as this that Proust transferred to the mouth of the Duchesse de Guermantes.

Again the snobbishness of the Guermantes is by no means typical. In 1908, as part of his composite book, Proust had planned an essay on one of his favourite subjects – genealogy. He did not write that essay, but he did put his genealogical gleanings into the brilliant dinner-table conversation where the Guermantes and their friends vie in citing high-born forebears and royal connections. But Paris, it needs to be said again, was a highly permeable society, loyal to Republican ideals and esteeming men on their merits; it is extremely doubtful whether in real life even Parisian blue-bloods would have indulged in such an orgy of blatant ancestor-worship.

When we turn up photographs of Proust's close friends – dowdy Madame Straus, with her melancholic eyes, down-turned twisted mouth and absurd hats; Reynaldo Hahn, at forty still with a youth's immature face, cigarette hanging from impertinent lips; Agostinelli, Proust's secretary, moon-faced and with vapid ox eyes; even the photograph of Proust himself in later life, seated hunched in Venice, with a small moustache and bowler-hatted, for all the world like Charlie Chaplin in one of his pathetic roles – we realize the immense amount of beauty and joy the novelist contributed to the characters of his novel from his own spirit, a spirit, as his letters reveal, that leaped, and continued year after year to leap, as though on a trampoline.

At the time he was completing his novel and arranging publication, this spirit showed itself in ways that, paradoxically, were to darken somewhat his sense of achievement. At the end of 1912 war in the Balkans caused stock markets to fall, but Proust felt sure they would recover. He bought heavily in gold shares and American railroad stocks. 'I don't know if it's true,' wrote Proust's financial adviser, 'that the Government's suppression of God has meant there is less belief in France, but I'm inclined to believe there's more credulity.' In early 1912 Proust finally had to sell, having made a very heavy loss of 40,000 francs. For a time he thought he was ruined.

Proust had employed as a chauffeur, during his summers in Cabourg, a young man from Monaco, Alfred Agostinelli. In January 1913 he engaged him as a manservant and trained him to be his secretary. He attributed to Agostinelli remarkable gifts of intelligence and sensibility, made him presents and, generally, flattered his vanity, with the result that Agostinelli decided he wanted to learn to fly an aeroplane – flying, we shall see in a later chapter, had become the vogue sport. Agostinelli used Proust's money to leave Paris for Nice, where he enrolled in a flying school. Months passed. Proust missed his secretary and tried to get him back. At first Agostinelli did not deign to answer his master's letters, and when he did, insolently sent his replies unstamped, so that Proust had to pay the postage.

Proust felt a strong attraction to Agostinelli as a person. But theirs was primarily a master–servant relationship and it seems very unlikely indeed that it was anything but Platonic. Nevertheless Proust had become dependent upon it, he wanted Agostinelli back and, other means having failed, did not hesitate to bribe him. Despite his recent financial losses, on 30 May 1914 Proust wrote to his friend saying that he had decided to give him an aeroplane costing 27,000 francs. That very day Agostinelli rashly ventured out to sea on his second solo flight, crashed and drowned.

Proust was heart-broken. He thought he would never get over his friend's death. But he had evolved a philosophy for dealing with loss. His feelings for his elusive friend, like the hawthorn at Illiers and the girls in flower at Cabourg, would slowly be transmuted into words, go to enrich his novel as he added to it in the war years, and with so much else of his life escape the destructive hand of time.

With the bulk of his novel down on paper, Proust began to take steps to get it published, starting with the nearly self-contained *Swann's Way*. This obliged him, in the first instance, to enlist help from friends. Emerging from his cork-lined room, the novelist became the suave man about town, and no one knew better than he that flowers or fruit for a lady had to come from Lemaître or Charton, compotes for a sick friend from Tanrade, that a handkerchief borrowed when he had forgotten his own should be returned between two lavender sachets from Houbigant.

Proust went to Madame de Caillavet's salon and there renewed relations with Anatole France, who had written the introduction to his first collection of journalism, and with her son Gaston, a successful playwright. He called several times on Comtesse Greffulhe and on the Rumanian-born Bibescos, persuading them to entertain to dinner the reading committee of the *Nouvelle Revue Française*, which he hoped would publish chapters of his novel.

By marrying the daughter of the owner, young Gaston Calmette had realized his ambition of becoming editor of *Le Figaro*, but at the cost of personal unhappiness: now taciturn, portly and in his fifties, he was in love with another woman and planning divorce. This was not the ideal moment to be asked to find a publisher for a novel about an unhappy marriage, but Proust had long cultivated Calmette and some years before given a memorable dinner for him at the Ritz. Now, in January 1913, Proust called on Calmette at the *Figaro* office, urging him to continue his efforts on behalf of his novel, and leaving on his desk a monogrammed cigarette case from Tiffany's – Proust had a naive belief in the power of expensive presents. The embarrassed editor did not even say thank you for the cigarette case but he did publish in *Le Figaro* four extracts from *Swann's Way*.

Proust next approached the publishing house of Fasquelle. Foreseeing reluctance to take on so long and demanding a book, he offered to bear the cost of printing. This proposal had the effect of making

Proust appear a dilettante, bent on vanity publication.

Fasquelle were slow and Proust became impatient. He had met Gaston Gallimard, publisher of the *NRF*, in Cabourg and had had him to dinner at his hotel, with Louisa de Mornand among the guests. Though it was still on offer to Fasquelle, Proust submitted *Swann's Way* to the *NRF*.

To André Gide, guiding spirit both of the publishing house and the review, Proust's name evoked a rich invalid who wrote *Figaro* articles about *le Tout Paris* or the æsthetic appreciation of churches, and clever parodies, whereas Gide's taste in contemporary fiction ran to serious-minded novels by working-class authors such as those of the shoemaker Charles-Louis Philippe. When Proust's manuscript came into his hands, Gide was doubtless also deterred by its length, both as a writer, since he practised concision, and as an editor, since the book could not conveniently be serialized. How much Gide read of it is unclear, probably not all; at any rate he rejected it. Later he was to admit his mistake and to prevail on Gallimard to buy the remaining volumes.

Fasquelle also turned down the novel, but Proust found an adventurous young publisher, Bernard Grasset, willing to take on *Swann's Way*. It appeared in November 1913, just when Proust felt 'insane with misery' at Agostinelli's departure to Nice. The novel was dedicated to Calmette, who had given Proust the joy of seeing his first articles in print. Acting as his own publicity agent, Proust sent copies to numerous influential friends, with the result that *Swann's Way* was widely reviewed, on the whole favourably, though the literary critic of *Le Temps* objected, with reason, that Swann's infatuation with a cocotte showed a naivety improbable in a Parisian of such extensive experience.

To Proust's satisfaction the first edition of 1750

copies sold out and the book went into a second edition, yet none of the reviewers realized that here was a novel different in kind from any of its predecessors. Indeed, it claimed to be more than just another novel, more than a piece of writing. It claimed to provide spiritual sustenance. In the course of the novel a man of letters, Legrandin, tells the young narrator how important it is to put feeling into what he writes and concludes with Christ's words: 'Do this and you will live.' In notes written in 1911, to the section expounding the belief that art is the sole reality, Proust gives the title 'Perpetual Adoration' in allusion to the name of an order of nuns who pray day and night before the Blessed Sacrament. In *Time Regained*, 'our true self that seemed dead, sometimes long dead, wakes and revives when receiving the heavenly food brought to it [by memory]'. In a memo to himself for the same volume: 'by far the most important point perhaps in the whole book', he must make clear that Swann had failed to realize the supraterrestrial implications of the little phrase in the Vinteuil Sonata, 'because that *gospel* was divulged later, when Swann was dead . . . before the *revelation* that might have touched him most deeply' (my italics). Proust went so far as to declare, in a letter published in *L'Intransigeant*, that he was offering readers 'the bread of angels', explaining his meaning with eight lines from Racine's hymn to Holy Communion, ending:

> *Approchez, voulez-vous vivre?*
> *Prenez, mangez, et vivez.*[1]

Starting with the intention of writing a metaphysical book, Proust ended in effect with a new creed: Man's apotheosis through art. Proust recognized that this was so: in a letter to Jacques Rivière he praises the young

[1] Come close: do you wish to live?
Take this, eat it and have life.

man for having understood that his book is a 'carefully constructed work of dogma': 'Apparently subjective and dilettante, it was a stage on the road to the most objective and *croyante* of conclusions.'

The terms Redemption and Salvation, it should be noted, are conspicuous by their absence from Proust's new creed, and it does not help to apply them to Proust the man. Proust was not in the business of rescuing himself from guilt; he was trying to rescue himself from the sterility imposed by his own nature and from the Christian God who had failed him.

CHAPTER 7

The Birth of Cubism: Pablo Picasso

English and American artists who have shown in Paris agree that it is an experience quite different from exhibiting in London or New York. Visitors to a Paris gallery – not all, but some – will volubly express their pleasure if they feel pleasure, talk about the works, argue about them, seek to meet the artist and learn more about him or her. The many newspaper and periodical critics discuss a talent at length, probe, find fault, take sides. Art enthusiasts living in the provinces who have seen reviews may write to the artist expressing their reactions too. They see the artist as a pathfinder, providing a visual reading of the world: and in an age of widespread unbelief the reading can have precious value for others.

So it was in 1900–14. Many Parisians were themselves painters, as were quite a few writers. Henry Ghéon exhibited at one of the salons, Henri Bataille before turning to the theatre made a name as a portraitist, and Georges Feydeau's talent with the brush led to his marrying the daughter of a fashionable artist, Carolus Duran. Those who did not paint had plenty of opportunity to see the many who did. At the two annual salons no less than seven thousand pictures were exhibited, and a third annual Salon d'Automne was to join them in 1903.

At the 1900 Universal Exhibition a rich retrospective

of French art showed the 'pathfinders' from 1800 to the Impressionists: David, Delacroix, Ingres, Corot, Manet. This dazzling line had been continued by Renoir, by Cézanne, who had shown the hard rock beneath Monet's field of poppies, and by Gauguin, who had sought religious mystery first in remote Brittany, then in remoter Tahiti.

But by 1900 the prolonged display of fireworks had died down. Renoir and Cézanne had made their main statements, unhappy Gauguin was on the other side of the world, alone, ill and soon to die, and the place of the giants had been taken by small derivative men. Some called themselves Symbolists, and produced visual equivalents of literary themes, close to Maeterlinck's *Bluebird of Happiness*. Some were primarily decorators, elaborating the languorous motifs of *art nouveau*: tendrils, dragonflies, lilies, swirling hair.

Perhaps the most fashionable young artists were a group headed by Paul Serusier, Maurice Denis, Pierre Bonnard and Edouard Vuillard. Formed in 1888 in Paris, they declared their intention of following Gauguin in his Brittany period by imbuing art with a tinge of religious – but not specifically Christian – mystery. They called themselves Nabis, from the Jewish word for Prophets, in that they viewed colour distortion as a kind of religious illumination. But in most important ways, though they claimed to look ahead, they really looked back. They too were literary painters, admirers of Arthurian and medieval legends. Many Nabis professed, or were sympathetic to, Theosophy, so they treated subjects as glimpses of a 'higher truth'.

A typical painting, *The Orchard of Wise Virgins* (1893) by Gide's friend, Maurice Denis, shows three girls in long white 'timeless' gowns seated, isolated, on fawn, flower-strewn grass amid slender flower-bearing trees. One girl has an open book on her lap. In the background four nude girls are bathing. Faintly Biblical, it might mean anything – or nothing, much like its sister art, Symbolist poetry.

Such a work – and it could be matched by many more – fears to confront real life or the human dilemma. It is Post-Impressionism fading away, like a consumptive, into a sad dream of the past. It is Romantic painting and in 1900 the ship of Paris had gybed and was now on a classical tack. People were facing up to reality and wanted art to do likewise.

If French painting were to be brought into the twentieth century, probably it would not be by any of the Nabis. It required a more direct vision. Three young men with such a vision were to appear, and one was a foreigner. Just as a Russian would jolt the sleepy world of Paris ballet, so a Spaniard was to revitalize the wishful-thinking art made fashionable by the Nabis. His development and influence were to continue far beyond 1914; here we are concerned only with his formation and his early years in Paris, where, combining his own heritage with elements in the French, he originated a new style of painting.

Pablo Ruiz was born in Malaga in 1881 into an honourable though not well-off Andalusian family. His father was a kindly academic art teacher. His mother's family stemmed from Genoa, hence her Italian-sounding maiden name of Picasso, adopted by her son at the time he left for Paris in preference to his legal surname, which was widespread and as undistinctive as, say, Smith or Brown. Pablo was the only son, and had two younger sisters. His early life was secure and, as far as we know, happy, but interrupted by moves, first to Corunna, then to Barcelona. Pablo did poorly at school and from the age of eleven was allowed to train as a painter. He made for his teachers drawings of an exceptionally high standard from models and, a sign that he really was a compulsive artist, packed into the first of the notebooks he was to carry all his life scenes that touched or amused him or caught his fancy.

The mood in Barcelona during Picasso's late teens was one of decline, defeat and decadence. Bandaged wounded were carried on stretchers off troopships, victims of the Cuban War Spain was losing to the United States. The Barcelonans sought independence for Catalonia and, denied it, vented frustration in violence. Even in France Barcelona had a bad name as the city of bombs. In the artists' café he frequented Picasso heard typical *fin de siècle* slogans, including Nietzsche's, that God is dead, and we await the new 'man-god', who will make reality bearable by bringing us scintillating art.

In Barcelona the art being produced, far from being scintillating, was either prudently academic or bordered on the grotesque or sickly. Antonio Gaudí's as yet unfinished Church of the Holy Family offered fiercely capricious Gothicized forms, and in his *art nouveau* houses, where a Frenchman might have used upflowing vegetal forms, Gaudí modelled his lop-sided balconies on lava and decaying fungi.

The Church in Spain, respected for its works of mercy, was derided by intellectuals as obscurantist. Picasso was not obliged by his parents to attend Mass, and went instead to the bullring. Bullfights – as visual dramas and as incitements to courage – were an important element in Picasso's formation and he came to value the conquering matador more than Christ crucified. In short he lost his faith, but religion runs deep in the Spanish consciousness and the hound of heaven was never quite to disappear from Picasso's life.

In 1900, the year of his nineteenth birthday, Picasso was a strongly built, muscular young man, hands and feet small and beautifully made, skin white and fine.

His most striking feature was his big black eyes, with a burning, passionate, sometimes wild look in them. He was noticeably short and felt this as something to be made up for.

His physique and especially his eyes suggested energy and this had already shown itself in the hundreds of paintings and drawings he had done, so many that friends considered him a prodigy. But between the sensitive, almost feminine hands and the masculine, assured, all-probing eyes lay a certain tension. This could appear as restlessness: Picasso usually had to be doing something and rather than remain still would sew one piece of cardboard to another.

What had he so far painted? Portraits of student friends, sketches of people in bars and cafés, beggars, the sick, bullfighters, self-portraits – lots of these. It was mainly human beings that interested him; he strove to catch in each a characteristic gesture or expression, and to convey it with feeling.

To satisfy teachers or the Establishment, Picasso had also painted academic pictures. *Science and Charity* shows a sick woman in bed, a doctor on one side, on the other a nun cradling the woman's child, a subject probably suggested by Picasso's father, who posed for the doctor. Well conveyed is the tension between the attitudes of doctor and nun, a tension apparent also like a coiled spring in simple notebook sketches.

Another academic work, painted at eighteen, entitled *Last Moments*, had been chosen to represent Spain at the Paris Exhibition. A woman lies on her deathbed, comforted by a priest, and on the wall hangs a large crucifix. Later, perhaps regretting its conventionality, Picasso was to paint it over but we know there was a lot of black in the picture. The titles of other Spanish works chosen to hang in the Exhibition – *Crippled Children Bathing*, *Salus Infirmorum*, *Leader of the Blind* – witness to the prevalent mood in Spain: moralizing, and even more morbid than usual. Picasso's picture conformed but perhaps had something extra, for it was to be singled out by a Paris critic as showing 'a real sense of grief'.

In October 1900 Picasso's parents came to Barcelona railway station to see their son off on the train to Paris. With him was a friend, a painter-poet named Carlos Casagemas: thin, stoop-shouldered, receding hair and chin, a long red-tipped nose, the first of many gloomy poets to attach themselves to the exuberant Picasso. Both wore identical new suits of black corduroy, with round collar buttoned up to the neck, convenient when you were poor and did not always have a clean shirt. Picasso's return ticket had been paid for by his parents; it was a big expense, but they wanted him to see the Exhibition and perhaps sell some of the paintings in the rack above his seat.

Next day Picasso and Casagemas arrived in the brightly lit, sophisticated city. They spoke no French and clung to the Spanish artistic colony, where they had introductions, lodging briefly in Montparnasse, then in Montmartre, still in part a village of windmills and vineyards. On 25 October Casagemas, who got easily worked up, wrote a letter from himself and Picasso to their Barcelona friends:

> We got together at *petit Pousset* . . . and all got drunk. [Miguel] Utrillo wrote nursery rhymes, Peio [Pompeo Gener, a writer] sang bawdy songs in Latin, Picasso made sketches of people, and I wrote verses of 11, 12, 14 and more syllables . . . Here there are real teachers everywhere. Soon the Exhibition will close and we still haven't seen more than the painting section . . . Yesterday we saw a horror drama at the Théâtre Montmartre.

Casagemas detailed the bloodshed, then described the prostitutes, subjects which held an unusual fascination for him. Picasso, who did not write easily – he was never to pen a correctly grammatical letter – illustrated the epistle with drawings of glamorous women.

For women were his prime discovery in Paris. Barcelona women divided into the nice kind, who dressed in black, wore no scent, never appeared in public alone, veiled their faces in church, and the other kind, the 'fallen'. In Paris Picasso discovered pretty women dressed in pinks, blues, greens, their hair becomingly arranged under enchanting hats, well groomed, smiling, at ease with men, companionable. In Barcelona – a rare instance of a female subject – he had painted his sister Lola in her First Communion dress; in Paris with gusto he now dashed off sketches and paintings of smart ladies glimpsed in the street, and *petites bourgeoises* enjoying themselves at café tables and in the Moulin de la Galette. Also, more to hand, were fun-loving models. With one of them, a girl probably of Spanish origin called Germaine Gargallo, Picasso soon formed a liaison. Casagemas did too, but his girl soon left him for another Spaniard.

The second thing Picasso found in Paris was a variety of innovative painting far beyond anything Barcelona could offer. Durand-Ruel showed the Nabis, who offered visual equivalents of Symbolist poetry; Ambroise Vollard showed Cézanne; elsewhere could be seen Toulouse-Lautrec and van Gogh. Picasso wasn't interested in the 'real teachers' praised by Casagemas, preferring to teach himself. Responsive to an extraordinary degree to the work of others, he began tossing off pictures in the style now of Cézanne, now of Toulouse-Lautrec, now of van Gogh. But not in the style of the Nabis. To satisfy the Establishment he had done a literary painting, to be seen in the Exhibition, but he knew now that literary painting was not for him.

The third thing Picasso found in Paris was dealers. Berthe Weill, a small woman of humble origins who kept her banknotes in the top of her stocking, agreed to show three of his bullfights in her tiny gallery. And there Picasso met Petrus Manyac, a Catalan industrialist turned art dealer, who liked Picasso's work and gave him a contract: 150 francs a month – just enough to live on – in return for his future production.

The fourth thing Picasso found in Paris is less easy to specify. It is evident in the tone of Casagemas's letter and in a few of Picasso's sketches and paintings: a glimpse of a way of life less harsh than Spain's, where people really warmed to the arts and made love without feeling guilt.

One thing Picasso didn't like, and that was Parisians' insistence on assigning painters to groups or schools. As regards art Picasso was a very private person. He was never to join a school or exhibit in the salons and though he had frequented Barcelona's earnestly decadent café, Quatre Gats, he wouldn't accept the label 'decadent' for himself or take decadence seriously. In fact, when painting a close friend of those days, a sad poet named Jaime Sabartés, Picasso 'took him off', showing Sabartés draped in a cloak, crowned with a wreath, holding an iris in his hand, standing in the midst of flames in a dark graveyard, and captioned it *Poeta decadente*. Life, in Picasso's view, was too rich for any coterie spirit.

When he returned home for Christmas Picasso had good reason to be pleased. Perhaps it was on this occasion that he slept late and found on waking that his mother had brushed his clothes and polished his shoes. He became very angry and almost reduced her to tears, because she had 'removed his Paris dust'. The incident has overtones. Picasso was always to dislike having his studio dusted or tidied and, once established, would part with great reluctance from a painting: signs of an unusually strong territorial sense.

For the next three years Picasso came and went between Spain and Paris, seeking to find his true artistic self among the influences he had absorbed, and to sell his work, the arrangement with Manyac having turned sour and an exhibition in 1901 by Ambroise Vollard, though praised by one leading critic, having proved a commercial failure.

In spring 1904 Picasso decided he could not do without the artistic and intellectual stimulus of Paris. He settled there, renting a run-down studio in Montmartre's rue Ravignan. He had become friendly with three poets, Max Jacob, Guillaume Apollinaire and André Salmon, and though he still opposed literary painting, Picasso chalked on his studio door *'Au rendez-vous des poètes'*. He evidently thought of himself as a poet by virtue of the intense feeling he imparted to his work at this time, and was reading, or hearing Jacob read, the poetry of Félicien Fagus and Paul Claudel.

In these early months Picasso still felt himself an outsider and, rather as Canaletto brought Venetian light to London, brought to Paris his Barcelonan 'real sense of grief'. A good many of his subjects came from his Spanish past – gaunt old men with tightly closed mouths, a blind man touching the bread and wine of his frugal meal; others belong to Montmartre, such as *Girl with a Raven*, modelled on the daughter of Frédé, owner of the local café, Le Lapin Agile. The joyful side of Paris had yet to be absorbed.

Being poor, he wore a workman's blue denims and, not to be disturbed, painted mainly at night. Salmon recalls visiting him: blue jacket open on a white shirt with a fringed flannel belt girding his hips . . . 'A paraffin lamp gave a weak light. To paint or to show his work Picasso lit a candle and held it up high while showing me his world of hungry people, cripples, mothers with no milk in their breasts, all painted in sad tones of blue.'

Picasso's liaison with the model Germaine lasted only a short time. Then his excitable friend Casagemas fell in love with her and the two began living together. As well as being plain, Casagemas was sexually unsatisfactory, perhaps even impotent, and despite his desperate pleas Germaine soon left him for someone else. Casagemas's interest in bloodshed and the macabre then took a terrifying turn. One evening in a café he pulled out a revolver and shot at Germaine. She ducked, the bullet just grazed her neck, but Casagemas thought he had hit her and shot himself dead.

Picasso felt the suicide deeply: the loss of a very dear friend and also because he had pushed Casagemas and Germaine together. Picasso enjoyed the company of women, needed them physically, found in them motifs and a stimulus. But he believed that the man must remain master – very Latin! Casagemas had made the error of becoming dependent, the woman had shown no pity, and Casagemas had died.

Picasso brooded on the suicide in many drawings and in five oil paintings, one of which, known as *La Vie*, stands out as a master work of this Blue Period. A sad, frail young man, unclothed save for a slip, to whose shoulder clings a nude girl, points a foreshortened finger in fear and accusation at a hard-faced woman holding a baby. Between accuser and accused are two canvases, one of lovers clinging together desperately, the other of a crouched figure apparently dying. If, as seems likely, the foreshortened finger symbolizes sexual inadequacy, the painting is an allegory of two kinds of love, one giving and tender but doomed, the other taking and heartless.

No less black is a portrait of Jaime Sabartés, the 'decadent poet', unprepossessing, short-sighted, melancholy, who replaced Casagemas as Picasso's closest Spanish friend. Picasso depicts the young poet, long fingers outstretched on a tankard of beer, chin cupped in his hand, staring bleakly at the floor – a masterly hieroglyph of loneliness.

No one in Paris was painting like this, for Picasso had brought with him in the folds of his black corduroy suit a Barcelonan sadness and the old century's sense of ageing. It was only in summer 1904 that Picasso really entered into the *joie de vivre* of Paris, and his mediator was a very pretty Parisienne.

Fernande Olivier was about Picasso's age – twenty-two – and her parents had a small business manufacturing artificial flowers. Very young she had married a sculptor and learned how to draw, prettily but with no marked talent. Now estranged from her husband, who had become unbalanced, Fernande lodged in one of the small rooms in 13 rue Ravignan. She was tall, with abundant light-brown hair tending to auburn and green almond-shaped eyes, placid and happy-go-lucky.

The two met at the single basement tap used by the lodgers of No. 13. They chatted, Picasso invited her to see his paintings, she accepted. She was struck by Picasso's vibrant dark eyes, and by his exuberant, masterful manner, which suited her easy-going style. Soon she became his mistress and a year later moved in with him.

Picasso treated Fernande possessively. Spanish-style, he would not let her go out alone and at the start at least it was he who did the shopping. Essentials only, for they were poor: food, wine, tobacco – Picasso smoked a pipe – and, were he lucky enough to sell an extra picture, eau de Cologne for Fernande, who loved scent. Occasionally there would be an evening at Le Lapin

Agile, where Frédé sang popular songs to a guitar and served a *combine* of Pernod, grenadine and cherry brandy, topped with a cherry to make it 'artistic'.

At that basement meeting, says Roland Dorgelès, a Montmartre acquaintance of Picasso, the tap became a classical fountain, Fernande's cheap jug an amphora, and Dorgelès means that through Fernande's slim good looks and the serenity and fun she brought him Picasso was able at last to lay aside his inheritance of gloom and embrace the classical tradition, symbolized in Paris by the female nude. In autumn 1904 he brightened his palette from ashen blue to ochre in order to paint, in three lovely canvases, a young woman sleeping in the presence of an onlooker. The tension which is Picasso's hallmark derives here from the sleeper's peacefulness contrasted with the watcher's concern not to wake her; for the first time Picasso's tenderness is happy, and there is a sensuality quite new to his work.

Just before Christmas 1904 Picasso visited a Spanish priest, Father Santol, a friend of his parents, who ran a home for down-and-outs in Avenue La Motte-Piquet. Though not a down-and-out, Picasso often went hungry and Father Santol gave him some money. Exultant, Picasso headed home across the Place des Invalides. There he encountered a troupe of travelling acrobats.

Picasso too was a poor travelling performer, trying to find fulfilment, by pleasing a blasé audience with difficult-to-achieve moments of balance-in-tension. He was deeply moved by the acrobats and began to sketch them. But then they packed up and travelled on. The theme would have been lost but for the fact that Paris possessed what Barcelona, even London, could not match – two, sometimes three, circuses, one of them, the Médrano, near rue Ravignan. Picasso started frequenting the Médrano; here he drew more acrobats, also harlequins, weight-lifters, other circus performers and their families.

When he came to work the sketches into paintings Picasso brightened his palette still further, moving from ochre to a soft warm rose. Three paintings in which this colour predominates are particularly successful. *Acrobat on a Ball* shows a slim young girl in tights, both arms in the air, balancing on a large ball, watched impassively by a heavy squat man seated on a square block.

In *Acrobat's Family with Ape* Picasso depicts a slim, thin-armed boyish acrobat, seated beside and tenderly watching his young wife, who is calming their restless baby. In the foreground, seated on the floor, an ape looks up at the couple with a puzzled air, lending a potentially trite family scene new wonder and an edge of mystery or a touch of Darwinism. Picasso's inclusion of the ape, like that of the raven in his portrait of Frédé's daughter, grew out of a close, though unsentimental, rapport with animals. He enjoyed a relationship where words were not required and during his years with Fernande he became the owner, in turn, of a white mouse, three cats, a dog and a monkey.

The third painting, *Family of Saltimbanques*, was painted near the end of this circus sequence, in late summer 1905. A heavily built weight-lifter, no longer young and wearing a jester's cap, stands with a tall young harlequin, two boys and a small girl who carries a basket of flowers: slightly apart and facing away from the troupe is seated a young woman wearing a hat whose shape echoes the basket of flowers. The five troupers have been compared to the fingers of a hand, and by Rilke to a D, standing, he fancied, for *Dastehen*, Thereness. In his fifth *Duino Elegy*, the masterpiece in verse inspired by Picasso's masterpiece in paint, Rilke took the acrobats to symbolize lovers who, in a place we know nothing about, on some indescribable carpet, are able to manage all the daring lofty figures of heart-flight they cannot achieve on earth:

> Would not the dead then fling their last,
>   their for ever reserved,
> ever-concealed, unknown to us, ever-valid
> coins of happiness down before the at last
> truthfully smiling pair on the quietened
> carpet?

One other work from the Rose Period should be mentioned: a rose-suffused golden gouache of Fernande nude. She stands, head bent, looking a little to one side, her hands clasped below her sex, completing an oval that begins at the neck and admirably suggesting calm. In the earlier portrayals of Fernande asleep Picasso had been a possessor, her body an object, but here he faces her directly, person to person. There is a new maturity.

In these and related works Picasso, at twenty-four, proved himself a master painter, in the classical style, of the human figure, able to depict groups in tension with a depth of tenderness perhaps unique in so young an artist. His subjects now are no longer old and worn out: they are young like himself, spare, keen, stripped to essentials, tooled to their craft, and the rose light suffusing them indicates if not quite hope, at least acceptance.

These paintings Picasso found he could sell. Early in 1906 Ambroise Vollard, much esteemed because he had championed Cézanne, came to his studio and bought thirty Picassos for 2,000 francs - enough to keep him and Fernande for three years. His dealers and friends naturally expected Picasso to continue painting similar masterpieces. Why then didn't he? Why did he now seek a wholly new line? The answer lies partly in Picasso's nature, partly in the nature of Paris.

One may start perhaps with Picasso's sense of humour. We have seen him poking fun at Sabartés's decadent pose and trappings. At the Médrano Circus he particularly enjoyed watching Grock. The clown's most famous act was the Great Violinist: lifting a fiddle to his shoulder with suitable flourishes, trying to play it; but the fiddle is wrong side up and Grock would go into wonderful agonies wondering where the strings had gone to. Picasso would roar with laughter also at the antics of his poet friend Max Jacob, who had a big bald head on narrow shoulders and a grave expression: Jacob would roll up his trousers, revealing hairy legs, and perform a dance with tiny steps and pointed toe; wearing a lady's hat and veil he would sing falsetto. Or, with a partner, enact an elocution class, with the pupil stammering so badly the teacher begins to stammer too.

One evening at the Lapin Agile three earnest young Germans leeched on to Picasso, questioning him about the meaning of a painting. Picasso told them that every painting must speak for itself, but the Germans persisted with their boring interrogation. Finally Picasso, who had been given a Browning automatic by a friend and happened to have it on him, pulled out the revolver and fired shots into the air which much to his amusement sent the Germans scurrying.

If laughter, as Bergson claimed in his much talked about book of that name, is often a healthy attempt to jolt people out of fixed, pretentious ways, Picasso's laughter was of that kind. But it went with a marked combativeness. At one point Picasso wanted to become a boxer and began taking boxing lessons, only to stop when he discovered he didn't like being on the receiving end of punches. According to Fernande, he had the habit of tearing someone apart as soon as he left the room. He could be wickedly funny about even his best friends. It was the trait Fernande liked least, but it was

173

essential to his character and to his view of the world. He wasn't interested in a kindly conventional fixed notion of people or things: as man and artist he must probe – laughingly, rudely, roughly, even daringly like a matador.

As for the part played by Paris in Picasso's artistic development, two aspects stand out.

First, Paris was a city of museums. In the Louvre it had the largest museum in the world, and more museums than London, Berlin or Rome, and it was continually getting new ones, for example the studio-house and its contents bequeathed by Gustave Moreau. In the Trocadéro it had several under one roof, including an Ethnographic Museum.

Paris was also the capital of a large overseas Empire. The North-West African part stretched from Mauretania to Gabon. In 1906, as part of its policy of keeping Germany out of that part of Africa, the French Government wished to arouse interest and pride in her colonies there. So the newspapers were making much of French Africa and its culture.

Picasso did not read the papers but his friends did and they kept him very much in touch. One afternoon, probably in 1906, Picasso's interest was aroused by the Ethnographic Museum, which was open three afternoons a week, and he went in. Most of the exhibits were from Africa. Wooden sculptures of squat human figures, many tribal masks. Some were grotesque, others hideous, all very strange indeed.

Picasso was not the first or the only young Parisian artist to set eyes on such works, a few of which were on sale in enterprising antique shops. But since, with his Spanish background, he was not afraid of the grotesque – indeed, one side of him liked it – nor of the hideous either, he was the first to take them seriously. He saw that they were not just oddities but works of art, albeit

174

in a strange idiom. And, as usual when impressed by a new style, he set himself to master it.

In 1907 Picasso sculpted three chunky wooden figures. They are so well done they could pass as African but they are important for other reasons. They show Picasso feeling his way into so-called Primitive art and they elicited, encouraged too, his skill as a sculptor. Hitherto he had done only a few works in this medium, but henceforth sculpture was to be important in itself and sometimes to influence his development as a painter.

Slightly earlier in date but representing a progress in development is the painting known as *Two Nudes*. It represents dumpy women with exaggerated breasts, heavy trunks and feet. They derive from primitive fertility figures and show Picasso carrying into his painting a quite different conception of the nude from that elicited by Fernande. These women are not pretty, it is not their role to be pretty. They are functional: child-bearers.

African masks are of two main kinds: plain coverings that hide the face, fantastic headpieces intended to terrorize. When painting the portrait of Gertrude Stein, an American resident who bought his work and became his friend, Picasso drew on the former. Gertrude Stein was a type new to Picasso: heavily built, formidably intellectual, with none of Fernande's smiling grace or femininity. She happened to have a regressive hair line that made her upper brow oval, and a thin straight mouth. After striving in vain to achieve a likeness Picasso hit on the idea of portraying the lady's face as a mask. Her eyes are shown peering from behind mask apertures, her hard straight mouth seems devoid of speech. It is the face of a person who hides her feelings, who is sexually closed. Gertrude Stein in fact was a lesbian and thus, automatically, 'under cover'. It is to

175

her credit that despite the unflattering portrayal she prized the painting for what it is, a deeply perceptive rendering of character.

The second kind of mask made a much stronger impact on Picasso. Here was art more terrifying even than Goya's man-eating giant in *The Horrors of War*. But Picasso had no experience of war and the grotesque, garishly painted face coverings in the Ethnographic Museum linked up with something else in his subconscious.

Picasso valued Fernande as a source of sexual pleasure and artistic inspiration. But he was unusually possessive towards her, wished her life to be subordinate to his. Because she was easy-going, the two got along well. At the same time Picasso knew there were other types of women: Germaine, whose unfeelingness had driven Casagemas to shoot himself; the whores of the Barcelona brothels he had frequented in his teens; Paris women not content to inspire their artist lovers but compelled to drain them, dry up their creativeness; harpy women; *Femina destruens*. Given Picasso's possessiveness, such women posed him with a greater than usual threat, and one of them he had already arraigned as the cold, hard-faced mother in *La Vie*.

In 1907 Picasso drew on his memories of a Barcelona brothel to paint his most deeply considered and revolutionary picture so far. It is a large canvas, some nine feet square, confronting us, close up, with five prostitutes in a tight group. Two are full face, with one or both arms raised to show off their breasts. They have long noses, long ears and big black staring eyes. A third prostitute, in profile on the left, has a head like an African statue and the fingers of her raised left hand are outspread threateningly, like a talon. On the right, one prostitute is standing, the other squatting on the floor, legs apart, knees raised. Instead of faces both have African terror-masks. The main colours are ochre, pink and blue, which by contrast set off the painting's jagged, sharp, aggressive lines, like a cracked mirror.

Almost as curious as the painting itself is the fact that Picasso, having shown it to a few close friends, did not pass it on to a dealer or hang it on his wall. He kept the painting rolled up in his studio. Perhaps he wanted to keep secret something so personal, perhaps he thought that to display in a city like Paris a work of such shattering misogyny would harm him commercially. The painting was to be shown only in 1916, when bombing from the air had jolted Paris into a new sobriety. The brothel is in Barcelona's Carrer d'Avinyo – the Catalan form of Avignon – and Picasso – with heavy irony – had privately referred to it as *Les Demoiselles d'Avignon*. André Salmon, in showing it, retained the title, which becomes meaningless unless its context and the irony are understood.

Something even more important was to emerge from Picasso's encounter with African art, and to understand how we must meet two who came often to the *Rendez-vous des poètes* and influenced Picasso's thinking.

First, Max Jacob, son of a Jewish tailor from Quimper, a confirmed bachelor of volatile character – 'I am half barbed wire, half cotton wool' – but also with a lively humour and by profession a poet, who sought to express his own harlequin character in verse that displaces the usual ordering of reality.

Jacob explained to a friend: 'Artists have been urged to "astound" [this was in 1907: so Diaghilev's command to Cocteau in 1912, 'Astound me,' did not originate with the Russian]. That is the wrong word . . . The basic emotion in æsthetics is doubt, and doubt is obtained by linking what is incompatible and by harmonizing different terminologies.' Including the jumbling of tenses.

Here, translated into English in order to make them less obscure, are lines from an unpunctuated poem by Jacob about Spain, dedicated to Picasso:

> Gipsies will go to the cinema
> Future goatskin flasks have giraffe necks
> Phrygian Catalans were selling snails
> The ships gave the wind their lateen sails
> Like horses' feet were their oars.[1]

This is verbal collage, a deliberate displacement of accepted notions and usage, with the aim of exciting wonder, and perhaps a smile. It was at the time a fresh way of treating experience, and Max Jacob passed it on to his painter friend.

As well as being a poet Max Jacob was a religious man, or rather a man in quest of religion. Because of this and his habit of raising his eyes to the sky he was known as 'Jacob's ladder'. One day in 1909 he returned to his room from the Bibliothèque Nationale, where he'd been working, removed his top hat and was about to put on his slippers when he had a visionary experience. On the wall, which had become for the moment a serene landscape, he seemed to see the figure of Christ in a long yellow silk gown. The figure turned towards him. Jacob fell on his knees in tears: 'In a minute I lived through a century. I became suddenly aware that until then I had been only an animal, and that now I was becoming a man. Two words filled my being: to die, to be born.'

---

[1] *Les gitanes iront au cinématographe*
Les chevreaux futures outres ont des cous de girafes
Des Catalans phrygiens vendaient des escargots
Les tartanes ont courbé des voiles de bateaux
Et les rames étaient des pattes des chevaux.

Under the influence of that experience Jacob wrote a wishful-thinking novel, *Saint Matorel*, about a Hamlet-like man who dies in a monastery, having converted one of his former companions. A few years later Jacob was to be baptized into the Catholic Church – but without having persuaded his companion, Picasso, technically a Catholic, to return to the fold. At Jacob's baptism Picasso did, however, stand godfather, not as a joke but because he was deeply fond of his 'brother' as he called Jacob on that occasion. But he himself had his own vision, not of Christ; what religion was for Jacob, art, widening and deepening, must be for him.

Picasso's other close poet friend, Guillaume Apollinaire, was, like Jacob and Picasso himself, also an outsider, being the natural son of an Italian army officer and a minor Polish noblewoman. With a pear-shaped head, dark expressive eyes, very short neck and tiny mouth, Apollinaire was odd-looking and like Jacob had a volatile character. 'He was never the same person twice,' a friend noticed, 'and he took great pleasure in disconcerting people.' He was a better poet than Jacob: imprisoned by mistake in connection with the theft from the Louvre by an Italian nationalist of the *Mona Lisa*, he wrote a poem on his experience containing the fine lines:

> *Que lentement passent les heures*
> *Comme passe un enterrement.*[1]

But in most of his verse Apollinaire brought together, like Jacob, incongruous ideas or objects – as in a second-hand shop, complained Duhamel – and in some dispensed with punctuation, all in the interests of eliciting wonder and a fresh view of reality.

---

[1] How slowly pass the hours,
Slowly as a funeral procession.

Such was the intellectual mood surrounding Picasso at the moment when he received a visit from a friend who brought with him a naval officer just back from exploration in Africa. The officer described to Picasso how on one occasion he had found himself among a tribe that produced sculpture and he was curious to discover their reactions to a photograph, something they'd never seen. So he held up a photograph of himself in uniform. One tribesman took it, looked at it, turned it this way and that, then returned it, bewildered. The explorer then began to explain that it was a picture of himself. The man laughed incredulously and, taking paper and pencil, began drawing the officer. He drew the head, body, legs, arms as he saw them in the syntax of tribal art, and held out the picture to the officer. Having looked at it again, though this time more attentively, he took it back in order to add a detail he had forgotten: the shiny buttons of the uniform. Instead of putting the buttons on the uniform he put them round the face. He also added the officer's chevrons, but put them at the side of his arms and over the head.

Here was an insight into the psychology of the tribal artist: here too was visual displacement akin to Jacob's and Apollinaire's. The event is described in detail in Fernande's Memoirs, evidently because she considered it important in Picasso's development.

How could the painter elicit wonder by displacement while still sticking close to reality – for Picasso had a fierce and abiding love for the given world? The answer appears to have been suggested in 1909, when Picasso made a bronze of a woman's head. The planes of the head are deeply, irregularly accentuated, so are those of the hair, rising from just above the eyes in sharp ridges and furrows. The nose is a long, lean curve. Light is reflected from some of the planes, while others remain in shadow, giving a recognizably female head some of

180

the qualities of a cult object and investing it with unprecedented density and depth.

In summer 1909 Picasso transposed this technique to a two-dimensional medium. He painted landscapes and fifteen portraits of Fernande in which faceting reinforces perspective to intensify mass and spatial depth. The contrasting rhythms of the facets revealed very successfully the structural element in the motif.

One of Picasso's close Paris acquaintances was his dealer, Ambroise Vollard. Born in far-off Réunion, trained as a lawyer, now aged forty-one, Vollard was a burly man with a striking head – squarish, square-jawed, bald, snub nose, wily tapering eyes, thin mouth with turned-down corners. As a champion of Cézanne he almost certainly warmed to Picasso's new style and would have been a sympathetic sitter.

Picasso painted Vollard's portrait in winter 1909. He now took a momentous step forward by dispensing altogether with perspective and to a large extent also with colour. Instead he conveyed the mass of Vollard's body with faceting: crystal-like polyhedrons of paint, some catching the light, others not. The background he rendered in dark grey polyhedrons. Whereas in a conventional perspective portrait the eye is drawn in through the frame to the subject's world, here Vollard seems to project out from the background towards the viewer. There is a gain in impact.

Picasso sold this painting to a wealthy Russian and at once painted another, in similar style, of a German collector, William Uhde. An artist less adventurous, less relentless in probing, would have been content to remain on this new summit. But again Picasso chose to go further. Having reduced three-dimensional subjects to polyhedrons – cubes, the critics called them – he began to experiment in further 'displacement', to borrow the term Jacob and Apollinaire used for setting something familiar in a fresh light. Picasso began a series of experimental works in which he sought to break down banal objects into basic shapes and volumes, a kind of pictorial lowest common denominator.

At this point in development Picasso again came under the influence of some of the other powerful creators at work in the city. The city attracted innovators as its Bourse attracted new money, and among the innovators working in Montmartre was Georges Braque. Born at Argenteuil, on the Seine, he had grown up in Le Havre, where his father was an interior decorator and a Sunday painter. After studying at Paris's Académie Humbert, Braque rented a studio near Picasso's, painting mainly landscapes and still lifes.

Braque was a tall, strong, serious man, as wary as Picasso was exuberant. Asked whether work was going well, he'd reply, 'Perhaps. Perhaps not. We'll see.' He had a stable marriage, played the flute and accordion, and had a lifelong love of very orderly composers: Bach, Rameau and Couperin.

Braque first came to Picasso's studio in 1907, brought there by Apollinaire. He saw, and said he disliked, Picasso's squat *Two Nudes*, yet went off to paint a big *Nude* much resembling it. In 1908 he was depicting landscapes in geometrical shapes and in 1909, independently of Picasso, evoking volumes in space with faceting.

Picasso liked Braque, esteemed him as a painter and perhaps realized that his own disruptive analysis of shapes could benefit from Braque's clear thinking and restraint. Braque for his part felt the attraction of Picasso's adventurous personality. In 1910 they pooled insights and skills and began to work, in Braque's phrase, 'like mountaineers roped together'.

They chose to paint mostly simple, familiar, easily identified objects, and it was doubtless Braque, with his

182

interest in music, who selected two that have become famous, the mandolin and the guitar. They approached such objects as primitive tribesmen might do who had no notion what they were or what they were for. They rendered the objects as chunky patches of light and shade, sometimes seen simultaneously from different angles, with perhaps a hint of what the subject might be – say the peg of a guitar – so that the viewer could build the patches into a concept. For a time Picasso and Braque did not sign their canvases, so aware were they of a common purpose. Indeed, Braque's *Woman with a Mandolin* might be a Picasso, just as Picasso's *Girl with a Mandolin* might be a Braque.

From the experiments of analytic Cubism, as this style came to be called, it would have been only a step to abstract art, but that step neither painter wished to take – both loved the real world too much. It was Braque who took the initiative in using the new discoveries as an ingredient in a still more original kind of painting.

Braque had learned from his interior-decorator father how to imitate in paint the grain of rare woods, polychrome marble and masonry, a technique much esteemed by Le Havre housewives. In September 1912 Braque bought in a shop in Avignon a wallpaper imitating oak panelling. Cutting it into shapes, he pasted them on to a charcoal drawing to make a picture of a bowl of fruit and a wineglass standing on a wooden table against a panelled wall.

It had been a basic assumption of Western art that the surface of a picture must be homogeneous. The introduction of actual wallpaper to the smooth surface of a drawing and, very soon, to paintings by both Braque and Picasso, effectively modified the nature of painting.

Picasso then proceeded to paste sheets of music, newspapers, even packets of cigarettes or tobacco on to his paintings. He made dozens of such collages, using cut-out newspaper to represent, say, a bottle. 'We tried to get rid of *trompe l'œil*,' he recalled, 'to find a *trompe-l'esprit* . . . If a piece of newspaper can become a bottle, that gives us something to think about in connection with both newspapers and bottles too.'

Collages were fun to make and they aided the development of Cubism by showing how floating planes can convey, simultaneously, several possible views of a subject. Collages also raised in an extreme form the question: When we look at something, how do we see it most truly, most authentically?

The Impressionists had said, Go into the open and catch fleeting light effects; what Picasso dismissively termed 'painting the weather'. The Nabis said, Link what you see to books you have liked. Proust said, Notice detail and aspects others have missed; and be aware that you see in terms of what you expect and what you recall.

Picasso's analysis of perception is very close to Proust's. He believes our sense impressions are fragmentary, incomplete and sometimes misleading, that often a small detail will assume inordinate importance, like Proust's madeleine. Sometimes what we see will fail totally to correspond with what we expected to see, creating a tension. Sometimes again we build up a scene in terms of a dominant expectation, even of a jealousy. That the semi-literate painter and the most over-literate writer should see the same way may be coincidence or it may be that both had learned indirectly from Bergson to pay scrupulous attention to the complex processes involved in a single act of perceiving.

In 1913, after a long absence, Picasso returned to his preferred subject – the human figure – and applied these insights in two canvases. The subject of the first is a woman in a petticoat seated in a magenta upholstered armchair. In such a subject, what will our eyes notice? Primarily, the woman's torso, because it is framed by the chair, whereas her head and feet will lose importance. And our view of the torso is dominated by the chair's upholstered texture. So Picasso paints the torso as an oval sharply segmented into angular and curved patterns, differently tinted to suggest different planes. The woman has been changed by the armchair, just as the chair has been by her: there is a tension between them.

Certain details catch our eye: the ripple of the woman's hair matched by her petticoat's scalloped hem, so Picasso paints these attentively. One other tension: in our image of an ideal woman her breasts are firm, fruit-like, but the unsupported breasts of a woman in negligée tend to droop. Picasso daringly paints both, thus conveying how, in the act of seeing, we may synthesize what we hope to find with what we actually find.

In a second major canvas of 1913, *The Card Player*, Picasso has asked himself, What happens when we watch a game of cards? He answers in effect that that odd duplicated half-figure on a court card may well come to fascinate us, to the point that we see the players as court cards. Picasso's picture shows a highly stylized face – a 'poker face', perhaps – and a body composed of curves and rectangles beside an imitation wood table on which are grouped a newspaper, a bottle, a glass and playing cards; the man's body curves round to end in geometric shapes suggestive of those composing the head. By making the figure almost reversible Picasso points up his perception of a card player merging his identity with the cards he holds, and with the game he is playing.

Braque meanwhile was applying Cubist techniques to the still life. In *Oval Still Life*, painted in 1914, he breaks down a violin into fragmented parts, identifiable by the volutes and the neck. At the right side of the picture is lettering: DUO POU. We assume that *Duo pour violon et piano* is intended and with this clue find at the top of the picture the suggestion of a piano keyboard. Then we realize the aptness of the disjointed violin, for when the duo is performed the violin's sounds are so intimately blended with the piano's as to produce a single beauty. The colours are blue and tan, the tonality very pale and delicate. Braque was to say of this kind of painting that 'instead of starting with the object, one goes towards it, the interesting thing being the route'. The route, that is, of interpretative, poetic perception.

Picasso's and Braque's discovery of how we actually perceive things or people is not unlike Proust's discoveries of how we come to love someone by combining sense impressions with background expectations and memories, and of how a sense impression can, involuntarily, evoke with poignant force a similar childhood impression. Like Proust, Picasso and Braque are drawing on the Bergsonian philosophers who freed man's spirit from late nineteenth-century determinism and proclaimed that all experiencing and thinking are, in part, creative activities.

Picasso's Cubist paintings are firmly rooted in the real world. He accepted that world joyfully, while providing a reading of it more sophisticated perhaps than any since Botticelli's Christian reading of pagan antiquity. One has to beware of anachronism. After the First World War and again after the Spanish Civil War Picasso's handling of his subject-matter was to change radically, but in 1913 and 1914 there is in his work no revolt against the real world, no distortion for

distortion's sake, no mark of aggressiveness or hate.
That kind of art was beginning to emerge elsewhere,
but not in Paris.

As his notebooks show, Picasso had long done naturalistic sketches and stylized versions of the same motif.
In this sense he was born bivisual, almost as Gide was
born bisexual, and he chose to fulfil both visions.
Henceforth in Picasso Mediterranean Man cohabits
with Montmartre Man. He is the first great artist
to express two separate visions, and as he developed,
he was to add more, one of them derived from the
repulsion expressed in *Les Demoiselles*. Shakespeare
had made masterworks in contrasting genres: Picasso
was to work concurrently in radically different and
eventually even in opposed styles. In so doing he would
demonstrate that a single individual may be not only
complex but even contradictory.

The single-mindedness with which Picasso pursued
the stylistic experiments leading to Cubism is, again,
perhaps unprecedented in the visual arts. Sketches,
drawings, sculpture, collages, paintings pour from his
hand. Nothing must interrupt it. His father dies:
Picasso does not attend the funeral, does not go to comfort his mother. The war when it comes will be merely a
disruption of his painting routine.

A comparison with Proust, writing page after page,
version after version, in his cork-lined bedroom suggests itself. Since in attitude to parents and in so much
else the ultra-refined Parisian and the Parisian by adop-
tion could hardly be more dissimilar, it is striking that
both should have thrown themselves into their work
with the same frenzy.

Various interpretations are possible. It may be that
maturing genius must hasten to justify its originality
lest it be condemned as foolishness or worse. It may
also be that while both men had enriching views of

experience to offer society, both distanced themselves from that society's religious belief. This set them inevitably on the defensive – even to small voices from their own boyhood – and perhaps acted as a further lash in the desperate, day-and-night quest for alternatives in art.

'You can't escape your period,' Picasso once said. 'Whether you take sides for or against, you're always inside it.' Through Cubism he and Braque gave expression to many of the values of a place and period, and as soon as this happened a 'school' arose, of interest to everyone in the arts save to Picasso and Braque, who believed that the mystery of artistic creation is non-communicable.

By 1912 the Cubists were an identifiable group, exhibiting in that year both at the Salon des Indépendants and the Salon d'Automne. They were publicized by Apollinaire though, according to Braque, the poet could not tell a Rubens from a Rembrandt. Two of the group call for special mention.

Juan Gris, a gentle penniless Spaniard from Madrid, had been Picasso's neighbour and good friend in Montmartre. He adopted analytic Cubism, then pasted papers, and finally synthetic Cubism, but unlike Picasso and Braque, 'I proceed from the general to the particular, by which I mean that I start with an abstraction to arrive at a true fact.' Gris idealizes and beautifies, while his preferred colours, powder blue and warm beige, are as feminine as his master's are male. His canvases are rightly described as decorative, but the best possess a rare gentle serenity characteristic of Gris the man.

Fernand Léger, on the other hand, was to take Cubism in an opposite direction. Born in the Norman town of Argentan, Léger came to Paris in 1900, worked as an architect's draughtsman and in 1906 became a full-time painter. In 1911 he met Picasso, Braque and their circle and began to evolve his personal variant of Cubism, holding a one-man show at Kahnweiler's the following year.

Whereas Picasso and Braque remained curiously un-interested in twentieth-century technology and by this date had not painted even a motor-car, Léger was one of the first to draw inspiration from machinery, the heavier the better, and in general from urban culture. Not for him, either, Gris's closed world where a fruit dish, glasses, a chair and a newspaper bask like Platonic ideas, but rather the jangling of chains on pulleys, the prehensile beaks of heavy cranes, the geometry of cogged factory machinery, drawing out the machine side of man. This chosen world Léger was to paint with intense primary colours, jagged lines and an accent of harshness.

There is no space to do more than mention lesser French artists who styled themselves Cubists: Albert Gleizes, Jean Metzinger, Jacques Villon and Robert Delaunay, the sculptors Henri Laurens and the Lithuanian-born Jacques Lipchitz. Reverberations too were set up outside France by pre-war Picasso or Cubist exhibitions: two in Amsterdam, two in Moscow, two in New York, three in London, six in Munich, including Picasso's first retrospective. Again lack of space pre-cludes more than a brief mention of one momentous result. The Dutch painter Piet Mondrian was so impressed by the 1911 Amsterdam exhibition that he moved to Paris and began working in the Cubist idiom, eventually taking it across the borderline to become one of the inventors – the other, independently, was Kandinsky in Bavaria – of abstract art. That was a path both Picasso and Braque had glimpsed and decided to shun. Nevertheless, but for them abstract painting would almost certainly not have arisen when it did.

Cubism changed the course of painting worldwide. It also changed the way we assess what we see, and, more generally, all our sense-impressions. In visual terms it revealed the complexity of the human spirit, so that men of 1912, looking back to the 1890s, an age that had believed itself sophisticated, thought: How naive! How lacking in subtlety!

CHAPTER 8

The Harmonious City: Charles Péguy

Strong anti-clerical feeling in France around 1900 had its origin in the Vatican Council of 1870, when Pius IX had proclaimed the dogma of papal infallibility, had castigated liberal democracy, and had urged on good Catholics a policy of non-cooperation with Republican government.

These pronouncements alarmed French politicians of the Left and Centre, who thought the Pope was trying to assert a direct claim on the allegiance of their people, especially through the army and education. Unmollified by Pope Leo XIII's later advice to French Catholics to accept the Republic, even a hostile Republic, the anti-clericals began to work on the assumption that political and social life, renewed by the achievements of science and reason, could provide a new basis for common effort in which there would be no place for God, as there had long been no place for the King.

The Catholic Church in France between 1870 and 1900 certainly had not endeared itself to most Frenchmen. It had backed Napoleon III's misguided invasion of Prussia, because Napoleon and his wife protected religion. The loss of Alsace-Lorraine having brought an influx of Jews to Paris, some Catholics, encouraged by members of the clergy, helped to start the anti-Semitic climate in which the charge against Dreyfus of spying for Germany came to be believed. When it seemed

191

Dreyfus had been framed, the Church stood shoulder to shoulder with the army in opposing a re-trial. The Church believed that workers' demands for improved conditions were inspired by atheistic Socialists, and chose to barricade itself with a bigoted bourgeoisie in a bastion of privilege. At the intellectual level it failed to answer Darwinism. Boutroux and Blondel, it is true, provided ways out of positivism, but the man who did most to rehabilitate free will, Henri Bergson, was Jewish. Young François Mauriac, who came from a Gascon landowning family, spoke for many in describing religion of the day as 'an insurance policy for this world and the next', and when a member of his family married a gynæcologist, a curious boy's enquiry elicited the information that the term meant 'throat doctor'.

The Catholic Church in 1900 had identified itself with monarchy, the Right, old-fashioned thinking, narrow-minded prudery and a social status quo. So that when a succession of Radical governments sought to curb its influence, probably a majority of Frenchmen believed the Church was only getting what it deserved.

The situation, from the Church's point of view, was very serious indeed. Plans were afoot to hand Church property over to the laity and to close hundreds of her schools. So from 1900 we find a number of attempts to save the French Church from ruin by bringing her into line with current thinking, intellectual or social.

The first attempt was made by eminent scholars. In 1902 Abbé Loisy, a Biblical specialist, published a book maintaining that the core of Christ's message was that the world would end imminently and be followed by the establishment of an earthly Kingdom of God. Since this did not happen, it followed that Christ's statements in general, and the Church's interpretation of them, could not be treated as absolutely true and therefore different in kind from human statements.

Edouard Le Roy, a mathematician, published a book in 1907 maintaining that dogmatic statements by Rome are not statements of objective truth, but serve merely as guidelines to prevent error and stimulate religious activity. In the same year Paul Bureau, a professor of the Institut Catholique, roundly criticized the Church's failure to come to terms with modern science and, furthermore, with the needs of the proletariat.

The aim behind such books was doubtless good, even necessary, but these men – there were only a handful of them – lacked the moderate, more tentative tone shown by Maurice Blondel and in England by the English Catholic writer, Friedrich von Hügel. As a result Pope Pius X in December 1907 condemned Modernism, as the movement had come to be called, for twisting unalterable truth to suit modern thought and for playing down the role of faith in any affirmation of religious truth. Loisy left the Church.

The second attempt aimed to bridge the gap between Catholics and workers. It took as its blueprint Leo XIII's 1891 encyclical *Rerum Novarum*, a remarkably bold document for its day, which called on Catholics to do away with social injustice and to ensure that workers had access to education and received fair wages.

The leader of this movement, Marc Sangnier, was born in 1873, the son of well-to-do Catholic parents. He studied philosophy with Maurice Blondel and adopted Blondel's view that thought is fulfilled only in action. At the Polytechnique he held discussions with Freemasons (shunned by most Catholics as dangerous), with free-thinkers, with Jews and, above all, with young workers, listening to their grievances and aspirations.

Sangnier was a plump young man, with a heavy face, blue eyes and fair, drooping moustache. He was a first-rate speaker, emotional rather than intellectual, and he possessed an aura of goodness and authority that encouraged people to open their hearts to him. He had a way of grasping a newcomer's hand in his own long white hands with a benign imperiousness that many young people found to their taste.

Though he had been intended for the army, in 1899 Sangnier decided to make a career of social work by founding a study circle for young workers. This grew and widened into the first of several People's Institutes, open to all – workers and students, Catholics and unbelievers – as an alternative to the Socialists' anti-Christian People's Universities.

Sangnier called his movement Le Sillon, The Furrow, and chose as its badge a blade of wheat encircled with a red ribbon. He described it as 'a friendship' or 'a life in common' and his basic idea was to treat the Republic as a friend, not like most Catholics as an irreconcilable enemy. It attacked the selfishness of the middle class, campaigned for fair wages and the right to strike. Taxed with the vagueness of his ideas, Sangnier would smile and nod agreement: 'Furthermore, we don't know where we are going.'

Clearly he was going forward. In 1902 he founded and edited a newspaper, *Le Sillon*. Four years later he had 500 study groups across France. He arranged for workers to be taken on cheap-rate outings to museums, cathedrals, factories, printing-works. He started a co-operative factory for shoes in Fougères, another for shirts in Nancy. He arranged for those so inclined an annual retreat in a monastery.

Down in Bordeaux nineteen-year-old François Mauriac, doe-eyed and so slim he was called 'Asparagus', joined Le Sillon, as did his brother Jean, a future priest. They sold its newspaper at street corners and François' first published piece appeared in another Sillon periodical. Entitled 'The Ivory Tower', it pits two men with contrasting views of life, one favouring isolation, the other the camaraderie of social work. When Marc Sangnier arrived for a meeting in nearby Langon, Mauriac lodged him in one of the family houses. Next morning Sangnier read his associates a work of his own in quasi-dramatic form, entitled *By Way of Death*. It was rather earnest. Asked what he thought of it, Mauriac, who had a flippant side, enquired, 'Where's the love interest?' - which didn't go down well.

As late as 1909 Mauriac attended a Week of Social Studies in Bordeaux. Yet another literary Frenchman never to have known his father, Mauriac champed under any authority, even in its benevolent form as practised by Sangnier, and the irony in him could not take undiluted moral earnestness. The Sillonists 'cannot sneeze without saying they're sacrificing themselves to social duty', and Mauriac, arriving in Paris, joined a frivolous set, sippers of iced Kümmel, before returning to Catholicism under the more sophisticated literary influence of Claudel.

By 1908 Sangnier had a powerful movement on his hands, but the amount of good he could do was, he decided, limited unless he entered politics. In that year he founded a new political party, the République Démocratique, to unite Catholics who wished to work constitutionally for social reform. In 1909 and 1910 he contested seats for the Chamber unsuccessfully, and in the latter year started a political newspaper, *La Démocratie*.

Sangnier now went beyond *Rerum Novarum* by declaring that the only truly Catholic form of government is democracy. Some of his followers went so far as to praise the theories of Danton and Robespierre as essentially Christian and to hail the 'mystic-souled Russian anarchists'. This antagonized many of the hierarchy who had hitherto supported Le Sillon's work, and thirty-one bishops forbade their flocks to have anything to do with the movement. Rome was informed. Pius X could not accept the view that the voice of the people is the voice of God. In a letter to the French episcopate dated 25 August 1910 he condemned Le Sillon.

Sangnier, with his closest friends, accepted this ruling. He wrote the Pope a letter of submission and brought Le Sillon to an end. But its nine years of existence had done much to reconcile Catholics with a social conscience to the Republic. Two examples are of interest. In 1906 the eleventh Duc de la Trémouille, a Catholic and owner of the Château Margaux vineyards, successfully stood for the Chamber on the Left of the Republican Party; in 1912 a quarter of the Ecole Normale Supérieure were practising Catholics – there had been only two or three in 1900 – mainly as a result of a Sillonist group founded in the college in 1906.

Another attempt to heal the split between Church and anti-clerical Republic came from Jacques Maritain. Born into a Protestant family with a strong social conscience, Maritain studied philosophy at the Sorbonne, where he became a Tolstoyan. With dark good looks and a winning manner, he played a prominent part in expanding People's Universities and helped his sister Jeanne edit a pacifist periodical for young people. He married a Russian fellow-student, Raïssa Osmansoff, who shared his concern for the working class. While in Heidelberg Jacques and Raïssa read Léon Bloy, a shrill, often self-pitying exponent of a view that equates the poor with Christ, and money, the product of the suffering of the poor, with the blood of Christ. Rather as an unlikely illuminist prose poem had prepared Claudel for conversion, so Bloy prepared the Maritains.

In 1906 the Protestant Tolstoyan and his Jewish wife joined the Catholic Church.

Jacques Maritain believed that the answer to France's social division lay in the works of Thomas Aquinas, freshly interpreted. In articles in *Revue de métaphysique et morale* and elsewhere he expounded Aquinas's teaching on fair wages and just government. He revealed an older mainstream Catholic tradition fairer to workers than the bourgeois-weighted theories of the French Right.

Maritain decided to go further and to try to heal the split between Catholics and unbelievers about the status of dogma, and this issue he believed turned on the status of knowledge. To Berkeley's theory that our sense-perceptions may not correspond to an actual world Dr Johnson had replied by kicking a stone, but Maritain saw that the current view that an individual does well to formulate his metaphysic exclusively on the basis of personal experience could not be contested so cavalierly.

The fountainhead of French thinking, René Descartes, had said, 'I think, therefore I am.' According to Maritain, if you accepted that, you could never escape the closed world of subjectivism. Thomas Aquinas on the other hand had approached the issue from the opposite direction, saying in effect: 'God *is*;' – and he proferred five proofs – 'and that fact guarantees our existence and that of the outside world.'

Maritain proposed to replace Descartes with Aquinas, to offer philosophic realism as a possible common ground between Catholics and agnostics. He maintained that only if you accept the objective reality of the external world can you accept the objective reality of certain truths, including those of Revelation.

Maritain's neo-Thomism proved very useful in loosening up rigid Catholic attitudes. With what may be called the hard-core Paris intellectuals it had less immediate impact. They were convinced – and had the weight of Bergson behind them – that thinking is a dynamic activity, partly conditioned by our body's practical needs, partly by desires below the threshold of consciousness. This was an age, by and large, permeated with subjectivism.

Marc Sangnier and Jacques Maritain came from well-to-do homes and achieved success in their lifetime. A third man who tried to bridge the gap between Catholicism and society came from a very poor home and his short life was marked by repeated failures and public indifference.

Charles Péguy's ancestors were peasants: vinegrowers in La Beauce, the plain south of Chartres. His father rose to become a cabinet maker, fought as a soldier during the siege of Paris and there contracted an illness from which two years later he died, leaving one son, aged ten months.

Charles Péguy was raised in a two-room thatched cottage in Orléans by his grandmother, who could neither read nor write, and by his mother, a forceful woman with a craggy face and prominent chin who worked sixteen hours a day as a charwoman and repairer of rush chairs, including those in Orléans cathedral, eventually saving enough, sou by sou, to buy her cottage and two other small houses.

It was a household entirely given to work. The widow Péguy never had time to play with her son, to go a walk with him, or to accompany him to Mass – although she saw that *he* went, and also to catechism. When he was old enough for school, Charles spent his free time preparing rushes for chair-repair, peeling potatoes, sweeping the cottage floor or polishing the scant furniture. Recreation consisted in joking with his mother and listening to his grandmother's stories, including terrifying ones about the Devil. Yet it was a contented home and Charles Péguy was to recall the intensity of his boyhood – the struggle just to survive, the need to work almost till one dropped, the pleasure in small things. 'We are formed,' he said, 'by the age of twelve.'

Péguy attended the lycée, won prizes, started a football team at a time when sport was almost unknown in schools, took part in the annual procession in honour of Jeanne d'Arc. He went off to do his military service and showed marked gifts of leadership, rising to be a sergeant. He then went on a scholarship to the Ecole Normale Supérieure to train as a top-grade school-master or don.

As a student Péguy joined the Society of St Vincent de Paul and visited the home-bound poor. He actively campaigned for Dreyfus and when the Church used its political power against the accused officer showed his disgust by joining the Socialists. He collected money for striking workers and any cause that stirred his social conscience. Already he had hopes of being a writer. After listening enthralled to a lecture by Bergson he went up to the philosopher: 'Sir, I hear you've inter-rupted your own work to devote yourself to your pupils. That's a mistake. You have a book to write and should let nothing stand in your way.' Bergson did not heed this advice but he and Péguy became friends.

Péguy came to know a shy fellow-student younger than he, Marcel Baudouin, who came from a middle-class family that prided itself on having taken a leading role in the 1848 Revolution and was now strongly Republican and anti-clerical. Péguy had a way of asking a new acquaintance, 'Are you ready to lay down your life for what you say?' And if the other said yes, 'Then we can talk.' Marcel Baudouin did say yes, and the two talked long hours into the night, planning to work for social justice in a 'Harmonious City' composed of friends 'pure in heart' – the expression was one of Péguy's favourites.

Marcel Baudouin went off to do his military service. He did not have Péguy's robust physique; he fell ill and died. He left a widowed mother and a sister, Charlotte.

Péguy had seen in Baudouin the perfect friend. Under the shock of his grief and perhaps misplaced loyalty he transferred some of his affection to Charlotte. More than anything, perhaps, he wanted to lend a helping hand. At any rate, he proposed to Charlotte. Péguy was a likeable young man, full of promise, anti-clerical, Republican. Charlotte accepted him and when Péguy was twenty-four the two were married civilly.

Péguy made another friend, this one older than he. Jean Jaurès modestly called himself 'an educated peasant' but he was an unequalled orator and a tireless political journalist whose Socialism sprang not from theory but from a warm virile kindliness and a deep sympathy with his fellow men. Jaurès furthermore hated war with all his honest soul and flattered himself he was in agreement with Bebel, the German Socialist, to stamp out war. Rising forty, with his long beard, Jaurès already exuded a reassuring grandparental benevolence that won the hearts of workers. He had achieved wide influence with his articles, and it was out of admiration for Jaurès that Péguy decided to found and edit a periodical that would work for his 'Harmonious City'.

On the first day of January 1900 Péguy was seated at a desk in a tiny rented room crowded with books, writing copy and correcting proofs for the first number. Aged twenty-six, he was short of stature, with square shoulders, a round head, hair cut very short, ruddy cheeks, short-sighted eyes with a strong yet gentle look; he wore a tight black jacket, black trousers baggy at the knees and black shoes with iron-edged heels to make them last. When he went out he wore a black felt hat or hooded cloak and carried a thick stick, held in the middle like a marshal's baton.

His handwriting was very strange. Elongated and extremely compressed, it suggested a row of tightly planted Lombardy poplars. The space between letters was almost nil, but between lines there were exaggeratedly large spaces. It was both showy and secretive. His signature too was unusual: written with an upward slope of 45 degrees, according to graphologists it reveals high ambition. Certainly the new periodical embodied ambition, for its first number, 144 pages, was entirely written by Péguy; moreover, to save money, he was himself setting up much of it, as well as correcting, with characteristic meticulousness, all galleys.

On 5 January 1900 the periodical went on sale. Entitled *Cahiers de la Quinzaine*, *Fortnightly Exercise Books*, priced at 1 fr.50, it had thirty-six paid-up subscribers, and it is a measure of Péguy's self-confidence that, though booksellers refused to stock it, he printed 1300 copies.

The front cover carried Péguy's name prominently, the back cover his editorial slogan: *The social revolution will be moral or nothing.* In the leading article, 'Letter from a Provincial', Péguy announced that his periodical would publish facts and documents, suppressing nothing, as a means to establishing a Harmonious City. In such an ideal city all wealth would be held in common. The citizens would work for a living, except for women, the old and the very young, but there would be no superior or inferior jobs. Each worker would choose his job or trade, the one for which he was best suited.

Machinery would provide an abundant pool of goods, from which each would help himself. Art, science and philosophy would be accessible to all and no one would try to exercise authority in such matters. The citizens would not make war, and, like Péguy himself, who had an iron constitution, would not fall ill; however, they would undergo experiences that bring spiritual joy and spiritual suffering. In the city everyone would be able to achieve the ideal of beauty and thereby self-fulfilment.

How would the city be established? By telling the truth and by friendship. Péguy himself had dozens of friends, some of whom had put up part of the money for printing the *Cahiers*. The rest came from Charlotte's dowry.

If Péguy's socialism was somewhat hazy, other articles in that first number were factual, hard-hitting and to the point, as were the articles in succeeding issues, twenty a year. One of them criticized the Church for pitting its political power against Dreyfus, another attacked Durkheim's sociology as a non-science aiming to displace the humanities. Soon the *Cahiers* had built up a circulation of 1000, mainly anti-clerical Republicans of the Left, just enough to earn Péguy a very modest living.

In 1902 Jaurès was elected to the Chamber and, behind the scenes, became an influential figure on the Left. Péguy expected Jaurès to ensure that the ministry headed by Emile Combes would carry out measures of social justice, but not so. Combes had begun to study for the priesthood, then left the seminary and qualified as a doctor of medicine. Now aged sixty-nine, a little man with white hair and goatee, he decided on draconian measures against the Church. He seems to have been motivated not by personal rancour but by the ideals of the 1789 Revolution, for that had been a protest against a privileged nobility and also, quite as much, against a

202

supranational Church; it was in defence of the latter that Louis XVI had gone to the guillotine.

Combes closed down 2500 Church schools and obliged thousands of teaching priests and nuns to leave France. He took buildings and valuables, such as works of art and reliquaries, from the Church authorities and transferred them to groups of the laity. He sent President Loubet to visit the King of Italy without calling on the Pope, thus causing a diplomatic rupture, first step to the separation of Church and State in December 1905. He initiated plans for turning over uneconomic churches to civil use, thus provoking Proust's *Figaro* protest, 'The Massacre of Churches'. Most galling of all, he allowed his Minister of War, General André, to employ Freemasons to inform secretly on the religious practices of army officers: those who went to Sunday Mass were listed in a file marked 'Carthage'; those who kept away from church were listed in a file marked 'Corinth', and only they received promotion.

Péguy's vestigial Catholicism was outraged. He watched with abhorrence. How far this was from the Harmonious City! He urged Jaurès to exercise restraint on Combes. Though not himself fiercely anti-clerical, Jaurès judged these measures – with the exception of General André's espionage – politically necessary and took no action. In 1904 Péguy therefore broke with Jaurès, and in the *Cahiers* attacked the Government's 'fanaticism'.

Anti-clericalism reached its paroxysm in a speech by the Minister of Work, René Viviani: 'We have rescued men's consciences from belief. When a poor fellow, tired by his day's work, knelt down, we lifted him up, we told him that behind the clouds there are only chimeras. Together, with a magnificent gesture, we have put out the lights in heaven and no one will turn them on again.'

Viviani's speech was deemed so stirring, so true,that the Government had it placarded throughout the country, but Péguy wrote: 'For the first time since the world began a romantic sees the gesture of putting out lights as splendid.... The municipal lamp-lighter puts out lamps as well as lighting them, yet until now lighting has been considered so much more honourable that we would have been ashamed to call him a lamp-extinguisher.'

Now that political Socialism had failed him, Péguy turned for support to his friends. Joseph Lotte, a jolly Breton who sang sea shanties, was a teacher in Coutances and received Péguy's confidences by letter. Other friends were Louis Baillet, a Benedictine who offered his Masses for Péguy's conversion; Romain Rolland, musicologist, biographer of Beethoven and novelist, who gave Péguy his best-selling novel, *Jean Christophe*, to be serialized in the *Cahiers* and so keep the periodical afloat. André Suarès was an essayist who delighted in a worm's-eye melancholic view of life and contributed wise articles on Ibsen, Tolstoy and Péguy's favourite Pascal. Bernard Lazare, plain-faced, bespectacled, was plagued with ill health, to the police a dangerous anarchist, to Péguy a dedicated champion of the Jewish people, 'carrying fifty centuries on his stooped shoulders'.

Suarès and Lazare, like another of Péguy's friends, Henri Bergson, were Jewish. 'Each person gets the Jews he deserves,' said Péguy, adding that he, who never had a sou, got poor Jews and found them good at their job and loyal friends.

After 1904 it was through such friends as these, and friends of these friends, that Péguy pinned his hopes of realizing the Harmonious City. Moral renewal must come from small groups, at 'parish level'. And Péguy was not just theorizing. As a member of the St Vincent de Paul Society, he had befriended, among others, an elderly destitute embroiderer, Madame Gorius. After leaving college Péguy continued to look after this house-bound woman, played cards with her, did her shopping and once brought her a bunch of her favourite wild flowers. This so touched Madame Gorius that she dried the flowers, kept them always and asked that they should be placed in her coffin.

Frenchmen tend to think they move forward exclusively by way of the intellect, but this is not so; their past has left a subsoil of Christianity, which keeps sending up shoots. Péguy's friend Romain Rolland has a relevant passage in a letter written at the height of anti-clericalism: 'The politicians believe that religious sentiment amounts to practical interests and material gain, and can be offended with impunity. They fail to see that it is the life-blood of half France (more than the life-blood, since eternal life is held to be involved).'

In the wake of his disillusion with the political Left, Péguy's residual faith began to re-assert itself. It was very much a boyhood faith – 'We are formed by the age of twelve.' He had a particular devotion to the Christ-child and his blessed Mother. We recall Claudel's conversion in Notre-Dame, driven by his love of the Christ-child's 'innocence and infancy'. Each period has a preferred aspect of Christianity and this one, perhaps as an antidote to its sophistication and complexity, prized the Christ-child. We find it again in the poetry of Jammes and in a comment by Picasso to Cocteau: 'The strength of Catholicism is that it started from nothing in the sense that God lay in a manger.'

As a boy Péguy had a cult of Jeanne d'Arc, whose cause of beatification, supported in particular out of guilt by the English, including the late Cardinal Newman, was being considered by Rome. More generally, Péguy had a deep trust in the saints. Always busy himself, he thought of them as busy: 'Paradise isn't a casino.

The saints spend their time importuning God to save us.' 'You can't imagine,' he told Joseph Lotte, 'what St Geneviève, St Aignan, St Louis and Jeanne d'Arc do for me and what they obtain! Also, I have an incredible guardian angel. He's even more cunning than me, *mon vieux*, I'm well looked after.'

By 1907 the Church, partly under the influence of Le Sillon, had found again a social conscience, and Péguy, who in a sense had been practising Franciscanism without knowing it, felt tempted to rejoin the flock. When Maritain told him of his conversion in Heidelberg, Péguy said, 'I've reached that point too. But don't tell anyone.' He needed time to prepare his subscribers, many of whom were free-thinkers, Protestants and Jews.

He needed time also to prepare his wife and mother-in-law. They applauded Combes's Church-bashing, and of Mère Baudouin, moreover, Péguy was very much afraid. Asked once whether he believed in the Devil, he replied, 'Of course. When I sit by my mother-in-law I have the impression he's in the next chair.' For Madame Baudouin was by no means pleased that Charlotte's dowry had vanished into the *Cahiers*, and that the editor-writer earned barely enough to keep his dependants fed and clothed in their small house in Lozère.

Jacques Maritain kept pressing Péguy to regularize his union and have his three children baptized, but Péguy gave evasive answers. One day Jacques' sister Jeanne came to Péguy. 'You are a despicable coward,' she charged. 'You want to serve two masters.'

'You had better go and make that sort of remark at Lozère.'

'Would you really like me to?'

'Yes, and don't let me hear any more about it.'

In the event it was Jacques who went, a know-all twenty-six, with the fervour of a new convert and the casuistry of one steeped in medieval canon law. He explained to Madame Baudouin and Charlotte that since they did not believe in Christianity baptism for them was an act with no meaning, so they might as well accede to Péguy's wishes. To which the women retorted that rather than allow baptismal water to touch their children's heads they would drown them. And nothing Maritain said could alter this stand.

Maritain returned chagrined. Then he proposed a canon law solution, *sanatio in radice*, whereby Péguy would petition Rome, and Rome, having examined the evidence, would declare his marriage valid. His children would remain unbaptized, but Péguy would again be in communion with the Church and be able to receive the sacraments.

Péguy liked things clear-cut, dramatic, if possible heroic, and Maritain's proposal did not appeal. It seemed to Péguy devious and underhand. Perhaps also he believed his return to the Church would break up his home. And there was a further factor that certainly inhibited him. His was essentially a religion of the heart – to Maritain he said, 'I'd give the whole *Summa* for the Hail Mary and Hail Holy Queen . . . In what Christ said there isn't one abstract word. Or in the Bible' – and he disliked the rational, dogmatic and 'official' aspects of the Church. Péguy believed that a Catholic should decide whether or not he was on the orthodox road by consulting friends, including his friends the saints. Jeanne d'Arc, he would say, didn't listen to her confessor, she listened to her saints. Subjectivism again!

This comes out in Péguy's defence of Bergson, the only philosopher he liked. Bergson described dogma as the symbolic transcription of mystical experience. He had now become so popular he was being read in seminaries, to the disquiet of Rome, who scented danger in such anti-intellectualism. Péguy chose to put his own writings at risk with Rome by defending Bergson in the *Cahiers*: 'It is a lie to call Bergson irrational. It is a new form of rationalism more supple than the old. It helps us look closely at present experience. It is centred on concrete facts, and so is an ally of Christianity, a religion of the present moment and of incarnation.' Despite Péguy's spirited defence, Rome placed Bergson's three major works to date on the Index of Prohibited Books.

Péguy still hesitated to rejoin the Church. Instead, in 1910, he expressed his faith and fervour in a new form by publishing a long poem cast as a play about the girl Jeanne d'Arc in Domrémy, and her vocation.

The Mystery of the Charity of Jeanne d'Arc is really a series of dialogues and meditations. In the first Jeanne is praying for France, ravaged by war, and begging God to send saints. Hauviette enters, a decent kindly peasant girl, who says her prayers twice daily without fuss, just as she eats her three meals. Jeanne, she declares, is different from other girls, for she's always praying, and seems to *see* those she prays to. Jeanne scoffs at this but repeats that a saint is needed, a saint of a new kind.

There follows a meditation on the suffering of France and how people have come to despair of salvation because they despair of the goodness of God. Jeanne's distress is interrupted by the entrance of a nun, Madame Gervaise, who tries to console Jeanne by saying that the physical destruction of France's churches leaves the inner Church unharmed.

Already, like Claudel's Violaine, Jeanne is showing readiness to embrace redemptive suffering. She reflects on the pains of Hell: if she can thereby save the damned from suffering, she prays, 'My God, throw my body into eternal flames.'

Jeanne believes she wouldn't have abandoned Christ

on Good Friday. 'St Francis wouldn't, nor St Clare. We are great criminals, great sinners. But we wouldn't have done that. I don't like the English, but I say the English wouldn't have let that happen.'

Péguy's play ends with Madame Gervaise urging Jeanne to let the will of God take its course; as for the perdition Jeanne foresees, can she be sure it will happen? 'In face of the eternal promises, what do we know, how can we judge?'

In a companion poem, *The Porch of the Mystery of the Second Virtue*, Péguy probes the paradox within those promises. It opens with God soliloquizing about the theological virtues. Faith and charity he can understand, but hope astonishes him: 'That these poor children seeing all that goes on should believe that tomorrow is better ... !' Charity only loves what *is*, but hope loves what *will be*.

God himself has opened his heart to hope by way of Jesus the bridge who, forever crucified, suffers from men's treacheries and rejoices at their acts of loyalty. Jesus has made himself men's slave and, in thus binding himself, has bound God. If man hopes, God hopes; man hopes in God, God in man; they will be able to save themselves only through each other. And so, by way of the heart of man, Jesus transforms the heart of God.

In a third poem, *The Mystery of the Holy Innocents*, Péguy urges us to live child-like in the present, undisturbed by excessive remorse or concern for the morrow and, again, he celebrates hope, this time hope of redemption. Péguy gives this soliloquy to God:

O nuit sera-t-il dit que je t'aurai créée la dernière.
Et que mon Paradis et que ma Béatitude
Ne sera qu'une grande nuit de clarté ...
Et tout s'achèverait de lassitude,
Cette énorme aventure,

Comme après une ardente moisson
La lente descension d'un grand soir d'été.
S'il n'y avait pas ma petite espérance.
C'est par ma petite espérance seule que l'éternité sera.
Et que la Béatitude sera.
Et que le Paradis sera. Et le ciel et tout.[1]

Péguy's cycle of poems sold badly and caused many *Cahiers* readers to cancel their subscriptions. Gide, however, in the *NRF* recognized their importance and their topicality. He remarked also on the repetitions – Péguy never said in one line what he could say in four – but generously compared them to litanies or Arabic songs.

Maurice Barrès received a review copy of the first poem. He disliked the author's longwindedness – 'When I read Péguy, I look at my watch' – and described his *Cahiers* articles as '*pot-au-feu* literature, he tosses in every available vegetable'. But the *Jeanne d'Arc* fitted in with a campaign he was conducting against the closure of churches, and in an article in *L'Echo de France* the famous patriot-novelist praised Péguy's poem.

Encouraged by this, Péguy entered his poem for the Académie Française prize of 10,000 francs, a sum that would end his poverty. Paul Bourget and Barrès promised him their votes, but another Academician, the leading Sorbonne historian, Ernest Lavisse, a pillar of the agnostic Establishment, campaigned against the poem. 'Péguy,' said Lavisse, 'is a Catholic anarchist who has

---

[1] O night, will it be said that you are my final creation?
That my Paradise and my beatitude
Will be no more than a luminous glow . . .
And that all will end in tiredness,
All this great adventure end
Like the slow descent of a summer's night
On a bright harvest?
It would be like that but for hope.
Eternity and beatitude will exist
Because of hope, and Paradise and Heaven too.

put holy water in his petrol bomb.' No one in Paris sur-
vives a *mot* like that. The Academicians took fright and
decided that year not to award any prize at all.

Péguy was furious. He knew his poem to be a great
work, as indeed it is. He attacked Lavisse in many an
article, calling him a 'fat gravedigger' who trimmed
his Establishment sails to the Sorbonne's Socialist
wind. When Fernand Laudet published in the *Revue
Hebdomadaire* an article criticizing Péguy for giving the
public only the legends about Jeanne d'Arc, Péguy
waded into Laudet with 200 pages of Swift-like venge-
ful invective. Péguy was a good friend, but he could be a
good hater too. For a full eighteen months after Lavisse
coined his *mot*, he could not bring himself to say the Our
Father, with its declaration of forgiveness.

Though at the personal level they brought him only
financial trouble and disappointment Péguy's poems
are an important contribution to the period. With those
of Jammes and Claudel they re-introduced Christian
belief and the note of mystery to a literature from which
those themes had long been absent. They are also
notably of their time. Proust had sought an absolute in
communion with his past self and his mother; Péguy
sought it in communion with the saint of his childhood
and with the Mother of God.

Right up to the eve of war Péguy failed to make his
mark on the larger public. He hoped his actress friend,
Madame Simone Casimir-Perier, would bring his
Jeanne d'Arc to the stage, but this did not happen. He
saw few signs of his Harmonious City rising. He did not
rejoin the Church, nor find domestic peace. Yet by a
small number he was revered, even loved, for his generous warmth and his integrity. One of those Péguy
helped was Jacques Rivière's brother-in-law, Alain-
Fournier, for whom he found a secretarial job in Paris.
The author of *Le Grand Meaulnes* spoke for quite a few

when he declared: 'I say, knowing what I'm saying, that not since Dostoievsky has there been a man who was so clearly a man of God.'

In February 1912 Péguy's eight-year-old son Patrick fell dangerously ill of typhoid. Péguy placed him under Our Lady's protection and vowed that if the boy recovered he would go on pilgrimage to Chartres, 'the one place in the world where everything becomes childlike'. The boy did recover, and Péguy set off. A reserve officer and a strong, fast walker, he covered the 144 kilometres from Paris to Chartres in three days. It was typical of Péguy to use demanding physical activity as a form of prayer and self-sacrifice, and to do so quite alone. Out of his walk came a new poem, *The Tapestry of Our Lady of Chartres*, in which Péguy the Parisian symbolically presents to Christ's mother the city he lives in, conceived as a ship laden with souls and men's sins, but also with redemptive grace.

In July 1913 in fulfilment of another vow Péguy repeated his walk from Paris to Chartres. Again his private intention doubled with a public statement. He was acting out, so to speak, the proposition that Paris can become the Harmonious City, but only by returning, step by step, to her Christian origins, so richly expressed in France's best cathedral.

Péguy's walks chimed in with similar themes in Claudel's poems and plays. They struck a chord in the young and were talked about approvingly. Less than thirteen months after his second walk Péguy was to leave Paris again, this time in uniform with his regiment for the Marne, and he was not to return. For all his stubbornness and tirades, he had been to dozens around him the ideal friend, a man pure in heart. Today his courage, his writings and his pioneer walks are remembered as thousands of young people set out every year on pilgrimage in the footsteps of Charles Péguy.

CHAPTER 9

A Music of Nuance: Claude Debussy

To turn from the articulate field of literature to the more emotive field of music is something of a knight's move, but it is eased by the fact that the period's most original musician found some of his inspiration in poetry and had an unusual gift for expressing in exact language his musical intentions.

Manuel Debussy and his wife Victorine were small tradespeople, who ran a china shop in pretty St-Germain-en-Laye. A former regular soldier, Manuel Debussy had dashing good looks but was weak and ineffective. Victorine, daughter of a wheelwright, was intelligent and ambitious for her children, the eldest of whom was christened Claude-Achille, Achille being her husband's heroic-sounding second name. In 1866, when Claude-Achille was four, the Debussys sold their china shop and moved to nearby Paris, where Manuel became a ledger accountant and fathered more children. Madame Debussy was of a nervous disposition. She found the duties of impoverished motherhood very onerous and sent all her children at various stages to make protracted stays with kinsfolk. Claude-Achille went to an aunt in Cannes, where his formal education suffered but his musical training began, with piano lessons from a teacher named Cerutti.

Debussy was a shy, dreamy, churlish boy but his mother detected quality and, when he returned to Paris, sent him for piano lessons to Madame Maute, a pupil of Chopin and mother-in-law of the poet Verlaine. Under this doubly artistic lady the boy made such good proress he entered the Conservatoire de Paris at eleven. There he won a second prize for piano but got bad marks for harmony. He read Hans Andersen and Dickens, his favourite being *Bleak House*. Occasionally he accompanied his father to performances of Donizetti's *The Daughter of the Regiment*, a favourite with the ex-soldier, and other light operas.

Debussy's amiable composition teacher, Ernest Guiraud, between games of billiards in the local café, gave his pupil advice. Entering for the coming *prix de Rome*, let him sacrifice his personal tastes to the academicism of the day. Debussy duly composed an elegant pastiche of Massenet, the cantata *L'Enfant Prodigue*, which won him the coveted prize of three years in Rome.

They proved a sad disappointment. Debussy was at twenty-five already solitary and independent. He disliked the regimented life of the Villa Médicis, its insipid food and equally insipid musical academicism. At least two of his obligatory compositions were rejected by the powers that be as unsatisfactory. Debussy believed he was wasting his time and at the end of his second year walked out.

Back in Paris Debussy led a Bohemian life, frequenting Le Chat Noir café, where Henri Rivière – no relation to Jacques – staged a shadow theatre and Madame Maute's son played the piano, and cabaret where Yvette Guilbert sang songs that would have made a monkey blush. Here he indulged a great fondness for Welsh rarebit washed down by pale ale, chain-smoked and talked, for preference, about Symbolist poetry.

He was a striking-looking man. He had a quite markedly protruding brow, modelled as though by

Rodin's thumbs and partly hidden by a fringe of black hair, pudgy cheeks, red sensual lips and a black beard. He dressed smartly, favouring green bow ties. With his often fierce expression he looked like an Assyrian. But behind lay a warm sensuousness that could be very tender. He loved cats, and later when he had his own home kept grey ones.

He had a few friends, original people mainly. One was Erik Satie, a little, prematurely bald man in bowler hat and galoshes, short-sighted eyes mischievous behind pince-nez, an odd blend of sharp intelligence and child-like naivety. In Venice he and Bakst observed the strutting, head-dipping pigeons. 'What are they doing?' asked Bakst, and Satie answered, 'Looking for messages to carry.' As a composer he had little success but comforted himself by saying, 'The public venerates boredom, for boredom is mysterious and profound.' Though he was more interested in adding to his un-rivalled collection of umbrellas than in finding a wife, Satie was at present courting Suzanne Valadon, mother of Maurice Utrillo and herself a painter.

A second close friend was Pierre Louÿs who, fasci-nated by the decadence of Hellenistic Alexandria, sought to re-live its pleasures in Algeria and to describe them in hothouse poems and novels. Louÿs for a time had sought the company of Gide, but Louÿs was hetero-sexual and amoral, and on the latter issue the more seri-ous Gide split with him. Debussy, who had few moral inhibitions, found Louys' quest of 'pagan pleasures' much to his taste and in 1897 set to music Louÿs' *Chansons de Bilitis*. Their friendship was to last well into the new century.

Debussy at twenty-six, answering another of the ever-popular questionnaires, said his favourite occupa-tion was reading, with a blended cigarette between his fingers, his favourite virtue pride, his favourite quality in a man will, and in a woman charm. His idea of happiness? To love. He preferred sensuous women with generous curves and determined character.

Debussy's first mistress was a grey-eyed blonde, Gabrielle Dupont. Then he fell for a singer, Thérèse Roger, and planned to marry her, only to break off the engagement and return to Gabrielle. They lived together until 1899, when, with Erik Satie as witness, Debussy married Lily Texier, seamstress daughter of a Burgundy station-master, whose abilities included a gift, prized by her husband, for making a good cup of tea. Tea mattered in a household where the income came from Debussy's piano lessons; as the composer put it, on the top floor of 58 rue Cardinet 'there was more love than beefsteaks'.

Another forceful young woman whom Debussy much liked was Camille Claudel. Her liaison with Rodin precluded any amorous attachment, but Debussy seems to have enjoyed watching her deft hands at work on clay in the *art nouveau* style, blending the human figure with fronds, flowers, flowing water. Debussy loved her *La Valse*, an example of which he bought and kept on his chimneypiece, and *La Petite Châtelaine*, a child gazing with puzzled eyes into the unknown. He also saw in Camille's studio her group called *Vagues*, water lifting to take the shape of young women, which Philippe Berthelot of the Quai d'Orsay was to buy, and the Japanese sea-prints of Hokusai.

Debussy's first important orchestral work, *Prélude à L'Après-Midi d'un Faune*, owes much to the composer's sensual nature and something to his friendships. Though the title comes from a Mallarmé poem, the notion of a compound earth deity is close to the bronzes Camille was making, while beings capable of enjoying pleasure without remorse were a favourite topic with Louÿs – he was soon to start a steamy periodical, *Le*

Centaure. Gide contributed to *Le Centaure* and his early prose poem, *Les Nourritures Terrestres*, published in 1896, which claimed that the earthly Paradise still exists for those willing to enjoy the pleasures of the flesh, is an almost exact literary equivalent of the flutes, warbling clarinet and harp arpeggio in Debussy's voluptuous score.

Debussy wanted to move on to human emotion, to people loving and clashing – in short to opera. And whoever, in the 1890s, wished to write opera had to come to terms with Wagner. Aged twenty-six, Debussy went to Bayreuth to listen to mythology and what he considered the sometimes forced recurrence of leitmotifs, but he said with a sigh to Louÿs, 'I don't see how one can go beyond *Tristan.*' He claimed to know the score of that opera by heart; later he came to like even more the Good Friday music from *Parsifal*.

Since Bayreuth and its revelation that opera could be almost a religious experience, Debussy had been gaining confidence. He believed it might be possible to learn from the stupendous German yet remain true to French moderation and elegance. He decided he wanted to treat a serious subject not overpoweringly but naturally, almost simply. He believed that since word, gesture and sound spring from a single source, all must be informed by a single mood.

After many hesitations Debussy chose as his libretto a *Tristan*-style play set in an undefined past age by Maurice Maeterlinck, about adultery ending in death. But whereas Maeterlinck concentrated on Destiny, Doom, and the Darker Domains of cosmic symbolism, Debussy intended to focus on character, particularly on the now hesitant, now daring, always tender love between Pelléas and Mélisande. By 1896 he had composed a piano score, but this was only the first stage in what was to prove a long ordeal.

Of the Paris Opéra Arnold Bennett wrote: 'From the tenor to the vendor of programmes there are twelve hundred priests and priestesses of art in the superb building. A few may be artists. But it is absolutely certain that all are bureaucrats.' Except that he called the building a railway station outside and a Turkish baths inside, Debussy would have agreed, and nowhere was bureaucracy so fossilized as in the choosing of operas. *Faust, Carmen* and *Manon*, plus works by Puccini and Verdi – these were the staple, because proven draws. Among the moderns Alfred Bruneau's operas were performed, because he used libretti by best-sellers such as Zola, and in February 1900 *Louise* was staged. This prettification of a Montmartre 'where every heart has a duty to love', by a younger contemporary, Gustave Charpentier, Debussy sat through in misery, wincing at its 'anæmic ditties' and maudlin sentiment; he winced still more when *Louise* was received with wild applause and, next day, with rapturous reviews.

Pelléas et Mélisande was the very opposite of safe. Being innovative, untopical and devoid of catchy tunes, it struck the bureaucrats as exceedingly risky and for long Debussy despaired of getting it performed. 'People don't like Beauty,' he complained, 'because it's irksome, it doesn't suit their mean little souls; with more works like *Louise* it will be impossible to pull them out of the mud.'

In June 1901 Debussy was in debt, and with doctors' bills to pay, for Lily had contracted tuberculosis. But with the turn of the century had come some appointments and a ray or two of adventure. The recently appointed director of the Opéra Comique, Albert Carré, admired *Pelléas* and decided to risk staging it. Debussy, overjoyed, hastened to orchestrate his piano score, while Carré and Messager, the likeable, intelligent conductor of the Opéra orchestra, looked for a singer capable of taking the demanding part of Mélisande.

Mary Garden was a pretty blonde Scots-born soprano with what was then the unusual quality in a singer of being both small-boned and slim. On the night of 13 April she had become a star by standing in for the usual soprano, who had lost her voice, in the role of Louise. She was a sweet, unassuming girl; Carré and Messager not only admired her voice but both in their different ways quickly fell in love with her. They persuaded Mary to come to Messager's Paris drawing-room with other potential cast members to hear Debussy play his score.

'As I listened,' Mary was to recall, 'I seemed to become someone else, someone inside me whose language and soul were akin to mine. When Debussy got to the fourth act I could no longer look at my score for tears . . . and as he played the death of Mélisande, I burst into the most awful sobbing, and Madame Messager began to sob along with me, and both of us fled into the next room.'

Having played to the end, Debussy turned. 'Mesdames et Messieurs, there you have my *Pelléas et Mélisande*. Everyone must forget that he is a singer before he can sing the music of Debussy.' He murmured a quick '*Au revoir*' and without another word was gone.

For a comparative newcomer like Mary Garden Debussy's cryptic command was awesome. Nevertheless, having studied her part, Mary Garden went along to attend for a trial in the Opéra rehearsal room. When she arrived after lunch Debussy was already there. After a quick exchange of greetings Debussy seated himself at the piano and Mary opened her score. 'We did the first act, Debussy singing the role of Golaud. His voice was husky and not strong . . . but he was a magnificent pianist. So there he sat, singing the part of Golaud, playing the piano and never making a word of comment. When we came to Pelléas, he sang that too, and all the other roles save mine.

'Then we came to the Tower scene. I was singing my lines when he got up abruptly and walked out of the room. I stayed a little while, waiting, quite bewildered, feeling I had offended him in some mysterious way and began to prepare myself for the shock of not singing Mélisande. I put on my hat and was about to leave when a boy came in. "Miss Garden, Monsieur Carré would like to see you in the office." When I walked in, there sat Debussy with Monsieur Carré. Rising from his chair, he came up to me and took both my hands in his.'

'Where were you born?' asked Debussy, and when Mary told him in Scotland, 'To think you had to come from the cold far North to create my Mélisande – because that's what you're going to do, Mademoiselle.'

He turned to Carré and raised his hands. 'I have nothing to tell her . . . What a strange person she is, this child.'

With that he fell silent, in his curious detached way took his hat and, mumbling 'Goodbye', walked out of Carré's office. Debussy had a disconcerting habit of suddenly walking out.

Maurice Maeterlinck had moved from Belgium to Paris. A tall, heavy man with a flattish, good-looking face and long, sleek hair, he was the same age as Debussy and had recently become famous with his poetic but well-researched *Life of the Bees*. He shared his apartment with a Norman girl, Georgette Leblanc, sister of the author of the Arsène Lupin mystery novels. Georgette had a good voice and had recently scored a success in the role of Carmen. Like Mary Garden she was slim, but in other ways her opposite, having a hard face with hollow cheeks and a domineering manner, which she used in order to get her way with Maeterlinck. This lady had set her heart on singing Mélisande.

In May 1901 Debussy had gone to Maeterlinck's flat and played him the piano score of *Pelléas*. Maeterlinck, who was not in the least musical, fell asleep before the end. What happened when he awoke is uncertain. Georgette says Maeterlinck proposed her for the leading role and Debussy agreed. Perhaps at that early stage, fearing a change of heart by Carré, and not wishing to alienate the famous author, Debussy did show undue acquiescence; at any rate Maeterlinck came to believe that his mistress would sing Mélisande.

On 29 December 1901 Maeterlinck opened his newspaper and on the arts page read that the Opéra had begun rehearsals of *Pelléas* with Mary Garden in the role of Mélisande. Urged on doubtless by his angry mistress, Maeterlinck stormed down to the theatre and broke in on Debussy and Carré. 'I won't have Mary Garden singing Mélisande,' he roared.

Surprise, consternation, alarm beset the two musicians. Debussy said he had no recollection whatever of having promised the role to Georgette; however, Maeterlinck, famous and influential, obviously had to be handled with care. Discussions ensued. Debussy suggested that Georgette should sing an act of *Pelléas* before a jury of musicians who had heard Mary, and they would choose. Georgette agreed, she sang the designated act and the jury decided they preferred the Scottish girl.

Maeterlinck still raged. He threatened a lawsuit, only to discover that in France a composer has more say over a joint work than a librettist. Believing his honour to be at stake, Maeterlinck then challenged Debussy to a duel.

Debussy was by no means an athlete, and being a heavy smoker had poor wind. He heard, moreover, that

Maeterlinck performed well with the sword. He decided not to live up to the name Achille. But he did agree when the obliging Carré, a reserve officer, proposed to pick up the gauntlet for him.

Maeterlinck had the support of Lugné-Poe of the raven head, who had originally produced the play *Pelléas*, and he now practised sword thrusts with Lugné in the latter's garden. However, for some unexplained reason the duel did not take place; instead Maeterlinck stormed up to Debussy's humble fifth-floor flat and threatened him with his heavy cane. Debussy could brave the critics, even the Opéra establishment, but this very large, angry Fleming with his raised weapon almost frightened the life out of him. He suddenly felt faint, collapsed into a chair and was revived by smelling salts from the ever-solicitous Lily.

Maeterlinck might write about the Bluebird of Happiness and childhood dreams but in real life he had a streak of meanness, and on that Georgette played. In mid-April 1902, sixteen days before the first performance, Maeterlinck published a letter in *Le Figaro*. By refusing his choice of actress, wrote Maeterlinck, Debussy and Carré 'shut me out from my own work which, thenceforward, they treated as occupied territory. Arbitrary and absurd cuts have been made . . . Bereft of all control over my work, I am reduced to hoping it will be an immediate and complete fiasco.'

Paris loved – still loves – an artistic scandal. Opinions polarized and hardened for or against *Pédéastre et Médisance*, as one wag called the opera. At the dress rehearsal an anti-Debussy faction handed out programmes lampooning the episodes, so that many in the audience approached the opera in ribald mood. When Mary Garden sang, '*Je ne suis pas heureuse*' with a slight Scottish accent, the audience mimicked her and when Pelléas caressed her golden hair, '*Il fait le coiffeur*' someone shouted, and laughter followed. During the intervals more than one fist-fight took place.

These were not the best of auspices for the first night on Monday 30 April. Debussy could not bring himself to watch and remained in Carré's office backstage, chain-smoking, while Carré busied himself with last-minute exhortations, hoping that the previous night's disturbance would not be repeated.

The opera is set in an island castle. Tender, guileless Mélisande has been tricked into marriage with Golaud. Golaud's half-brother, Pelléas, falls in love with her and she with him. Golaud surprises the guilty pair, kills the one and wounds the other, who dies afterwards.

To this unoriginal nineteenth-century subject Debussy brought freshness, sincerity, depth of feeling and all the resources of early twentieth-century musical technique. Instead of self-contained melodic arias he created what he termed an overall dramatic melody, of which the characters' singing and recitative are parts. He put in no dances, little noise, few perfect cadences, but he did put in silences, especially when Mélisande is on stage. Power he achieved not with a battery of horns and timpani but through restraint and reticence.

The first-night audience gave Pelléas a fair hearing. Between puzzlement and wonder they listened responsively to the lines of greatest emotion: '*On s'embarquerait sans le savoir, et l'on ne reviendrait plus*'; '*Si j'étais Dieu, j'aurais pitié du cœur des hommes*', and when the curtain fell on the last of twelve scenes it was plain they were deeply divided.

'Sung conversation' was the summing-up by an influential writer of the realist school, Jules Renard. 'I waited for a rhyme that never came. A succession of notes like the noise of the wind . . . I prefer the wind. In music I like a tune that sounds familiar. The scenery was beautiful, but as Lucien Guitry reminded me, it's bad business to put beautiful scenery in a show that's sure to flop, and as he sat through the piece Guitry heaved enormous sighs of boredom.' Another of the old school, Théodore Dubois, went still further – he forbade his Conservatoire students to listen to so unorthodox a work.

The young and musically more refined felt differently. Maurice Ravel attended every performance, Romain Rolland called it the most original opera since opera was invented, while the poet Fernand Gregh wrote:

> As the gentlemen of 1636 all identified with the Cid, and the romantics of 1830 with Hernani, so we young people saw ourselves as Pelléas. The most moving lines were carried by Debussy's music into our lives and even today serve as passwords . . . We left the theatre heads ablaze, drunk with harmonies, laden with musical and visual images, even with ideas. For a masterpiece is an intellectual centre from which radiate all kinds of theories and thoughts.

Gregh's view was to prove correct: *Pelléas* quickly became a favourite and by Christmas 1906 would reach a fiftieth performance.

At the turn of the century the state of French orchestral music looked dim: Franck was dead, Saint-Saëns in his mid-sixties, Fauré and Satie were writing mainly chamber or vocal pieces. Better work was being done across the Rhine. But in 1900 Debussy carried a stage further the instrumental colour and rich harmonies of *L'Après-Midi* by composing *Nocturnes*, three short pieces – '*Nuages*', '*Fêtes*', '*Sirènes*' – and after his success with

Pelléas he began to contemplate a full-scale orchestral work.

Debussy had a horror of feeling shut in, of crowds, of being too hot. The music of his day he considered too closeted. He felt an urge to open windows wide. Pelléas and Mélisande long to get away from their suffocating island castle to the sea, and that was Debussy's own wish.

As a boy he had responded to the quiet Mediterranean at Cannes, later he had gazed on the fiercer North Sea from the Brittany ports of St Lunaire and Cancale. If he weren't a composer, he once said, he would have liked to be a sailor. Certainly he found deep satisfaction in the movement of water, and in the movement of Nature generally. He saw Nature in early twentieth-century terms, no longer as hostile lumps of inert, heavy matter, but as pulsating atoms, each with its energy composed of movement. It was the privilege of musicians, Debussy wrote, 'to give rhythm to the universe's immense palpitations'. He compared the energy within Nature to a music 'that produces the movement of waters, the curves taken by shifting breezes; nothing is more musical than a sunset'.

It was when he came to putting such feelings into sound that Debussy showed his originality. He disliked the birdsong, lowing cattle and storm in Beethoven's Sixth Symphony. Music, he said, 'is not the expression of a sentiment, it is the sentiment itself'. He wanted to get through to the bare flesh of emotion – *his* emotion as he watched the sea: 'truly the part of Nature that most cuts you down to size'.

Debussy began composing the three Symphonic Sketches, *La Mer*, at the home of his wife Lily's parents in the Burgundy hills during summer 1903. But the sea was present vicariously in reproductions of paintings by his favourite Turner and of Hokusai's *The Hollow of the Wave off Kanagawa*, first shown him by Camille Claudel. Debussy finished the score on Sunday, 5 March 1905, at six in the evening.

The apparent asymmetry and tonal instability of *La Mer*, unprecedented in French music at that date, led some to speak of Debussy the dreamer, jotting down sensations haphazard, regardless of classical proportions. But a recent analysis by a musicologist, Roy Howat, has shown how cannily *La Mer* is constructed, in particular how Debussy, perhaps by design, perhaps in subconscious response to his training, makes use of the Golden Section. This is the method of dividing a fixed length in two so that the ratio of the shorter part to the longer equals the ratio of the longer part to the entire length. The dividing-point approximates to a little under two-thirds of the whole length.

The Golden Section is found in some natural objects, such as certain sea shells, and in much visual art, for example in Hokusai's *The Hollow of the Wave*, which Debussy thought relevant enough to reproduce on the cover of his score. It lends a work of art an underlying pattern that viewers or audiences of any civilization appear to have found, or continue to find, specially satisfying.

The first sketch of *La Mer*, 'From Dawn to Noon on the Sea', comprises an Introduction, two Principal Sections, a Transition and a Coda. Each is constructed differently, with its own themes, keys and metres, yet, as Roy Howat shows, the Introduction and two Principal Sections consist of ABCBA arch forms, suggestive of a wave, and these are structured according to the Golden Section. In the first Principal Section the turning-point of the arch occurs at unit 66 out of 107 units. The Golden Section is also found to determine the climaxes of the dynamic shape of the Sketch as a whole. It also underlies the Third Sketch, 'Dialogue of the Sea and the

Wind'. The tidal motion pervading all the sections is neither fortuitous nor chaotic, it results from the careful application of soundly classical proportions, though these are concealed under a rich and varied texture.

La Mer received its first performance at a Paris concert on 15 October 1905. Its fluid rhythm and polyphonal harmony were too innovative for most, one critic complaining: 'I don't hear or see or feel the sea', by which he meant the stock maritime equivalents. But when Debussy conducted it at two subsequent concerts in January 1908 the piece came into its own, and was applauded in particular by the discerning Chinese-born critic, Louis Laloy: 'Without in any way abandoning his delicate sensitiveness, perhaps unequalled in the world of art, his style has become concise, decided, positive, complete.'

Though not as poor as Péguy, Debussy had to earn his living the hard way, teaching the piano. By one of his pupils, a certain Raoul Bardac, he was invited to the Bardac home near the Bois de Boulogne; there he met Sigismond, a financier, and his wife Emma, née Moyse, of Bordeaux. This lady was an excellent amateur musician; she had received the dedication of Gabriel Fauré's Verlaine song-cycle, La Bonne Chanson, and had been the first to sing it in public. In 1903 she was aged about forty-one, a couple of years older than Debussy, distinguished-looking though not beautiful, well dressed, cultivated. She no longer loved her elderly husband and she appreciated, as did many women, Debussy's gipsy good looks. Later, to an acquaintance who described Debussy as 'so softly affectionate', Emma replied, 'No, Madame, he is cuddly.'

Debussy and Lily had shared four years of impoverished marriage, and one year of Lily's illness. According to Mary Garden, Madame Debussy was sweet and looked after her husband attentively as though he were a child. But she was not musical, not very sensitive: she slammed doors and her voice grated on Debussy. Emma on the other hand had style and could talk intelligently about his work. Emma apears to have taken the first step and Debussy, whose record of faithfulness was not good, responded.

By himself Debussy would probably not have dared to propose elopement to a social superior with two grown-up children. A single divorce was scandal enough, a double one would be socially ostracizing. There was the money question too. If Emma left Sigismond she would suffer financially, and Debussy's earnings were small.

Emma seems to have wished to take the risk. She had a very rich uncle Osiris, who was old; when he died he would, she believed, leave her a substantial sum. Until then they would somehow manage.

On Bastille Day 1904 Debussy left Paris with Emma and took the boat to Jersey. They spent a holiday on the island and when it was over Debussy did not return to Lily. Deciding she could not face life without Debussy, Lily bought a revolver, tried it out by firing a shot into the wall, then pointed it, as she thought, at her heart and pulled the trigger.

That same afternoon Debussy received a note delivered by messenger: 'When you get this, Claude, I shall be dead. Please come to me. I want no hands to touch me but yours.' Debussy rushed to the flat and found Lily prostrate amid neighbours, but still breathing – the bullet had entered under her left breast and missed the heart. 'Claude,' she whispered, 'if you're coming back to me, take me to hospital. If not, leave me here to die.'

Without a word Debussy rushed down the stairs and called an ambulance. At the hospital, after two hours' wait, the surgeon came to Debussy, now accompanied by friends. 'We are happy to tell you that your wife will live.'

Debussy looked up at the doctor, Mary Garden recalled, 'and in his husky voice muttered just one word, "*Merci*". Then he walked out of the hospital and out of the lives of us all.'

Sigismond left the Bardac house at 24 Square du Bois-de-Boulogne and Claude Debussy moved in. For the first time in his life he had elegant and comfortable surroundings. He had a big workroom with a fireplace and orange curtains. On the mantel he placed Camille's bronze, *La Valse*, and a Buddha; on his work-table a Chinese wooden frog, called Arkel, which he believed brought him good luck. For if Debussy had no belief in God he had a strong belief in certain superstitions and, for example, would never cut the string on a parcel, convinced it would bring bad luck. While composing at a black upright piano he chain-smoked, rolling his own cigarette in ungummed paper and bringing it to his mouth, a friend noticed, in a flowing, curved movement, like a line in a drawing by his favourite Leonardo. At intervals he would dash off an affectionate note to be taken by the maid to Emma in another part of the house, signed 'Your old pianist'. If he and Emma wished to go to the centre of Paris, a car and chauffeur were waiting.

Debussy's desertion of Lily, his divorce from her and later his marriage to Emma in 1908 were censured by all his friends save Erik Satie and the critic Laloy, and by most of his acquaintances save Proust, who described the second marriage as 'a hot-house necessary for the full development of his genius'. Art the absolute . . .

Hothouse for genius or not, Debussy undoubtedly loved Emma. The deep affection suffusing his letters is unmistakable. Nevertheless, one does not marry a socially superior, well-off lady without having to make certain sacrifices. Emma had an ailing mother living with her whom Debussy mentions caustically as being in 'a state of suspended animation' and in summer he who loathed crowds was hauled off by Emma to noisy fashionable seaside resorts. In 1905 a daughter had been born, Claude-Emma; Debussy doted on her but a nurse had to be found and wages too. Uncle Osiris finally died, but left his millions to the Institut Pasteur. The big house, the servants, the motor-car and chauffeur had to be paid for, and the marriage that was to solve Debussy's money troubles soon began to aggravate them.

Debussy had deeper worries as well. Something in his temperament compelled him continually to wish to break new ground: 'My desire always to go further and beyond is for me the bread and wine of life.' We shall find this drive again; we have already seen it in Picasso, for example, and in both men it was supplemented by an army of critics clamouring for innovation. They were a sharp, noisy, impatient lot, the Paris critics, quick to spot signs of a creative artist repeating himself.

Debussy had in mind to write a large-scale musical work using words from Poe's 'Fall of the House of Usher', in which the castle-home of a decadent old family collapses and crushes the family's last member and the tomb of his sister. But somehow he could make no headway. Everything about 'Usher' belongs to the *fin du 19ème* and to Debussy's taste, as an adolescent, for the darker side of Symbolism. It went clear against the grain of the new, more affirmative artistic values, and this surely is why Debussy dried up, and why in 1909 we find him confiding his wretchedness to a friend: 'One gives orders to a person who doesn't obey and this person is oneself! How difficult it is to say, "You're

behaving like an idiot"; one goes on dreaming in a
vicious circle: like sad wooden fairground horses, with
no music and no riders.'

While 'Usher' refused to take shape, critics complained that he had bartered his genius for bourgeois
bliss, and bills to be paid poured in. Debussy decided to
undertake conducting engagements abroad, uncon-
genial but well paid, and in 1910, while he was on tour
in Vienna, he received a letter from someone he'd never
met which was to set the fairground horses turning
again and to stir him to a new kind of music.

Gabriele d'Annunzio was the most famous living Italian writer. A sensuous poet – 'Sing of biting the fruits of
earth with sound white hungry teeth' – a dramatist, a
novelist whose heroes are self-seeking and amoral, and
also a self-styled Great Lover, who had wooed, won and
discarded the actress Eleonora Duse, d'Annunzio was a
short, strongly-built man with bald pate, prominent
eyes and a fair beard, pointed and scented. He had
lately moved to France in order to escape his debtors
and there his keen nose for the latest fashion had
picked up the scent of Péguy's poem on Jeanne d'Arc
and Claudel's *Tidings*, not yet performed but much discussed.

D'Annunzio's letter from Arcachon to Debussy may
be given in full, since its style points up by contrast
Parisian restraint:

> *Mon cher Maître*,
> One day long ago, on the hill of Settignano
> where the most melodious of Tuscan sculptors
> was born, Gabriel Mourey [translator of Poe
> and Swinburne] spoke to me in moving terms
> about you and about Tristan [l'Hermite, lines
> by whom Debussy had set to music]. I knew
> your music and already loved it. I belonged to

a little group in Florence where certain serious-minded artists played your music and welcomed your innovations.

Then as now I suffered from not being able to write music for my tragedies. And I dreamed of being able to meet you.

This summer, while I was drafting a *Mystère* that has long been in my mind, a lady friend sang to me the most beautiful of your songs with the spiritual intensity they require. My writing, as it took shape, trembled at the sound, sometimes. But I did not dare to hope for your music.

Do you like my poetry?

In Paris, a fortnight ago, I wanted to come and knock at your door. Someone told me you were out of town.

Now I can no longer keep silent. Will you see me and hear me speak about this piece of writing and my dream?

Send me a brief word at once and I shall come.

At least I shall have the joy of expressing to you my gratitude for the beautiful thoughts that you have sometimes fostered in my agitated mind.

Gabriele d'Annunzio.

To this somewhat disingenuous letter – d'Annunzio had already unsuccessfully approached two other composers – Debussy replied courteously and when the Frenchman returned to Paris, d'Annunzio called on him. His *Mystère*, he explained, was a ballet-drama, libretto in French unrhymed octo-syllabics by himself, depicting the conversion, trial and glorious martyrdom of the Roman officer Sebastian. The name part would

232

be played by a woman, who would both dance and speak in recitative. There would be trendy allusions to Frazer's recent comparison, in *The Golden Bough*, of Christ to Adonis. The work would be long, in five 'mansions' or acts, but the music should last a total of about one hour, and it was this music, which would blend with words, dance, drama and action, that the Italian asked Debussy to compose.

The subject could hardly have been further from doom-laden, despairing 'Usher'. Debussy, moreover, was not a Christian: he could not, he said, abide the idea of a God over him or of being one of a crowd in an afterlife. But he found himself responding to the 'intense life' of the libretto – Sebastian dances on burning coals, Christ's shroud is unfolded before him by a woman possessed – and to Sebastian's heroism, an equivalent of Debussy's own long struggle for recognition, and indeed to the affirmative mood, for in the last scene Sebastian is welcomed to heaven by choirs of angels. Debussy agreed enthusiastically to write the music.

He began on 9 January 1911 with the musically most important third act, where Diocletian questions Sebastian, is captivated by his beauty and offers to make him a god if he recants; Sebastian stands firm while the women of Byblos hail him in his suffering as Adonis and try to crush him under their heavy jewels and finery. Debussy sent his music to d'Annunzio page by page, corrected in pencil, for the work was due to go into rehearsal in May. The part of Sebastian would be taken by a Russian dancer, Ida Rubinstein.

As word got about that the music was brilliant, singers clamoured for a part. One evening the vocal director's doorbell rang; the maid opened and reported: 'Please, sir, it's a lady come to see if the Marquis of Saint-Sébasto's heart is full [*cœur* for *chœur*].' In the opposite direction Archbishop Amette, very popular because of the help he had given the homeless in the massive Seine flood of 1910, objected to the androgynous quality of this Sebastian and urged his flock to stay away.

Le Tout Paris none the less filled the big Châtelet theatre for the first night of *The Martyrdom of St Sebastian*. Even fifteen years earlier the idea of huge resources and all the best talent being given to such a subject would have been unthinkable. Since then Gide's Alissa, Claudel's Violaine and Péguy's Jeanne had prepared the way for this, the most ample lyric treatment of redemptive suffering. Ida Rubinstein in her scarab-like armour danced faultlessly through the very long work, the audience's attention being held by miracles, magic, lavish costumes and spectacular stage effects; indeed Henri Ghéon complained that they obscured Sebastian's inner drama. Some of the Italian's imagery, too, grated on Parisians' sensibility: to the mother of the prisoners he is guarding Sebastian says, 'I know I shall touch the red heart in your dry breast, swelling now with milk of sorrow.'

These and other imperfections were more than outweighed by Debussy's score: 'a melodic precision,' wrote the composer Gaston Carraud, 'a breadth of inspiration, a boldness of colouring and accent, such as Debussy has never before exhibited'. Much admired were the recurring Sebastian theme – a distinctive, spread dominant eleventh chord – the moment in Act II when the Magic Chamber floods with light, the voice of the possessed woman 'whose song floats on the air like a loosened scarf', the sensual lamentations of the women of Byblos who warble of grief and love like wounded cooing doves, the dazzling magnificence of Paradise, with its fierce act of faith and the savage joy of its psalms. For Elisabeth de Gramont, 'the music makes you believe in heaven since it takes you there'.

Before and after the success of *Sebastian* Debussy was making important innovations in music for the piano. He achieved harmonies of hitherto unprecedented colour and complexity and in *'Pagodes'*, one of *Estampes*, written in 1903, he used a Chinese five-note scale, reminiscent of the Cambodian and Javanese dances he had seen at the Exhibitions of 1889 and 1900. To most of his piano pieces he gave a title – a clue less to the subject than to the mood engendered in the composer by his subject – and many of these concern water: *'Jardins sous la Pluie'*, *'Ondine'*, *'Reflets dans l'Eau'*. Debussy conveys in quite a new way the nuances of a refined sensibility before the half-movements of water in the half-tones of sunshine or moonlight. It was here that he found an absolute, constantly alluring, constantly eluding final definition. As he once remarked, he made a religion of Nature's mysteries.

Bergson, incidentally, was very fond of Debussy's music and so much enjoyed the first night of *Pelléas* that he returned for the second performance. He told his friend and translator, Benrubi, that an article by Paul Landormy pointing out the affinity between Bergsonism and the music of Debussy was on the whole correct. According to Landormy the affinity lies in 'the infinitely delicate task of discovering the freshness and spontaneity of feeling, unencumbered by the interpretations of common sense.'

The theme of a cathedral submerged by the waves had been treated quite often by poets, for example in Rimbaud's *Illuminations*, and had become almost a stock metaphor for a residual Christianity, invisible but not wholly silenced; because of this perhaps, and almost certainly because it was such an eloquent image of the mysterious intermediate worlds he loved, Debussy felt drawn to the theme. One of his early songs, to his own words, refers to bell-buoys, 'carillons of the floating churches, angelus of the waves'; but his master-piece here is the tenth of the *Préludes*: 'The Cathedral Submerged by the Sea'. Some of the harmonies in this and other *Préludes* seemed at the time bewilderingly discordant, but in his piano music, as in *La Mer*, Debussy never really renounced the classical tradition, unlike Schoenberg for instance, who in 1908 broke through into atonality.

In a city mainly concerned with adult pleasures, Debussy is a pleasing example of an artist who catered for children. He loved talking and playing with his daughter, Chou-chou as he called her, he wrote her charming letters, quoted her sayings to friends, bought children's books for her – mainly English, for the French are deficient in this genre – and wrote music to please her. *Children's Corner Suite*, which includes 'The Golliwog's Cakewalk', he dedicated to Chou-chou.

One of the books Debussy bought was Barrie's *Peter Pan in Kensington Gardens*, with illustrations by Arthur Rackham. His 'Fairies are exquisite dancers' depicts a fairy dancing on a thread of spider web, while the spider plays a bass fiddle. This inspired the sixteenth of Debussy's *Préludes*, published in 1913, and provides an example of Debussy transmuting the tenuous delicacy of visual image into the subtle tones of the piano.

In his vocal music also during these years of maturity Debussy reached the heights. As a young man he had set to music Verlaine and Mallarmé, but a change in taste at the turn of the century brought much earlier writers into favour, the chanteuse Yvette Guilbert, for example, forsaking bawdy songs for medieval ballads. In May 1910 Debussy wrote *Trois Ballades de François Villon*, the second of which, addressed to Our Lady by Villon's mother, a poor old woman, is particularly admired, a

modal melody in the vocal part alternating with a hesi-
tating, psalm-like recitative.

Of no less high quality is '*Auprès de cette grotte
sombre*', the first of three songs with words from *Le
Promenoir des deux Amants*, a deceptively simple poem
set near water by the early seventeenth-century writer
Tristan l'Hermite. In the opinion of one connoisseur of
Debussy, Roland-Manuel, this is the most beautiful
French melody ever written.

Debussy had often drawn inspiration from literature
and, on the eve of the war, could rightly claim to have
returned it with interest. To mention only two, André
Gide found solace in playing Debussy's piano works, *La
Mer* became one of the models for the Vinteuil Septet in
A la Recherche du Temps Perdu, and one of the operas
Marcel Proust enjoyed on Théâtrephone was *Pelléas et
Mélisande*.

Throughout these years of maturity Debussy drew on
a pool of values from which not only writers but, as we
shall see, non-literary men of influence, including
statesmen, also drew. They include an affirmative attitude to life, a response to the flux of Nature such as
Claudel shows in his *Five Great Odes*, and to some
degree a recognition of the redemptive value of suffering. Moreover, as Fernand Gregh had written à propos
Pelléas, a musical masterpiece is 'an intellectual centre
from which radiate all kinds of theories and thoughts',
and through his diverse masterpieces Debussy did
much to spread those values. Some of the ladies who
played his *Etudes* and *Préludes* on their drawing-room
piano, or sang his songs, and some of those who listened, learned what Gregh calls 'the passwords' of the
age. They would also have become more aware, through
the nuances of Debussy's music, of subtleties in the
world around them and of finer gradations of feeling.

CHAPTER 10

The Russian Connection

Among the city's foreign residents and visitors Parisians warmed particularly to the Russians, who often really did conform to our stereotyped image of what they would be doing in that place and period: sailors from the visiting Imperial fleet flocking to Montmartre cafés to enjoy red wine from the bottle and chant Cossack songs, or Grand Dukes, Princes and Imperial Army officers drinking champagne from crystal glasses in Maxim's and tossing louis d'or to their pretty lady friends to retrieve under the raspberry-coloured banquettes. On leaving the restaurant these larger-than-life men tipped Gérard the doorman so lavishly that he was able to retire on his savings to a château in the Pyrenees.

Parisians when they chose could be wild, but rarely on the scale of these Russians. A group of officers would hire a private room, imbibe prodigiously, turn out the lights, then blaze away with their revolvers, causing considerable damage to the furnishings for which their equerries paid handsomely, and sometimes to themselves. Prince Orloff, a valued resident, had been dismissed from the Imperial Army for challenging a German officer to a duel of liqueur glasses of Cointreau; after eighty glasses the German collapsed, but Orloff went on to drink one hundred and twelve – and walked away, unsteadily but beaming. Then there was Grand Duke Serge, who one evening presented his mistress, Augustine de Lierre, with a platter of oysters, and when

238

the lady opened these, to her surprise and delight in each she found one or more pearls, enough to make a valuable necklace.

No country is more interested in royalty than a Republic. The arrival of a member of the Imperial family, even if only to take tea at the Bristol on his way to Nice, was reported in France's Press with adulation. The Tsar's efforts to mend his ramshackle political structure were highly praised, and when he paid a state visit, boxes at the Comédie Française were requisitioned. The most famous of the demi-mondaines, La Belle Otéro, whose performance of the fandango on a table-top at Maxim's had made her the talk of the town, was one of those evicted. As the bedmate of at least three Kings on their visits to Paris, the Spanish dancer could afford a haughty line. Stopping before the Tsar, when he had taken his seat in the theatre, she said loudly, 'All right, I'll leave. But never again will I eat caviar.'

The favour paid by President Loubet to the Russian pavilion at the 1900 Exhibition has been noticed, while the name of the beautiful bridge he had inaugurated, Pont Alexander III, reminded those who crossed it that the Russians were not just colourful spenders but France's allies. Strong ones, surely: had not Russians achieved the near-impossible by obliging the great Napoleon to retreat!

Tsar Nicholas II decided in 1904 to expand militarily in Outer Mongolia. He seized Port Arthur on the Pacific. Japan considered her ties with Korea threatened and made war on Russia. Japan was inferior in numbers, Russia in training, equipment and communications.

The Tsar was in his palace playing a game of billiards when an aide whispered that his Navy Minister would like a word. 'This isn't the day I see my Navy Minister,' said the Tsar reprovingly and continued his game. The news the Minister had wished to impart was the sinking of the Imperial fleet at Tsushima.

Why had it been sunk? Partly because Grand Duke Alexis had been Admiral in charge of the navy budget. Over the years he had handed in reports for vast expenses, but no new Russian ship took the sea. Alexis's mistress was an actress named Bletta and after Russia's defeat, while Alexis withdrew to Paris, St Petersburgers referred to her diamond necklace as 'the Pacific fleet'.

That same ominous year, 1905, saw crowds in St Petersburg demonstrate angrily in favour of a more liberal constitution; troops opened fire, many in the crowd died: that was 'Bloody Sunday'. Down in Odessa sailors on the battleship *Potemkin* mutinied, and again men died.

Here was a major military upset combined with an alarming crack in the social fabric, and to no other country did the implications matter more than to France. Buoyed by her alliance with an apparently strong Russia, France had been pursuing a high-handed policy in the Mediterranean, and in this same year 1905 had been ruffled by Kaiser Wilhelm's landing in Tangier, described earlier, and his speech protesting that policy.

One might have expected a cool, grave scrutiny of the new situation and its dangers. Not so. In 1905 the French were enjoying prosperity. New inventions, we shall see, were engendering new industries. The renewal in literature and the arts and a flourishing theatre drew civilized visitors and their money from every continent. There was a tenacious view that the French had all the answers, that nothing could go wrong.

In the press, therefore, writers glossed over events in

Russia. They believed that by granting a Duma, or Parliament, the Tsar had satisfied internal grievances. As for the defeat, a well-known French general writing in *Revue des Deux Mondes* found it encouraging: the Japanese had shown what could be done by a force inferior in numbers but with good morale – the position of the French army vis-à-vis the German. One of the few practical lessons learned was that Lépine, the Prefect of Paris, attributing the Japanese victory to training in ju-jitsu, sent fifteen of his policemen to learn this martial art from a Parisian, Monsieur Regnier, who changed his name to Ré Nié.

What of the Paris bankers and financiers who, since the signing of the Russian alliance in 1893, had advanced money, some of which had disappeared into Grand Ducal pockets, some into the maw of bureaucracy, some to funding the Tsar's 'Great Experiment' of reforming education and workers' conditions? These men adopted an attitude of sang-froid, which filtered, as they hoped, into the press and prevented panic selling on the Bourse. But in the privacy of their boardrooms these men were very worried indeed. They and their clients had hundreds of millions of francs invested in Russia.

Against this background, in spring 1909, a Russian impresario arrived in Paris. Aged thirty-five, Serge Diaghilev was a strongly built man of medium height, with thick glossy black hair, full cheeks, dark intelligent eyes, the right tilted more than the left, sensuous lips, of which the lower slightly protruded, white teeth that showed often in his confident smile. The son of a cavalry officer, raised by a musical mother, at twenty-three he had found his vocation: 'I intend to be a Mæcenas. I have everything necessary except the money – but that will come.'

Come it had – from diverse sources, first to found a

241

periodical of the arts that had lasted six years, then to fund his work as a freelance impresario. Through his influential friend, Grand Duke Vladimir, Diaghilev had secured a subsidy from the Government to stage a festival of Russian music in Paris and, a year later, a festival of Russian opera. For 1909 he had scheduled his most ambitious project yet: taking to Paris a company to perform ballet. Then, in March, Grand Duke Vladimir died, the Imperial Government cancelled his subsidy, and this was why Serge Diaghilev had entered the drawing-room of perhaps the richest and certainly the haughtiest lady in Paris.

Elisabeth de Caraman-Chimay, as she was before her marriage, came from one of France's distinguished families, and with her straight back, high-bridged nose and cold dark eyes, looked the part. 'Beautiful lily, whose black pistils are your eyes,' wrote her poet cousin, Robert de Montesquiou. She had married handsome, red-bearded Comte Henri Greffulhe, a descendant of Louis XV and one of the Mailly sisters, and the heir of Dutch bankers. A Deputy and a home-lover, Henri Greffulhe had a big house in rue d'Astorg and a château, Boisboudran, where Elisabeth had made a Japanese Trianon, with red lacquer bridge, pagoda and a lawn on which perched bronze cranes. Henri liked to be in bed with his wife by 11.30 except when entertaining his equals, or royalty: he and Elisabeth had given dinner to King Edward VII and Queen Alexandra on their visit to Paris.

It took Proust three years to be invited to Elisabeth de Greffulhe's home; Diaghilev managed it in three weeks. The lady's first impression was that here was a shady adventurer. 'I kept wondering what on earth he wanted. There he sat, staring at one of the statues in my drawing-room. Suddenly he got up and began studying my pictures and, I must say, some of the things he said were extraordinarily interesting . . . When he went to the piano and began playing pieces by Russian composers I had never heard of, I began to understand him and why he had come.'

Diaghilev's first request to Comtesse Greffulhe had merely been that she add her name to the list of honorary presidents of his art festival. Now he had a request of wholly different magnitude. He wanted her husband to put up money – all the money – to bring a ballet company – dancers and all the attendant personnel, a total of eighty – from St Petersburg to Paris for a six-week season at the large and expensive Théâtre du Châtelet.

On the face of it Diaghilev's proposal was preposterous. Why should a shrewd French banker put up a quarter of a million francs to transport a troupe of foreigners to a city already brimful of artistic excellence? Why, that is, unless the bringing of these exotics would help to brighten influential Frenchmen's image of Russia, lately further clouded by the fact that the Duma of 1906, from which much had been expected, and the Duma of 1907 had both had to be dissolved. If Paris, which thought so largely in artistic terms, were to receive proof of Russia's excellence in one of the arts, that could have a threefold effect: raise from their current low level the value of Russian bonds, make it possible to float new loans to the ever-needy Bear, and restore credibility to France's expansionist foreign policy in the Mediterranean, where bankers and industrialists were waiting impatiently to scoop up big profits.

In any such dilemma a banker will consult fellow-bankers and this is what Comte Greffulhe now did. He spoke to colleagues who knew more about the arts than he; from them he heard high praise of Diaghilev's ability; indeed he found unexpected support for Diaghilev's daring plan.

Greffulhe decided to form a consortium. Its members'

names were recorded by Diaghilev's friend, Serge Lifar: André Benac, a banker friend of Proust's parents; Isaac de Camondo, a banker who collected Impressionists and tried his hand at opera; Henri Deutsch de la Meurthe, oil tycoon and aficionado of aviation; Arthur Raffalovitch, financier and philanthropist; Henri de Rothschild, of the banking family, doctor of medicine and playwright; and finally Basil Zaharoff, builder of warships and arms supplier. These were the men who, with Henri Greffulhe, put up a quarter of a million francs to bring the Russian ballet to Paris, and their prime motive was political-financial.

Once he had money in his pocket Diaghilev became Mæcenas more than ever before. Indulging his passion for beauty and perfection, he ordered the Châtelet redecorated from proscenium arch right up to the seats in the gallery. He took out the first five rows of stalls, losing of course part of his take, extended the stage forward and had it refloored with best pine. He brought from St Petersburg Russian technicians, under E. Valz, a wizard of stage effects, and told him to do what the French had pronounced impossible, get two fountains of real water playing on stage in time for the first production. He commissioned a coltish *enfant terrible*, Jean Cocteau, to design a programme; he toured Paris, buying up any and every object he thought might enrich his productions.

Diaghilev operated from a room in the Hôtel de Hollande encumbered by trunks only half unpacked, the table cluttered with letters, programme proofs and box files, drawings for costumes and sets on the chairs and against the walls. To a visitor he would say, 'Come in and sit down. No – for God's sake don't put your hat on the bed, it's unlucky! It means death; no – no – not on the table either – that means poverty.'

For this dynamic man who swept all human obstacles

before him fretted over a hundred superstitious fears. He counted paving stones, avoided black cats and open ladders, never signed a contract on a Monday, believing it unlucky, would surprise friends by suddenly raising the first two fingers of his right hand against some unassuming little man in the room who, he swore, had the evil eye. This fear reached its funniest when he crossed the Atlantic. Frightened by rough seas, Diaghilev made his moujik servant go down on his knees and pray, while he, Diaghilev, a non-believer, lay on his bed in agonies for both.

A similar contradiction informed Diaghilev's ways with money. While spending thousands on this or that prop, he jibbed at handing over small amounts of cash. He would jot down the amount on his shirt cuff, saying he would settle it later, then send the shirt to the laundry, thereby in both senses wiping out the debt.

Diaghilev went to the Gare du Nord to meet his dancers and take them to the Comtesse Greffulhe's welcoming dinner at the Crillon: the men ill at ease in badly cut blue suits, the girls fresh-complexioned and demure. 'Paris never recovered from the fact,' noted Arnold Bennett, 'that when they were not dancing these lovely girls were just honest misses, with apparently no taste for banknotes and spiced meats.'

Then came the task of integrating the company into an unfamiliar theatre, of marshalling the talents of his brilliant aides. Michael Fokine was only twenty-nine; thin, highly-strung, in his cotton tunic looking like a fencing-master, he was difficult to work with, but possessed a rare gift for translating a period or a country not his own into dance movement. Léon Bakst – real name Lev Rosenberg – was red-haired, with a prominent forehead and bright, shrewd eyes with wrinkled lids that gave him a sceptical look behind his spectacles. Bakst liked to do every part of the costuming himself, from earrings to shoelaces, even the making of wigs. In spare moments they dashed off amused drawings of one another, and of Diaghilev, a habit picked up by Cocteau, who attended rehearsals, for as the drum-beat pervades Africa, so creativity pervaded Diaghilev's chosen world.

Parisians talked about the coming opening with only mild interest. If there was one art form that left them cold it was ballet. The Paris Ballet belonged structurally to the Opéra, whose director, a retired barrister with little interest in dance, treated the Ballet as Cinderella. An ungifted Belgian named Joseph Hansen, rising sixty, had a virtual monopoly on new ballets, of which in the first eight years of the century he treated Paris to a niggardly four, three being choreographed by himself. Hansen studiedly ignored Isadora Duncan's innovations: dancing barefoot in loose chiton; he demanded, whatever the subject, dances on the points, costumes based on the tutu. Music was composed to the choreographer's dictation, while the scene-painter would trot out the same old heavy realism with no reference to either costume designer or choreographer.

As Degas' paintings bear witness, the company was almost exclusively female. Buxom women often danced the male roles, and the few males on the roster were so little considered that in an Assembly debate on the Opéra budget one Deputy proposed that men dancers, 'whose only job is to support the ballerinas', should be replaced by omnibus conductors at 3 francs a night.

Diaghilev operated on quite other principles. 'Beauty in art is feeling,' he said, 'told in images.' And that feeling could be best achieved by one mind – Diaghilev's – coordinating all the arts involved – music, setting, costumes, choreography, leading dancers and every member of the corps de ballet. In place of creaking fiveacters he chose, or commissioned, short pieces in a single setting, he did away with conventionalized mime, he re-introduced the leading male dancer and he drew the corps de ballet into the main action. Realistic scenery he replaced by poetic settings that worked with score and costumes to convey that dominant feeling he wished to impart.

Diaghilev chose to open with a classical ballet treated in this new style. On 19 May 1909 the curtain rose on *Le Pavillon d'Armide*, music by Tcherepnin, story by Gautier, decor by Alexandre Benois. Karalli and Nijinsky danced the leading roles, real water danced from the two fountains, as Beaugency looks at a tapestry of Armida and her court and dreams that he is the crusader, Rinaldo, succumbing to her charms.

This Franco-Italian subject Diaghilev followed with a more specifically Russian offering: the *Polovtsian Dances* from *Prince Igor*, music by Borodin, decor by Roerich. Here with a vigour not hitherto seen in Paris male dancers stamped out rhythms that seemed to bring the steppes to the Seine.

Diaghilev's third major production was a ballet evoking an Oriental land in a past age. *Cleopatra*, with music by Arensky in a setting by Bakst, starred Nijinsky and Ida Rubinstein, who had a slim flat-breasted body sustained uniquely by champagne and biscuits. She made her entrance carried in a glistening coffer against a setting of giant figures hewn from tawny rock. 'Four slaves,' Cocteau recalled, 'unwound no less than eleven veils from a swathed figure. The twelfth, dark blue veil Cleopatra undid herself, letting it fall with a sweeping circular gesture . . . to reveal her face set off by a small blue wig from which on each side hung short golden braids.' Another in the audience, Reynaldo Hahn, compared his emotion that night to the elders of Troy when they first beheld Helen.

To these offerings Parisians responded only in so far as their limited understanding of ballet allowed. What they warmed to most were the settings: colourful, rich, imaginative. After that, the combination of art forms to make a single, flowing impact. The innovative choreography and fine points of the dancing rather passed them by. Indeed *Mercure de France* did not even refer to the season, probably because it had no ballet critic.

The box office did good business, but Diaghilev had spent so recklessly that even Gabriel Astruc, 'the Astute', whom Elisabeth Greffulhe had prudently appointed as manager to the company, had to go round hat in hand. 'Camondo and Benac smiled, Henri Deutsch scolded me in a friendly fashion, Henri de Rothschild made his cheque into round figures, and Jupiter-Zaharoff frowned.' Even so, there remained a deficit of 60,000 francs, writs flew on all sides and Diaghilev, according to Astruc, was caught by his creditors at the railway station. There his mixture of hauteur and bluff evidently worked and he succeeded in regaining Russia to organize his next season.

Diaghilev returned in May 1910 to a city that had done its homework on the subject of ballet, bringing a production that flourished in one dazzling tour de force all his company's aces: powerful rhythmical dancing, exotic atmosphere, lavish costumes. *Scheherazade* had music by Rimsky-Korsakov, choreography by Fokine, decor and costumes by Bakst. In the role of the Gold Negro Nijinsky made his entrance 'like a flashing parabola', said Cocteau; passion stirs in the harem, a frantic orgy ensues; then comes the reckoning. As Arnold Bennett noted, 'The eunuchs pursued the fragile and beautiful odalisques with frenzy; in an instant the seraglio was strewn with murdered girls in all the abandoned postures of death. And then silence, save for the hard breathing of the executioners! . . . A thrill! It would seem incredible that such a spectacle should give pleasure. Yet it unquestionably did, and very exquisite pleasure.'

So, too, thought Picasso; difficult to please, he called Diaghilev's *Scheherazade* a masterpiece, while Proust said, 'I never saw anything so beautiful,' and Henri Ghéon wrote in *Nouvelle Revue Française*: 'Its supreme quality is that of seeming indivisible, of being one with the work it represents, even to the point of seeming to issue from the very music itself before melting back into the colour of the settings.'

Suddenly the full importance of the Ballets Russes came home. Here was an extension of the realm of beauty: power, brilliance, teamwork, lavishness. The Russians knew their business. On 19 May 1910 Russian Bonds dated 1889 rose to 94½ compared with a low on 15 December 1906 of 77¼. The bankers exchanged smiles of satisfaction and thereafter Diaghilev had no trouble getting his annual subsidy, though he did continue to overspend it.

The 1912 season featured *L'Après-Midi d'un Faune*. It was Léon Bakst, apparently, who had the idea that all figures should move in profile, like an animated classical bas-relief. Diaghilev had a possessive attachment to Nijinsky and allowed the young dancer to choreograph Debussy's score. Nijinsky's knowledge of music proved to be as defective as his French; he wished to turn a voluptuous piece into something overtly erotic, and Debussy found collaboration distinctly wearing to his nerves.

On 19 May 1912 *L'Après-Midi* opened at the Châtelet. A faun lazily playing on his flute on a hot summer afternoon is taken unawares by nymphs on their way to bathe. With one of them the faun becomes amorously involved; he courts her with leaps over the stream: they link arms and dance; then, frightened, the nymph leaves the stage, while the faun, outstretched on the grass, passionately fondles the scarf she has dropped.

Nijinsky chose to dance without a jockstrap and to make his final embrace of the scarf erotic in the extreme. He was booed by many in the audience, and sharply criticized by *Le Temps*, which extended its strictures to other Diaghilev productions: 'The stigma of the Barbarian is common to them all.' Proust's protector, Gaston Calmette, wrote in *Le Figaro*:

> Those who speak of art and poetry in connection with this ballet are making fun of us . . . We saw a faun, incontinent, vile – his gestures smacking of erotic bestiality and heavy shamelessness . . . The body of an ill-made beast, hideous from the front, even more hideous in profile.

The Russian Embassy, alarmed that all Diaghilev's good work for Russian–French friendship would be undone at a stroke, quickly intervened and persuaded Nijinsky to tone down his eroticism.

Then, surprisingly, Auguste Rodin thought fit to speak his word. At seventy-one he was himself something of a faun out to grass, though he still made portrait busts, notably one of Clemenceau of which the fierce little politician complained, 'Rodin makes me look like a Mongolian general.' In *Le Matin* the sculptor spoke up for the ballet: 'When he lies full length on the rock, one leg bent, flute to his lips, as the curtain rises, you would think Nijinsky a statue, and nothing could stir the soul more than the movement with which, at the close, he throws himself down on the ground and passionately embraces the discarded scarf.'

Diaghilev's feelings about Rodin's intervention were mixed, for the sculptor had begun to make a statue of Nijinsky and the dancer went often to sit. Though

Rodin was wholly heterosexual, Diaghilev did not always behave rationally and now became fiercely jealous. One hot July day the Russian arrived earlier than expected in Rodin's studio in the beautiful nineteenth-century Hôtel Biron to find Nijinsky stretched on a couch, covered by a shawl, Rodin curled at his feet. Overcome by heat, wine and hours of posing and fashioning clay, both were fast asleep. Diaghilev left them undisturbed and shortly thereafter persuaded his protégé to end the sittings. The statue was never made; however, J. E. Blanche, who had painted Gide and his circle of Algeria-lovers, did a good large painting of Nijinsky in his costume for *Les Orientales*, one hand tilted flat to his chin, which Winnaretta de Polignac, an admirer of both artist and subject, purchased for her home.

Among the composers whom Diaghilev persuaded to write music for his Ballets Russes was a young St Petersburger – in 1910 aged twenty-eight – slim, slightly built and pale, flattened-down hair parted in the middle, big nose, full lips. According to Debussy, Igor Stravinsky was socially gauche, kissing ladies' hands while treading on their toes. After a lonely childhood in which he would spend hours watching seagulls gliding above the grey Neva, he had married his first cousin, Catherine, a pale, fragile, very religious girl: a marriage reminiscent of Gide's except that it bore fruit in two children. Stravinsky had studied under Rimsky-Korsakov and the contemporary who most influenced him was Debussy, but whereas the Frenchman subordinated melody to harmony, the Russian subordinated it to rhythm.

In 1910 Diaghilev suggested to Stravinsky that he write a ballet on the legend of the Firebird. Stravinsky liked the idea, Diaghilev commissioned the work and it was to receive a performance as a ballet in Paris in June 1910. According to Serge Lifar, it was Diaghilev who then proposed a ballet about a primitive rite set in pre-civilized Russia.

What, we may ask, prompted Diaghilev to propose a subject so alien to his own character and tastes, so unusual in itself at that time and in ballet wholly unprecedented? The answer can be only conjecture; nevertheless certain circumstantial facts may throw light on Diaghilev's thinking.

The Russian impresario, we know, was not an originator intellectually; his originality lay elsewhere, notably in an ability to gauge Paris's mood – for only by stimulating the easily bored city could he draw in customers. He was a man who read the newspapers not for yesterday's news but for tomorrow's topic of conversation, who invited to dinner clever young men who would toss him ideas gleaned from lively Sorbonne periodicals like the *Revue du Mois*.

Now the first decade of the century saw a sudden revival of interest in prehistory. The paintings of bison and hunting scenes in Altamira, formerly considered forgeries, were now authoritatively stated to be genuine. Here was high-quality visual art going back 40,000 years. More prehistoric art was found in Ariège in 1906–8, and in interpreting it scholars used the seventh volume of James Frazer's *Golden Bough*: entitled *Spirits of the Corn and of the Wild*, it describes how certain primitive peoples ensure a harvest by killing one or more young victims.

Side by side with this awakening interest in primitive rites and art went the growing preoccupation with a woman's redemptive suffering: Jeanne d'Arc, Violaine, the woman dancer who portrayed Sebastian.

Russia had no tradition of a girl sacrificing herself to

ensure the return of spring: indeed, anthropologists would consider such a ritual extremely improbable and Frazer cites only one case of a girl victim – among the Pawnee Indians of North America. But Diaghilev was not concerned with factual truth; what moved him, as he himself admitted, was truthful feeling. His favourite music, for instance, was *La Bohème*. So it may well have been he who put to Stravinsky the idea of a girl being chosen by the elders of her people to dance herself to death, thus ensuring the return of spring.

The probability of that kind of genesis is increased by Stravinsky's comment that his French title for the work is best translated *The Coronation of Spring*. Coronation implies a triumph, redemption by a girl victim on a cosmic scale.

Here a comparison with Picasso's masked prostitutes in *Les Demoiselles d'Avignon* suggests itself. In neither work is the primitivism authentic, for men in Africa wear masks, not women. Primitivism in both has come from a foreigner using Parisian modes but drawing on insights formed in a less refined society.

In keeping with this unauthentic theme Stravinsky drew little on authentic popular music. 'The opening bassoon melody in *Le Sacre*,' he confessed, 'is the only folk music in that work. It came from an anthology of Lithuanian folk music I found in Warsaw.' This melody leads into a prelude suggesting the stirring of vegetal life – a very excited stirring, for this is a sudden Russian spring. Adolescent groups perform dances before adoring the earth. In Part II one of the girls is chosen for sacrifice, then dances with increasing frenzy until she falls dead. The onlookers hold up their hands, signifying that the sacrifice has been duly made.

Like most highly original works, Stravinsky's could have occurred only when and where it did. Likely sources in the thinking of the time have been mentioned; as for the music, Stravinsky confessed it owes more to Debussy than to anyone except himself. Nevertheless, just as d'Annunzio in *The Martyrdom of St Sebastian* is demonstrably an Italian working in Paris, so Stravinsky, particularly here, is a Russian working in Paris, in touch with a particular public's sensibility, values and attitudes, adapting his native talents accordingly. Only when backed by the large sums Frenchmen were willing to supply could Diaghilev, a freelance using a theatre he could fill with an informed, responsive, comparatively open-minded audience, provide the benevolent terrain required by a work as original as this.

The ballet received its first performance on 29 May 1913 in the Théâtre des Champs-Elysées, itself a pioneer building in ferro-concrete. 'The audience remained quiet for the first two minutes,' Pierre Monteux, the conductor, recalled. 'Then came boos and cat-calls from the gallery, soon after from the lower floors. Neighbours began to hit each other over the head with fists, canes or whatever came to hand. Soon this anger was concentrated against the dancers, and then, more particularly, against the orchestra . . . Everything available was tossed in our direction, but we continued to play on.' Stravinsky went backstage in a fury to find Diaghilev flicking the house lights in a last effort to quiet the audience. For the rest of the performance he stood in the wings behind Nijinsky, holding the ends of his tail-coat as he stood swaying on a chair shouting numbers to the dancers, like a coxswain.

The jeering and fights – gendarmes had to intervene – were occasioned less by the innovation of subject and musical technique than by what was felt to be 'barbarian' exaggeration of emotion and rhythm. For reasons, partly political, that will emerge in later chapters, Parisians were becoming much concerned, in this second decade, to defend French classicism, which they might have defined as a life-affirming subject treated without undue emotion.

After the performance Stravinsky, Diaghilev and Nijinsky went to a restaurant. So far from weeping and reciting Pushkin in the Bois de Boulogne, as legend has it, Diaghilev's only comment was: 'Exactly what I wanted.' He was thinking of the publicity.

Under the stress of attacks from critics, who described his music as *Le Massacre du Printemps*, Stravinsky went down with typhus. Diaghilev, who had a horror of illness, declined to visit him, but Ravel went and, like the child he in many ways was, burst into tears, which almost frightened the remaining life out of the sick man.

Debussy meanwhile applauded *Le Sacre*: 'Primitive music with every modern convenience,' and received as a gift from the composer the four-hand score. Satie too recognized the status of the ballet but had to be funny: '*Coup de théâtre*: we've just heard that *Sacre du Printemps* is an American publicity stunt, organized by Galeries Lafayette to make their arch-rival's latest fashions appear ridiculous.'

As well as bringing Russian ballet to Paris, Diaghilev stimulated French ballet and commissioned works from French composers. In the latter role he had an indispensable collaborator in Misia, the young lady of Polish descent who enjoyed riding the 'Trans-Siberian' at the 1900 Exhibition. Daughter of a sculptor and grand-daughter of a famous Belgian cellist, Misia had been born in Russia in March 1872, the same month and year as Diaghilev; like the impresario she lost her mother at birth and acquired a stepmother who encouraged her musical talents.

In 1908 Misia was aged thirty-six. She had expressive
dark almond eyes, a tilted-up, bridgeless nose and
abundant chestnut hair piled like a brioche. Without
possessing beauty or, in most people's eyes, sexual
attractiveness, she was extremely popular, for she radi-
ated *joie de vivre* and had a rare gift for interesting others
in her enthusiasms.

After her divorce from Natanson, Misia had married
a newspaper proprietor, Alfred Edwards; she was separated from him and now living with the man who was to
become her third husband, José Sert: short and squat,
with a nobbly bald head, who looked, said Dali, like a
potato. Sert dressed in cape and sombrero, told cruel,
bizarre stories, and was busy on a commission from the
King of Spain to decorate the cathedral of Vich, near
Barcelona. Sert had shown the first of his frescoes at the
Salon d'Automne and the critics deemed them heavy
and vulgar, as indeed they are. But Sert had a thick skin
and just shrugged. Also, he had a lot of money. Misia
was fond of saying, 'I've had only husbands, never
lovers;' she might have added that all the husbands
were very rich.

Not that Misia wanted money for herself. True, she
had her pianos, and a flat in the Rue de Rivoli which she
later exchanged for one in Quai Voltaire, but she only
wanted money to help artists. Her approach to them,
and indeed to art, was quite as high-handed as
Diaghilev's. Having commissioned Bonnard to paint a
frieze for her apartment, she found the long straight
edges of his canvas monotonous and cut them into scalloped shapes. When friends complained of her lack of
respect, she replied, 'I don't respect art; I love it.'

In 1908 Misia, accompanied by Sert, went on from a
performance of *Boris Godunov* to sup on fresh sole with
Diaghilev at Prunier's. Informed and open-minded
about all the arts, she responded quickly and whole-

heartedly to Diaghilev's ambitions for 'total' ballet, while the impresario felt an increasing affinity with Misia. She was, he said, the only woman he could ever have imagined marrying – the sister he never had.

Misia gave the Russian a promise to help him when his company arrived, and she fulfilled it, haranguing friends whom she received in bed – she seldom rose before noon – canvassing the influential in the afternoon, buying up empty seats, taking poor arthritic Auguste Renoir in 1911 to performances of Stravinsky's *Petrouchka* and of *Spectre de la Rose*, in which Nijinsky in a costume of curling petals, conveying the impression, thought Cocteau, of some melancholy, imperious scent, performed his most celebrated leap.

At the first performance of the former ballet the Châtelet house lights had been dimmed for twenty minutes, but the curtain had not risen and the audience grew restive. Into Misia's box raced Diaghilev in tailcoat. 'Can you give me 4000 francs, at once, to pay for the costumes?' Misia's car was waiting, she sent it home for the money and ten minutes later the curtain rose on Admiralty Square, St Petersburg. Modifying a *mot* Debussy applied to Cocteau, we may say 'Diaghilev was a great man, and Misia his prophet.'

Misia's other role was to help her musical friends participate in the Diaghilev Phenomenon. Of these the most gifted was Maurice Ravel. Three years younger than Misia, Ravel was the son of a Swiss mining engineer who had won a piano prize at the Geneva Conservatory, and a Basque mother who sang Maurice and his baby brother to sleep with Basque and Spanish lullabies. Maurice attended the Paris Conservatoire, where his teacher was Fauré, and there began to produce work of considerable invention, more precise and drier than Debussy's. Without the advice Debussy had received from Guiraud, he failed to win a *prix de Rome*, much to Misia's indignation, for at this stage he had already written *Pavane for a dead Infanta*.

Maurice Ravel was a small man, short and lean, who looked like a stable-lad or, as one friend said, like a fox-cub, his most marked feature a long straight nose. He dressed fastidiously in suits cut by Gaillard, with tie, handkerchief and socks matching. He lived in the country west of Paris with his mother and, when she died, alone. Like Misia, he got out of bed late, worked during the afternoon and around seven, throwing a few clothes over his pyjamas, would go for a long walk in his beloved woods, 'working his music' until perhaps midnight.

Ravel liked small things: bonsai trees, blue pansies, toys, intricate gadgets, insects, particularly marching ants. He liked mixing original cocktails to which he gave names like Phi-Phi and Valencia. He filled his small living-room with inexpensive Japanese-style objects, and if a visitor happened to praise one Ravel delightedly pounced: 'It's a fake!' He loved being with children. When Misia's half-brother Cipa, a Borodin fanatic crippled by polio, and his Polish wife Ida went for a holiday to Spain, it was to their friend Ravel that they entrusted their small children, Mimie and Jean. Ravel amused them by cutting out paper dolls, taking part in their pillow-fights, catching dragonflies which he called 'chipolatas with wings' and composing a suite of five pieces for piano duet inspired by Perrault's Mother Goose stories.

Yet this playful person was exceedingly clever and knew every musical trick in the book. When Vaughan Williams, three years his senior, went to stay with Ravel in 1908, he wrote home that his visit was proving both pleasurable – he was invited by Ravel to spend one evening with some 'rather jolly tarts' – and musically fruitful. 'But I feel that only ten years with Ravel would teach me all I want,' while Debussy compared Ravel to a magician in his ability to conjure up strange flowers round the legs of a perfectly ordinary chair.

Misia convinced Diaghilev that if he wished to consolidate his company's initial success he should commission not only Russian composers but French ones too. She introduced her small reserved French friend to the large flamboyant Russian and from the meeting issued a commission to compose a score on the subject of Daphnis and Chloë.

'I was less concerned,' Ravel recalled, 'with being accurate in archaic detail than with loyalty to the Greece of my dreams, which in many ways resembled that imagined and depicted by the French artists of the latter part of the eighteenth century.' He might have added that the god in his ballet is more suggestive of Christian France than of pagan Greece.

The finished work, which took Ravel three years and was dedicated to Diaghilev, had its first performance in 1912, with choreography by Fokine. The ballet depicts the love of a shepherd, Daphnis, for a nymph, Chloë. Pirates invade their island home and carry off Chloë. The god Pan, who dominates the setting in the form of a huge rock, is asked to intervene; because he loves the nymph Syrinx, Pan is moved by Chloë's plight, he frightens off the pirates and restores the nymph to her shepherd, their reunion being celebrated with a bacchanale.

Despite occasional echoes of the *Polovtsian Dances* and *Scheherazade*, Ravel's score is highly original, very Parisian in its subtlety and refinement, and with moments of power. The long symphonic interlude that introduces the third scene has been called the most full-blooded, eloquent and stirring evocation of dawn ever written.

Through Misia's agency Diaghilev commissioned

two other Frenchmen to write scores for his company. Reynaldo Hahn composed music for *Le Dieu Bleu*, yet another ballet with a religious theme, this one concerning the love-affair of an intending Siamese priest, in which Fokine drew on youthful memories of Siamese dancers who had visited St Petersburg, adding a most original 'dance of the hands', and Bakst once more provided strongly coloured exoticism. But Hahn's gift was for pure melody, not dance rhythm, and the production in 1912 met with only moderate success.

More important was Debussy's *Jeux*, commissioned by Diaghilev with a scenario by Nijinsky, for this was the first ballet to take a modern subject. Three tennis-players, a boy and two girls, meet by chance in a garden at nightfall. They are looking for a lost tennis ball. The boy flirts with both girls but cannot decide which to choose, and they depart in different directions. For this deliberately undramatic action and inconclusive ending Debussy provided a score lasting fifteen minutes yet containing twenty-three different motifs, subtly inter-related. Though it is too oblique to work perfectly on the stage, Stravinsky said that *Jeux* 'discovers a whole new world of nuances and fluidity. These qualities are French, even peculiarly French perhaps, but they are new.'

Diaghilev's success prompted the formation of other companies, stimulated the French state ballet director-ate to relearn the art of expressing feeling with the whole body and, across the whole board, the com-missioning of new work. One French composer who wrote an important ballet for a company other than Diaghilev's was André Roussel. Starting out as a naval officer, Roussel studied and later taught at the Schola Cantorum; he had heard temple music on a naval visit to India and was one of the rare composers to bring authentic Eastern modes to French ears.

Roussel's ballet, *Ariadne's Web*, takes us into a world like La Fontaine's. The protagonists are all insects. A spider catches a butterfly and prepares to make a meal of it, only to have its prey rescued by mantises, who at the end kill the spider. There is no Eastern music in this particular work, but there is much delicacy, charm and small-scale drama.

More ambitious in theme and scale was a score for ballet by Paul Dukas, who taught composition at the Paris Conservatory and was so severe on his own compositions that he burned most of them, believing them to fall short of his high standards. One that escaped the flames was *La Péri* which, choreographed by Clustine, was performed by Trouhanova's Paris company in 1912.

We enter the East once more. Alexander, conqueror of India, still young but failing in health, wanders in search of the Flower of Immortality. He finds it in the hand of a sleeping Peri, or fairy, and steals it. The Peri wakes; she is beautiful; Alexander begins to lust after her, whereupon the flower in his fingers dulls from emerald-green to purple. The Peri realizes that he is not ready yet for the flower. She implores him to return it, and when he refuses, dances before him, ever more alluringly, until she falls into his arms. She then manages to seize the flower and departs. Alexander feels his life ebbing, but as the Peri leaves she holds the flower towards him as if in promise of immortality. Dukas' masterly instrumentation conveys a variety of intense feeling, from the voluptuous to the frenzied and the intensely spiritual.

A consortium of bankers had brought the Ballets Russes to Paris, hoping to help boost the image of Russia, the rouble and, with it, much else. They succeeded.

Diaghilev's company was not the only factor at work, but it was one of the most important. Again Arnold Bennett, with his nose for money, got the point: 'And this was Russia! This was the country that had made such a deadly and disgusting mess of the Russo-Japanese War.' By 1913 the image of the sinking of the Russian fleet had been superseded by that of Nijinsky's powerful leap in *Le Spectre de la Rose*. Russian bonds continued strong, Frenchmen readily invested in new loans to the Tsar and supported a French policy grounded in confidence in Russia's military might.

The six-season connection with Russia also left its mark on the host city. With Cocteau as their unofficial publicity agent, rather as Apollinaire was for Cubism, the Ballets Russes gave Parisians a taste for luxury, for colour, for Oriental styles, more powerful kinds of dance. As we shall see, the Russian connection helped to change their style of party, and way of dressing. It added another brilliant art form to those already on offer, this one particularly compelling, since it compounded several arts, thereby increasing at any one session the dose of joy. By 1912 Paris had begun to assume the aspect of Armida's pavilion – a place of 'leisurely luxury art' as Ravel was to describe it retrospectively in the 'twenties – a crystallization of the intense experience Proust said was elicited by involuntary memory, but this one repeated evening after evening as the curtain rose on yet another never-never world.

CHAPTER 11

A World on the Move

The scientific scene in France towards the turn of the century shows characteristics that set it off from such scenes elsewhere. To start with, Paris was the undisputed centre, what Cambridge was to England and Chicago, in physics, to the United States. This links with something else: French science was Government-funded, and directed to educating top men for state service – itself an ideal of the Revolution. As the 1900 Exhibition programme said: 'The gateway to progress is Education.'

The prestige subjects of French science were, since Lavoisier, metrology – the exact measurement of matter, including gases – and, since Pascal, mathematics. In 1900 France's most eminent man of science was Henri Poincaré, author of more than four hundred mathematical papers and, incidentally, a forthright opponent of Peano's and Russell's formalism.

The Second International Congress of Mathematicians held in Paris in 1900 addressed itself to the most famous open problem in pure mathematics – the Riemann hypothesis, first raised in 1859 by the German Bernhard Riemann. The hypothesis is concerned with the distribution of the prime numbers amongst all whole numbers, and asserts that all of the many solutions have a certain form, but since there are infinitely many the hypothesis cannot be proved by direct computations. During this decade remarkable progress with the problem was to be made, but only now, eighty years after, computers are giving signs of solving it.

Pure science ranked higher than practical inventions. Charles Cros had conceived the principle of the phonograph, but Thomas Edison actually made it, and many other examples could be cited. But because of its orientation towards training state employees, pure science had inadequate facilities. Pierre Curie, a pure physicist, had to spend much of his working life as director of the Ecole de Physique et Chimie Industrielle; the last word is the operative one, and Curie's brief was to train engineers.

Another feature of French science is that, as with businesses and artisan work, it tended to run in families. Henri Becquerel, who discovered the strange properties of uranium, was the son and grandson of physicists; Jean Perrin, one of the leading physicists in 1900, had a son Francis who attained fame in the same field.

As in other areas of French civilization, the chrysalis of the extremely important discoveries of the new century lies in the last years of the old, and a convenient starting point is 1894. In that year the director of research in the Ecole de Physique was the aforementioned Pierre Curie. Son and grandson of doctors of medicine, Pierre had been educated with his elder brother Jacques at home, taken his *licence* at eighteen, and with Jacques, also a physicist, had done brilliant work in crystallography and magnetism. Now aged thirty-five, he had a long handsome face, serious eyes, close-cropped hair and a Van Dyck beard. In character he was reserved, unselfish, idealistic. His hobby was natural history, and on country walks he rarely met a flower, plant or insect he could not identify. His annual salary was a pitiful 3600 francs, one of the reasons he lived with his parents.

Among Pierre Curie's students that year was a Polish girl of twenty-seven. Marie Sklodowska was the daughter of a Warsaw teacher, living in what the Russian authorities called 'the territory of the Vistula', for Poland was now part of Russia, and the freedom of its people much restricted. Marie had spent several humiliating Jane Eyre-like years as a governess in order to save enough money to study science in Paris – for Poles a 'promised city'. She lived with her elder sister, wife of a Polish doctor practising in Paris, and for all her needs had just 3 francs a day. She was a shy, serious girl with grey eyes, fair frizzy hair and a determined chin. She was studying magnetism in metals for a doctorate, and had impressed her teachers by her memory, power of concentration and zest for learning.

These two high-minded people soon fell in love, and the following summer were married. They set up home in a small flat in rue de la Glacière. In September 1895 Pierre was appointed professor, at a salary of 6000 francs, and while he taught, Marie worked in the laboratory of the Ecole de Physique. They were visibly very happy, in fact their love for each other became a byword in their group of physicist friends. These were headed by Jean Perrin, known from his pear-drop face and halo of frizzy hair as 'the archangel', Paul Langevin, a handsome extrovert specialist in the movement of particles in gases and liquids, and Gabriel Lippman, inventor of instruments, whose method for reproducing colours photographically was to win him a Nobel Prize.

Uranium, which Becquerel had found to emit luminescence and, in total darkness, rays penetrating enough to expose a photographic plate wrapped in black paper, was then the foremost topic. Marie set herself to measure, with a sophisticated instrument invented by Pierre, the speed of the electricity so discharged. She found two unexpected things: that it did not vary with temperature, nor did it vary as between pure uranium and uranium in a compound. After more tests she realized that the speed of electricity depended on only one thing: the actual weight, in the samples, of pure uranium. She and Pierre discussed this and concluded that the electricity must originate at the heart of the metal, the uranium atoms themselves. To this power within uranium they gave the name 'radioactivity'.

In April 1898 Marie asked her friend, Gabriel Lippman, a member of the Academy of Sciences, to make this report on her behalf in the Academy's *Proceedings*: 'Two minerals containing uranium: pitchblende (oxide of uranium), and chalcolite (phosphate of copper and uranyl), are much more radioactive than pure uranium. This remarkable fact suggests that they may contain an element much more active than uranium.'

Pierre became so excited that he dropped his own work on crystals to help his wife track down the new element, to which patriotically Marie intended to give the name polonium. However, to separate polonium from the bismuth it closely resembles proved beyond their joint powers; polonium is a shortlived element and even now has not been isolated in a pure state.

This disappointment was balanced by another discovery, reported in December to the Academy: evidence of 'a new substance containing a new element, which we propose to name radium . . . It contains a large amount of barium [a silver-white metallic element], yet is highly radioactive. The radioactivity of radium must therefore be enormous.'

Enormous also was to prove the task of isolating radium in sufficiently pure a condition to measure its atomic state and so convince chemists that it really existed. Marie estimated she might have to treat hundredweights, perhaps tons, of pitchblende in order to procure a few grains of radium.

The Curies applied to the Sorbonne for premises, only to be told none were available. The only place they could find was a wooden shed formerly belonging to the medical department, in a yard of the Ecole de Physique. It had no proper windows, the skylight leaked. In summer it was like a hothouse; in winter, despite an old-fashioned cast-iron stove, like a refrigerator.

The Curies took over this shed and then one day a wagon deposited a load of shining blackish pitchblende from mines in St Joachimsthal, a gift of the Austrian Government. This ore, and many further loads of it, would have to be sifted, a kilogram at a time.

Marie's notebooks survive. On one page, in her regular sloping hand, weights, measurements, observations; opposite, Pierre's upright hand and diagrams. In another notebook Marie entered, week by week, the weight of her little daughter Irène, born in 1897, the number of her teeth, her first words, her liking for tapioca. In the margin of a third book, a cookery book, she wrote a recipe for redcurrant jelly, using fruit bought cheap at Les Halles, for she and Pierre could still not afford expensive purchases, and their one treat was a summer holiday bicycling in Auvergne or Brittany.

With only one part-time assistant Marie sifted the pitchblende, trying to separate radium from barium. One year passed, a second. Pierre who, according to Marie, had a 'geometric' mind, drawn to the shapes taken by phenomena rather than to their material reality, advised Marie to abandon her quest. He still did not know the extent of her tenacity.

After four years' hard work and exhausted physically, early in 1902 Marie succeeded in isolating a tenth of a gram of radium, not the metal but a pure salt of radium, white powder resembling table salt. On 28

March she established its atomic weight, entering in her notebook: Ra – 225.93.

This queer foundling of a substance was full of surprises: heavier than lead but continually 'busy', in darkness it emitted enough bluish phosphorescent light to read by; it emitted heat, enough in one hour to melt its own weight of ice; it discharged electricity, it coloured a glass phial mauvish-violet. And, as Pierre found when he exposed his arm to the salt, it made the skin red, as though burned, yet he felt no pain. It took six weeks for most of the skin to grow again, but a square centimetre in the centre remained a greyish colour and would not heal, 'indicating some damage at a deeper level'.

The burning properties were elucidated by the Curies' friend Paul Villard. Using a sample containing radium lent by Marie, Villard sent radiation consecutively through two photographic plates.He concluded that radium emitted three kinds of rays – the so-called alpha and beta rays identified by Rutherford – and a third kind, gamma rays, penetrating and burning, akin, thought Villard, to X-rays.

In 1903 for their discovery of radioactivity Pierre and Marie Curie were awarded, jointly with Henri Becquerel, the third Nobel Prize for Physics. Overnight the husband and wife team became famous and President Loubet honoured their leaky shed with a visit. The following year Pierre assumed the Chair of Physics in the Sorbonne, salary 10,000 francs and a laboratory of his own. He ordered a modern bathroom for the house they now shared with his widower father. Another daughter was born.

Because of Marie's weakened health the Curies went to Stockholm only in June 1905. There in his thank-you speech Pierre said: 'In the hands of evil men radium can become very dangerous . . . Nobel's discoveries show that explosives have allowed men to undertake admirable works, but they are also a terrible means of destruction in the hands of war-makers . . . I am one of those who, like Nobel, believe that humanity will draw more benefit than harm from new discoveries.'

Experiments showed that radium's intrusive gamma rays could penetrate the body to destroy hidden harmful cells such as cancer. When an industrialist, Armet de l'Isle, built a factory near Paris to extract radium for medical use, the Curies claimed no royalties and refused to take out any patents.

On Thursday of Easter Week 1906, after lunching with a group of science teachers, Pierre Curie set out for the Institut, by way of rue Dauphine. It began to rain and Pierre put up his umbrella. The street was crowded. Pierre started to cross it, while a two-horse wagon carrying military equipment approached, hidden from Pierre by his umbrella. The driver tried to pull in his horses but too late. Pierre was knocked down, and the wagon's left rear wheel passed over his skull.

For eleven years the Curies had lived and worked together united by their love for each other and their quest for knowledge. Marie was stricken and would never recover her gaiety. She continued her research but her spare-time thoughts centred on Pierre, and she wrote to him, almost daily, in a little grey notebook.

A fortnight after the funeral: 'My Pierre, I think of you non-stop, my head is burning and I feel I'm going mad. I don't understand how it can be that I have to live without seeing you, without smiling at my life's sweet companion.'

On 13 May: 'My little Pierre, I want you to know that the laburnum, wisteria and hawthorn are in flower, the irises coming out. You would have loved them. I want you to know too that I've been appointed to your chair and some people have been mad enough to congratulate me.'

On 6 November 1906 the ubiquitous Elisabeth Greffulhe was among the notabilities in the front row to hear the first lady to teach at the Sorbonne deliver her inaugural speech. Marie walked slowly to the long table, laid her notes on it, and began in a quiet, monotonous voice: 'When we look at the progress made in physics . . .' This was the last sentence Pierre had spoken in that hall.

'Her face is strange and ageless,' said the *Figaro* correspondent, 'her deep-set grey eyes strained from reading or weeping; above a high brow her greying hair is combed back into a knot; her face is calm and pale, her lips pursed.'

The most important topic now was the nature of the atom. In various papers Marie explained how radioactivity substantiated the connection between matter and electricity, a field where the French expert was Paul Langevin, who in his laboratory at the Collège de France was studying ions in gases, liquids and dielectrics. Paul Langevin had an uneducated wife who nagged him to take a better-paid job. Unhappy at home, Paul appears to have become attracted to Marie and she, perhaps inadvisedly, wrote to him more than once supporting him in his wish to get a divorce.

The affair came to a head in 1911. Paul Langevin petitioned for divorce, his wife announced that Marie had stolen her husband. Marie denied it, and won support from certain of the Republican newspapers. But the extreme right-wing press attacked Marie, calling her a 'wog' and demanding her resignation. Raymond Poincaré, a very able barrister-politician and a cousin of Henri the mathematician, agreed to represent Langevin and to protect Marie's name. Langevin secured the divorce, but not before much mud-slinging and no less than three duels.

In that same year Marie was proposed for membership of the Academy of Sciences but lost to Edouard Branly, who invented the coherer, an essential in radio-communication. Marie, however, received the 1911 Nobel Prize for Chemistry for her discovery of polonium and radium, the only woman ever to win a Nobel Prize twice.

Part of the prize money Marie gave to the building of an Institute of Radium, where she and others would have laboratory facilities. It was built in a street named after Pierre Curie and inaugurated in 1914. Present was Marie's daughter Irène, seventeen, who was to marry Frédéric Joliot: husband and wife worked together and Joliot would one day receive a Nobel Prize for discovering the existence of the neutron. Another 'family business'.

The years from Marie's discovery of radium to the outbreak of war brought elucidation of the nature of matter. Rutherford in Cambridge fired at a target of thin gold foil high-speed helium nuclei – the alpha rays thrown out by radioactive elements – and was astonished to find that a few came straight back. He concluded, correctly, that all the atom's mass, and all its positive charge, must be concentrated at the centre, in a 'nucleus', while practically the entire volume of the atom around it is empty space, containing just orbiting electrons, moving around the nucleus. Electricity, then, was not a fairy dancing on top of rock-hard matter such as the previous generation had believed; but under its whirling petticoats itself a force of perhaps stupendous power.

In Zürich, working alone but aware of the Curies' research, Albert Einstein made two no less revolutionary claims about the nature of matter. The mass of a body, he declared, is increased by the energy of motion; and there is an equivalence between mass and energy. Scientists were saying in effect: 'Behind the apparently solid and unchanging lies a sequence of changes.' This endorsed and stimulated further the work of creative artists who were exploring the succession of selves, or the juxtaposition of selves, within a person.

In the field of chemistry the French did less well than in physics. Because they linked research closely to industry it was the Germans who excelled in developing dyes and fertilizers, and they who scooped the Nobel prizes. Again, in technology linked to heavy industry based on substantial capital investment, such as the manufacture of electric generators and electric locomotives, Germans led. Where the French came into their own was in the development of the motor-car, for this could be done fairly cheaply within a family business.

Opinions differ about which nation contributed most to its invention, but the French were among the most active in developing the motor-car. In 1900 Amédée Bollée, a bell-founder's son, was producing beautifully made cars of advanced design, and his brother Léon unusually silent cars, engine noise being blanked off by sound-absorbent material. Fernand Charron, former champion cyclist, was building CGV racing cars, later sold in England as Charrons. Alexander Darracq, a former bicycle manufacturer, produced a light Bollée under licence and was tooling up for the racing cars that were to make him a millionaire. Comte Albert de Dion, in conjunction with a former toymaker, Georges Bouton, offered racing motor-tricycles and a small, inexpensive 3½ h.p. single-cylinder car which was to win world success.

Delahaye had turned from agricultural machinery to the production of rugged little one- and two-cylinder cars, engines cooled by water tubes running the length of the chassis. The firm of Gobron-Brillié offered, in various models, a unique opposed-piston engine. The American-founded Hotchkiss artillery company were building a prototype 50 h.p. car, the first of many models noted for durability. Panhard-Levassor, originally makers of woodworking machinery, produced a wide range of high-class automobiles. Armand Peugeot, of a well-known ironmongery family, was building four-speed cars with automatic inlet valves. Louis Renault, of whom more later, was offering an advanced 3½ h.p. car with a de Dion engine, while Léon Serpollet, a poor workman's son, with financial help from a rich American, was producing steam cars quite as good as most petrol-driven vehicles.

In those days there was no question of going to a showroom and choosing a car ready to drive away. You decided the make of car that would suit your needs, then ordered the *carrosserie* or body, which would be custom-built. Such was the demand in 1900 you would have to wait up to twenty-two months for delivery. Manufacturers of motor-car bodies sought the advice of couturiers and allowed for the height of ladies' hats. La Belle Otéro's blue Mercedes was so high and narrow that it sometimes flopped on its side rounding a curve.

When your motor-car was ready, you would have to register it. If a Parisian you would receive a number and one of five letters: E, G, I, U or X. The number of Octave Mirbeau's Charron was 628–E8; we happen to know because he used the number as the title of a book about the pleasures of touring. You also paid an annual motor-car tax: in 1900 this was 120 francs for a small model, 240 for a large.

French cars, unlike British or German, ran on *essence minérale* – benzine distilled from coal-tar, which came from the mines. So to obtain a driving licence (not necessary across the Channel until the late 1920s) you went for a test to the Mines Department. Having passed your test you went to the police, who issued you with a *Certificat de capacité pour conduite d'une voiture*. Then the Conseil d'Etat sanctioned the word *automobile* and decreed that it should be feminine.

Paris in the days of electric cars must surely have been delightful, but from 1901 the *essence*-driven *teuf-teuf* prevailed. In 1907 the French capital counted 4000 *teuf-teufs*, one-sixth the number of horse-drawn private carriages and fiacres. The Montmartre/St-Germain-des-Prés line was served by the first 'autobus', holding thirty passengers, a 35 h.p. motor capable of 20 kilometres per hour having replaced the two Percheron cart horses. The journey took twenty-five minutes instead of forty-five, but the bus stopped at fixed points, not as before when the passenger wished.

The character of the city changed. 'In our beautiful avenues of chestnut and plane trees, Paris's finery,' wrote Léontine de Caillavet to a friend, 'automobiles stir up so much dust, emit so many petrol fumes, they've put an end to our peace and joy.' But the future lay with the intruder. Already a Paris court had ruled that owners of horses had a responsibility to train their animals not to shy at the *teuf-teuf*.

If you wished to venture further afield, you bought a goatskin coat with the fur outside, fur boots to the knee, leather helmet and a stout pair of goggles. Unless you happened to be mechanically minded you also engaged a mechanic, to cope with almost certain trouble. Charles Rolls, driving a Panhard from Paris to Le Havre in winter 1900, had the following mishaps: 'joints of water gone, bad junction to be replaced, bad cut in tyre of off front wheel; chain loose, burst of back tyre, mackintosh loose and wound up in shreds on pump, leaking cylinder, whole upper ends of cylinders red-hot, pump jammed, leaks in radiator pipes, ignition tube burst twice, oil on the brakes, another tyre burst.'

Pneumatic tyres, made by the Michelin brothers and, in England, by Dunlop, were as yet not very sturdy: a suffragette once punctured the tyre of a police car with a safety-pin. Tyres were the motorist's biggest single expense, and might cost him 2000 francs annually.

Even so, according to Filson Young's *The Complete Motorist* (1904):

> France as far as automobilism is concerned is 20 years ahead of England . . . The great *routes nationales* might have been engineered with a prophetic eye to the new locomotion. Motoring . . . has become part of the life of the people. In the remotest villages, and in the humblest inns, *essence* can always be bought; capable mechanics abound, and the hotel keepers, alive to their own best interest, charge nothing for putting up a car for the night.

In 1907 Octave Mirbeau, aged fifty-nine, author of novels and plays, set off in his 40 h.p. Charron Grande Vitesse to tour France. His cheerful chauffeur, Charles Brosette, son of a blacksmith, was good at repairs, though, as Mirbeau knew, he fiddled the petrol bills. Their tour took them to the Auvergne and Savoie. Though obliged to divide his attention between the lubricator, volt-meter, oil-pressure gauge and the scenery Mirbeau valued the motor-car because unlike the train it put him in direct touch with people. He has a perceptive comment too on how movement changed appearances. Though averaging only about thirty kilometres per hour, he found movement 'put things into a new relief, giving me an impression that objects and persons were not just static but intensely active'.

Mirbeau noticed the reactions of animals encountered on country roads. Geese he found intelligent: they got into line on the verge. Piglets liked running after the car. Cows hogged the centre of the road but were less easily frightened than horses, according to Mirbeau a motorist's prime danger. 'The horse sees only what is on its right and left, like a politician in the House.'

Mirbeau found provincial hotels so poor he sometimes preferred to sleep in his car. But by and large he enjoyed his tour and, dedicating the book that resulted to Fernand Charron, who built his vehicle, Mirbeau wrote: 'I owe you many joys and new impressions, a whole new order of precious encounters that books cannot provide.'

Proust was another who used the motor-car for new experiences. He prized it, he says, because it gave access to the pretty hidden corners which long ago had been visible from a stage-coach but which had lately become invisible from a railway train. It brought to transport in effect that suppleness Bergson had rediscovered – and praised – in the psyche.

That motor mechanics, *garagistes* and salesmen were an upwardly mobile group emerges from Feydeau's farce, *Le Circuit* (1909). Etienne is a clever mechanic turned shady salesman bent on getting to the top in the motoring business: 'It has all the advantages of a liberal profession and is a *sport* too.' Etienne's skill, know-how, thick moustache and confident manner bring him success with the ladies, including the mistress of the motor manufacturer for whom he drives. The play ends with racing cars tearing through a Breton village, a dog getting run over, two cars crashing and Etienne arriving first: not a parvenu, as he proudly puts it, but a *sportsman*!

Whereas the British excelled at luxury cars such as the Rolls-Royce 'Silver Ghost' of 1906–7 and the Germans at solid, durable vehicles like the Mercedes built by

Daimler from 1901, the French led in racing cars. From 1900 the Panhard, Mors and de Dietrich were invincible, and were joined in 1912 by the 4½-litre Peugeot, raced with much success by Georges Boillot.

The long straight French roads and large regions of flat country were well suited to motor races, and it was French organizations that sponsored the top competitions, most starting or ending in Paris. One of the most famous was the Paris–Vienna race of 1902, which Marcel Renault won at a speed faster than the Arlberg Express. The most ambitious was a Peking–Paris race, across two continents, sponsored in 1907 by *Le Matin*.

At first the Chinese were suspicious of the project: *chi-chos*, as they called motor-cars, were obviously bent on discovering routes for invasion. But, reassured by the French Minister and others, they and the Russians eventually agreed to cooperate by stockpiling fuel at intervals on the route.

Twenty-five cars entered but only five presented themselves in the Chinese capital. These were: a 6 h.p. Contal tricycle, two 10 h.p. de Dion-Boutons, one 15 h.p. Dutch-built Spyker, and a 40 h.p. Itala. The French were counting on a light car, though slower, getting out of difficulties more easily than a heavy vehicle. After many adventures, including the collapse of a bridge in Trans-Baikalia when the car overturned, and the breaking of a wheel, which a Russian carter-blacksmith re-made, the four-cylinder Itala, driven by Prince Scipione Borghese, won the race, arriving in Paris exactly two months after leaving Peking.

The man who altered the direction of motor-car manufacturing, Louis Renault, was born in Paris in 1877, the son of a middle-class button-manufacturer. Early interested in machines, he started work in the Paris boiler company of Delaunay-Belleville and, after military service, constructed a *voiturette* from his own designs. Instead of having the engine connected by belt or chain to a central axle, from which another chain imparted the drive to the rear wheels, Renault introduced direct drive by cardan shaft and bevel pinions. His car weighed 550 lbs and its ¾ h.p. de Dion engine could push it to 48 kilometres per hour. At twenty-one, with his brother Marcel, Louis founded Renault Frères which in two years built and sold two hundred such cars.

Most French motor manufacturers were light-hearted, happy-go-lucky men, motivated more by adventure than profit. Louis Renault was different. A wiry, muscular, sallow-faced man with hollow cheeks and tight mouth, he lived for the business of producing, in his big Billancourt factory, large numbers of inexpensive cars. Immensely hard-working, he got along on five hours' sleep, his one relaxation a long liaison with the Opéra Comique singer, Jeanne Hatto. After his brother Marcel was killed in the 1903 Paris–Madrid race, Louis took sole control: he would turn up in some unexpected part of the factory and if he found a workman idle would dismiss him on the spot. Employees regretted the traditional friendly ways of a small business, and labour relations at Renault were often troubled.

However, the company prospered. Renault's distinctive 'Alligator' bonnet appeared all over Europe. By 1906 he had supplied Paris with 1500 two-cylinder taxis at 3800 francs apiece, and also its first autobus. In 1907 the 'Red Renault' taxis were on the streets of London; and in that year he began making aero engines. By 1912, out of a French production of 50,000 vehicles, Renault was making 10,000.

Though he was never to be popular as a boss, Renault

has his place in the history of Paris, first for having introduced to his Billancourt factory the technique of the future, mass production; secondly because, as we shall see, his little red taxis were one day literally to be the saving of Paris.

In the other machine that has become an integral part of modern life – the aeroplane – the French were again to the fore. The seminal date is 17 December 1903, when the Wright brothers made the first powered flight at Kitty Hawk. If the Americans' success attracted no commercial interest at home, in France it was either ignored, doubted or disputed – the French have a long tradition of turning a blind eye to non-Gallic invention. In and around Paris eager young men continued to bend over drawing-boards and to study the lift of box-kites in the belief that one of them would be the very first to fly a powered machine.

The chrysalis of the aeroplane was the hot air balloon, which its inventors, the Montgolfier brothers, had demonstrated in the forecourt of the château of Versailles before Louis XVI: it had ascended on a short successful journey carrying a sheep, a duck and a cock. A hundred and seventeen years later, at the Paris Exhibition, the balloon was still very much in evidence and among those who made an ascent was the fastidious – and loquacious – Comte Robert de Montesquiou. One evening he dwelled too long on the complex emotions of an æsthete in space: 'And I felt the earth draw away from me,' whereupon the satirical artist Forain muttered in a corner, 'The earth too!'

Alberto Santos-Dumont, youngest child of Brazil's coffee king, after studying in Paris, had elected to stay on and experiment in powered flight. Small, thin, reserved and elegantly dressed, Santos-Dumont had two useful advantages: his light weight – 110 lbs – and a full purse. He designed and built his own balloon of varnished light Japanese silk, the envelope weighing only 31 lbs, under which he slung a bicycle and a small engine. At the Exhibition the twenty-seven-year-old Brazilian made several ascents, seated on the bicycle, steering by the handlebars, and winding his 66 lbs of ballast in and out as required.

By 1906 Santos-Dumont had come to the conclusion that the powered balloon would never provide sufficient speed or manœuvrability, and switched to designing a winged machine based on the box-kite. What he finally constructed was a biplane, driven by a pusher engine mounted between the wings, which were at the back of the aeroplane, while the fuselage – struts of fabric-covered pine braced with piano wire – extended forward and came to a head in a small box-kite that could be swivelled left and right and up and down. In October 1906, in Bagatelle Park, Santos-Dumont flew this tail-first hybrid a distance of 60 metres, so making the first powered flight in Europe and winning a prize of 3000 francs offered by a rich Deputy, racehorse owner and aviation enthusiast of Irish descent named Ernest Archdeacon. In November Santos-Dumont did even better – 220 metres.

A less cumbersome design was needed, and it is no accident that progress in this direction was to come largely from young men with artistic training, for an aeroplane, no less than a building or painting, depends on balance and economy of means.

Gabriel Voisin, born in Lyon in 1880, had studied architecture at the Atelier Godefroy in Paris; in his spare time, with his younger brother Charles, a hydrographer, he built a steamboat and a glider, which the brothers flew from the top of a quarry. In 1905 Gabriel built and flew for a short distance on the Seine an aeroplane with floats. The following year, with Charles and two workmen, Gabriel founded Voisin Frères, in order to build what he called the *Standard*: a dumpy biplane with wings forward, a pusher engine and a rudder for lateral as well as directional control. It looked like an object in a Cubist painting.

Léon Delagrange then became prominent. He was a sculptor who had known Voisin at the Beaux-Arts but his passion was aviation. He ordered a plane from Voisin, but when he flew it at Vincennes in February 1907 it split in two and crashed. Delagrange emerged unhurt and the following month at Bagatelle flew a similar plane 85 metres. This was the first flight to be filmed – by Gaumont. In April the following year, at Issy, Delagrange set two records: a distance of just under 4 kilometres, and length of time airborne: six and a half minutes.

The flying machine still did not have an accepted name. In 1908 Academicians, questioned by *L'Auto*, proposed: *aéro, philair, autoplaneuse, alérion, icarien, velivole* – d'Annunzio's suggestion – *aéromobile, avion*, and even *vol-au-vent*! But *aéroplane* got most votes.

Horses had regularly received the Church's blessing and Monseigneur Amette, Archbishop of Paris, agreed to bless two new aeroplanes and the first aerodrome, Port-Aviation, near Juvisy, south of the capital. 'No event,' said Amette, 'better deserves the Church's benediction than the conquest of the air: man imitates God in everything and God has the wind for wings.' Nice points for theological discussion.

The year 1908 saw important successes by two flying men new to the public. Wilbur Wright, exasperated by long fruitless dealings with the United States army, came to France to try to agree the production of Wright airplanes under licence. On 8 August 1908 at a racecourse near Le Mans Wright made the first public display of his *Flyer* biplane, a model much improved of course on his Kitty Hawk original. In the next five months Wright made over 100 flights. Aged forty-one, bald, gaunt and with piercing hawk eyes, he made a favourable impression both on the public and on a French syndicate, with whom he came to an agreement for building the *Flyer*.

On her way to her château at Josselin the Duchesse de Rohan stopped to meet the aviator. Hoping for a *mot* to tell at her next party, she said, '*Dites-moi*, Monsieur Wright, you were drawn to make your interesting experiments in France because it's the country that most readily offers a man glory?'

'No, ma'am,' replied the American. 'Because it offered me a contract.'

The other aviator was Henry Farman. Son of an English journalist working for a London newspaper, Farman was educated at home. One of his earliest recollections was of flying a kite made of newspaper and laths at Boulogne-sur-Mer. Farman was encouraged by his father to develop his naturally good physique by practising sports. At eighteen he won the Paris-Clermont Ferrand bicycle race against seventy-five competitors. With his younger brother Maurice he specialized in tandem races, at which the pair were never beaten.

Henry Farman entered Gustave Courtois' studio as an art student. He remained five years until he was told that in order to excel he must give all his time to art and abandon cycling. Farman decided instead to abandon art. He joined another brother, Dick, selling cars on a commission basis and turned to motor-racing. After a crash in 1905, when he ended in the branches of a tree, he complied with his parents' plea to abandon motor-racing and promptly took up flying.

Like most of these early flyers Farman was lean, light

and athletic. Mechanical know-how mattered less than good balance, litheness, quick reflexes and the ability to 'ride' a machine in its often bumpy flight like a good steeplechaser. One example from the other side of the Channel is Vernon Castle, slim and athletic, celebrated as a tango dancer, who was to enlist in the Royal Flying Corps and prove himself an excellent pilot. The RFC actually looked for good horsemen and said that mechanical knowledge as such was no help.

Ernest Archdeacon died of a heart attack while watching a close-run horse race at Auteuil, but his name remained in the Deutsch-Archdeacon prize offered to the first plane, starting from a given spot, that succeeded in flying round a flagstaff 500 metres away and returning to the start without touching the ground. In a biplane built by Voisin Frères, driven by a V8 Antoinette, Farman won this prize in January 1908. He then went off to the United States to give flying displays. He also made a far-reaching innovation by fitting ailerons to his Voisin, which had previously relied on its rudder for both lateral and directional control. In 1909 Farman started manufacturing his own planes. With his brother Dick he also wrote one of the earliest books on flying, *The Aviator's Companion*.

The next giant in French aviation was Louis Blériot. Two years older than Farman, son of a Cambrai businessman, Blériot started a successful business of his own manufacturing acetylene headlights for motorcars. He made a very happy marriage to a colonel's daughter, who bore him six children and, when he turned to flying, lent him constant support in his long, costly experiments. In 1906 Blériot went into partnership with Gabriel Voisin but at this stage – he would change later – he wanted complicated heavy engines, whereas Voisin preferred light ones and a year later the two separated. The following year Blériot built a monoplane with steering rudder in front, the so-called 'Duck'. This unwieldy machine repeatedly crashed. Only in 1908, after further experiments and mishaps – he had fifty crashes in his flying career – did Blériot build what was to become the aeroplane of the future – a monoplane stabilized by a horizontal tail and steered by a vertical rudder.

The *Daily Mail* offered a prize of £1000 to the first person to fly the Channel. Hubert Latham, a young associate of the Voisins with ample private means, attempted the journey on 19 July 1909, but 18 kilometres out his Antoinette engine failed, he came down in the sea and was rescued by his escort.

Six days later, after waiting seventy-two hours for storm clouds to clear and a strong wind to drop, Blériot hobbled across a makeshift airfield near Calais to his plane. He was on crutches, for the previous month, while competing in an air race above Douai, the asbestos covering his exhaust had slipped off, causing his right foot to be burned to the bone. Blériot's plane was an improved version of his 1908 monoplane, driven by a three-cylinder 25 h.p. Anzani engine (not yet paid for), the total weight of the machine being 660 lbs.

At 4.35 a.m. his mechanic spun the propeller, the engine revved and Blériot taxied the machine on its bicycle wheels down the field. He rose into the air and headed out to sea at an altitude of about 100 metres. Soon he met unexpected head-on squalls. He carried only 17 litres of *essence* and did not know how to swim, but he battled on to reach the white cliffs. At 5.12 he landed near Dover Castle. The crossing had lasted 37 minutes. As soldiers ran up to congratulate him, Blériot said in English: 'Be good enough to hand me my crutches.' It was a full hour and a half later before an escorting destroyer arrived, bringing Alicia Blériot to congratulate her husband.

Back in Paris Blériot received a hero's welcome, the Légion d'Honneur and telegrams from Latham, Farman and Santos-Dumont who, sadly, was falling victim to multiple sclerosis. Blériot's plane went on display at Selfridges, and at Paris's first Salon de l'Aviation.

Blériot's success brought home to Frenchmen that flying had come to stay. The aeroplane took its place in the man in the street's vocabulary and in the *Bottin Mondain* a plane-owner, like a yacht-owner, might now signal the fact in his entry with a small pictogram.

Flying, moreover, changed man's view of himself. He was no longer, like all objects on earth and most creatures, bound by the laws of gravity. He could soar into the air and survey his habitat from the superior position formerly accorded to God and the angels. As prophets in 1900, half in hope, half in conviction, had predicted, Mind had triumphed over Matter. To the French, who had taken the lead and in 1911 had more than three times the number of certified pilots as England and Germany combined, the achievement imparted an immense, largely justifiable pride.

Three fields of innovation here considered, radioactivity as a key to the nature of the atom, motoring and flying, have certain features in common. All are concerned with displacement in space: of particles from radioactive elements, of man on four wheels on the ground, of man in three-dimensional space. The overall result was to replace mass by energy as a dominant concept in thinking, imagining and the stream of consciousness technique. Nature was seen to be 'on the move', notably by Debussy, and it seemed to follow that man was doing the right thing in getting on the move too.

One further consequence ensued. Since, as Bergson

had shown, we habitually apply spatial imagery to our view of time, men began to attach increased value to the period towards which they were being displaced. The Fall, so to speak, had been reversed by Flight, and a habit took root – it is still with us – of believing that the innovations of tomorrow would in themselves constitute Progress or induce Progress The new cult word was given a capital first letter but left vague. For some Frenchmen Progress meant an advance towards social and international harmony, but to others, as we shall see, it meant France's resumption of her former role as the leading political power in Europe.

CHAPTER 12

Parisiennes

Since 1610 when Madame de Rambouillet decorated the salon of her new house near the Louvre with soft blue hangings and insisted that male guests make their points with wit, not the sword, Parisian ladies have played an influential role in intellectual, literary and artistic life. Particularly active during the Romantic Movement, in the late nineteenth century they became less so; the prominent names then were political hostesses and the courtesans who gave visiting royalty and Grand Dukes a good time in return for pearls and diamonds.

The early twentieth century by contrast saw Parisiennes more actively participating in creative work than ever before. This was expected of them. The bronze chariot horses commissioned to crown the Grand Palais are led in triumph by women, while above the main entrance to the Exhibition stood a Parisienne, whose arts she seemed to be protecting with her skirts.

A word about the background. Octave Mirbeau put it provocatively when opposing the candidature of two women writers for a place on a Literary Society committee: 'Woman is not a brain,' he said, 'she is a sex and that is much more splendid. She has only one role: to make love, that is, to perpetuate the species. Woman is unsuited to everything except love and motherhood.'

What Mirbeau had in mind was the home, but the home is so fundamental to French life that they have no word for it! *'L'intérieur'* connotes its visible side; its invisible side is conveyed by speaking of mother and children. And it was the mother who saw to the upbringing of her daughters in middle- and upper-class homes, she who either gave lessons or engaged a visiting teacher, she who taught them to sew and to make dresses from paper patterns, to play the piano and to sing a little, accomplishments so general that once a week on the top half of the page listing share prices *Figaro* published a song with its musical score: this a mother would cut out, back with cardboard and place in a folder in the piano stool for future use.

A young teenager would be shielded from novels by Balzac and Zola. For amusement she had bicycling and games such as diabolo, which came in in 1907 – an hour-glass-shaped bobbin is balanced and spun on a string suspended from two sticks. If she showed signs of being very bright she might attend a girls-only lycée or similar institution. If very bright indeed, she would go to university.

But her destination in most cases was marriage and the founding of a new *intérieur*. From the age of seventeen there would be arranged meetings – *entrevues* – with young men of whom her parents approved and whose parents would be satisfied with her dowry. Few families put financial consideration before their children's happiness; nevertheless, without a dowry a girl of the bourgeoisie was virtually unmarriageable. Octave Mirbeau mischievously printed on his *faire-part* that he was marrying Mademoiselle so-and-so 'despite her huge fortune'.

Once married, a young wife became almost a bondswoman. She might not open a bank account in her own name, and only in 1907 would she be granted control over her own earnings. Even when legally separated, a woman could not 'give, remove, mortgage or acquire' possessions without her husband acting for her or giving his consent.

Yet the American novelist Edith Wharton, who in 1906 rented an apartment in rue de Varenne, recognized that the Parisienne was accorded a status and power in the family that remained unacknowledged by the law. In Paris, she writes, 'as soon as a woman has personality, social circumstances permit her to make it felt'. In the French capital men and women interacted, whereas 'it is because American women are each other's only audience, and to a great extent each other's only companions, that they seem, compared to women who play an intellectual and social part in the lives of men, like children in a baby-school'.

Edith Wharton admired the Frenchwoman's 'power of absorbed and intellectual attention to male conversation', her sense of continuing tradition and forms, her taste and æsthetic values. She might have been describing Madeleine Gide or Emma Debussy.

In this chapter we will look at a number of Parisian women, first one from the Left Bank, secondly, several from the Right, then at fashions in dress, interiors and dancing, and finally at the movements for women's rights.

Marguerite Appell was the daughter of a mathematician, later Rector of the Sorbonne, and was born in 1883 in the château of Saint-Germain-en-Laye, where her maternal grandfather held the post of curator. She was one of four children, lived at 6 rue Le Verrier, in the university district, and received her primary education from a teacher who came three times weekly, and from her father who read aloud to her. She had much tenderness in her make-up and was very fond of Dickens: at ten she could discuss with her father all the characters in *Great Expectations, Little Dorrit* and *Bleak House*. She liked telling stories to her younger siblings and took the lead in producing a little home magazine that ran to four numbers.

Her father, though not a practising Catholic, greatly loved his mother who was, and for that reason he saw to it that Marguerite made her First Communion and at twelve sent her as a boarder to the convent in Saint-Germain. There she showed herself a leader. At fifteen, like Sarah Bernhardt in similar circumstances, she wished absolutely to become a nun. But a wise priest showed her that she did not have a vocation and at fifteen and a half, schooling complete, she returned home.

Without being very pretty, Marguerite had a pleasing face, a well-shaped body and a sense of humour. The first young man to attract her was Pierre, son of the philosopher Emile Boutroux. He was pale, delicate, sensitive – but did not like dancing, which the lively Marguerite adored. Pierre faded out and was replaced by Emile Borel, a brilliant mathematician, tall, dark, with a thick beard, who did like dancing. The son of a Protestant clergyman, Emile was thirteen years older than Marguerite and looking for an intelligent wife. Marguerite satisfied him on this score and on others, and in one of those formal letters expected of suitors he wrote to Monsieur and Madame Appell requesting Marguerite's hand.

Emile and Marguerite spent their honeymoon in Italy. Emile had an iron constitution and a passion for museums; Marguerite shared neither of these attributes. As a result she returned to Paris exhausted. There she had a miscarriage and lost her chance of ever having the four children she wanted. However, she was not a complainer. She set herself to looking after a husband she greatly esteemed, even if there was no strong physical attraction on either side, and to running well her fifth-floor flat in 30 Boulevard Saint-Germain. That meant, thriftily.

There is a revealing story of women of Grenelle, one of the city's poorer districts, coming to the waste land of the Champ-de-Mars in 1902 after the Exhibition buildings had been pulled down, to gather burdock to ease their rheumatism and grass to feed the rabbits they reared for the pot. Marguerite did not have to go as far as they, but she did have to plan the spending of every franc.

She had a maid but did her own shopping. Milk was not delivered to the door but there were milk-vending machines: *Le Bon Lait Maggi pasteurisé et contrôlé*. Fresh vegetables came up daily. Bakers offered squat English loaves – *pain de mie* – as well as crusty French bread, for despite the animosity engendered by the Boer War things English were fashionable.

When she received Emile's Sorbonne friends, who included Jean Perrin and Paul Langevin, Marguerite wore a dress made for her by 'a little woman' and served simple three-course meals: *vol-au-vent aux filets de soles à la sauce rose*, a roast garnished with vegetables and a dessert. In this she typified a fashion for light food in tasty sauces, a speciality of Proust's Françoise, for example, being *cardons à la moëlle*: cardoons look like celery and taste like artichokes; *sauce à la moëlle* is a beef stock with carrots, onions and madeira.

After coffee Marguerite might be asked to go to the piano to accompany Perrin and Langevin in a favourite duet, '*In lichter Waffen Scheine*', from *Lohengrin*. Like many dons, they treated Wagner's Grail operas as a substitute for their lost faith. After the singing exuberant Jean Perrin, in his velvet, would say, '*Agitons des idées générales*' and they would join in one of those abstract discussions dear to French intellectuals, such as what point does political open-mindedness become betrayal of principles.

Emile was actively Left-wing – in later life he was to sit as a Deputy. For the moment he gave unpaid talks for the People's University. Marguerite would accompany him to the kitchen of a working-class home, where, surrounded by workmen and their wives, he would discourse on a mathematical subject. Charles Péguy and Jacques Maritain, known then as the blue-eyed anarchist, might join them or drop in at the flat afterwards to discuss Socialism.

Marguerite and Emile adopted Emile's orphaned twelve-year-old nephew, Fernand, they moved to a larger flat and Marguerite became in almost every respect his mother. When Emile won a 10,000-franc science prize, husband and wife used the money to found and jointly edit a new periodical, *Revue du Mois*. It published articles of general interest, mainly by dons, about the exciting scientific discoveries of the day: it also dealt with trade unionism – high praise here for German achievements – with international affairs, and with new novels and plays. Distributed by the prestigious Librairie Alcan, its orange cover was to be seen in many French homes, along with those of *Mercure de France* and *Revue des deux mondes*.

Among contributors to the *Revue* were Pierre Curie and Paul Painlevé, a pioneer of aerodynamics and from 1910 a much-liked Deputy for the Fifth Arrondissement. Both became friends and Marguerite helped Painlevé in his election campaign. Under the name Camille Marbo she also published several novels in the Dickens vein and became quite influential in the literary world. So that when Marie Curie got involved in the Langevin divorce and looked like losing her chair, Marguerite went to Louise Cruppi. This lady, of classic good looks, was a pianist of concert hall standard. She made her drawing-room a meeting-place for artists – her daughter was to marry the sculptor Paul Landowski – and was a good friend to Fauré, Debussy and Ravel. She held recitals in her home and even had short operas performed there. This respected lady was able to get the attacks on Marie halted.

Anatole France was one of the famous Marguerite met. Complimenting her on her shoulders and ankles, he spoke suggestively about sexual pleasure with a cynicism that displeased her: 'I'm sure there are things you don't know. Such a pity . . .'

By 1912 Marguerite was buying dresses from a couturier – her friends approved the loose-fitting line – and giving formal six-course dinners with place cards. Among her *ananas* (pineapples) – the mode word for what we would call lions – were Paul Painlevé, the dramatist J. H. Rosny *aîné*, Fernand Gregh the poet, young Edouard Herriot, a future Mayor of Lyon, and Philippe Berthelot, pillar of the Quai d'Orsay and ubiquitous guest.

Such in brief was the career during the early 1900s of an intelligent young woman, not an intellectual but devoted to spreading knowledge, and concerned for the poor. She was less independent than women in the Fabian and Bloomsbury groups, yet she seems to have been content with what was granted her. Choosing his wife's *nom de plume* Emile said, 'I want you to have a personality separate from mine,' yet it was he who, after she'd had a tiring day, would carry her in his arms up five flights of stairs.

Religion, as the agnostic Romain Rolland said, was still a strong force with more than half the people of France, and he was thinking specially of women. It was Parisiennes, led by a Deputy's wife, the Comtesse de

Mun, who demonstrated against the closing of religious schools and the transfer of Church property to associations of laity. It was they who formed a majority at Sunday Mass, they who went to talks on the Christian life, among the most popular being those by the Abbé Huvelin in the crypt of St-Augustin and later published.

One passage in these talks expresses the mood of optimism then so prized in the city. 'I cannot bear people to be pessimistic,' says the good Abbé at Pentecost, 'to think disparagingly of humanity, to see in it only its ugliness; emphatically, no! Human nature is beautiful, it is great, it is noble, because, if it will have it so, the Holy Spirit is perpetually at work in it.'

A second symptomatic note occurs in a talk entitled 'Mothers who are too "masterful" '. The Abbé describes 'mothers who long too restlessly, too eagerly, too intensely, to plan the future of their children; who work for that, not according to God's plan, but according to a plan which is entirely of their own devising . . . If everything does not turn out exactly as they wish, there is sorrow, despair, and a sort of frenzy.'

This masterfulness is rather common in our period. It could be the result of early widowhood – Gide's mother, of a husband absorbed by his career – Proust's mother, though her domination was of a gentler kind; and of a *mariage de raison*, where the wife turned her affection from an inadequate husband to a chosen son; as the birth rate was low, there would often be just one son, and he would attend day school, sleeping at home. Evidently the Abbé Huvelin had seen the damage and hastened to warn against it.

Because arranged marriages did not always turn out well, many Parisians, for a long or short period, kept a mistress. English or American visitors expressed surprise at the number of plays on the Paris stage based on the 'eternal triangle'. They considered it a contrived situation. But in fact the dilemmas of a wife with an unfaithful husband or of a wife who became another man's mistress were among the most actual for many in the audience. Of the men met in this book more than half had mistresses, a higher proportion than emerges from similar cross-sections in London or Berlin. But most Parisiennes accepted the situation. The Church was still a strong force in their lives, even if they did not go to Mass, and the Church forbade divorce. Also, they believed divorce would harm their children, and, with a knowledge of human nature which Anglo-Saxons termed cynical, they believed that home would eventually reassert its power, that the wanderer would settle down. Often he did. Jean Perrin, for instance, had a succession of love-affairs, but stayed with Henriette and was a model father. Again, by not expecting too much, wives achieved quite a lot.

In order to keep their good looks ladies who could afford it went to Sarah Bernhardt's preferred dietician, Dr Caissarato, and like Sarah, gave up sweets, tea and coffee; they took baths of rosemary and milk, or hyssop and porridge oats, and to discourage wrinkles coated their faces with ground almonds and rosewater. To preserve their figure they would ride in the Bois or use one of the new electric vibromasseurs.

They also tried to keep their minds fit. By contrast with German ladies, who limited themselves to cooking, cradles and church, and to the women of the so-called 'Souls' in England, for whom games, charades, amateur theatricals and country pursuits loomed large, they attended the three annual salons (ten thousand paintings!), the series of concerts called Pasdeloup, Lamoureux and Colonne, lectures at the Collège de France by Bergson and Henri Poincaré. And if they were very well off indeed, they gave parties at which rising artistes performed.

Princesse de Polignac, née Winnaretta Singer of the sewing machine family, was a very rich widow, masterful yet kindly, who looked like Dante and whose ambition, says Stravinsky, was to have her bust next to Richelieu's in the Louvre. With the Duchesse d'Uzès and Comtesse Greffulhe the Princess was one of Paris's leading patrons of music and dance. When twenty-two-year-old Isadora Duncan was brought over from London by Charles Hallé and danced to Chopin's preludes and waltzes at one of the Friday evenings given by Madame Saint-Marceaux, wife of the sculptor of *La Danse* on the Opéra building, the Princess saw her, went to her studio, patiently listened to Isadora's theories – how her centre of action was not at the base of the spine, as with ballerinas, but the solar plexus – invited Isadora to her home and, after leaving an envelope containing 2000 francs, departed as unobtrusively as she entered.

Isadora danced several times at the Princess's house, her rendering of Botticelli's *Primavera* being much applauded. 'Inspiration is given out by the thousand volt per second from Miss Duncan,' said the young stage-manager Gordon Craig, and another who fell in love with her was Winnaretta's brother, Paris. Isadora was very maternal but not the marrying kind: she and Paris – her Lohengrin, she called him – formed a long, stable liaison and had two sweet children: the odiously named Doodle, and Patrick.

Another who performed at Winnaretta's parties we have already met in Proust's circle. A protégé of Massenet, smallish, with thick, very long eyebrows, small moustache, cigarette dangling from his lips, Reynaldo Hahn would sit at the piano, head tilted slightly back, and 'from the hurt mouth – a little disdainfully – comes the saddest and warmest sound that ever was,' wrote Proust.

Hahn's music was uncomplicated: pure melody. His seven *Chansons grises*, written before he was seventeen, include '*Cimetière de campagne*', in which he recalls how, as a child, wearing a cassock, he would serve Mass, and in the background is heard the ding-dong of a church bell. These songs, says Proust, filled his audience's eyes with tears. For most of those present, as for the composer himself, Christianity was a part of the lost world of childhood and to that extent of æsthetic-nostalgic value. Adult Catholicism, with its prohibition of divorce and saccharine Saint-Sulpice statuary, appealed to few of them. As Hahn wrote to his sister: 'My soul is inherently religious. But Rome has filled me with disgust . . . If I had children, I would try to teach them a *vague but deep belief*.' After purring in front of the great ladies all evening, Hahn would hurry to Proust's apartment to retail cattish stories about them, forgetting how much these society hostesses contributed to the interaction of the arts – visual, verbal and musical – characteristic of the period.

Misia Godebaska was another who encouraged musical talent. She took Maurice Ravel for a cruise on her second husband's yacht and invited the gifted young to perform at her parties. Misia 'laughs and clucks and coos,' Gide cattily noticed, 'puffing out her neck and letting her head roll on her bare shoulders'; this easy informality, as we saw, won her the friendship of Diaghilev and his company and, more surprisingly, of cool, formal Lady Ripon, one of the few English ladies really to belong to Paris society.

In 1911 Lady Ripon took the Ballets Russes to London and at one party there, according to Stravinsky, proposed a parlour game (very un-Parisian, this) 'in which we were all to decide what sort of animal each of us most resembled. Lady Ripon initiated it by saying that "Diaghilev looks like a bulldog and Stravinsky like a *renard*. Now, Monsieur Nijinsky, what do you think I look like?" Nijinsky thought a moment, then spoke the awful, exact truth: "*Vous, Madame – chameau*" – just the three words; Nijinsky did not speak much French. Lady Ripon did not expect that, of course, and in spite of her repeating: "A camel!? How amusing! I declare! Really? A camel?" – she was flustered all evening.' For *chameau* also means bitch and Lady Ripon's morals were not of the strictest.

Leading Paris literary hostesses were the Duchesse de Rohan and the Comtesse de Béarn, both belonging to the very highest society. Each of these ladies had her 'day', when she was at home to visitors, and this was published in a directory, while she saw to it that the press announced children's tea-parties, coming-out balls, masked balls, fancy-dress balls and the like.

Behaviour had to conform to exact rules. When calling, for instance, a gentleman must carry his hat and stick in his left hand and keep his gloves on, even when shaking hands. At the conclusion of a call a card was *not* left in the hall as in England, but when the persons one was calling on happened to be 'not at home' one left a card with corner turned up (*bristol corné*). A titled couple abbreviated their title on a joint card, for example B^{on} et B^{onne} de la Rochette, whereas on individual cards it was *de rigueur* to put Baron (or Baronne) in full.

Not everyone took the minutiae of etiquette so seriously. The humorist Allais, finding nothing grander to put on his calling card, inscribed it:

MONSIEUR ALPHONSE ALLAIS

Customer of the Gas Company.

At afternoon parties lady guests took their umbrella or parasol with them into the drawing-room, at least Proust's Duchesse de Guermantes does, and men took their top hats with them. Perhaps this evinces a strong sense of property and the need of highly strung people to have something to toy with. A week after a ball one paid a call on those who gave it: this was known as the *visite de digestion*!

There were also a number of minor points of etiquette: one never said *'de la soupe'*, always *'du potage'*, never *'du café'*, but *'une tasse de café'* and for some obscure reason *poireaux* was pronounced *poreaux*.

Prominent in the literary world, though not of such high rank as the ladies mentioned, was the Comtesse de Noailles. Born Anna Elisabeth de Brancovan in Paris in 1876, which makes her seven years older than Marguerite Borel, she was the daughter of an émigré Rumanian cavalry officer and a Greek lady, whose father was Musurus Bey of Constantinople, an astronomer-poet known in that city as Nostradamus. Anna was a small, delicate child, often ill, who loved flowers, music – Paderewski would often call and play – and the scenery of Lake Geneva where the family spent their summers. She received her education at home. A pretty young girl, her shiny black wavy hair worn Alsatian-style in long plaits, she loved dancing and was much courted. At twenty-one she married Comte Mathieu de Noailles. He had a distinguished name and an affable manner; he dabbled in politics as a Radical Socialist, gave Anna a son and sheltered her in her chosen career of poet.

Anna published her first book, *Le Cœur innombrable*, in 1901, and her best book, *Les Vivants et les Morts*, in 1913. Language and form are uninventive; all her own are the musical cadences and distinctively feminine sensibility. She writes best of Mediterranean landscapes, of flowers, their scents and the memories they evoke, of her almost voluptuous pleasure in Nature, and of her regret that that pleasure must end.

The attachment to pleasure is her strength but also her limitation, for she can seldom see beyond it. Watching poor, sad-looking Venetian women hurrying to church, she begs God quickly to satisfy all their longings, 'since the only real cure is joy'.

In one of her best poems Anna de Noailles reproaches God with taking pleasure in beautiful misty landscapes, in the play of birds and butterflies, while remaining indifferent to man's never satisfied longings. Since she does not believe in an after-life, death becomes the arch-enemy, and yet by its very finality attracts her. She thrills to a soldiers' marching song: *'Cet appel exaltait mieux que vivre'*, and about the battlefields of Alsace-Lorraine writes:

> *Leur pays et leur cœur s'endorment deux à deux,*
> *Et leur rêve est entré dans la nuit nuptiale . . .*[1]

Anna de Noailles happened also to possess a flamboyant personality, and through the combination made her mark on Paris. With her fringe, big brown eyes, wide nostrils and jowled cheeks she resembled a poodle, but she was intensely alive, intensely voluble. She loved what she called conversation, which others called monologue, for she poured forth talk, like a torrent. She also carried with her a sheaf of verses, in large writing on pale blue vellum, and if not in the mood for conversation would start reading these aloud.

---

[1] Their country and their heart sleep side by side,
And their dream has become a wedding night . . .

Anna wanted fame for herself and bowed down before fame in others. She is said to have made Bergson blush, when they first met, by advancing towards him in three stages, halting three times, each time with a greeting: *'Monsieur! . . . Maître . . . Acropole de la pensée!'* She loved power also. She fell in love with the nationalist politician, Maurice Barrès, who treated her roughly, and wrote a novel about him, entitled *La Domination*, in which she reveals a taste for subjection, what a friend termed her Oriental side.

She was not very intelligent. She believed that science would lead to the rule of justice and pity, to a future 'like summer that never ends'. She wrote a silly novel about a nun who receives her lover in her cell, interspersed with rather extravagant praise of Nature; of it her friend Abbé Mugnier said: 'She goes one better than St Francis. To the melon she says "You are my brother", to the raspberry, "You are my sister".' But the author of a fine line – *'Le paradis, c'est vous, beaux cieux lourds de nuages'* – considered that she possessed special insight into metaphysical matters. Once, brandishing a chair, she chased Jean Cocteau along the corridor, angry because he had written a letter to Jacques Maritain on some point of theology: 'It's as simple as this,' she shouted at Cocteau. 'If God were to exist, I should be the first to be informed.'

Anna de Noailles loved to dance, and with her light agile body performed well. But she did not go out a great deal. Most often she received friends reclining on her Louis XV bed. In praising joy of every kind, tinged with regret that death is the end, she spoke for her milieu in the 1900s. She became a darling of the salons and was invited to read her poems at the Collège de France. We shall meet her again presently in a political role.

As well as adding her own distinctive voice to the literary chorus, Anna de Noailles played a prominent part in helping other women writers, either as friend or as hostess.

One whom she protected was Gabrielle Colette. Daughter of a free-thinking Paris-born mother and a bankrupt Burgundy tax-collector who had lost a leg against the Austrians, Colette spent a happy childhood in the Yonne before marrying, young, a man socially above her. Henry Gauthier-Villars wrote a famous column of musical criticism, *Letters of an Usherette*, under the name Willy. A shameless exhibitionist who paid newspapers to write about him – 'only God and Alfred Dreyfus are as well known' – Willy was also a self-styled Don Juan and a literary pirate. Discovering his young wife's literary gifts, he placed her each day under lock and key in order to turn out Claudine novels, which he published under his own name and the profits from which went into his own pockets.

In 1900 Paris was reading *Claudine à l'école*, which had caused a sensation by describing a Burgundy village school where the girl pupils have a crush on their women teachers; the fresh innocence of its heroine, Claudine, being contrasted with the perversity of Luce, a country girl who sells her favours to an old protector and plays out his sexual fantasies.

In 1901 Willy, aged forty-two, and Colette, aged twenty-eight, set up home in rue de Courcelles. They became prominent figures in Paris. At one of the tables of the Palais de Glace, Cocteau recalls, would sit Willy, 'with his huge moustache, his Tartarin beard, his glance lively under his heavy eyelids, his Lavalière cravat, his episcopal hands folded atop his walking stick', and next to him Colette, 'thin, thin. Like a baby fox in cycling costume,' with her ever-present bulldog, Toby. And no woman in Paris, it was said, had a glance as sweet as hers.

Colette took to the stage, playing Claudine and acting

in mimes. She toured France and mixed with all sorts. In 1906 she escaped bondage to her bullying, exploitive husband and went to live with a lesbian, the highly eccentric Marquise Mathilde de Belbœuf, great-granddaughter of the Empress Josephine, until her divorce from Willy should come through. In a typical gesture Willy, on his next train journey, seated himself in a 'Women Only' compartment and met all protests with the cool claim: 'I am the Marquise de Belbœuf.'

Though the discovery of Sappho's poems in the 1890s had shown that lesbianism had flourished in classical Greece and was perhaps less heinous than the Old Testament made out, Colette had put herself beyond the pale. Only a very few enlightened hostesses would receive her. One who befriended her was the mannish woman novelist, Rachilde, literary editor of *Mercure de France*, who kept as pets two black sewer rats, Kyrie and Eleison. Warmer and less alarming was the friendship accorded her by Anna de Noailles. Both ladies shared a sensuous fondness for flowers, shrubs, plants, small animals, for chocolate, for cream and, of course, for language. Colette would never forget Anna's kindness.

As for her novels, Claudine's zest for life and affection for animals pleased readers, though basically she is an amoral little piece who declares, 'Vice is the evil we do without pleasure.' The critic Jean Larnac disapproved of the propensity of Colette and other female writers to dwell on their childhood and adolescence: 'It almost seems that youth is their most precious possession ... so eagerly do they indulge in describing tomboy delights in the garden, in the woods, at the seashore, without a thought for anything but their own sensual gratification in fresh air and the beauties of nature.' Larnac would have preferred them to extol love, marriage and maternity!

The ladies who held, or went to, salon receptions set great store by dress, for, says the English-born Daisy of Pless, Parisiennes tried to shine in three things: repartee, clothes and popularity. To which one may add Gertrude Stein's remark: 'Fashion is the real thing in abstraction. The one thing that has no practical side to it and so quite naturally Paris which has always made fashions was where everybody went in 1900.'

The leading couturiers were Jean Worth, who dressed royalty and opera stars; Madame Paquin, high society and actresses, her establishment in rue de la Paix next door to Worth's. The three Callot sisters, daughters of an antique dealer, favoured velvet for day, overhung with beads or tiers of lace, heavy satin for evening, while Jacques Doucet specialized in day dresses and fine lingerie.

From 1900 to 1908 the Silhouette Serpentine or Swan Bend prevailed. Based on a very tight corset, prominent bust and behind, it was beginning to appear to the young heavy and overblown. Colours were invariably pale. Spring and autumn fashions varied details of cut and accessory only. Hats, wide-brimmed and heaped with ornaments, were important. In 1906 Elisabeth Greffulhe founded 'A league for small hats', and with friends put together a number which they sold for charity, but she failed to reverse the trend.

Enfin vint Poiret. A draper's son, Paul Poiret as a boy frequented the Louvre and theatres. At nineteen he joined Doucet and was allowed to dress Bernhardt for *L'Aiglon*: it was he who conceived her scarf knotted at the waist, which became famous. After military service and a short spell at Worth, Paul Poiret opened his own shop. The actress Réjane patronized him and he was launched.

Poiret was a burly fellow who loved good cooking and came to resemble a sculptured Assyrian bull. He chose as his wife a textile manufacturer's daughter, Denise, slender and petite, with a small bust. Such a girl could never look well in the capacious matronly gowns of the day, and it was initially to set off Denise's figure that Poiret revolutionized couture.

He began quietly in 1906 by designing loose, instead of fitted coats. Two years later, from a new establishment in the Faubourg Saint-Honoré, he daringly launched his Empire line: high waist, almost no bust, narrow, straight and simple. Dispensing altogether with the old-style waist-constricting corset, he straightened the traditional S into an exclamation mark.

With this revolution in line went a revolution in colour. 'Nuances of nymph's thigh,' says Poiret, 'lilacs, swooning mauves, tender blue hortensias, niles, maizes, straws, all that was soft, washed-out and insipid, was held in honour. I threw into this sheepcote a few rough wolves: reds, greens, violets, royal blues, that made all the rest sing loud. I had to wake up the good people of Lyon, whose stomach is a bit heavy, and put a little gaiety, a little new freshness into their colour schemes. There were orange and lemon crêpe de Chines which they would not have dared to imagine.'

Poiret launched his combination of Empire line and bold colours with a showmanship learned from frequenting the theatre. In the large garden of his establishment he presented fashion parades, backing them up with a de luxe booklet entitled *Les Robes de Paul Poiret* in an edition of 250 copies at 40 francs. The ten plates by Paul Iribe had no elaborate backgrounds, no swirling figures, just models standing still, their dresses depicted simply.

Poiret's new style, dubbed *le vague*, had to contend with the Tanagra line, launched by Madame Paquin in the same year, which while retaining the Swan Bend, lowered the neckline considerably (a very transparent lace bodice saved propriety), and featured a skirt without petticoats that clung to the hips. The Tanagra line was more becoming than *le vague* and might well have won the day but for the first Ballets Russes. On a wave of enthusiasm for Bakst's loose Oriental costumes in rich colours *le vague* caught on with a speed that surprised even Poiret.

Poiret undoubtedly helped to create a new type of Parisienne, more natural in appearance than before, able to move more freely and drawing on bold colours to express the vitality that had replaced decorativeness as a desideratum. But the couturier was also meeting a need. Women now needed to be mobile, whether climbing on to the top deck of a bus (here young English and American visitors had shown the way) or hurrying up and down Métro staircases. If their motor-car broke down, they might have to walk quite far for help; at an air display they would rove the extensive aerodrome, chatting to brave young pilots and climbing into their machines. These and similar activities would not have been possible in a tight corset and heavy multiple petticoats.

Poiret was very much the pasha. Wearing a colourful Chinese-style brocade jacket he would stride up and down his establishment telling his mannequins exactly how to pose and at anything second-rate inclined to lose his temper. Almost as superstitious as Diaghilev, whenever he saw a pack of cards he would turn one up: a club or heart, he would be happy all day; but a spade would plunge him into gloom – so sometimes his mannequins would stack the cards. He saw himself as a 'pure' artist and invited Dunoyer de Segonzac and Picasso to his dinners, much to the annoyance of Apollinaire, who thought Poiret just a showman. In fact, like Diaghilev, he was both.

In 1910, invited by the Freudenberg brothers, who

ran the Herman Gerson dress business, Poiret went to Berlin, taking with him his latest collection and eight mannequins. There he met the Kaiser's son, Prince Eitel, and was pleasurably surprised to find he knew more about Parisian fashion and art than most Frenchmen. Poiret was particularly struck by the excellent new villas going up in the pinewoods round Berlin. He was also invited by Mrs Asquith to put on a show at 'Gowning Street', as the press renamed Number 10, much to the disgruntlement of British designers, for it was a time of crisis for their textile and dress trade.

As his fame grew, Poiret opened up an interior decoration business named Martine, after one of his daughters, and a scent business, named Rosine, after a second daughter. The first couturier to launch into this field, Poiret had his biggest success with *Le Fruit Défendu*, which smelled of peaches.

Despite so many activities, including the founding of a Syndicat to check the pirating of Parisian fashions by New York department stores, Poiret continued to design highly innovative clothes. The chronology goes like this:

1909: the slender, straight line already described, jackets up to 40 inches long, as in the past the hem a shade below the ankle, domed hat with a droopy wide brim. Described by Eve Lavallière as 'The Mushroom Look'.

1910: the hobble skirt. A woman could walk only by taking tiny steps. Despite protests, it became fashionable, modified however by discreet pleats at the side or a concealed slit.

1911: Turkish-style trousers. When his mannequins showed them off at the Auteuil races, people laughed and scoffed '*Au harem! Enlevez ça!*' The fashion failed to catch on.

1912: small fur hats.

Spring 1913: very high-heeled shoes, skirts with several shaped panels or with a corkscrew line, hats with a feather at the back pointing straight up. Dressed like this it was fashionable to hold the body slightly backwards, knees bent.

Spring 1914: double skirts, the inner one narrow, slit at both sides, the outer one flared and shorter by 10 inches. Aigrettes. On the cheeks violet instead of rouge.

Jean Worth says fashion changes speeded up between 1908 and 1914. Whereas before 1908 a girl could decently wear a frock from the previous summer, after that date she felt obliged to dress in the fashion of the moment. Proust speaks of similar changes and how they were attributed by some to the tempo of modern living, based on the motor-car and telephone. He denies any causal link and sees fashion either as a swing of the pendulum or, as he puts it, 'such theories and notions of "schools" devour each other like microbes and globules, and by their struggle ensure the continuity of life'. Proust's simile has itself become outmoded. We know now that an organism's antibodies act not at random but in order to protect identity and survival value. Fashion in clothes would appear to be intimately linked to a society's view of itself and to its dominant tone and images. In our period fashion expresses not only a need for mobility but also, in its colours, the exuberant joyousness proclaimed most notably by Anna de Noailles.

'Dressing well,' said Poiret, 'means heightening one's individuality,' to which Jean Worth added an important rider: 'The reason the Frenchwoman is so well dressed as a rule is that she is immensely critical of her appearance.' Others were critical too – we are a long way from English tolerance – none more so than the four top cari-

caturists who could be seen, most days, in the Avenue
du Bois, studying form. Helleu, his yellowish face
framed by a black beard, long and lean; Forain, who
drew for *Figaro*, his hands clasped behind his back
under his coat making a kind of bustle; Boldini – 'a
Paganini of the peignoir' – with his broad forehead,
large eyes and darting gestures, like a hermit crab; Sem,
his big umbrella under one arm, wearing a brown rain-
coat, like a bespectacled marmoset, throwing out harsh
comments in a Périgord accent. It was Sem who almost
sank the hobble-skirt by drawing a caricature of ladies
so dressed – but with horses' legs and horses' hooves.
'His talent is such,' asserted the painter la Gandara,
'that . . . we shall never be able to see a pretty woman
except through Sem's eyes, with all those minor imperfections he can insinuate so subtly.'

If new fashions provided subjects for sharp wit, they
also encouraged those social occasions where they
could be admired. Poiret loved throwing parties. In
1911, the year he published his second luxury book, *Les
Choses de Paul Poiret*, with plates by young Georges
Lepape, he gave a 'Thousand and Two Nights' Ball',
at which fashions in the book came to life: jewelled
turbans, bead-trimmed tunics worn with slave bangles
and harem slippers. The following year Poiret designed
the costumes for Félicité de Chabrillan's Persian Ball, at
which Félicité dressed as Scheherazade and several
ladies came as exotic birds, notably Elisabeth de
Gramont as a bird of paradise.

At these parties, when the dresses had evoked
surprise, discussion, comparison and copy for the gossip columnists, guests began to dance. About dance
Elisabeth de Gramont, an intelligent society commen-
tator, has a striking image: in Steinlen's *fin de siècle*
drawings illustrating the songs of Montmartre his
women slouch, their shoulders droop beneath capes or

boas, they sit sipping absinthe in the wan light shed by
gas-globes; then, with the turn of the century, electric
light is switched on, the women straighten up and begin
to dance, bouncing energetically, swaying, swinging.
Or, if the party's mood is more restrained, they move
into a square dance for four persons – the quadrille. But
whether it be quadrille or waltz, Parisians dance their
way into the twentieth century.

New dances appear: in 1903 the cakewalk; soon
afterwards Debussy included in his *Children's Corner* a
'Golliwog's Cakewalk'. In 1910 the cakewalk yields to
another American importation, the boston, which is a
variation of the waltz, and in 1911 to the Argentinian
tango.

In its native form the tango is danced to guitar and
bandoneon. In 1907 Camille de Rhynan, a French
dancer and composer, modified this for the ballroom. A
couple of years later he won a dancing competition
organized by a leading newspaper for a range of dances
including the tango, and so launched a fashion. Tango
parties began to be organized in private houses with
an Argentinian boy playing the piano, while in Montmartre, at the El Garron and La Feria cafés, Almanos
and Odette danced to popular tango tunes, notably '*El
Irresistible*' and '*El Choclo*'.

The tango consists of a shuffle, a whirl, a dip and a
swing, the dip being considered daring or indecent
according to your point of view, like the waltz a hundred years earlier. The tango was frowned on by the
Church and in Germany forbidden to army officers in
uniform. But in Paris it thrived. To dance it well you
wore a brightly coloured slim-line dress with, for the
period, quite a short skirt deeply slit at the sides.

*   *   *

Closely related to changes in dress were changes in the decorative arts. Perceptive visitors to the 1900 Exhibition had believed the future lay with *art nouveau*, whose leading practitioner was Emile Gallé of Nancy. Over his studio door Gallé inscribed these lines: 'Our roots are deep in the woods/Among the mosses, close to the springs,' thereby declaring his belief that the artist must return to nature, notably to the flowing curves of water and plants, but at the back of Gallé's mind were the Symbolist poets and *their* view of nature as a place where one mused, dreamed and evoked rather than stated.

Out of this creed developed an art of tendrils, whiplash lines, dragonflies, dream-maidens, *femmes-fleurs*, in which curves and convolutions triumphed.

Gallé started as a glass designer and the best *art nouveau* was small-scale: glass, jewellery, bronze and gilt bronze. The dancer Loie Fuller, whirling in long loose tunic, became a model for many statuettes, and also for a fine bronze table lamp by Raoul Larche. These had a vogue beyond France: Charles Sykes's 'Spirit of Ecstasy', the mascot for Rolls-Royce, derives from such work, although Sykes's model was not Loie but Lord Montagu's secretary. Young René Lalique, working for Robert de Montesquiou among others, produced innovative jewellery, notably about 1900 a silver and cast glass pendant brooch of a *femme-fleur*. In such work, incidentally, there is an absence of those religious themes to be found in England's Arts and Crafts Movement.

The best *art nouveau* furniture are small pieces, stools and the like, where tendril lines are appropriate. Larger pieces, like an asymmetrical pearwood cabinet with whiplash supports by Hector Guimard, designer of the Métro entrances, served to show that *art nouveau* was in several respects ill-suited to the twentieth century.

311

Doing away with straight lines and right-angles made for an uncertain, unrobust-looking product at a period that prized confidence and action. Dreamy woodland and mossy springs no longer struck a chord in an age of the pulsating atom, the motor-car and the aeroplane. Certainly *art nouveau* did well to challenge the historicism of French furniture since 1870 and its lack of refinement, but to challenge it effectively something stronger was required.

A new style meeting new needs emerged between 1905 and 1908. Termed Art Deco, it reasserted respect for tradition and discipline by drawing on Louis XVI work and First Empire sobriety. It aimed at producing strong but light pieces, symmetrical, spare in line but in surface sumptuous.

Louis Majorelle, born in 1859 and working in Nancy under the influence of Gallé, started as an *art nouveau* devotee. A corner table made by him has a top in the form of a water-lily leaf, even to the extent of slightly curved rims; the splayed legs terminate in small water-lily leaves. Around 1910, in a volte-face comparable to Poiret's streamlining of the Swan lady, Majorelle turned from the motifs of garden and pond and began to produce pieces with sober functional lines, attractive by virtue of exotic woods and discreet rich inlays. A leading Parisian maker of jewellery, clocks, light fittings and furniture, Paul Follot, followed a similar evolution.

The new wave of furniture makers was helped by the founding of the Salon d'Automne, which accorded their work equal place with painting and sculpture, and by the patronage of rich couturiers. André Groult, married to Poiret's sister Nicole, was one of the first to seek to harmonize all elements in a room: to this end in 1912 he commissioned a group of artists to produce a much-admired range of new and colourful fabric designs. In the same year Jacques Doucet commissioned Paul Iribe to furnish his new apartment at 46 Avenue du Bois. Iribe looked like a seminarist and spoke in whispers, but he was a Titan determined to sweep pretentious, overblown clutter from French homes. One of Iribe's pieces, a little commode on tall, slim, very slightly curved legs, is overlaid with shagreen and decorated with nine small rose blooms on almost straight, very thin stems, mere lines. On a white bergère of the same period by Iribe similar radiating very thin lines divide the high back; the legs are short, the arms terminate in whorl mouldings. These pieces are small-scale, equivalents, say, of a Debussy *Etude*, but they are strongly conceived, concentrated, clean-cut, the meandering fussy detail of *art nouveau* firmly pruned back.

Jacques-Emile Ruhlmann and Clément Rousseau are two others who made pioneer Art Deco furniture in exotic woods, decorated with restrained stylized floral motifs, often in marquetry.

The swing to Art Deco took place at the same time as the constricting corset was shed and the slender lady came into vogue, dressed in Empire line. The two events are part of a general trend towards lightness, mobility, rich colour. These qualities we shall meet again in Matisse. Proust, too, evidently warmed to the trend, for he bought long slim notebooks in which to jot down thoughts for his novel, and on the cover of one is a girl in a new slender-line bustless dress. In a way impossible twelve years earlier she is light and elusive, as Albertine is in the later novel. Once again fashion in one field, like an electro-magnetic current, is seen to affect fashion in adjacent fields.

In furnishing their homes tastefully, in expressing their personality through attractive clothes and accessories and, of course, in bringing up their children, married Frenchwomen exercised a great deal of freedom. Many found in such activities all the freedom they wanted. Others, such as Marguerite Borel and Anna de Noailles, chose to lead full lives partly outside the home. They reconciled the demands of family and work without suffering from legal or social constrictions. But both happened to belong to groups tolerant of enterprising women. Elsewhere in Paris old taboos prevailed.

One class of men, for instance, wished to keep women hobbled precisely because they had such a high opinion of them. Early in 1902 young Louis Gillet wrote to Romain Rolland: 'I am ashamed of being only a man: a woman, a real woman, seems to me a goddess. But I am unspeakably shocked by feminist ideas. I would recoil in horror from a woman doctor or a woman lawyer and I don't understand either how they are allowed to do paid jobs in a workshop, to become cogs in the social machine when in fact they are society's soul and conscience, its music.'

The year following that pronouncement saw, in fact, a steady growth in the number of professional and career women. The ban on women lawyers had been lifted in December 1900 and thereafter quite a number of French Portias came forward. Marie Curie in 1906 opened the way to university teaching jobs. There were more women doctors. Frenchwomen came late to sport but at the 1912 Olympics the women's tennis singles was won by Marguerite Broquedis. More women published distinctively feminine novels. Just as the Salon d'Automne had raised interior designers to the level of painters, so the founding of the Femina prize in 1905 by the women's magazine, *Vie Heureuse*, for the best literary work in the past year by a member of either sex rewarded books that the markedly male Goncourt might have turned down. The Femina jury of twenty-one women, presided over by Anna de Noailles, gave the prize in 1910 to Marguerite Audoux's *Marie Claire*, a real-life novel of value about growing up in a Bourges orphanage, and in 1913 to Marguerite Borel's *La Statue Voilée*.

At the economic level, women got their working day reduced from eleven hours to ten in 1904. In 1907 a married woman was granted sole right to her earnings. In 1910 she might take eight weeks' unpaid maternity leave. In 1913 a minimum salary was set for women working at home.

Yet in various ways the single woman especially was a second-class citizen. In his 1912 play *La Femme Seule* Eugène Brieux, a leading campaigner for social justice, depicted her plight in the shape of a Parisian girl of twenty-three, Thérèse, whose parents have died and who is living with her godparents. She is engaged to a young man, René. Unexpectedly the family notary absconds with a large sum, including her dowry. René yields to his parents when they disapprove of an impecunious marriage. Thérèse's godparents suggest moving to Evreux; but she declines. To their dismay she is going to live alone in Paris and work on a new periodical, *Femme Libre*.

Act II shows Thérèse doing well in her job. Then the editor sexually harasses her and she is obliged to leave. She cannot find other work nor, as a single woman, cheap accommodation.

Act III shows her in Evreux, living with her godparents but self-supporting. She organizes a women's trade union on a small scale which succeeds so well that union leaders in Paris take fright and send a delegation to threaten Thérèse. She stands her ground until, at last, the workers she has tried to help, misled by the delegation, destroy the women's workroom. Thérèse is beaten, but only for the moment. She will return to Paris, regain her independence and perhaps, as an equal now, rejoin René. But before taking the train, she declaims prophetically:

> The sons of middle-class families who haven't enough stamina to marry girls without dowries will be sure to find those same girls later – girls whom they forced to go to work! . . . A new era has begun. In every land, among rich and poor, out of every home deserted by drunkards or left empty by those who fear the tribulations of marriage, a woman will rise up and leave, and come and take her place beside you, in the factory, in the workshop, in the office. You wouldn't take her as a housewife, and she refuses to prostitute herself to you – she will be a working woman, a competitor, and a successful competitor! – Goodbye!

The battle in France for equal legal rights took place against a world background of prejudice. In 1908 in New York City the Sullivan Ordinance forbade women to smoke in public, Mayor Markbreit of Cincinnati declared flatly: 'No woman is physically fit enough to run an auto,' and Grover Cleveland, former President, wrote in the October 1905 issue of *Ladies' Home Journal*: 'Sensible and responsible women do not want to vote. The relative positions to be assumed by man and woman in the working out of our civilization were assigned long ago by a higher intelligence than ours.' In Germany too women had second-class status while in England, though suffragettes were on the march, women were denied many of the rights long taken for granted by men.

In France prejudice was no less strong but issued from different traditions. When a feminist writer,

Pauline Savari, put herself forward for the Academy, the Duc d'Aumâle retorted: 'Women are not eligible because one becomes a French citizen only by doing one's military service.' The Duke's argument was often used against feminist calls for the vote – in the 1900s usually only the vote in municipal elections. The feminist reply was: 'The Frenchwoman pays taxes and buys war loans which have always been a way of participating in national defence. Maternity is her everyday battlefield.' Madeleine Pelletier, a feminist doctor of medicine, said she favoured military service for women if it meant full rights.

Frenchwomen pressed much less hard than their counterparts across the Channel for the vote in general elections, preferring to win the municipal vote first and to campaign against particular injustices such as the schoolteacher abroad who, in marrying a non-French colleague, loses her nationality, or the wife who, on divorcing, loses her dowry, and the free-thinker who lives apart from her Catholic husband but cannot obtain a divorce. Feminist organizations disapproved of the suffragettes' extreme methods and preferred to campaign legally under the slogan 'Equality in dissimilarity'. But they met a big obstacle in the Radicals' anti-clericalism. Speaking to a lady friend in 1909, Georges Clemenceau said Poiret should be decorated for freeing women from the corset and its attendant 'hypocrisy', but 'to entrust the destiny of government to the votes of women, influenced as they are from the sacristy, would be to return to the Middle Ages'.

In the quest for women's rights Catholics rather dragged their feet, Marc Sangnier of Le Sillon declaring in 1904 that it was women's role to suffer! Socialists promised more, but when it came to the point gave the sex struggle second place to the class war. In fact

Madeleine Pelletier, of working-class Paris origins, and politically of the extreme Left, declared a woman to be much better off in a middle-class family than in the proletariat, and the last thing she wanted for women was a collectivist society.

Louise Cruppi, as well as being the wife of a Cabinet Minister and presiding over a musical salon, tried to get over her grief at the death of her young son by immersing herself in the feminist movement. She wrote a novel about women's rights, *Avant l'Heure*, became president of the Association to Help Women Students in Paris, and in a well-documented book made known in France the greater freedom enjoyed by Scandinavian women. It was mainly individual moderates such as she, the Comtesse Marie de Villermont and Elisabeth Renaud, and small periodicals like *La Française*, that enlightened opinion and ensured that a bill proposing to give women the municipal vote was placed on the Parliamentary agenda. But by then the year was 1914 and amid more pressing concerns the bill had to be put aside. Thirty-one years would elapse before Frenchwomen got their vote in both municipal and national elections.

Parisiennes, in these opening years of the century, differentiated themselves a little more from men and, in so doing, became more interesting to men and to one another. They described feelings, insights and aspirations which hitherto had not been put into words. They emerged from a clutter of heavy curtains, vases and pot-plants, from the constrictions of *le petit calice*, as it was euphemistically termed, to be lithe, independent, free-ranging, more sincere. Many doubtless became more satisfactory wives, thereby refuting Claudel's claim that love and marriage must be mutually exclusive.

CHAPTER 13

Theatre: the Sublime and the Ridiculous

Paris's forty-odd theatres annually staged a hundred or so new plays, the most popular of which might run for two hundred performances. The best work of Corneille, Racine and Molière was kept alive by the subsidized Comédie Française, thus ensuring a backbone of tradition, while one or two 'fringe' companies, like Lugné-Poe's Œuvre and, later, Copeau's Vieux Colombier, fostered innovation. Leading performers enjoyed high esteem. Notable among the men were Lucien Guitry and the Rumanian-born de Max; among the ladies, Gabrielle Réjane, who played in light comedies; Jeanne Granier, both on and off the stage a favourite with the Prince of Wales; and Julia Bartet, whose dazzling clothes sense prompted the quip: 'Hand Bartet Racine and she'll give you back Paquin [her favourite couturier].'

But the queen of the Paris theatre was Sarah Bernhardt. Illegitimate daughter of a Dutch Jewish lady by a Norman naval officer named Morel, Rosine Bernard was born in Paris. She received a convent education and, like Marguerite Appell, went through a phase of wanting to be a nun. She won a place in the Conservatoire, where her teachers thought her too thin and tense to do well. But at twenty-five she proved them wrong when she appeared in Coppée's short poetic *Le Passant* as Zanetto, a teenage Tuscan minstrel who by his sweet innocence disarms the evil designs of a mature lady. From this success she went on to play classic roles with the Comédie Française, most notably Phèdre. She had left that company to star in contemporary plays and, most recently, to acquire and manage her own playhouse.

The huge old Théâtre des Nations on the Place du Châtelet Sarah bought and redecorated, replacing the immemorial red with upholstery and hangings of yellow velvet. In the large foyer she commissioned painter friends to depict her famous roles, such as Lorenzaccio, Theodora and Phèdre. From her dressing-room, where she installed a bath, she had three large ante-rooms lead down to a dining-room with a table for twelve; here every Sunday she invited to dinner close friends, authors and leading actors.

In the Théâtre Sarah Bernhardt, as it now was, eight days before Christmas 1899, Sarah gathered her company about her. In her twenties she had been exceptionally slim – 'Madame Sarah needs no umbrella, she walks between the raindrops;' now, at fifty-five, her figure was still willowy, her arms slender – but she had the beginnings of plumpness around the stomach, which she declined to corset. The voice that thrilled audiences has been preserved in a recording of *Phèdre*. Her delivery was akin if not to singing, at least to *recitativo* in opera, and to a modern ear that kind of delivery impoverishes nuances of expression.

Her love-life had not been happy. Very young, she had had a brief affair with the Prince de Ligne and borne him a son, Maurice, whom she spoiled and who was forever running up debts. At thirty-eight she had married a handsome Greek actor but within one year they separated. Thereafter she preferred intense Platonic friendships with much younger men.

Her present favourite, Edmond Rostand, born in

Marseille and now aged twenty-four, was handsome, slim, smartly turned out, afire with the verve and loquacity of the South. Four years earlier his *Princesse Lointaine* had been produced by Sarah. She had lost 200,000 francs on this dream fantasy, but money to her counted for less than art and glory, and in her poet's new play, which he was now to read to the company, she saw promise of both.

Napoleon's son, the Duc de Reichstadt, is fighting ill-health and confinement in the palace of Schönbrunn, unloved by his silly mother Marie Louise, tyrannized by the wily Chancellor of Austria Metternich, obsessed by the legend of his father and dreams of re-establishing the Empire of France with himself, the rightful heir, at its head, to lead the Grande Armée to a repetition of the old glories.

Rehearsals began, the cast was called for 1.00 p.m., and minor players appeared then. Lucien Guitry, who played the faithful Flambeau, one of Napoleon's old Grognards, arrived about three. At 3.45 Madame Sarah made her entrance, and the whole company, some fifty persons, kissed her hand in turn. She changed into male clothes and work began, only to be suspended at five for Madame Sarah's cup of tea, watched by others, we are told, with patience and tender respect.

More rehearsing took place, interrupted by the great lady's evening performance – for Sarah continued to direct and act in her regular repertory – after which rehearsing would resume till after midnight.

The pressure was relieved by occasional fun. In a scene on the plain of Wagram Napoleon's son is called to mount a horse. Sarah Bernhardt could ride side-saddle but here she must sit astride; she demanded the tamest horse in Paris. A slow-lumbering nag was found and led on stage.

This animal Sarah studied dubiously. She ordered

the thunder machine sounded. The drowsy horse did not stir. She then had the cast form a circle and rush at the horse, shouting *'Vive l'Empereur!'* This we are told galvanized the horse, which was evidently a Republican, for it expressed its opinion of Empire in farmyard style, and the cast went into fits. When Rostand announced that Flambeau too must ride a horse, Sarah decided she would rearrange the scene on foot. Then she tore off to Vienna to study Schönbrunn and its park, taking with her Rostand. Live horses on stage had to wait for Diaghilev.

L'Aiglon – The Eaglet – opened in time for the Exhibition, on 17 March 1900. Distrusting hooks and buttons, Sarah had herself sewn into her tight-fitting uniform of pure white, relieved by colourful medals and black stock, its high collar setting off her slim, hollow-cheeked face, very pale, and its reddish-blonde mop of hair. Her suppleness allowed her to play convincingly the lively little boy of early scenes, jumping on to the knees of his grandfather Franz Josef, arranging his toy soldiers in order of battle and being surprised by Metternich. 'Where are the Austrians?' he asks, and the boy replies, 'They have all fled.' Later, ambitious for glory, he surveys the deserted battlefield of Wagram and speaks the resounding line, 'Paris, I already hear your bells.' In the final act when the young eagle, balked of his dreams of glory, dies of consumption, it was said that she drew a last breath, 'dying as angels die if they were allowed to'.

The play's theme exactly suited Paris's mood. People wanted and were prepared to work for a new greatness. What form it might take they were not sure, but greatness was their goal; and those who felt rancour about Alsace-Lorraine took pleasure in seeing the Austrians cast as villains. Rostand's poetically emotional approach to this history was original, and was matched by Sarah's acting. She made the aspiring young Aiglon someone with whom the audience could identify. When played in London, Graham Robertson complained, 'It's like standing before a beautiful waterfall. Pretty soon one wants to leave.' But in Paris for almost a year audiences loved every minute of the four hours.

Organizing the production of an original work puts immense strain on the creator, as Stravinsky had found. On opening night Rostand, never robust, contracted pneumonia and spent the spring convalescing with his family. There was nothing new for Sarah in life emulating art. She would drive to Montmorency in her two-horse landau, swathed even on a warm day in a chinchilla wrap, to see 'her poet' and leave on his table a bunch of Napoleon violets.

Sarah Bernhardt was a rare blend of refined artistry, panache and shrewdness. She had been blessed with almost tireless energy and Napoleon's knack of being able to renew it with twenty minutes' instant sleep. She knew she possessed exceptional gifts and that the public wished to be dazzled by them. Yet she possessed a sense of humour and, quite often, an endearing modesty. She admitted that her energy often overflowed into inconsistency. 'I promise everything with the firm intention of keeping my promise, and two hours later I've forgotten. If friends remind me, I tear my hair and invent excuses.' To a sixteen-year-old who after a single meeting begged a signed photograph, she sent one inscribed: 'To Michel Georges-Michel, a charming friend to whom I owe all.'

At various times, she took up painting, the piano, writing, pistol-shooting, alligator-hunting. She became a good enough sculptress to be able to show *art nouveau* ornaments shaped like flowers and small animals at the 1900 Exhibition. For a time she kept a tame lion in her house. 'If there's anything more remarkable than watching Sarah act,' said Sardou, 'it's watching her live.'

In August, when theatres closed, Sarah took ship for Belle Isle, off the south coast of Brittany. As she crossed the drawbridge of her house a servant unfurled from the flagstaff her personal self-designed standard. Up at six, she would don fisherman's clothes and a white beret, sling a gun over her shoulder and, accompanied by two huge mastiffs and a black boy servant, hurry to the beach to shoot duck. Then perhaps to her nearby farm to collect fresh eggs and milk, or to make her own butter, which meant in effect to persuade a compliant house guest or two to work the churn. The rest of the morning she might spend sketching in the company of her lifelong companion, Georges Clairin, a docile portrait-painter, and Louise Abbéma, also a painter, who, as she aged, in her blunt-peaked yachtsman's cap more and more resembled a Japanese admiral.

Lunch at one was served on Quimper plates. Sarah ate sparingly, mainly caviar, oysters and sorbets, but insisted on sampling each course and, if not perfect, on summoning the cook and berating her publicly. In the afternoon there would be tennis or shrimping or perhaps the reception of a visiting dignitary; on one occasion King Edward VII. When storms almost wiped out the Belle Isle fishing fleet in 1911, it was she who organized a theatrical gala and sent the proceeds to be distributed among the needy. Money for Sarah meant gold in a chamois bag or brass-bound strongbox, easy to give or spend, and so despite huge earnings all her life she was on the verge of financial ruin.

Evenings were given over to cards, dominoes or a performance by a guest. One evening Reynaldo Hahn started to play and hum the Habañero from *Carmen*, whereupon Sarah's son Maurice seized his mother's scarf and went into a Spanish dance, his two young daughters imitating him. Another time, Sarah asked Hahn if he'd care to hear one of her musical compositions. This turned out to be 'The Dance of the Bears', made up to amuse Maurice when he was a child. 'You see?' she said proudly. 'The left hand doesn't move at all. It just keeps on repeating the same note.'

In September she would return to Paris, resume her fourteen-hour schedule and create another role, for her big theatre had to be filled. With a flair for gauging public taste, in 1903 she played the lead in Sardou's *The Witch*. Set in Toledo during the Inquisition, Zoraya, a Moorish gipsy, is accused of sorcery and condemned to the stake by Cardinal Ximenes, the Grand Inquisitor. At the height of anti-clerical measures the play proved a success. Later, when the Government overreached itself, Sarah chose to satisfy the tide of reaction: she became Teresa of Avila in a play by Catulle Mendès.

Her stage was the world. She played the main Continental cities, she played London, where the actress Madge Kendal, though an admirer, complained that Bernhardt acted in roles requiring such displays of passion that Mrs Kendal felt she could not take her daughter to see her, to which Sarah replied, 'But Madam, remember that were it not for passion, you would have no daughter to bring.'

On her sixth United States tour in 1905, accompanied by fifty trunks, five servants, a secretary and a masseur, she played *L'Aiglon*, crossing the continent to applause. People stayed away from other theatres, so as to have money to see Sarah as Napoleon II. The managers of all the playhouses in the West became so alarmed that they arranged to boycott the French actress. Sarah's reply was to play in a transportable canvas theatre with room for 4800 seats. In Houston and Dallas more money was taken than ever before – up to $9000 a performance – and altogether on this tour 'under canvas' she played sixty-two cities.

In South America the Germans might have commercial hegemony, but the French led in the arts and Sarah, very patriotic, saw her tour there as part of France's 'civilizing mission'. In 1905 she played several Latin-American countries, ending in Rio de Janeiro. In the last scene of her farewell performance in *La Tosca*, she had to escape the police by jumping through a high window. She was meant to land on mattresses but for some reason her right knee hit the stage and she fainted with the pain.

Next day, against all advice, she embarked for New York, and the ship's doctor came to examine her knee, but he happened to have dirty hands and fingernails, and Sarah vowed this unclean person should never touch her. At the end of the three-week voyage her knee had become so swollen she could not open on the announced night. Thereafter all walking caused her pain.

Sarah decided to defy this disability. She would continue acting, continue living to the hilt. More than that, though now past sixty, she would defy the ageing process by spending as much time as possible with the young. So she trained promising actors and actresses, and at home looked after – with much good sense – Maurice's granddaughters, whose mother had died. She had them call her '*Grand*', short for *Grandmère*, but not without another connotation.

At Belle Isle she continued to play tennis doubles, taking her stand gallantly at the net. But opponents knew that balls had to be placed within her reach, otherwise she'd throw down her racquet and walk off. For age was bringing to the fore the selfish side of Sarah's character. In her mid-sixties she chose as her leading man an empty-headed, conceited but very handsome actor of Greek-Dutch parentage, Lou Tellegen. Soon the two were inseparable.

In 1909 Sarah again showed her flair for gauging public opinion. This was the year when the Pope beatified Jeanne d'Arc, and many Frenchmen chose to see the Maid of Orleans as a symbol of France's perennial innocence and courage in the face of warlike neighbours: in 1431 the English *goddams*, in 1909 the Kaiser. There was, as we shall see later, perhaps more than a little narcissism in this, but the fact of the new popularity of the shepherdess-soldier is undeniable, and Sarah chose to meet and further define it by staging Emile Moreau's simple yet moving *Trial of Jeanne d'Arc*.

By then aged sixty-five, Sarah did not hesitate to take the part of Joan. So the play's great moment falls not when Joan is condemned or burned, but when she is led before her judges and the heavy iron fetters are removed from her aching wrists.

> 'What is your name?'
> 'Joan.'
> 'Your age?'
> 'Nineteen.'

This drew from the house a gasp not of incredulity, but of wonder and admiration, then a moment's silence, followed by loud clapping.

Parisians in the past had fêted young stars of genius – the Spanish-born soprano La Malibran, Sarah herself – but now for the first time they offered incense to a woman in her sixties. By bringing to life Napoleon II and Jeanne d'Arc she had come to personify the honour of France. Moreover, she had made of her life a work of art. Now she was defying time by remaining continuously youthful, achieving Proust's ideal of apotheosis through art. Parisians applauded. They called her the Eighth Wonder of the World, they called her Divine.

When she was seventy and still playing leading roles, though soon her leg would have to be amputated and replaced with an artificial limb, the various aspects of her life since 1900 came together. The Government decided to put their seal on the public's acclaim. Protocol did not allow them to honour her as an actress, but in recognition of her services as a nurse in the 1870-71 war and as a purveyor of French civilization abroad, Sarah Bernhardt received the scarlet ribbon of the order established by the Emperor Napoleon, the Légion d'Honneur.

In the *Revue de Paris* for February 1900 Georges Bourdon, former production manager of the Odéon, wrote an article comparing London and Paris theatres. London, he noted, dispensed with a prompter's box bang in the centre of the stage, which was a feature of Paris theatres, except Sarah Bernhardt's. London scenery had more realistic detail than Paris's, it was changed faster and better lit. The standard of comfort for the audience was higher in London. Bourdon might have added that both cities were dominated by actor-managers and the star system. Both cities had censorship, the Lord Chamberlain mainly concerned with sexual mores, the paid delegates of Paris's Assembly with protecting the Establishment. But in 1906, as an economy measure, the Assembly was to abolish censorship.

In the first decade of the new century Londoners went to see the witty paradoxes of Oscar Wilde, J. M. Barrie's fey sentiment and 'little mothers', the well-tooled dramas of Pinero and Jones. They also went to plays by two foreigners that challenged their accepted standards, the Norwegian Ibsen and the Irishman

Bernard Shaw. Parisians by contrast never took to Ibsen, whom they found gloomy, and Shaw's *Candida* irritated them: how could a woman in her right mind prefer a weak man to a strong one? They preferred comedy by Frenchmen about subjects within a framework of accepted French values. The productions of Sarah Bernhardt and the Comédie Française apart, by far the greater number of successes on the Paris stage at this time were comedies of character.

The master of this genre, Tristan Bernard, was born in Besançon in 1866, came to Paris at fourteen, studied for the Bar, then began to run his father's aluminium factory. But Bernard was less drawn to business than to bicycling; he became for a time sports manager of the cycling arena, Buffalo Vélodrome, and in that role was portrayed by Toulouse-Lautrec – legs astride, back arched, black beard thrust forcefully forward. For this bicycle-racing enthusiast also loved the arts, particularly poetry, and would read aloud his favourites: La Fontaine, Hugo and Verlaine.

Tristan Bernard had a love of nonsense and the joyousness of a child let loose to play. One day on a busy street he was accidentally hit and knocked down by a grandfather clock a workman was carrying on his shoulders. Instead of getting angry Bernard rose to his feet, brushed off the dust and said to the workman, 'Why don't you wear a watch like everyone else?' At home – he made a happy marriage at twenty-one – he would rise in the middle of a meal to throw a napkin over his arm to imitate a pompous head waiter or, during a dinner-party, disappear from the room to return a minute later as a trapper from the frozen North, swathed in the furs of lady guests. Taking tea one day with a stingy hostess, Bernard was offered a plate of *babas au rhum* – each cake cut in two. Helping himself, Bernard said politely, 'Thank you, Madame, I will have a *ba*.' 'I'll never grow into second childhood,' he declared, 'I've never emerged from the first.'

At twenty-three Bernard wrote his first successful comedy, *L'Anglais tel qu'on le parle*, featuring a so-called interpreter who cannot speak or understand English. The humour in this and subsequent plays is of the easy, jolly kind called *l'esprit boulevardier*. Its tone comes through in a piece Bernard wrote for a periodical, 'Genesis, French-style':

> The first day of Creation would have been a Sunday.
> Work would have begun on Monday at 2 p.m.
> Without delay a commission for the Sun and the Moon would have been appointed;
> then a commission for the Stars;
> then various zoological commissions, not forgetting the ornithological and ichthyological sub-commissions.
> Following that, the setting up of a commission for the creation of man, a technical committee for putting man to sleep, a special commission to study the removal of ribs, then the high commission for the creation of woman.
> By 3 p.m. on Saturday nothing would have been done.
> To the roll of drums the President of the Republic would have arrived to inaugurate a collection of tarpaulins and a heap of rubble which, by special dispensation, would no longer be called Chaos, but have the new name Universe.
> Most important of all, the world henceforth would have an administrative existence.

Bernard took endless pains polishing his plays but, as a true boulevardier, pretended to be lazy. To someone who suggested coming to see him, he would say, 'Please do. Preferably in the morning. That's when I work.'

Like Shaw's *Pygmalion*, the subject of Bernard's best play was suggested by a professor friend. André Godfernaux specialized in incapacity of the will and from his descriptions of patients Bernard conceived the eponymous Triplepatte, an inconsequential, weak-willed but well-meaning nobleman, so named after one of his steeplechasers that refuses to jump unless given the whip.

The play opens at a spa, where the tone is set by a forceful doctor who prescribes for patients the opposite of what they expect: 'Otherwise you wouldn't need me.' Triplepatte drifts in. He is in debt and needs money. Though he is not at all attracted to marriage, his friends decide that marry he must. The girl proposed is Yvonne, the eighteen-year-old daughter of a morbidly shy financier.

In Act II Triplepatte arrives for a party at Yvonne's house and gets talking to Yvonne's father, neither knowing who the other is. 'You're thinking of marrying,' the father exclaims, 'yet you don't like parties! Once married, it'll be nothing but going to parties and giving them. At present you can stay away. But then, you won't have any choice!' After which Triplepatte bolts, only to be stopped at the gate and brought back to meet Yvonne.

Act III, in his bedroom, shows Triplepatte, the reluctant bridegroom; in Act IV, at the *mairie* the bride and the guests await Triplepatte who eventually arrives in his slippers, having mislaid his shoes, and declares that he cannot bring himself to tie the knot.

During the final act Triplepatte and Yvonne at last find themselves alone. They agree that had there been less talk and had they been less pushed around they might have become fond of each other. And in the last moments Triplepatte suggests that it is not too late.

Triplepatte was the hit of 1905, and later produced as *Toddles* in London, that city and Berlin being much readier than Paris to stage foreign successes.

Bernard's closest friend was Lucien Guitry, a square-jawed colossus who had played Flambeau in *L'Aiglon* and from 1902 directed the esteemed Théâtre de la Renaissance. Lucien Guitry affected a Buffalo Bill hat and, it is said, wished you '*Bonjour*' in so expansive a manner he seemed to hand you the day on a plate. He owned an early *teuf-teuf*, an open Panhard with rear entrance to the back seat and a fashionable wicker umbrella-holder strapped to the side. He would invite Bernard to tour the countryside, Guitry consulting one of the as yet rudimentary road maps and shouting directions to his begoggled chauffeur in his mighty actor's voice. On one occasion Guitry announced triumphantly: 'We have arrived in Cervic.' Bernard, who had caught sight of a name on the town hall, stroked his long black beard and said quietly, 'Yes, but the locals call it Villeneuve.'

Guitry gave twice-weekly lunches at his apartment in the Place Vendôme, where the guests were Bernard, the bony-cheeked, often tart diarist Jules Renard, and a gentle, monocled, almost bald playwright from Provence, Albert Capus. An early practitioner of *franglais*, Capus once entered a coiffeur's shop, explaining to his friends, '*Je vais me faire dresser le hair*' – dresser meaning to stand on end. Later he emerged, looking very displeased. 'I shall never set a hair in there again.'

Capus's *La Châtelaine* depicts a charming young hero who frees his equally charming heroine from family harassments. He declares at one point what in effect was Capus's philosophy: 'Let's be happy. Happy at any price. And the more we love life, the more it will make us happy.' Capus, like Bernard, was quite without rancour. It was said that he would ridicule the Government in a new play and the next night sit down to a game of poker with the President. Proust, like Capus a practitioner of *franglais* – he calls a lift-boy *un liftier* or even *un lift* – enjoyed *La Châtelaine* so much – it was one of the successes of 1902 – he mentions it in his novel. Happiness became so much the fashion in the theatre that a long-running comedy of 1905, by Francis de Croisset, was actually entitled *Le Bonheur, Madame*.

Many Paris theatres were owned or managed by Jews, and some of the leading playwrights were Jewish: Bernard, Bernstein and Porto-Riche – a purveyor of 'stern' drama – to mention only three. An unkind joke went as follows: Maeterlinck cannot be elected to the Academy because he is Belgian, Porto-Riche because he is Jewish and Anna de Noailles because she is a woman; Francis de Croisset – real name Franz Wiener – cannot be elected because he is all three. Croisset was one of Proust's friends and contributed something to the character of Bloch in Proust's novel.

Bernard's chief rivals in the business of making Paris smile were the co-authors Flers and Caillavet. The Marquis Robert de Flers – one day to co-edit *Le Figaro* with Capus – was a most likeable man, one of Proust's most loyal friends and a model for his stylish officer, Saint-Loup. Gaston de Caillavet was the son of Léontine Arman de Caillavet, whose literary salon, presided over by Anatole France, was graced by Bernard and Lucien Guitry. Both young men had wanted to be historians, but joined forces in 1900 to write a ballet comic opera, *The Labours of Hercules*. Their best work came after the abolition of censorship in 1906, when they felt free to satirize the Légion d'Honneur in *Le Bois Sacré*, the Académie Française in *L'Habit Vert*, and Republican France's fondness for royalty in *Le Roi*. 'Our system works so well,' said Caillavet, 'that I'm unable to tell which part of a play is mine, which my partner's! The dialogue? We talk it to each other.'

Hardly a year had passed without the visit to Paris of one of those major or minor monarchs courted by the French Government as possible allies. With Edward VII partly in mind, Flers and Caillavet chose to make King Jean IV in *Le Roi* a middle-aged, still pleasure-loving charmer who in his youth had had an affair with an actress, Thérèse. Thérèse is now the mistress of a powerful Left-wing Deputy, Bourdier. Bourdier returns home to find the King's hat in his drawing-room. Thérèse comes down and tries to explain, while Bourdier is given a marvellous opportunity to depict a whole range of emotion by repeating a single word.

> BOURDIER: The name of that man, that – ? I must know!
> (*The King appears, smiling complacently.*)
> THERESE (*introducing the two men*): His Majesty the King of Ardagne – Monsieur Bourdier, a friend of mine.
> BOURDIER (*astonished*): Ah! (*There is a moment's embarrassment.*)
> THE KING: How are you?
> BOURDIER (*furiously*): Sire!
> THERESE: Do you know what His Majesty condescended to say the moment you arrived? Well, he expressed a desire to make your acquaintance.
> BOURDIER (*softening*): Sire!
> THE KING: Yes, I was looking forward to that privilege. In what way can I be of service to you, my dear Bourdier?

BOURDIER (*diminuendo*): Sire!

THERESE: His Majesty was kind enough to think of allowing you to invite him to a grand hunt and dinner-party at your château at Gourville.

BOURDIER (*almost meekly*): Sire!

THERESE: And further: His Majesty, who has only one more day to dispose of . . . offers you all of next Sunday, the day he originally intended to spend with the Marquis de Charnarande.

BOURDIER (*bowing, vastly pleased*): Sire!

THE KING: Don't thank me! Don't – And now, good-bye – till Sunday! I shall be most pleased to see you then. Don't come to the door – I couldn't think of letting you – ! Goodbye, dear old Bourdier!

BOURDIER: Sire. (*The King extends his hand to Bourdier: Bourdier hesitates, not knowing whether to kiss or shake it.*)

THE KING: Shake! One doesn't kiss kings' hands – in private!

THERESE: Sire – pardon him. Monsieur Bourdier is ill acquainted with the forms – he is a Socialist –

THE KING: So am I!

The King transfers his attentions to another lady and in the last act is persuaded by her to sign a treaty for which his Government has, for some time, been angling. Politics is treated as an adjunct of the bedroom.

Quite as handsome, debonair, assured and teasing as Flers and Caillavet was the master of farce, Georges Feydeau. The son of a prolific but not successful novelist, Feydeau was born in Paris in 1862. After the Lycée Saint-Louis, where he was noted only for laziness, he did much amateur acting and wrote light one-act plays. During a year's military service he continued writing, then became for a time a racing correspondent. One day, it is said, too busy on a new play to study form, he put the following note in his column: 'Abundance of other news obliges us to hold over till tomorrow our selections for today's meeting.'

Feydeau cut a dashing figure on the Boulevards. Very good-looking, with strong white teeth, wavy chestnut hair and a full moustache, he had much success with the girls before – and also after – his marriage at twenty-seven to Marianne Carolus Duran. Despite his quiet charm, he cannot have been an easy husband, for he stayed in bed till well after noon, and left the house at six for his apéritif at the Café Napolitain, then for dinner at Maxim's. Here, at his permanently reserved table, until two in the morning, to the strains of a gipsy orchestra playing Paul Delmet's sentimental tunes and the popping of champagne corks, Feydeau would observe closely the mixture of upper-class Parisians, *nouveaux riches*, Russians, gigolos, kept women, artists, bookmakers, journalists, politicians, con men and detectives, a frenzied whirl punctuated by comings and goings, where every glance, every facial expression was multiplied and intensified by the mirror walls. This became the stuff of Feydeau's farces.

One of his hits takes its name from the restaurant. *La Dame de chez Maxim* is a tart whom Petypon, a young married man, picks up on a wild evening and brings home. Found in Petypon's bed by the young man's uncle, a general just home from many years in Africa, the tart had to be passed off as Madame Petypon and is brought to a wedding reception at a château in Touraine where everything she says and does, however vulgar or outrageous, is deemed by the provincial ladies to be the height of fashion – just because she's from Paris.

La Puce à l'Oreille – That Starts Me Thinking – also

turns on mistaken identities and a wildly farcical *maison de passe*, where a customer can escape any unwelcome intruder by pushing a button that swings round one entire wall of the room, transferring him to the bedroom adjoining and bringing the inmate of that room on to the stage. The farce depends on split-second timing, so Paris's stage mechanics were evidently on the mend.

If we compare Feydeau to a great immediate predecessor, Courteline, we see that Feydeau is original in two respects. His farces are much faster: they mirror the new tempo in Paris, speeded up by electricity, telephone and motor-car, and to that extent reveal a complexity we have met elsewhere in the arts. Alfred Capus was to say that the society of his day did not readily lend itself to the dramatist because, 'to use a metaphor from photography, it will never sit still long enough to be snapped'. Secondly, they are warmer. Courteline's *Boubouroche* (1893) depicts a gullibly sentimental petit bourgeois, roundly deceived by his girlfriend, who ends by believing her lies. It is a cruel comedy. Feydeau on the other hand extols sentiment, and if he puts a husband in an absurd situation he does so in order to laugh with him rather than against him. For example, *Léonie est en avance* is about a phantom pregnancy: the wife, supported by her mother and midwife, expresses the wish to see her husband put a chamber pot on his head. The husband at first declines, but then, informed that a pregnant wife's urges must be satisfied in the interests of the child, he crowns himself with the chamber pot which, of course, gets stuck on his head.

Beds, it has been said, are Feydeau's most versatile prop. They serve for sleeping in, hiding in and under, bouncing on and as an unreliable platform to declaim from. They also played an increasing part in Feydeau's private life. Womanizing, his preference for living at night and disastrous speculation on the stock exchange put such a strain on his marriage that in 1909, after a violent quarrel with Marianne, Feydeau went to live permanently in the Hôtel Terminus, near the Gare Saint-Lazare. As a rising young playwright, Lucien Guitry's son Sacha, was to put it, the burdens of marriage are too heavy to be borne by two people alone.

Commenting on the change in Paris theatre since *fin de siècle* social realism as practised by Octave Mirbeau and various followers of Zola, the theatre critic of the *Revue des Deux Mondes* wrote in 1905:

> Everyone knows that one of the dominant tendencies in today's theatre is optimism. After being down in the dumps for a decade our theatre paints life in rosy colours. It portrays only nice characters, generous souls, motivated by tact and unselfishness, simple yet noble.

'Nice characters' is perhaps a backhanded compliment. Shaw could have made *Le Roi* a devastating attack on double standards in French foreign policy instead of the gentle satire it is. Did French dramatists pull their punches because they had an eye on a seat in the Academy? This seems unlikely. Eugène Brieux outspokenly attacked the French judiciary in *Red Robes* (1900) and hypocrisy about venereal disease in *Damaged Goods* (1902), yet ended by wearing the sword and bottle-green uniform. The truth seems to be that writers for the stage imbibed the prevailing bonhomie they helped to diffuse.

In order to fill out this record, we should notice the three leading serious dramatists. Eugène Brieux, who has been mentioned, was the self-educated son of a carpenter who was a journalist and later editor of Rouen's

La Nouvelliste. He came to know at first hand the various social evils he exposed on the stage. If there is much sermonizing, there are also well-observed portraits of peasants and bourgeois.

Henry Bernstein, the tall, stooping son of a New York banker, continued the *fin-de-siècle* Zolaesque 'down-in-the-dumps' play. Bernstein was noted for his superstition – he gave his plays six-letter titles, believing that number to be lucky – and into most he introduced a 'good-luck' subordinate character named Zambeau, Zamo or the equivalent. He was also noted for his combativeness – he fought several duels – and he excelled at drawing characters like himself driven by strong passions: lust, avarice, greed, sadism.

His plays incurred Proust's displeasure: 'In La Fontaine and Florian animals speak like men and women. In Bernstein men and women speak like gorillas, pigs, wild beasts.' In this Proust was expressing contemporary taste. Slice-of-life plays now had only a small following: Paris audiences preferred to spend their evening watching either the sublime or the ridiculous.

The third serious dramatist, Henry Bataille, was a Rousseauist who pitted social convention against true feeling, notably a woman's driving need to love and cling to love once given. His *Marche Nuptiale* depicts a young couple from the provinces who come to Paris, fortified against the battles of life with a little money and infinite hope.

Bataille's most successful play, *The Nude Woman*, tells of an unassuming young model whose sculptor husband, spoiled by success, is attracted to a Princess. In the key scene the sculptor, Pierre, has to choose. Lolette, the model, invokes her husband's duty to stay with her. He replies:

'Now, now, talk to me about love if you like, but not about duty! . . . I have made you, helped you rise in the world. I leave you on a higher level than when I found you – life is richer in resources than you imagined. You can build up again your social position, find – as everyone can – someone else to love, someone better than I. You will be happier, much happier.'

Lolette tries unsuccessfully to commit suicide and in hospital is rescued from despair by the timely arrival of a less selfish man friend. A kindred subject was made by Ibsen into a masterpiece, *When We Dead Awaken*. Bataille does not quite do that, but Lolette is a character of true pathos and charm. The fact that Bataille based his play on Debussy's desertion of his first wife contributed to its success.

Cinematography had been invented in 1895 by the Lumière brothers of Besançon, and the cinema industry was developed in France mainly by Léon Gaumont of Paris, who was responsible for the first experimental talkies, in 1902, and for colour films in 1912. During the first fourteen years of the new century France poured talent and energy into the new medium, and there is hardly one type of later film, save perhaps the Western, that did not originate with these pioneers.

The cinema grew out of the theatre, drew its audiences from playgoers and often made cinemas out of former music-halls or theatres. Like a theatre, the prestige cinemas had an orchestra. The Pathé cinema near the Invalides, one of Paris's thirty-seven cinemas in 1913, employed an orchestra of sixty and boasted the world's largest screen. France by then had three hundred cinemas.

Cinema personnel came from the theatres. Georges Meliès had started as a conjuror, then produced magic and mystery shows. In 1900 he turned to cinema, became a pioneer of trick photography and turned out hundreds of 'magic' films, including ghosts, produced by double exposure, and science-fiction like *A Trip to the Moon* (1902), with thirty scenes.

Louis Feuillade was one of the few who went straight into films. After trying to become a Catholic priest, he served as an army sergeant, then made a successful film series about an insupportable spoiled brat. He found his true bent in *Fantomas* (1913–14), a series of episodes featuring a master criminal who continually eludes his sworn enemy, Inspector Juve.

Historical drama also made the passage to celluloid. *The Assassination of the Duc de Guise* (1908) was followed by Sarah Bernhardt playing Queen Elizabeth opposite the inseparable Lou Tellegen as Essex, this subject suiting the Entente Cordiale. The honour and glory of France, as in *L'Aiglon*, continued to the fore, as in *The Siege of Calais* (1911), featuring the heroism of the town's burghers depicted already in bronze by Rodin.

Emotional drama along the lines of Bataille's *Marche Nuptiale* went easily into film, though Mugnier complained that the heroines, unable to voice their feelings, overdid the heavy breathing. A favourite setting was Brittany, recognized since the Pont-Aven painters as a region of simple, touching faith. Apollinaire co-authored with André Billy a script, *La Bréhantine*: though never shot, it gives a good idea of this type of film.

Aline Le Briant is a lighthouse-keeper on the Isle of Bréhat. She makes of the lighthouse a chapel of remembrance for her fiancé, Yves le Maris, who has disappeared. A novelist visits the lighthouse. He happens to know Yves, who is living a debauched life in Paris. He says nothing but uses the subject for a novel. Aline reads the novel, serialized in a newspaper; she understands, writes a note of explanation to the novelist and commits suicide. The novelist brings Yves to the lonely island where, chastened, he settles down with his uncle to lead a reformed life.

Comedy, however, was the staple of early French cinema: in the first decade hundreds of short films were shot echoing stage vaudevilles and farces. André Deed, originally a music-hall acrobat, created a favourite character, Boireau, a simpleton who wherever he goes creates chaos. In one film Boireau eats garlic, making his breath so pungent everyone he speaks to collapses. Finally he addresses a cab horse, whereupon the horse backs away, with its cab, up a steep hill, for trick photography was a feature of Deed's films.

Charles Prince, born in 1872, was tall, chubby-cheeked, short-nosed, with a smile for everyone. After training at the Conservatoire, where he won first prize for comedy, he made a name on the stage and played the lead in Feydeau's *Le Circuit*. Entering films, he countered Deed's knockabout with a quieter comic character, Rigardin, a moonish bourgeois who pines after young ladies and occasionally succeeds with them. Prince made more than two hundred Rigardin films and by 1914 was France's most popular film actor.

Prince's friend and rival, Max Linder, was born in 1883 of a well-to-do wine-growing family near Bordeaux. After a moderately successful stage career in 1905 he switched to films as an extra and became famous as Max, a debonair young man about town, with long moustache, plastered-down hair, hooded eyes that roll romantically, roguishly or knowingly. In *Max Takes a Bath* he goes to a shop and buys a bathtub. How to get it home? He decides to carry it: The tap is on the landing outside his flat. Max carries water from the tap to the bath in a small carafe. Deciding this method is too slow, he drags the bath on to the landing, fills it and gets in. Other tenants of the block pass, see him, protest, call the police. The police carry Max to the station in his bath. There he keeps them at bay by splashing water, escapes, carrying the bath over his head beetle-like on all fours. He continues like this along a street and finally up the side of a building – more trick photography. Finally from the roof he drops the bath on the policemen, foiling their attempts to climb up the side of the building.

In 1909 twenty-year-old Charles Chaplin crossed the Channel to play the Folies Bergère. For his curtain-raiser, according to Georges-Michel, who saw it, bowler-hatted and twirling a cane, he pelted a group of singers with oranges; then in a little blue beribboned sweater he performed a comic boxing act. It may have been in this year that he watched Max Linder. Later he said that seeing Max's films led him to take up a cinema career, and there are many resemblances between Chaplin's early style and that of the Frenchman, who was eventually to go to Hollywood, though without repeating the success he had in France.

Technically this early cinema requires no apology. Though a single camera limits the visual interest, the photography has sharpness and depth, the film is fine-grained, sometimes sepia. As for the mood, this comedy is neither cruel nor bitter. Generally there is an affectionate dwelling on idiosyncrasy. One sees, in germ, the films of Raimu and Tati.

Though silent film lends itself to comedy, the French choice of that genre was by no means inevitable, as one sees by comparing it with early German cinema. That too grew out of certain favourite stage themes, such as the Doppelgänger, anguish, bloodshed, latent anti-Semitism. The German film *The Student from Prague* shows the student selling his reflection to the Devil, while in *The Golem* a rabbi, aided by black magic, brings to life a clay monster, believing he will free the Jewish

343

people, but the monster turns against his creator, wreaking destruction in the ghetto.

The cinema altered Paris by bringing a world of laughter to those who could not afford the theatre. 'M. Ollinger-Jacob,' joked Erik Satie, 'charming director of "The Greatest Cinema in the Whole World", will show you leading comics, drama, travel, fairy stories, artistic films and much else. The price of seats is ludicrously cheap and families of more than a hundred get a special reduction. M. Ollinger-Jacob is a philanthropist-cum-benefactor of suffering humanity; by means of thermo-cinematographic treatment he cures the worst cases of hypochondria and extreme neurasthenia. Numerous letters and attestations.'

For a decade and a half the theatre and its young sister-art provided Paris with literally thousands of productions, most expressing a rosy view of life, where individual foibles were laughed at – but gently – and underlying values rarely questioned. Because people went so often, to some extent this rosy view coloured their thinking in the real world. As Satie observed, it soothed them. It helped to make them believe that France was still as powerful as in the days of Corneille and Napoleon, and did well to pursue honour and grandeur. Indeed, Paris's best actress pursued both with zest; moreover, she defied the years, as Proust wished all art to do, and by portraying sublime heights of passion at sixty suggested that art could improve upon life.

Some in her audiences chose to model their behaviour on the divine Sarah. Wives defending their honour with revolver shots are far from rare in the press, and later we shall see a Cabinet Minister's wife do just that. The majority, however, tended to see amusing, gently mannered comedy as a paradigm for their own lives. Nothing could go gravely awry, somehow the dramatist would contrive a happy ending. For the world of the Paris theatre, like the medieval image of Eden, was a garden enclosed, delectable, artistically compelling, with no visible serpent.

CHAPTER 14

Celebration with Colour

In the late nineteenth and early twentieth centuries it could be said that the art for which the French showed most talent was painting. Certainly it was the medium into which they poured their lark song. Under the weight of the association of words in a language little changed since Villon, a lyric poet's soaring often, in spite of itself, dips to regret – with the Romantics, indeed, to bathos – whereas among painters from the young Renoir in 1865 for half a century the lyrical note is pretty well sustained. This chapter will describe some of the artists who, taking a different line from the Cubists, achieved that most difficult feat in a mature civilization – they saw freshly a variety of subjects and, elated by their discovery, celebrated them, most often by innovative use of colour.

It begins once again in the 1890s, with an ageing teacher and a situation that struck brighter members of the young generation as a dead end. Gustave Moreau painted pictures in which he believed he was conveying a world of high thinking and deep spirituality. A French Pre-Raphaelite but without Christian belief, whose meticulous brush owed much to the fifteenth-century Andrea Mantegna, grey-haired Moreau turned out crowded, detailed, hothouse scenes featuring various 'eternal women' laden with jewellery, in antique poses and timeless backgrounds, in a snaky epicene rhythm close to Beardsley's. He depicted slender male figures too, in a world at once ancient and modern. 'He'd have us believe the gods sported watch-chains,' snapped Degas.

Moreau's 'eternal women' were often *femmes fatales*, as deadly in an antique way as Zola's Nana in a modern. One disturbing canvas shows a Cat being metamorphosed into a Woman, and a favourite subject is Salome carrying on a platter the head of John the Baptist. Viewers did not need Freud to tell them that Moreau suffered from a possessive mother, whom he adored yet detested for in effect castrating him.

It is typical of the *fin de siècle* Establishment that in 1892, aged sixty-six, Moreau was appointed a professor at the Ecole des Beaux-Arts, and there guided some of the Nabis into historical painting with Symbolic overtones, while preparing to endow the city of Paris with his house and a collection of his works, for Moreau possessed ample means, indeed this had allowed him to pursue, undistracted, his vision of seductive-destructive women.

In 1897 Moreau's most gifted student was a certain Henri Matisse. The son of a grain dealer in the far north of France – Flanders – Matisse had started as a solicitor's clerk in Saint-Quentin. During a convalescence from appendicitis – very fashionable at that time – he tried his hand at painting – his mother, as a hobby, painted plates – liked it, and when he returned to work went for an hour early each morning to the town art school, where he learned to draw from casts. At twenty-one he gave up the solicitor's office, went to Paris and entered the Académie Julian, from where he migrated to the Beaux-Arts.

Matisse was slight of build and had a big head, with plain, easily forgettable features. He had brown hair, soon to grow thin, moustache and beard. His blue eyes were slightly short-sighted. He spoke in a precise, opinionated way and had an air of quiet dignity that was to earn him the nickname 'Doctor'. Like Ingres, he played the violin. He was virile, enjoyed the company of women, and made friends easily.

Matisse liked Moreau the man but disliked Moreau the painter, whose linear, story-telling canvases seemed to a new generation so contrived, so far from real life and so morbid. But Moreau surprisingly gave Matisse two good pieces of advice. One was 'Follow your innermost feeling,' which the professor had been doing in a way, in his oft-repeated Salomes; the other was 'Go down into the street.' The bookish septuagenarian was saying in effect, Do what I never dared to do, come to terms with the world you live in.

Matisse was to heed both counsels, but for the moment he had other things on his mind. Seldom afraid to take risks, at twenty-nine Matisse took a very big risk indeed. He had as yet no clear idea of how he wanted to paint and believed himself to be a slow developer. He had no job, only a small allowance from his father and an illegitimate daughter to support. But he proposed marriage to a beautiful tall girl from Toulouse, Amélie Parayre. As Gertrude Stein noticed, Amélie had 'a profound feeling for life', clapped on a hat and jabbed in its pin with verve, kept her flat spotless, cooked memorable jugged hare in Perpignan style and served it with a full-bodied Pyrenees wine called Rancio; also she was willing to pose by the hour for her husband.

Soon after marrying, Matisse fell ill of acute bronchitis and had to go to Switzerland to convalesce, Amélie saving the day by opening a little fashion shop. All his life Matisse was to be subject to bronchial trouble. We have noticed Proust's asthma; André Gide suffered nervous and pulmonary weekness and was turned down for military service; many other creative young men were 'highly strung' to the verge of chronic illness. The fact that French schoolboys played almost no outdoor sport probably made matters worse. Indeed, the enlightened Duc de Cossé-Brissac sent his sons to school at Ladycross, in Sussex, specifically so that their bodies should be strengthened by football and cricket, but in our period few, even among the well-to-do, followed the Duke's lead.

Back home, in early 1900 Matisse went to work in Jambon's theatrical workshop on the Buttes Chaumont, painting an enormous laurel frieze to adorn the Grand Palais for the coming Exhibition. He earned one franc an hour and was glad of the money. With him toiled another former pupil of Moreau, Albert Marquet from Bordeaux. Marquet had a sharp eye for the humorous and was able to catch the amusing side of a character in half a dozen strokes; Matisse had no such ready response and was still learning. Like Picasso, he felt he must open himself to as many influences as possible before deciding on his own road.

From 1900 to 1905 Matisse 'went down into the street', or rather the stock image of Paris streets and public places. He painted the Moulin de la Galette and the Cirque Médrano; at the Petit Casino he sketched cabaret *artistes* Paula Brebion, Gabrielle Lange and Mistinguett. He painted panoramas of Paris and landscapes too.

His real dilemma lay in the choice not so much of subject as of style. Matisse felt drawn to vivid colours. It was in his 'innermost being', to use Moreau's phrase. He liked vivid colours for themselves and because through them he believed he could express his joyful response to a subject. For Matisse possessed large resources of *joie de vivre*. He was encouraged by Turner's paintings – the orange sunsets, not the misty, muted landscapes – which he had come to love on his honeymoon in London, and by an exhibition of Islamic art in Paris in 1903, where he had seen miniatures whose primary colours were laid in flat patches without gradation, not necessarily corresponding to colours in real life.

Drawing on one or both of these influences and on his own instinct Matisse produced a few original works in these early years. One is a view of Notre-Dame from his top-floor studio flat in Quai Saint-Michel. The *quais*, a bridge and the cathedral towers are arranged to form an autonomous pattern, and melt into a morning sky of mauve rose. This is close in colouring to Picasso's Rose Period harlequins and, since Matisse did not yet know Picasso's work, is a pointer to mood, pink/rose, at least since Piero della Francesca's *Resurrection*, being the colour of promise and hope.

The Japanese Lady beside Water is just recognizable by her hairstyle and kimono, but there is no line separating her from the garden and water: person and setting have merged in a joyful shimmering pattern of reds, pinks, mauves, violets and greens, laid on thick and unshaded.

A few of these paintings Matisse managed to sell to one or two of Montmartre's colourful small dealers, including Berthe Weill who could manage only 20 francs apiece for them but she did pay cash, as usual lifting her skirt to extract the money from the top of her stocking and handing it over with a quip. Vollard – 'a wily fox' Matisse called him – took some of his work at a better price. With thrifty housekeeping the Matisses could afford to go for the summer of 1905 to the fishing port of Collioure, in Amélie's part of France.

Matisse was a man of the north. He had grown up in rainy summers and snowy winters under a sky most often grey. It had left him with a yearning for colour and he would have understood – though not fully agreed with – the Dutch colourist Van Dongen's *mot*: 'Painting is an invention of men from the north.' In

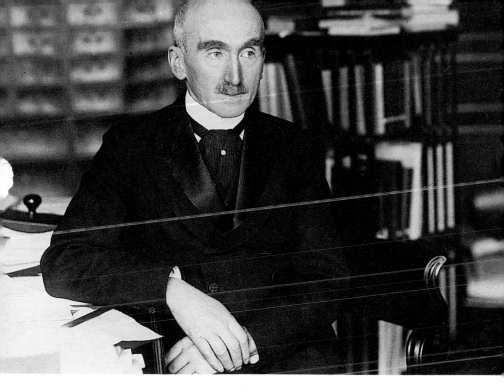

Three philosophers who helped to create a climate of opinion: Henri Bergson (above), the most influential thinker in Paris since Voltaire, drew even society ladies to his lectures; Emile Boutroux (below left), professor at the Sorbonne, was one of the young Proust's heroes; Maurice Blondel (below right) taught that thinking is incomplete unless it results in action.

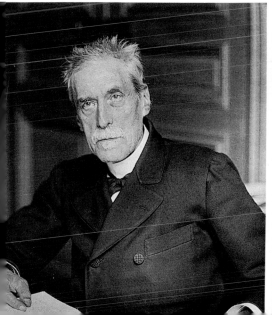

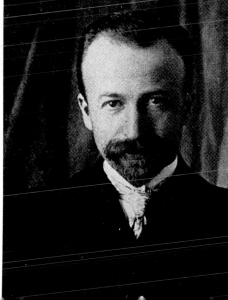

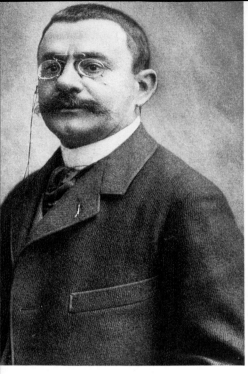
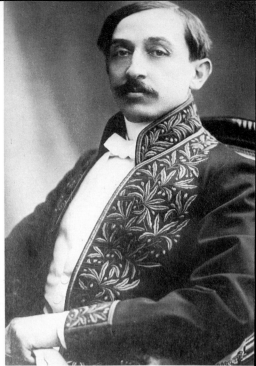

Leading nationalists: Théophile Delcassé (above left), Foreign Minister for seven years, believed Germany was preparing for a war of extermination against France; Maurice Barrès (above right) in the uniform of the Académie Française, was a novelist, a deputy, and a president of the League of Patriots; Raymond Poincaré (below left) had been evacuated from his native Lorraine during the Franco-Prussian War, an event which coloured his subsequent stance towards Germany; Philippe Berthelot of the Quai d'Orsay (below right) shaped the French take-over of Morocco.

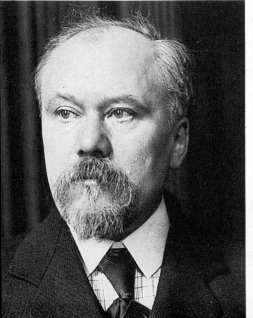
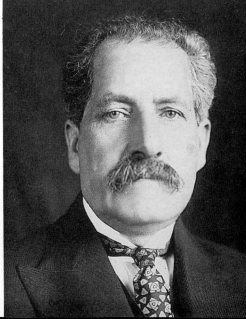

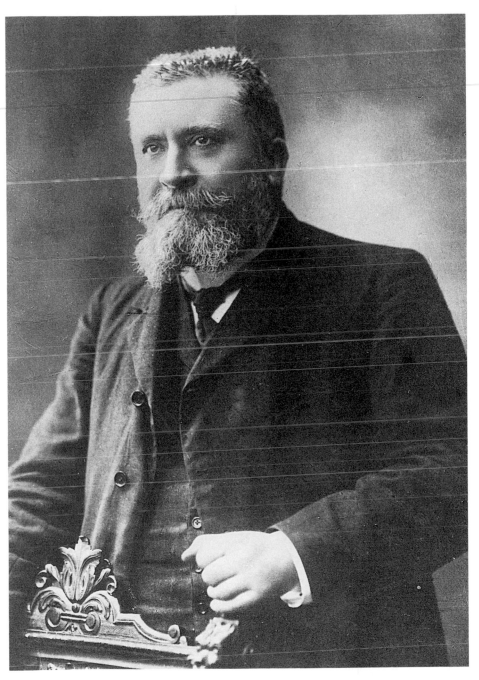

Jean Jaurès, founder of *L'Humanité*, Socialist and tireless advocate of détente with Germany.

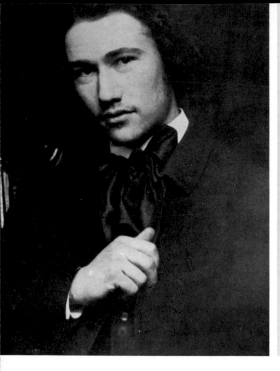
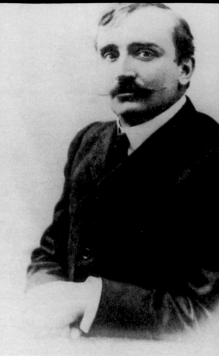

Four writers with spiritual aims: André Gide (above left) argued that homosexuality was compatible with the Gospels; his friend, Paul Claudel (above right), wrote poetry and plays with a Catholic content; Marcel Proust (below left) described his great novel as 'a carefully constructed work of dogma'; Charles Péguy (below right) celebrated in one of his long poems Jeanne d'Arc, beatified in 1909.

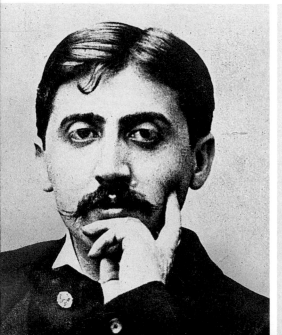
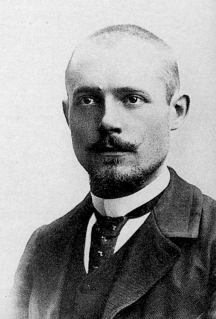

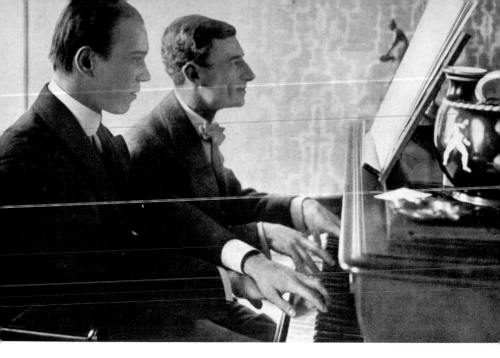

Three prominent composers who took ballet music seriously: Claude Debussy (below left), whose *L'Après-Midi d'un Faune*, danced by Nijinsky, was denounced by some as 'barbarously erotic'; Reynaldo Hahn (below right), whose *Le Dieu Bleu* was also performed by the Ballets Russes; as was *Daphnis and Chloë* by Maurice Ravel (above), photographed here with Nijinsky by their friend Igor Stravinsky.

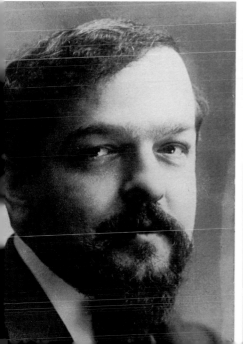

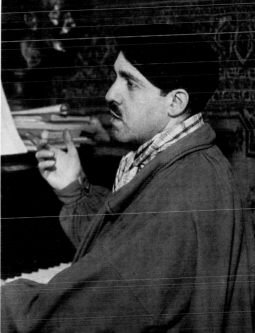

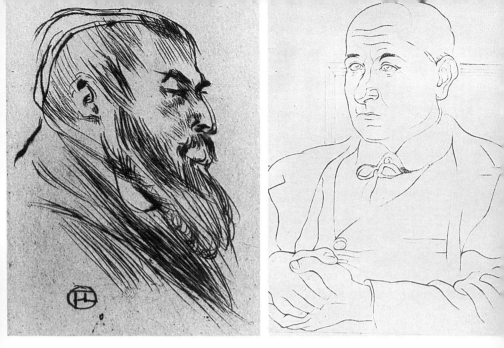

Marie Laurencin's group portrait of 1908 (below) reveals her sense of fun: the artist stands beside the poet Apollinaire, seated, and flanked by Picasso in profile holding his dog, and his mistress Fernande Olivier. *Copyright ARS N.Y./ADAGP.*

Max Jacob (above right) delighted Picasso with parodies and grotesque dances. *Copyright 1990 ARS N.Y./ADAGP.*

(Above left) Tristan Bernard, the wit and playwright.

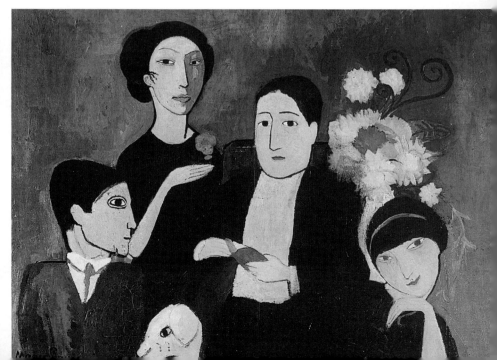

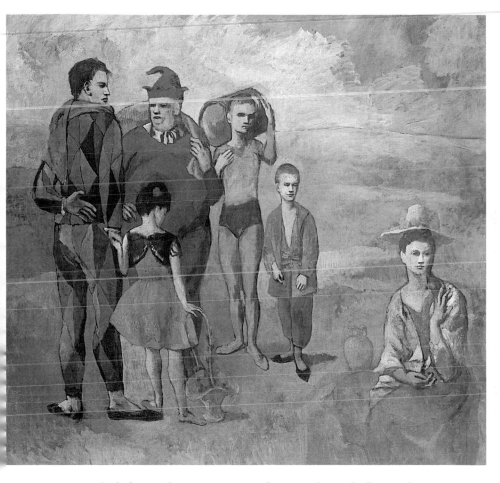

Circuses were a lively feature of Paris. Picasso enjoyed going to them and talking to the performers. *Family of Saltimbanques*, painted in 1905, belongs to his Rose Period. *National Gallery of Art, Washington; Chester Dale Collection. Copyright 1990 ARS N.Y./SPADEM.*

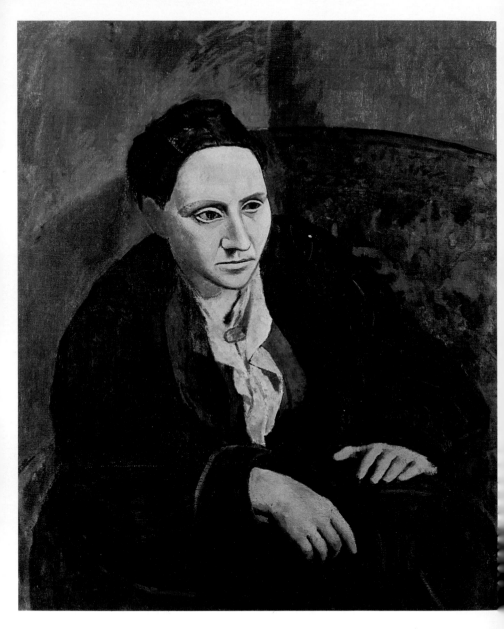

Gertrude Stein, friend and patron of Matisse and Picasso, who painted this mask-like portrait of her. *Copyright 1990 ARS N.Y./SPADEM.*

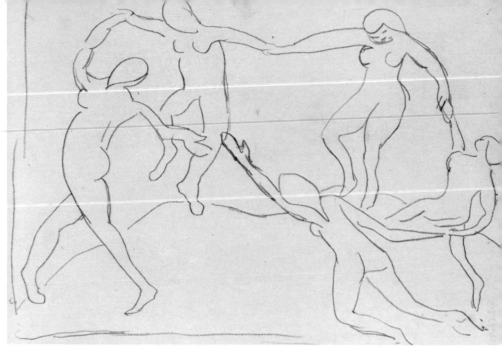

Henri Matisse captures the vigorous movement of dancers such as Nijinsky in this *Study* (above) based on his big mural *La Danse*. (*1909, pencil, 21.8 x 35.1 cm. Collection, the Museum of Modern Art, New York. Gift of Pierre Matisse*). *Copyright 1990 Les Heritiers Matisse/ARS N.Y.* His *Le Bonheur de Vivre* (below) defies established rules of perspective and foreshortening; the dominant colours are mauve, orange and green. It was hailed by Apollinaire as 'Instinct Regained!'

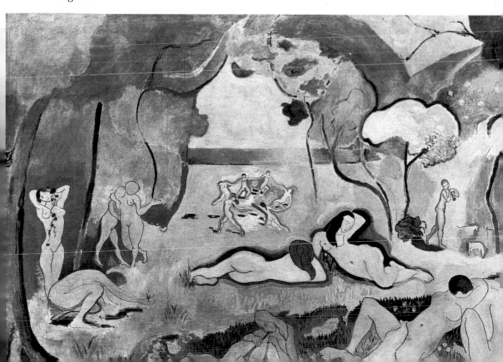

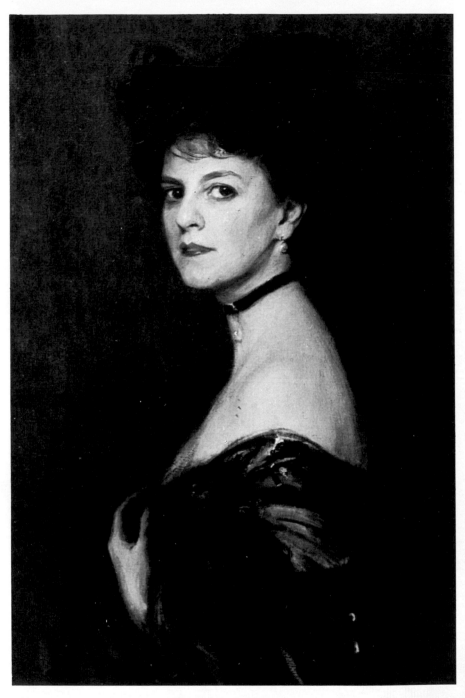

Elisabeth Greffulhe, with her husband the banker Comte Henri Greffulhe, worked for the Triple Entente by entertaining Edward VII and bringing the Ballets Russes to Paris.

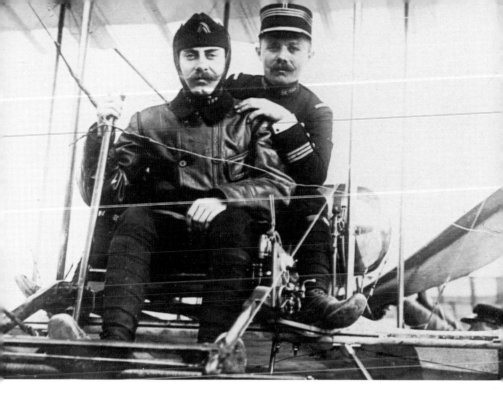

Henry Farman (above), an Englishman resident in Paris, was a champion cyclist before designing and piloting aeroplanes, seen here with a military passenger; Louis Blériot, the first to fly the English Channel, was hailed as a hero on his return to Paris (below).

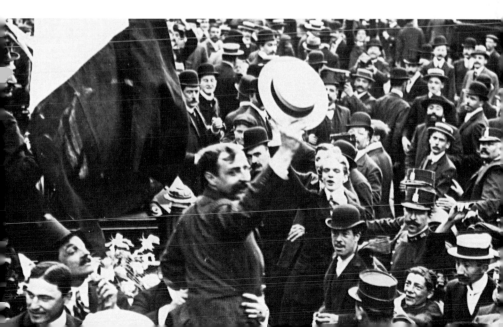

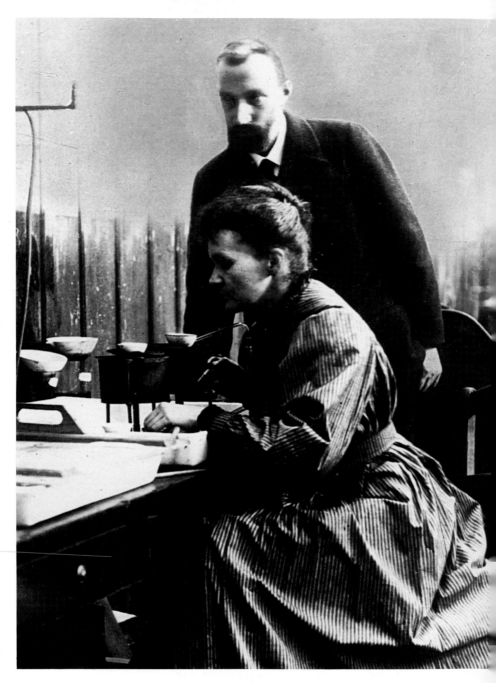

Pierre and Marie Curie discovered radioactivity and shared, with Henry
Becquerel, the Nobel Prize for Physics. Their happy marriage ended with
Pierre's death in a road accident at the age of forty-seven.

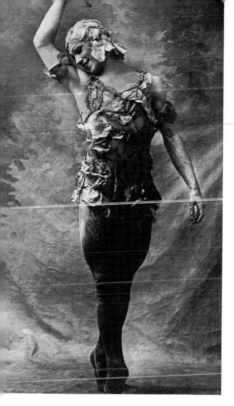

In the title role of *Le Spectre de la Rose* Nijinsky (left), 'like some melancholy, imperious scent', performed his most spectacular leap.

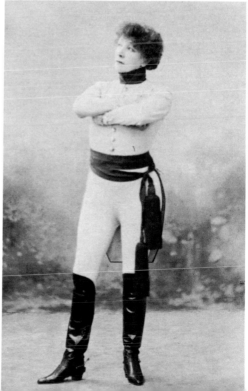

Sarah Bernhardt (right) as Napoleon II in the stage success of 1900, Edmond Rostand's *L'Aiglon*.

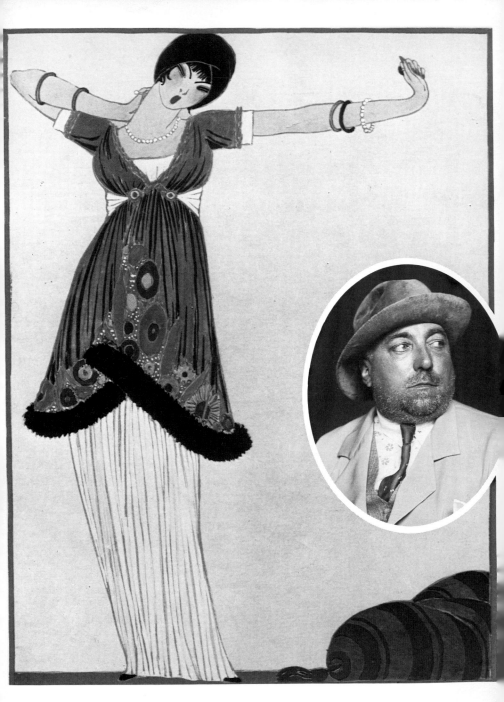

Paul Poiret (inset) helped free Parisian women from the corseted Swan Look, and popularised high waists, a slim line, and bold colours. Here an evening gown designed by Poiret in 1912 is sketched by Georges Lepape with the title *Lassitude*.

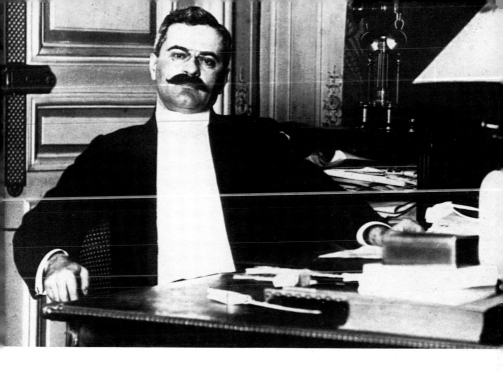

Gaston Calmette (above), editor of *Le Figaro*, waged a muck-raking campaign
against Finance Minister Joseph Caillaux (below left). Madame Caillaux
(below right), bought a revolver, drove to the *Figaro* office, and shot Calmette dead.

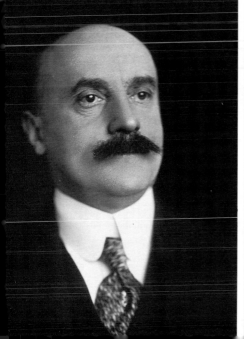

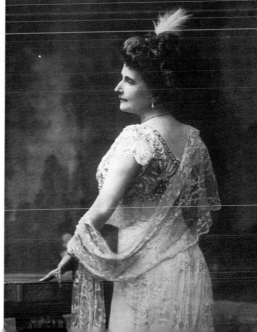

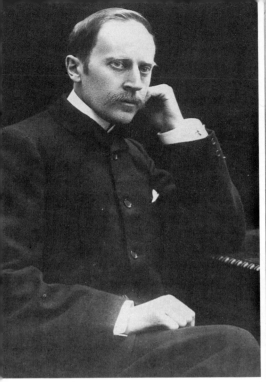
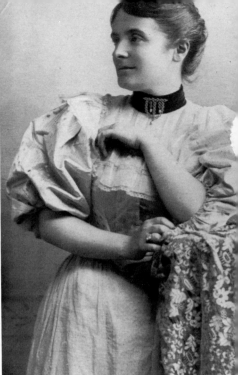

Four far-sighted Parisians: Romain Rolland (above left), novelist and music historian, worked for détente with Germany, as did the abbé Mugnier, the spiritual director of several society ladies and friend of Proust, here (below right) in a portrait by the Comtesse Greffulhe. Anna de Noailles (below left), a poet and hostess, was another friend of Mugnier's. Louise Cruppi (above right), wife of a Foreign Minister, was encouraged in her campaign for women's rights by Rolland.

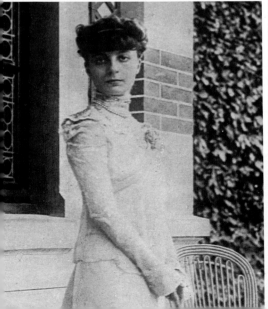
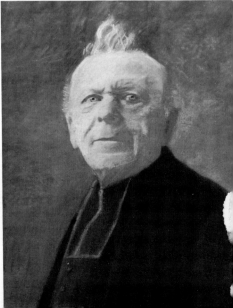

Paris he had been painting the world as he would have liked it to be; here in Collioure he found that world actually existent. It was a turning-point.

That summer Matisse painted *Open Window, Collioure*. The two halves of a window are open; on the sill are flowers in pots; outside, framed by foliage, fishing boats in harbour. Like an opened reliquary, the open windows seem to reveal, just for us, a secret, and the secret is that the world consists of bright colours, jostling one another like the bobbing boats.

Of that summer Matisse wrote, 'I worked as I felt, by colour alone,' and the painter André Derain, an eternal student who seems to have strayed from a Tchekov play and who had taken Matisse as his mentor, explained to another of his mentors, dour Maurice Vlaminck, that working with Matisse had taught him the negation of shadow in the accepted sense. 'Here the light is very strong, the shadows very bright. Shadow is a whole world of brightness and luminosity opposed to sunlight.'

In September 1905 Matisse exhibited his latest work at the Salon d'Automne in the Grand Palais. It might have been lost amid the thousands of more conventional pictures but for the fact that half a dozen young artists were also showing pictures heaped with red, yellow and vermilion. They included Derain and Marquet, who, besides the Exhibition frieze, had done serious paintings with Matisse and learned from him; both favoured waterside subjects; Georges Rouault, who as an apprentice glazier had repaired stained glass at Chartres and there acquired a taste for primary, contrasting colours and for a thick line, which he used to depict fairground people and outcasts. Also of the number was Derain's friend, Maurice Vlaminck, a true eccentric, professional wrestler and active member of the Anarchist Movement, who liked painting heavy

Seine barges and threw vermilion and violet on to his canvas as other anarchists threw bombs, to break up the Establishment.

It so happened that pictures by all the bold colourists were hung in one room. A leading art critic, Louis Vauxcelles of *Gil Blas*, entered this world of yellow seas, green skies and an inordinate amount of red. Then his attention turned to a bust in the same room by a contemporary named Marque, showing a child's head treated in the Florentine style. Vauxcelles exclaimed: '*Donatello au milieu des fauves*' - Donatello in the wild beasts' den.

The label stuck. Matisse and the colourists came to be known as Les Fauves, and some of their pictures were reproduced, grouped on one page, in *L'Illustration*. But Les Fauves were not truly a group, they were individuals trying to shake off the past through a highly personal use of colour.

Vauxcelles intended his epithet to be reproving. To apply colour emotionally, arbitrarily, was to deny the primacy of the subject and therefore to infringe the first principle of classicism - an attitude unacceptable to Paris critics and to the public whose taste they formed. Matisse's *Femme au chapeau*, a portrait of Amélie in a smart hat, her hair vermilion and green shadows on her face, excited such derision viewers tried to scratch off the paint with fingernails. Green face indeed!

If Les Fauves was the label that stuck, other criticisms were more to the point. Matisse and the colourists were called The Incoherents or The Invertebrates. Matisse's work to date had in truth shown structural looseness and when, in the winter of 1905-6, he began work on an ambitious canvas, he tried to remedy the deficiency.

The subject is a seaside scene, nudes on the ground against a sweeping arch of rocks; beyond the arch, beside the sea, other nude figures are dancing. These

elements Matisse builds up in a series of flowing arabesques that impart a unifying strength. He accentuates
the curves of the women's hips and breasts, and
duplicates them in the curves of the landscape. He
exaggerates the height of the central dancing figure in
order to provide a strong vertical. There is certainly no
incoherence here.

This work Matisse entitled *La Joie de Vivre* – it is
known aslso as *Le Bonheur de Vivre* – and Apollinaire
hailed it: 'Instinct regained!' The title tells something
about Matisse and something too about a mood in Paris
we have already met: in Picasso's Rose Period, in Gide's
celebration of sensuous pleasure, and in Debussy's *La
Mer*.

Two very intelligent well-off Americans of German
parentage, Gertrude Stein and her brother Leo, two
years her senior, had come to live in Paris, convinced
that this was the city where literary and artistic history
was being made in a new, distinctively twentieth-
century mode. Gertrude had studied under William
James, and thus became interested in the way instinct
and reason join to form value judgments, and, generally, in an analysis of perception. Now in her early
thirties, Gertrude was short, stout, with a strong big
head, a voice like heavy velvet and a hearty laugh.
Leo was tall, thin, sad-looking, with a long reddish
beard and gold-rimmed spectacles. Both dressed in
brown corduroy and wore leather-strapped sandals –
Gertrude's had pointed toes like gondola prows – which
elicited a couplet from Apollinaire:

> *Leurs pieds sont chaussés de sandales bacchiques,*
> *Ils lèvent vers le ciel des yeux scientifiques.*[1]

[1] Their feet are shod in Bacchic sandals,
They raise erudite eyes to heaven.

The Steins had begun to collect art, had bought *Femme au chapeau*, and now bought *La Joie de vivre*.

Gertrude and Leo invited Henri Matisse and Amélie to their apartment at 27 rue de Fleurus. The four quickly became friends. Gertrude was beginning also to buy Picassos. She won Picasso's gratitude by passing on to him the Baltimore Sunday *Sun* which ran a comic strip, 'The Katzenjammer Kids', on which he doted, and she also introduced the Spaniard to Matisse. They showed each other polite respect, as did Proust and Debussy, even exchanged pictures but never became close. The North and South Poles, someone quipped.

Gertrude Stein liked Picasso's effrontery, his inner unease. To Matisse she said, 'There is nothing in you that fights itself,' which was true in the sense that Matisse sought to become submissive and humble before a subject – only then, he confessed, 'do I feel as though I were being helped by someone who makes me do things beyond my power'. But Gertrude liked Matisse's quiet assurance and when she forged a style for her experimental writing she described it as 'a noble combination of Swift and Matisse', meaning that, while satirizing the pretentious, she elicited wonder from the everyday. In *Tender Buttons* she offers neat little *aperçus*: 'Celery tastes tastes where in curled lashes and little bits and mostly in remains.'

Gertrude Stein, through friends, arranged for Matisse to exhibit engravings, lithographs, watercolours and drawings at New York's Gallery 291, and when in the same year, 1908, Matisse opened a private art school in a former convent at 35 Boulevard des Invalides, Gertrude urged her young American acquaintances to enroll. 'All Matisse's pupils come from Massachusetts,' claimed one humorist, relishing the bizarre place-name. In fact they came from many states, and from lands as distant as Sweden and Hungary: 120 in all during the four years the school functioned.

What did 'the Doctor' teach his students? 'The model . . . must make an impression on you, awaken in you an emotion that you then seek to express.' 'Photography has been bad for our imagination because it has depicted things unemotionally' – perhaps unfair to Atget and others. Classical perspective should be replaced by the 'perspective of feeling', with value counting for more than magnitude, colours for the background usually as vivid as for the foreground. Genius usually includes a grain of the irrational, and Matisse's grain appears in this maxim: 'All human shapes are convex, there are no concave lines' – surely untrue, witness the nudes with pinched faces being painted at that very moment in Montmartre by Modigliani.

In this his busiest year Matisse took time to visit Italy. Picasso, finding himself in a strange place, sketched from life, but Matisse, who travelled more than the Spaniard, preferred to memorize impressions and draw on them later. With his predilection for full-bodied women one might have expected him to warm to Veronese and Titian, but the Italian painters he fell in love with were Duccio and the early Primitives who had celebrated the spiritual in gold and blue.

Nineteen hundred and eight was Matisse's *annus mirabilis*, for he then received his most important commission so far. There lived in Paris an odd, extremely rich textile dealer, Sergei Shchukine. Aged fifty-nine, he had sharp eyes under beetle brows and spoke with a stutter. He ate no meat and belonged to the sect of Old Believers. Half the year he travelled, usually in his favourite Egypt, and his aims in life were to fill his Moscow house – for he kept a residence there as well as one in Paris – with the best contemporary art and to dazzle friends by showing it to them. He had started well in 1897 by buying Monet's *Lilas d'Argenteuil*, then acquired work by Degas, Cézanne and Gauguin. He didn't consult dealers or connoisseurs, having un-shakable faith in his own judgment backed by his love of Egypt's robust sculpture and the bold colouring of its frescoes. His commission to Matisse was for two large panels to go in his Moscow home.

For some years Matisse had felt a growing fascination with brightly-woven textiles and the part they play in the domestic scene. A visit to the Biskra in North Africa which André Gide and friends had made almost a place of pagan pilgrimage offered him an experience of simplicity, of few objects and strong light. In *The Dessert, Red Harmony*, intended for Shchukine's dining-room, Matisse gives pride of place to a boldly designed tablecloth, the pattern of which is almost matched by the wall covering and carpet. On the cloth stand two carafes and two pedestal dishes of fruit. In one a lady is arranging fruit, but it is not she who dominates the scene. The textiles do that, by their strong colour and assured pattern. The lady's hair, in three curved tiers, seems to be just one more phrase in the flow of bright arabesques, and even the trees we glimpse through a window are brought into line with the red harmony.

Matisse's other painting for Shchukine's house is a very large panel, 2.60 × 3.90 metres: *The Dance*. The subject – five figures performing a vigorous round dance – is so simple only the most sophisticated treat-ment could make it original. Matisse takes a viewpoint slightly above ground level, so that the circle appears oval. Each dancer is at the most extended point of a demanding movement, and each point is different. The foreground dancer, whom we see from the back, is lunging for, but has not yet caught, his neighbour's outstretched hand, so the circle is still open, for the viewer vicariously to join. Shoulders, arms, legs and feet – all are straining to the full, while the figures veer to the edge of the panel, as though about to break through it. This is the vigour of Ballets Russes captured in line and colour.

Matisse sold no less than thirty-seven paintings to Sergei Shchukine. He and Picasso found the Russian and the Americans, Gertrude and Leo Stein, their most loyal customers, and one wonders why it fell to foreigners to buy the two leading painters in Paris. The answer may lie in Kipling's already quoted description of the French: 'First to follow Truth and last to leave old truths behind.' The cultivated Parisian, down the ages, has been conservative. He values tradition, trusts the Old Masters. It was this very conservatism in noncreative Parisians that made innovation possible for the creators. Sorties into no-man's-land can be launched only from positions of strength.

In 1911–12, under the title *Large Still Life with Aubergines*, Matisse painted his Collioure studio. It might have been thought that after Chardin nothing remained to be elicited from this genre, but Matisse knew better. Three violet-coloured aubergines and two figs lie beside a terracotta statuette on a red tablecloth in front of a boldly designed blue and green screen. The carpet and wall-covering are coffee-bean brown, with mauve petals in clusters of five. Matisse reveals to us how our impression of a room grows out of a focal point of colour: here the undulant aubergines. Colour is the essential datum of Nature, from the earth and its fruits radiating outward into the textiles we weave and wear, the furniture we make.

By 1914 there existed a recognizable world of Matisse. In it the sun is high and bright, in several

senses windows are open on to trees and balconies
hung with flowers. Inside, the room has been arranged,
clearly, by a woman. She may or may not be present, but
she has marked the room with her taste and made it welcoming. There is fruit in a bowl, a vase of flowers.
Strongly coloured wallpaper and chair coverings and
tablecloths are as much a reflection of her warm character as her dress or jewellery. They say to the sun Yes. It
is an open, trusting world, in which outside and inside
are on intimate terms.

Raoul Dufy was born eight years after Matisse. He too
was a northerner, but from Le Havre, where his father
had a small metals business. One of a large family,
Raoul had to leave school at fourteen to take work in a
firm of coffee importers. This job gave him occasion to
see much of the busy port – fishing boats with brown
sails, steamships loading and unloading cargoes from
the Americas. He started to draw these scenes and at
twenty-three won a scholarship to the Ecole des Beaux-
Arts. Moreau had been succeeded by another who went
in for depicting decapitation, Léon Bonnat; under
Bonnat young Dufy studied but the artist he came to
hero-worship dwelled in the Louvre, by name Claude
Lorrain.

Dufy was a good-looking young fellow, with striking
blue eyes, slightly turned-up nose, fair curly hair and
an innocent expression. He liked to be neatly turned
out and even if he had no money for his next meal his
down-at-heel shoes would be polished and shining. He
was cheerful and had more than his share of idealism,
hence perhaps his fondness for Claude's dreamy landscapes, which Ravel too loved. He found it easy to like
people, was wholly lacking in envy, and wherever he
went won friends.

After the Beaux-Arts Dufy began painting seascapes and seaside resorts around Le Havre in the style of the pre-Impressionist Norman, Boudin. In 1904 he teamed up with another sea-lover, Albert Marquet who, under Matisse's influence, was using impasto to depict colours reflected in shimmering water, and urged Dufy to do likewise. One day, Dufy was to recall, while working at Sainte-Adresse, 'I drew the contours of each object in black mixed with white, each time leaving in the middle the white of the paper which I then coloured with a specific and quite intense tone . . . Blue, green, ochre, not much else. The result surprised me but I had discovered what I was looking for . . . my reality.'

In 1905, at a Paris exhibition, Dufy saw a seascape with nudes by Matisse, *Luxe, Calme et Volupté*, all in the flaming colours of a Turner; he liked it so much he decided to stop painting in the style of Boudin and to follow the way hinted at by Marquet and made plain by Matisse.

With his cheerful temperament, his liking for his fellow-men and for seaside towns, Dufy began to paint holiday resorts in an extended palette that now included red. In summer the resorts were full of Parisians, who arrived by train and, now, by motor-car. *The Posters at Trouville* (1906) shows visitors on the promenade, a gaily striped bathing tent, bold posters and a flag advertising *Le Journal*. Flags by the sea had been around since Sisley, but for Dufy they had the fascination of a toy for a child or a mandala for a contemplative and he was to make them almost a signature. *The Regattas* (1907) depicts yachts of Le Havre, a flag and, in the foreground, smartly dressed spectators – a visual twin of Proust's Balbec.

In 1908 Dufy withdrew from this holiday world. He discovered Cubism and spent the summer of that year with Georges Braque at L'Estaque near Marseille, leaving aside Fauvist primary colours for sober ochre, dusty green, grey; and undulant curves for hard straight lines. To be close to Braque and Picasso Dufy rented a small studio near the Lapin Agile. He was thirty-one years old, almost without a sou and wholly unable to choose between Fauvism and Cubism.

Quite a few painters in Montmartre, during the first decade of the century, experienced the hardship Dufy now encountered, and we have vignettes of how they sought to get enough to eat. Maurice Vlaminck won prizes in bicycle races; during the 1900 Exhibition, wearing a red jacket, he played gipsy music on the violin in a smart restaurant. His disciple Derain earned money as a professional boxer, and when that source dried up he and Vlaminck would fantasize about which of them would become famous first. Fame, Derain decided, would be having one's photo in a newspaper, and the loser would stand the winner a good meal. 'Agreed,' said Vlaminck. 'Wait,' said Derain, recalling the other's anarchist activities. 'If you murder a concierge or derail a train, that doesn't count.'

A fortnight passed. Then Vlaminck came round to Derain's studio flourishing *Le Petit Journal*. 'How about this!'

Page four carried a photo of Vlaminck endorsing one of the popular medicines of the day, Pink Pills for Pale People. 'Since taking Pink Pills I've recovered my health, resumed all my occupations. Signed: Vlaminck, artist painter.' Derain acknowledged defeat and paid for the meal.

While Derain was doing his military service, Vlaminck decided to write an erotic novel and got Derain to illustrate it. Entitled *From One Bed to the Next*, it sold quite well and almost alone among hacks Vlaminck succeeded in getting paid by his tight-fisted publisher, putting his huge wrestler's hands on the desk and saying quietly, 'Pay up or I'll throw you and your chair out of the window.'

Van Dongen, a red-bearded Fauvist, also made money by writing titillating pieces; his appeared in *Frou-Frou*, a precursor of *Playboy*, and he wrote satires too for the humorous *L'Assiette au Beurre*. The Dutchman's other sources of income were unloading vegetables at Les Halles and selling newspapers at the street corner. In the evening he would slope off to paint the low life that fascinated him in fairs, cabarets and cafés, managing to sell just enough to keep his wife and daughter in their one room in the Bateau Lavoir.

One of the most colourful of Montmartre's impoverished was Suzanne Valadon's illegitimate son, to whom a Spanish painter-poet, Miguel Utrillo, had lent his surname. Young Maurice Utrillo was in several senses a boy of the streets, who saw more of cafés than the schoolroom. He received informal art lessons but could not settle to productive work. He developed a taste for red wine, first by the glass, then by the bottle.

Among the kindly residents on the north side of Montmartre was a former gendarme turned wineseller. In 1911 *le père* Gay took in Maurice as a lodger above his shop at the corner of rue du Mont-Cenis and rue Paul-Feral. Gently, but with a firm hand, Gay provided Utrillo, then aged twenty-eight, with canvases and paints and told him to get to work. When Utrillo protested that he didn't have a subject, Gay bought him picture-postcards. With these to guide him, soon Utrillo was turning out paintings of Montmartre's streets, some with the dome of Sacré-Cœur in the background, in which he revealed the power and variety latent in the pigment white.

Every so often Utrillo would rebel. He would overturn furniture and threaten to break up Gay's house, whereupon the unruffled former gendarme calmed the rebel with a bottle of red wine. Then Utrillo would resume the rendering of a line of houses which to passers-by might look drab but which to a former boy of the streets had been a playground. Through his empathy for them and his skill he made them one of the best-known emblems of Paris around 1910. Gay sold them for 50 to a 100 francs apiece.

Utrillo performed well on the piano. Vlaminck's violin-playing has been noticed; Derain built himself an organ on which he played his favourite plainchant; Dufy, if he sold a painting, spent part of the money on a ticket to a concert. The similarity often noticed between Fauvist colour schemes and Debussy's tone painting may owe something to the painters' informed appreciation of innovations by living composers.

Sometimes Utrillo would take leave from his easel by way of the window and hurry down to Marie Vizier's cabaret. There his favourite drinking companion was a figure-painter who had arrived from his native Italy in 1906. Since the Renaissance young Frenchmen had been hurrying eagerly to Italy to learn, but now Italians were coming to Paris, even so assured a talent as Giorgio de Chirico, believing their training incomplete until they had worked in the city by the Seine.

Young Modigliani specialized in female nudes with elongated bodies and pinched faces. Though practically no one bought his work, Utrillo recognized its quality, and perhaps too a poignant note not unlike his own. According to Georges-Michel, their first meeting was quite dramatic. To begin with, as a token of their mutual admiration, they exchanged coats. Then one said to the other: 'You are the world's greatest painter.'

'No. *You* are the world's greatest painter.'

'I forbid you to contradict me.'

'Say that again and I'll hit you!'

'The world's greatest . . .'

The fight started and lasted till they were both exhausted. In a nearby bistro they made it up. There they consumed a large number of bottles of wine, and exchanged coats several more times. Then they went out.

'You're the world's greatest painter, admit it.'

'No. You are.'

And they were at it again, landing up in the gutter, where they went to sleep, and woke at dawn to find that the few francs in their pockets had been stolen.

The incident illustrates the faith and courage that carried these impoverished painters through their Spartan youthful years, though it does have a latent sadness, for Modigliani was to become so discouraged by lack of recognition that eventually he became a drug addict and took his own life.

In 1908 Raoul Dufy was trying to make ends meet on 100 francs a month: 'I couldn't afford to buy colours, so I concentrated on drawing.' When Apollinaire showed interest in his draughtsmanship and asked him to illustrate with woodcuts a Bestiary of charming animal poems by himself, Dufy agreed and thought things might be looking up. He should have known that Apollinaire's books were almost invariably remaindered, and the 120 copies of the Bestiary made neither of them money.

Dufy was still hovering between Cubism and Fauvism – Derain was another in the same dilemma – still, at thirty-one, experimenting. He chose this inauspicious moment to fall in love with a girl called Emilienne Brison and to marry her. But Paris had one or two safety-nets for endangered talent. The State had given young Dufy a scholarship, and now under an endowment by a Paris magistrate aptly named Bonjean, Raoul and Emilienne were offered board and lodging for a year in a fine house near Paris, virtually a Villa

Médicis *à la française*. Here Dufy survived until another rescuer came along – Paul Poiret. The couturier recognized in Dufy a kindred lover of vibrant colour, and a strong decorative talent. In 1910 he commissioned him to design a heading for his writing-paper and, the following year, to paint the awning for his Persian-style gala, The Thousand and Second Night, inspired by Ballets Russes productions. Dufy having given satisfaction in these humble tasks, Poiret put up money for a small workshop in Avenue de Clichy and commissioned Dufy to design and print four textile wall-coverings, one of them a seascape, then more textiles for his fashion house. Dufy won favour with these and got an important commission from a leading textile manufacturer, Bianchini.

Designing textiles strengthened Dufy's taste for vivid colours and distanced him from Cubism. By 1913, aged thirty-six, he may be said to have found his centre as an artist. In that year he painted *The Public Garden, Hyères*. Such places tend to be dusty and run-down, but Dufy singles out the curving palm tree branches, the angle of a balcony, a wrought-iron bandstand and with a touch even lighter than usual makes the garden a quiet place with a soul that we long to visit.

Dufy continued to paint regattas and the sea; blue, he held, is the only colour to keep its individuality, however dark or pale. Later he was to extend his range to racecourses and paddocks, to concert halls and galas, to all occasions of joyful elegance. He is the celebrant, in this decade, of nature on holiday. His style, of considered slightness, fluid, spontaneous, joyful and wittily allusive, is as difficult to achieve as a perfectly risen soufflé or a suite by Ravel; one stroke of colour too many and the picture becomes a poster; too little and it lapses into preciousness.

*   *   *

Among the many painters Dufy met when living in Montmartre was one gifted woman. Marie Laurencin was born in Paris in 1883. She hardly knew her father, who was a Deputy from Picardy named Alfred Toulet, for he was already married to a niece of well-known General Tisserand when Marie arrived. Marie's mother, Norman with a dash of Creole blood, had wanted to become a Carmelite nun; she gave her daughter a good education at the Lycée Lamartine and on Sundays would chant to her the *Dies Iræ.* From the Lycée Marie went on to the Académie Julian. She had a lovely slim figure and a regular oval face with dark eyes, but her Creole ancestry showed in frizzy hair and rather full lips: pretty without being beautiful was the general opinion. She had a happy temperament: forever skipping and singing. At the Académie Julian she became fond of Persian miniatures, and of rococo, whose soft colours quite early she adopted as her own.

'I had left a little portrait of myself,' she later recalled, 'in pink, white and black in the cloakroom at the art class where I was studying, and the next day it was gone. Braque had taken it to the Moulin de la Galette to show his painter friends. He returned it, saying, "Petite Laurencin, you have real talent. You must keep it up, and come to see us, too." '

Marie did go to see Braque and his group, including Picasso. She was a determined young lady, who claimed she never did what she didn't want to. And she knew very early that Cubism wasn't for her. She saw the world as a place where one hopped and skipped and sang to oneself, light in body and texture, softly curved. The colours she found in it were not the bold male colours of Matisse but soft pastels, the colours of sugared almonds. Because she belonged temperamentally with the Fauves, Rodin named Marie 'Fauvette', which happens to mean 'Warbler'. This designation she gladly accepted, for her talent, as she prettily put it, ranged between a flutter and a coo.

Marie Laurencin painted young women, girls, children, ponies, dogs, doves peeping through flowers, pianos, guitars and flimsy muslin curtains. All her women's heads were modelled, she said, on her grey-eyed cat Possiquatte, but this is not to be taken literally, any more than her claim not to like the country because there is too much air and the milk smells of cows. Her preferred medium is watercolour, her tones pale pink, pale blue, pale green, pale grey: as Cocteau said, Marie Laurencin discovered that grey has shades. She claimed to paint 'by ear' – meaning that she had to listen to her subject talking while she painted his or her portrait. Hence, she explained, her failure to make a satisfactory painting of the Blessed Virgin. If she had been born deaf, she claimed, she could not have become an artist.

Her originality is that she is the first women to paint wholly as a woman, expressing her very feminine sensibility not in terms invented by men but in her own. She claimed, for instance, that women do not have noses, at least in the way that men have them: structurally they are less evident in the face and their lines are softened further by powder or make-up. The girls and women she painted that way have an unprecedented *douceur*.

Tenderness is the mood she likes to convey. Tenderness flowing between young women, and between young mothers and children. Tenderness often in the lightest of touches and gentlest of glances. There is here no attempt to assert or define, just suggestions, hints below the surface of the conceptual: not boudoir decoration, as is sometimes said, but truly feminine painting, content to be such.

In her early twenties Marie met the *éminence grise* of foreign policy, Philippe Berthelot, who lived on the Left

Bank and mingled from choice with artists and writers. Berthelot fell in love with Marie Laurencin perhaps as much for the pretty girls in her watercolours as for herself. She evidently fell in love with this handsome, very assured, much older man and for two years was his mistress. Then Hélène Berthelot persuaded Philippe to end the liaison.

Marie Laurencin became the object of Apollinaire's affection. Apollinaire too was an assured and ardent lover; also he could appreciate the poetry in Marie and in her work. But he was domineering, fussy about his personal possessions and had a cruel streak. He also had a difficult mother who wanted her only son, with, as she too often reminded him, her own noble Polish blood in his veins, to marry a girl with money. Marie also had a determined mother who frowned on the notion of her daughter marrying a penniless writer.

Marie's love-affair with Apollinaire lasted a year and a half and meant more to her than any other. If we know little about it, at least it has left us a remarkable painting by Marie, dating from 1908. Beside a seated Apollinaire, who has a tiny mouth and no neck, stands Marie in a tongue-in-cheek hieratic pose, flanked by Picasso in profile with an eye like that on a Mediterranean fishing boat, holding his dog, who resembles a lamb, and Fernande Olivier, with a vase of flowers near her head looking like a rococo hat. It is a work that tells us much about the painters of Montmartre, their friendships and fun.

By 1910 each of the artists who had been labelled Fauves had worked his way out of the extreme Fauve position. Vlaminck, who had painted Derain with a mauve moustache, was using dark, inky lines to depict bare trees, lonely roads and canals in Flanders. Derain, who had painted Vlaminck with an orange moustache and the River Thames green, was emerging from Cubism into a still personal, but restrained use of colour. Marquet was painting quayside scenes in colours that correspond to those in real life, while Rouault was choosing to arouse pity in his viewer by distorting the human figure – he had crossed into Expressionism. But the challenge of Fauvism and its claim that traditional art was dead, that museums are cemeteries – these were not forgotten, and they appeared in a sensational new form in 1909 when an Italian, Filippo Marinetti, published in *Le Figaro* the manifesto of Futurism.

The essence of modern life, said Marinetti, is Speed; Futurist writers and painters should leave traditional subjects for racing cars and fast trains. Let them get to grips with energy, with the exhilarating whirl of machinery, in which man's future lay. Moonlight must be killed.

The fun lurking in Marie Laurencin's painting of herself and her friends went hand in hand with a fervent belief in certain artistic principles. Marie as a 'Fauvette' might not warm to Picasso's Cubism but she recognized it as an authentic development of the exploration of the human figure. Her friends too stood by certain canons, however uncanonical they might be in the margin. A theory like Futurism which would displace man and nature from the centre of the stage seemed to them a direct threat to everything Parisian artists had achieved in the current decade. In 1905 Vauxcelles had reproved the Fauves; in 1910 a group of Montmartre artists decided to reprove Futurism.

Early in 1910 an unknown calling himself Joachim-Raphael Boronali launched in the press a manifesto for a new artistic movement which he termed Excessism. 'Excess in everything is strength. The sun is never too strong, the sky too green, the distant sea too red, darkness too thickly black. Destroy museums, trample on their absurd exhibits. End draughtsmanship, shading, careful finish; instead, dazzle and roar.'

Excessism began to be talked about. At the Salon des Indépendants, which opened in March, a painting by Joachim-Raphael Boronali aroused much controversy. Entitled *And the Sun Slept on the Adriatic*, it was a morass of colour, but the artist claimed that it embodied the principles of Excessism. A number of critics hailed the work and the public, beguiled by the bold manifesto, spoke of a new masterpiece.

A fortnight later the secret came out. Boronali, far from being a new Italian genius, was an anagram of Aliboron, a Montmartre wag. Under the attesting eye of a bailiff Aliboron and friends had arranged for a donkey called Lolo, belonging to the owner of the Lapin Agile, to have a paintbrush attached to its tail; dipping this in various pots of paint, the donkey had whisked its tail over the canvas, back and forth, to produce *And the Sun Slept on the Adriatic*. Thereafter Futurism never had quite the same glamour for French artists.

When does innovation break the bounds of restraint? When does personal bent become eccentricity? When does respect for the subject – a cardinal principle of classicism – disappear under emotion felt by the artist? How does one distil from ephemera a satisfying timeless or supra-temporal quality?

The Colourists here described no less than the Cubists grappled with such questions, often without articulating them. As the Impressionists had rescued painting of the 1860s from studio drapes and props and paid models by going into the fields, so the Colourists rescued it from the dim and decadent literary-historicism of *fin de siècle*. Moreau's Salomé yielded to Matisse's Amélie, arranging her interior as tastefully as she would her own clothes, designed perhaps by Dufy, and to Marie Laurencin's tender, fun-loving schoolgirls.

The fresh, life-affirming note, whose emblems are sunshine and unbanal colours, is very pronounced in Matisse, Dufy and Laurencin. It did not just happen. It was already being sounded in sister arts, in Claudel's *Five Great Odes*, which celebrate an immense and spacious world, West and East in counterpoint, and in Debussy's rich harmonies. Partly the Colourists were responding to a mood, partly they helped further to define it. Matisse's uncluttered interiors prepared the way for Art Deco, his *La Danse* cleared the ground for the daring tango, and Ravel may well have found the nymphs for *Daphnis and Chloë* in Marie Laurencin's bare-armed young girls. Precisely because it was sounded in so many different forms at once, the note of joyful assurance took a firm hold on Parisian imaginations.

CHAPTER 15

Attitudes to Germany

On the hill of Sainte-Geneviève the Sorbonne has welcomed foreign students since the days of Roger Bacon, Albertus Magnus and Thomas Aquinas in the thirteenth century. Its outlook has always been more international than that of the National Assembly at the bottom of the hill on the banks of the Seine, and so it was in the 1900s. A number of liberal-minded men with first-hand knowledge of Germany and a grounding in German history taught there. They included Henri Lichtenberger, author of a standard book on modern Germany, Lucien Herr, librarian of the Ecole Normale and secretary of the *Revue de Paris*, and Félicien Challaye, who had widened his views by travel to Japan and wrote for the *Revue du mois*. These men were advocates of Franco-German friendship.

They were not starry-eyed. They admitted that Germans enjoyed less freedom of speech than Frenchmen save at election time, and their press had less influence on the Government. The Reichstag could pass a resolution but unless it was endorsed by the Government – headed by the Chancellor, himself chosen by the Emperor – it would never become law. But the Frenchmen pointed out that though politically less advanced, in social welfare schemes the Germans led the world. Lloyd George was to be so impressed by Germany's national insurance for the old that he adopted the scheme for Britain.

When *Le Figaro* ran contentious articles by a French journalist, Jean Huret, drawing attention to Berlin's 'bridges and gas lamps decorated with emblems of war: helmets, lances, sabres, shields, drums and trumpets . . . on Sundays, at the Zeughaus, Berlin's military museum, one meets schoolchildren hearing from their teachers the story of the regimental flags and machine-guns on display', the Sorbonne savants explained that Germany's social structure derived, historically, from military service, but that any danger was offset by the influence of the Churches, stronger there than in anti-clerical France, and by a deeply inculcated moral conviction that the sword might be drawn only in a just cause.

Charles Andler, perhaps the most brilliant Sorbonne expert on Germany, came from Strasbourg, where his father had owned a pharmacy. In 1870 invading Prussians shelled streets near the Andler flat and for weeks the family lay low in a cellar. French youths residing in Alsace were liable for service in the German army, and to save his son from this Andler *père* moved to the Haute Saône, then to Paris. Charles studied philosophy – and learned to be generous-minded – under Emile Boutroux and like many during that low tide of faith exchanged Christianity for Socialism, which then meant Marxism. He called on Engels in London and translated *The Communist Manifesto*. He rose to become professor of German studies and an expert on Nietzsche; he also wrote books on Kant and on German Socialism.

In 1905 Andler was aged thirty-nine, good-looking, with shy eyes, a kindly expression, thick hair, moustache and small beard. He was happily married to the daughter of an Alsace pastor and had two children. Harsh boyhood experiences of the invading Prussians had left Maurice Barrès and the ex-Minister of Education, Raymond Poincaré, bitter, but Andler either felt no bitterness or surmounted it. Indeed, he fervently believed that the 800,000 Frenchmen who voted Socialist should work closely with Germany's four million Socialists to renounce war and press their governments to disarm. He himself often crossed the Rhine to lecture on Nietzsche and work for détente with his many friends there.

One Easter recess, at the request of the vice-chancellor, Andler led twenty law students on a visit to Cologne, Berlin and Hamburg. They were made a fuss of and shown round the Kaiser Friedrich Museum by the director in person. In replying to toasts at a dinner, on advice from the hard-line Ambassador Jules Cambon, Andler limited himself to polite remarks about the host country.

On his return, to his astonishment, Andler found himself attacked for these politenesses. In the *Echo de Paris* the stridently nationalist novelist-Deputy, Maurice Barrès, called Andler a humanitarian-anarchist, whose support for Dreyfus had 'Germanized' him and who, though born in Alsace, was ready to abandon that province and Lorraine to their fate in order to pursue the chimera of Franco-German understanding. Barrès demanded that the university dissociate itself from such a person, for 'fathers do not accept that their sons should be taught to betray them'. Barrès's call was heeded by many students; demonstrations were organized against the 'traitor' and for fully two weeks there were scuffles and fights outside lecture halls.

The incident shows how high feeling ran. Anyone who worked for détente required courage and Andler had plenty. He stood by his remarks and continued to pay regular visits to Germany. Though he wrote little for the general public, he was seen by Socialists in both countries as a fearless and effective bridge-builder.

One of Andler's Socialist friends at the Sorbonne did

write - most successfully - for the general public. Romain Rolland, only son of a Burgundian notary, received a somewhat pampered upbringing. He did brilliantly at school and won a coveted place in the Ecole Normale, his indulgent parents moving to Paris solely in order to give him a home there. Tolstoy was then the fashion; young Rolland wrote to the famous novelist and received a friendly answer, which gave him *cachet* and helped him to exchange his Catholicism for Socialism: 'What does the existence or non-existence of God matter, if the soul is divine!'

Rolland played the piano outstandingly well, had a first-rate critical brain and as a Socialist was *persona grata* in the senior common room. He won a place as university lecturer, first in art history, then in music. His Socialism he expressed in a series of plays extolling Danton and other heroes of the Revolution. They exude high thinking but proved virtually unstageable.

Rolland married a Jewish girl, Clotilde, daughter of Professor Bréal of the Sorbonne, and the young couple used to stay regularly with Clotilde's German uncle in Mainz. This uncle loved music as much as young Rolland. Here the Frenchman conceived his vocation: he would work for peace through friendship with cultivated Germans.

Rolland was a tall, slim man with delicate, handsome features, a fine nose and rather deep-set gentle blue eyes - 'the clearest and kindest eyes I have ever seen', said a friend. He spoke very softly, followed a vegetarian diet, neither smoked nor drank and worked an eighteen-hour day. Believing like his kin-spirit Rilke that an artistic career was incompatible with marriage, Rolland separated from Clotilde in 1900, when he was aged thirty-four, though the two were to remain friends. Thereafter he formed warm brother-sister relationships, notably with the beautiful pianist and champion of women's rights, Louise Cruppi.

Rolland's first major contribution to détente was to write a Life of Ludwig van Beethoven. He brought to his task musical erudition, sympathetic understanding and a clear style. He did more, he was the first writer to cast Beethoven not only as a hero in spirit and creativity but as no less a hero than Julius Cæsar, say, or Danton. The biography appeared in 1903; it proved a critical and popular success, though the malicious said its readers were mainly repressed women who saw in the composer of the *Moonlight Sonata* a dream lover.

Rolland's next venture in the cause of Franco-German understanding was a novel, *Jean Christophe*. The hero is a high-minded young Rhineland composer, Johann Christopher Krafft who, after an unhappy childhood, sets himself the task of expressing in art moral truth. Arriving penniless in Paris, he is befriended by Olivier Jeannin, a sensitive music-loving teacher from the provinces. 'Olivier had serenity of mind and a sickly body, John Christopher mighty strength and a storming soul.' Johann Christopher falls in love with Olivier's sister, Antoinette, and when she dies of tuberculosis, continues to love her in Olivier, who resembles his sister in looks.

The two friends room together. The German comes to appreciate in Olivier the France of the provinces, Catholic, bent on furthering social justice, while Olivier appreciates the German's courage and creative energy.

The friends disagree on one crucial issue: whether historically Alsace deserves to be called French or German. Olivier declares that after forty years Alsatians still persist in their refusal to become Germans save in name. 'It was possible,' he tells his Rhineland friend, 'for a great people to renounce the thought of vengeance for such a crime, but quite impossible for them to

express their adhesion to it without dishonour.'
Neither can accept the other's views on Alsace-
Lorraine; nevertheless, their friendship-in-music en-
dures and is charted through six volumes.

The first part of *Jean Christophe* appeared in 1904 in
the *Cahiers* edited by Rolland's friend, Charles Péguy,
and volumes appeared until 1912. The novel found
many readers in France and helped to foster a more positive and appreciative attitude to Germany. It should be
noted, however, that Rolland, gentle Germanophile
though he was, did not yield an inch on Alsace-
Lorraine. Only a very few Socialists were ready to do
that and most influential Sorbonne professors would
have endorsed Olivier's stand. A leading historian, not
a man of the Left or Right, Ernest Lavisse, for example,
welcomed the new century with an article in *Revue de
Paris*: 'The French and German peoples are formed by
their differing genius for complementing one another,
and are destined to the joint leadership of humanity' (in
1900 Britain was expected to be defeated by the Boers).
But, added Lavisse, no alliance can be formed between
the two neighbours until Alsace-Lorraine is returned to
France.

Jean Christophe was welcomed also by the German-
speaking public. During a stay in Florence a young
literary Viennese Jew, Stefan Zweig, chanced on,
and hailed, the first instalment: 'Here was the man, the
poet, who brought all the moral forces into play . . . a
soaring faith in the unifying mission of art . . . it was
the first consciously European novel . . . the first
decisive appeal towards brotherhood, more effective
because it reached broader masses than the hymns of
Verhaeren, more penetrating than all the protests and
pamphlets . . .'

A further unique feature of *Jean Christophe* is that
while writing his novel Romain Rolland was also living

376

it. He is Olivier, and Johann Christopher is – in part – Richard Strauss. The two came to know each other at the turn of the century, when the already famous Munich-born composer was thirty-six and Rolland two years younger. In March 1900 they visited the Louvre together and Rolland began making notes in his diary. Strauss, says the Frenchman, looks like a young bullock, has fair hair, a small nose and is tall. He has great energy, a tendency to over-excitement controlled by an effort of will, an amiable 'South German buffoonery'. 'His great virtue is sincerity, absolute frankness . . . I much enjoyed getting to know him better.'

The Boer War was on. Most Germans, including the Kaiser, backed the Boers, but Strauss said to Rolland, 'The English are very civilized and very strong. It's a thoroughly good thing that the stronger should triumph' – a comment Rolland naturally deplored as 'mistaken Nietzscheism'. Rolland admired much of Strauss's work, notably his heroic tone-poems, considered him the heir, in part, of Beethoven, and was pleased to have him as a friend, a remarkably loyal friend, as it turned out. Nevertheless, Rolland could not resist noting in his diary: 'Strauss behaves badly at table, sitting with his legs crossed at the side, holds his plate near his chin to eat, stuffs himself with sweets like a baby.'

In May 1905, in the belief that 'Music accomplishes the highest of missions; it acts as a link between peoples,' a German committee in Strasbourg organized a Festival of Music at which French and German works would be played. Rolland arranged to attend this memorable event as correspondent for the *Revue de Paris*.

Strauss opened the Strasbourg Festival by conducting Weber's Overture to *Oberon*, and in the second concert conducted his own *Sinfonia Domestica*. Rolland in his article praises the Festival's aim, praises his friend's symphony, then fires a salvo of complaints. Why had Charpentier been chosen as one of France's composers instead of, say, Debussy? Why had only five of Franck's eight *Béatitudes* been performed? It rather looked like an attempt to discredit France. As for the modern German composers represented, 'Mahler,' wrote Rolland crossly, 'is hypnotized by the prevalent German need to seem strong, but in my view he is unsure of himself, ironic, sad, agitated, the soul of a Viennese musician striving after Wagner's grandiosity.' In Hugo Wolf 'one looks in vain for a melody that is really original and strong'. German composers, he suggests, have it too easy, they are victims of their country's musical facility, and he ends by declaring, in italics, *'There is too much music in Germany.'*

The carping note was to reappear in Rolland's friendship with Strauss, but for the moment things went smoothly. Strauss began to write the score of *Salomé*, using Oscar Wilde's French text. He did not know where the stress fell on a large number of French words and phrases, and Rolland offered to help. A long correspondence ensued, in which Rolland proved himself sensitive and extremely helpful. On 2 August 1905, for example, Strauss is fretting about the pronunciation of *cheveux*, citing two pages from Debussy's *Pelléas*, where *cheveux* is stressed in three different ways. Which is correct? Rolland replies: 'The stress in *cheveux* falls on the second syllable. But someone in love will say *"tes ché věux"*. There is a barely perceptible quiver of voice and lips, as though he were saying "your *dear* hair".'

When Strauss finished his score he sent Rolland an engraved portrait of himself, inscribed 'to my collaborator'. Rolland was touched; the friendship prospered. But Rolland could not restrain his tendency to criticize. A high-point of Wilde's text is a scene where

Herod describes the moon as a mad, naked woman seeking lovers, and Strauss brings out with horrible vividness the prevailing air of insanity. Rolland told Strauss bluntly that he disapproved of the mood imparted to the Bible story by Wilde. 'It's not a question of bourgeois morality, it's a question of health . . . I'm afraid . . . you've been taken in by decadent German literature . . . There are forces that burn, others that fecundate . . In your *Domestica*, in *Death and Transfiguration*, in *A Hero's Life* there are beneficent forces.' And when *Salomé* had its Paris première, Rolland described it to a sisterly friend as 'a barbarous work'.

To explore madness or, as Strauss was to do in *Elektra*, depict extreme violence on stage, is surely not necessarily a sign of barbarism; it can in fact produce a more complete catharsis than the plays of Racine which were Rolland's ideal. But Rolland did not see this. He continued to criticize Strauss for, in effect, not being sufficiently French, by which he meant life-affirming and joyful. Once, watching him conduct, Rolland thought Strauss looked 'like a barbarian from Asia, one of those Huns that settled in Germany'. Presumably he did not voice this opinion to Strauss, for the two remained on good terms.

Rolland also worked for détente by instilling his beliefs in his pupils. Of these the one we know best is Louis Gillet, a good-looking young Catholic bourgeois of great charm, later an art historian, whose friends included Péguy and Marc Sangnier and who was later to become a trusted adviser to Rodin. In 1900, aged twenty-four, Louis Gillet went to Greifswald in Pomerania to teach French at the university there. He went with Rolland's blessing, an unofficial ambassador of goodwill, so to speak, with instructions to write often.

Gillet complied. He wrote to Rolland about the jovial

beer-drinking, the obligatory fencing which scarred so many faces on the left side – we learn from an English lady travel writer that German girls preferred young men with these marks of bravery. Gillet particularly admired German zest on the dance floor: 'When these philologists waltz, I feel their religious blood begins to pulsate.'

Gradually Gillet's enthusiasm cools. A keen admirer of Rolland's French Revolution plays, Gillet dislikes the Germans' claims that 'the keystone of modern history is not the Revolution but the emergence of the German Empire'. But instead of arguing the point Gillet pontificates:

> In the history of Europe I see only one country – France – that has always thought of the good of others . . . That great conqueror Bonaparte carried in his head the plans of a . . . world civilization . . . The Germans were great once . . . How is it that Beethoven's archangels have fallen from heaven? . . . The most ghastly thing is that these huckstering tenors continue to speak as though they were Crusaders, and the big corporal thinks he's Charlemagne.

Gillet overlooks the fact that France had been a nation for centuries, Germany for barely fifty years. The individual German states were both provincial and parochial, and certainly had no grand designs before Prussia under Bismarck; Austria was a much more dangerous entity to Napoleon than a non-existent 'Germany'. One might have expected Rolland to have pointed this out, or at least to have urged on his young friend less self-righteousness and a more open mind. Not so. 'Perhaps,' replied the musicologist gravely, 'under the grossness of the German hide you will find some deep and loyal soul. Look well: it would be a great happiness for you. Personally, I'm not too confident.' And he agreed with Gillet: 'We French are, we must be, the world's conscience.'

The stock portrait of Romain Rolland as a benign European above and beyond national frontiers – a portrait he himself was later to publicize – turns out to be exaggerated. Rolland was ready to hold out his hand to Germany only on the basis that French culture of his day was superior to German. He who praised the soul as divine believed the French soul more divine than any other.

Had *Jean Christophe* been a great moral novel in a class, say, with Tolstoy's *Resurrection*, it might have won Parisian minds to détente. But its characterization is thin – also, for today's readers there are too many tears – and the ever-critical Parisians told its author so. As for Rolland's friendship with Strauss, its importance lay mainly in a small Sorbonne circle. Rolland in short was a focal point for Franco-German friendship through art without ever becoming a really effective force in Paris life, and therefore in French politics. Rolland shrank from the hurly-burly of politics, and never used his close friendship with Madame Cruppi to influence the lady's husband, a Minister of Foreign Affairs.

What was the attitude of Marcel Proust to Germany? We know that he took an interest in the historical rivalry of France and the Holy Roman Empire – mentioned on the very first page of *A la Recherche* – and the comparative merits of their civilizations as expressed in the arts. We know that he kept in touch with public events: immediately on waking – around seven in the evening, for he wrote his novel at night – he read the newspaper, starting with the financial pages, because his income came from shares, prices of which rose and fell in line with international affairs. It is surprising, therefore, how little there is in his novel about Germany. He treats at length the Dreyfus affair, but in terms of its anti-Semitism, though quite as important in the public's estimation was the charge that an Army captain had sold his country's secrets not just to any foreign power but to arch-enemy Germany.

The explanation seems to be threefold. Proust saw foreign affairs through the eyes of his friend Calmette's *Figaro*, which mentioned Germany as little as possible. *Le Figaro*, incidentally, backed Delcassé to the hilt, even after he resigned. Secondly, the set Proust admired and aspired to belong to was firmly in favour of a foreign policy of grandeur. The Greffulhes put money into the Russian alliance and by entertaining Edward VII forwarded the Entente. Hugo Finaly, father of Proust's boyhood friend, Horace, headed the Banque Paribas which, we shall see, was to invest profitably in Morocco. Then again, Jewish people were not kindly disposed to Germany because several thousand Jews had chosen to leave their homes in Alsace – many settling in Paris – rather than live under German rule.

Thirdly, Proust was engaged in writing a novel which would exalt joyfulness-in-art as an absolute that lifts the reader above present reality, away from his fellows. In such a world the harsh competitiveness of international politics would have been out of place.

Nevertheless in his novel Proust does touch – obliquely, even lightly – on foreign affairs. In depicting Ambassador Norpois as self-satisfied, spineless and cliché-bound Proust was showing his own low opinion of diplomacy, which recurs when he compares Albertine's insincerity in her relations with the narrator to Delcassé's 'game of bluff' with Germany over Morocco, and, on another page, when he has Saint-

Loup liken German threats over Morocco to a game of
poker. Proust implies that international diplomacy is a
verbal thrust-and-parry in which neither side will dare
to pierce to the heart. As such it resembles the narrator's
unconsummated love. But at no point does he recognize
that Delcassé's 'game of bluff' might be exacerbating
German touchiness, and therefore be better compared
to Russian roulette.

Proust describes a party at the Guermantes' at which
guests discuss the character of the Kaiser. The statues of
Hohenzollern rulers and generals which Wilhelm had
chosen to line Berlin's Siegesallee were considered pretentious, so it was axiomatic in France that Wilhelm
had poor taste, and this emerges in a remark by one of
the guests:

'Every time I dine at Potsdam and the Emperor says,
"You must see this play or that play, it's brilliant," I take
good care not to go to it, and when I hear him berate an
exhibition of paintings, I hurry to see it.'

The Guermantes agree that despite his lack of taste
Wilhelm is very intelligent and a man of peace. True, in
opening a hospital he may vaunt German military
might, but that is just his manner, and indeed rather
amusing.

Proust's view of foreign policy in terms of per-
sonalities recurs when he introduces into his novel one
of Wilhelm's close advisers, Prince von Faffenheim,
probably modelled on Chancellor von Bülow. Despite
an atrocious French accent, it is the Prince's ambition to
be elected an associate foreign member of the prestigious Académie des Sciences Morales et Politiques. He
tries to achieve this by writing in the *Revue des Deux
Mondes* an article about his political career and including in it flattering remarks about Monsieur de Norpois,
who controls ten of the Académie's votes. Unmoved,
Norpois remains evasive. Finally the Prince finds an

apparently better way. He asks Norpois to introduce him to the elderly flower-painting Marquise de Ville-parisis, then invites that lady to a dinner at which she will meet the Queen of England; duly grateful, the Marquise tells Norpois to act. Whether he does so is left unsaid; probably he doesn't. An inspection of Académie records shows that between 1900 and 1914 two Americans, one Rumanian, Xenopol, not heard of since, and two Russians were elected associate foreign members, but not a single German. Even the dizzy heights of the Académie were not above rancour.

Proust was a man of peace. If he hurt someone, even involuntarily, he went through agonies. He was not taken in by those who claimed a future war would be over in a month, he said it would be worse than Götterdämmerung. Proust understood that many Germans besides Bülow longed to be 'recognized' by the French as civilizers, not just as soldiers; indeed Wilhelm II, who loved decorations and orders, particularly wished to receive the cordon of the Légion d'Honneur. Proust had written brave articles calling for the preservation of cathedrals as places of worship; he might well have written articles calling for institutional France to recognize well-intentioned merit across the Rhine. Perhaps he believed it would be impossible to get such articles into print. At all events the most intelligent writer of his day chose to take no part in the debate about France's foreign policy and Franco-German relations.

The German pavilion at the 1900 Exhibition gave pride of place to French paintings commissioned for Schönbrunn by Frederick the Great. If this was a friendly sign that Germany still recognized France's leadership in the arts, it went unremarked in Paris, but it did set a few Parisians thinking of the days when a

Frenchman had gone to Prussia to 'enlighten' a versatile monarch, and to ask 'Who among our contemporaries is qualified to go to Berlin in the 1900s and repeat Voltaire's success?'

One man well qualified was André Gide. He enjoyed German literature, which he read in the original, thanks to his governess, Miss Shackleton, played much German music on the piano, Bach for preference, was a friend of Charles Andler and had a Goethe specialist as a brother-in-law. He knew his Nietzsche and had based his play *King Candaulus* on Nietzsche's boutade: 'Generosity carried to the point of vice'. *Candaulus* had interested a German producer and been performed in Berlin as well as in Paris. Gide liked the work of Stefan George, which exalts beautiful youth as the new twentieth-century god, and he was to meet the poet in April 1908. He was friendly with Rilke and introduced the young Austrian's book about Paris to French readers. Furthermore, Gide was a good mixer and a practical man who had been mayor of his local village.

Was he open-minded enough? The answer emerges from Gide's comment on *Jean Christophe*: a book of wishful thinking, 'the illusion of a generous . . . mind', and from his reply to *Mercure de France*'s questionnaire in 1902 about the value of German culture. Gide replied that what he had most learned from Goethe, Heine, Schopenhauer and Nietzsche was their admiration of France! Gide went on to say that Cartesianism, which he here identifies with French classicism, is the only discipline neutral and general enough to become the basis of European culture.

Classicism in literature, for Gide, is a French creation, a French possession. In holding such a view Gide was not alone. Rolland thought the same about classicism in music: writing of Beethoven's *Missa Solemnis*, he says, 'There has always been something romantic about German music; classical music is our invention.' So the French must have the last word about literary style. For Gide, as for Rolland, the criterion of beauty is a line of longitude passing through Paris.

Gide in truth at this stage of his life read widely but in practice was not very open-minded. Much later in its history the *Nouvelle Revue Française* was to win a reputation for publishing the best young foreign writers, but in its early years Gide accepted little original work from abroad, and some, like a chapter from Chesterton's *Orthodoxy*, because pressed by Claudel. In sixty issues Gide had only half a dozen German books reviewed, mainly those that showed French 'moderation', and none by the peace-loving Jewish poet Franz Werfel, the Expressionists, Trakl and Stadler, or Thomas Mann, whose *Death in Venice* was to appear in 1912.

Gide did publish in the *NRF* one essay expressing a German point of view: Kurt Singer's reply to a claim by Gide that French as a language was superior to German. Singer argued that whereas French had emerged from laws and conventions prescribed by an aristocracy, German had sprung from individuals expressing their inner life. Its prefixes and prepositions gave it greater energy and movement than French. Singer denied that French was the more lucid language; the difference lay rather in the fact that Frenchmen's thinking happened to be more sociable and therefore communicable than Germans'.

No one replied to Singer: a rare case in this period of a German being allowed the last word in a French periodical.

Gide was a prodigious correspondent. He wrote more letters to friends than anyone probably since Voltaire. He kept a Journal in which he recorded a wide spectrum of observations, feelings and judgments. In all these millions of words it would be reasonable to expect some comment, some reaction to, say, Japan's defeat of Russia in 1905, the Kaiser's shock visit to Tangier, and the resignation of Delcassé. These events were fully reported in the press. Now not only does Gide fail to mention them but in all his thousands of letters there is barely a mention of Germany and Germans.

The same holds true of the pre-1914 correspondence of Gide's friends with *their* friends. The Jammes–Fontaine letters are silent on Germany, the Jacques Rivière–Alain-Fournier are silent too, as are the Suarès–Péguy letters. A similar silence is found in other groups: the letters between Vlaminck and Derain, Max Jacob's letters to various friends and those of Apollinaire. By contrast, earlier writers and painters – Diderot, Lamartine and Hugo, Courbet and Pissarro – had taken an active interest in their country's affairs.

When we look for an explanation, we find a clue in the correspondence of Madame de Caillavet, the well-known hostess who in politics was left of centre, with Georg Brandes, a public-spirited Danish-born man of letters. The correspondence contains much mutual flattery: she speaks of his 'generous soul', his 'Promethean flame', he of her intelligence; and both puff incense at Madame de Caillavet's lover, Anatole France.

There is no mention in the correspondence of Germany, but in 1903 Brandes strikes a rare serious note. He has been talking with an Armenian friend living in exile, Nazarbek, who has written a play about the Turkish massacre of Armenians in 1895 – a horrifying early example of genocide. Brandes suggests that Madame de Caillavet might ask Anatole France (who in old age held Socialist views) to help get it performed.

This was a reasonable request, given the additional fact that the lady's son was a playwright. But several weeks pass before she thinks fit to answer, and she does so in an unusually tart tone:

> I advise you to steer clear of Armenians . . . Tell
> this enemy of your repose that [Anatole] France
> cannot possibly get your play put on in any
> Paris theatre . . . Don't let's have another word
> about Armenia, it spoils our correspondence.

'Enemy of your repose' – the phrase reveals a marked
lack of public spirit. The Abbé Mugnier, so closely in
touch with the influential, noted other examples in his
diary and thought selfishness in Paris was growing:

> The word most often on the lips of today's
> unmarried girls is 'fun'. 'Are you having fun?'
> . . . When they marry and set up home, they
> are more concerned to have a 'garage' than a
> nursery. 'No children, two motor-cars.'

Anything that disturbed 'fun' or, if one were older,
'repose', such as the fate of the Armenians, or indeed the
plan to end the independence of Morocco, was best kept
out of sight and out of mind.

By no means a majority of the influential writers and
artists were as selfish as that. Gide for example tirelessly exerted himself on behalf of his many friends; his
letters are full of practical help for those less fortunate
than he. Claudel too was a generous friend. As consul in
Tientsin, Claudel's job was to secure the refitting of
China's naval base there for French contractors in face
of still active German competition, so he knew first-
hand about Franco-German commercial rivalry. Yet his
Journal, almost as full as Gide's, while giving much
space to the Old Testament Israelites' struggle with
their neighbours, is silent on Germany, as are his
letters.

In a journal or a letter one tends to comment on what
is unusual, disconcerting or irritating. If it is not motivated by selfishness, the silence of these sources on Ger-

many – and Morocco – is best explained, I think, by the fact that creative Parisians had no quarrel with a foreign policy aimed at discomfiting Germany. They probably thought of it seldom but in effect they gave it tacit approval. Indeed, the influential Parisians we have met were, each in his or her way, trying to forward French civilization and, for the French, foreign policy is not just power politics, it is France's self-styled 'civilizing mission' at work. The more the writers, painters, composers achieved, the more logical it seemed to them that France should expand geographically. Barrès put it in a nutshell when he declared that France was the heir of Rome, and therefore heir to Rome's Empire, which had included Tunisia, Algeria and Morocco.

That is one aspect of the strange silence. Another is the fact that for creative Parisians the world consisted of Paris. To get a book published, a play or a musical composition performed, they had to intrigue, pull strings, make and keep influential friends. The Paris Opéra was riddled with intrigue, each prominent official trying to get his mistress into the production; Richard Strauss, who seldom complained to Rolland, did complain about this à propos the casting of *Salomé*. In these circumstances they had little or no time to look beyond the capital. Far from thinking in terms of following Voltaire to Berlin and working there for détente, Gide had his work cut out just surviving amid the infighting, backbiting literary coteries.

Finally, there is the nature of Paris's mood at the dawn of the century. By and large, whether it was the novel or poetry or ballet or theatre or the paintings of Matisse, creative people had embarked on a quest for joy. Not for sensuous pleasure, but for an intellectual and spiritual joy that could provide the equivalent of lost religious absolutes. Because of the sheer intensity it generated in itself, their sensibility was virtually incapable of escaping for long from the subjective into the distantly objective.

Given the absence elsewhere – one might almost say in another world – of so many of the writers esteemed in Paris, it fell to a hard-hitting journalist Deputy, a leader of the Socialist Party, to question the policy of alliance with Russia and friendship with England as springboards for expansion in Morocco, which Delcassé had inaugurated, and which he and his circle in the Quai d'Orsay continued to push even after he had been obliged to resign.

Jean Jaurès was the son of a roadmender-cum-pedlar from a poor region of France: Castres in the Tarn. He showed brilliance at school, came first in the Ecole Normale exam – Bergson came second – and after graduation became philosophy master at the lycée in Toulouse. At twenty-six he was elected to the Assembly. He joined the Socialists, lost his seat but in 1902 was re-elected.

In that year Jaurès was aged forty-three. Like his roadmender father, he was powerfully built, stocky, broad-shouldered, with a short neck. His big long head, squared at the top, had regular features, its close-cropped hair offset by a bushy beard. His expression was benevolent: he is described as looking 'like an amiable bear'. He was married and had two daughters. Though not a believer, he allowed his wife to give the girls a religious education and to let them make their First Communion. For this he was much criticized by the hard Socialist Left.

The heart of Jaurès's character and the basis of his politics was a genuine, unforced affection for his fellow-men. In one of his earliest speeches he said, naively perhaps but without pretension: 'Each time I

390

meet an honest man I feel that much richer.' The same warm feeling, especially for those who were as poor as he had been as a child, comes out in his abiding love for Flemish primitive paintings. It prompted him also to become a Socialist, and to live his Socialism. Even when famous, he travelled to and from the Assembly by bus. He enjoyed fine food and could name the best vintages of Bordeaux and Burgundy, but he lived mainly on snacks at a café near the Assembly, dunking a sweet biscuit into *café au lait*. And in the Socialist Deputy something of the young academic philosopher remained, for Jaurès was absent-minded and would leave his umbrella on the bus, just as in his small house in Passy he would mislay his slippers.

Jaurès possessed quite exceptional energy. In 1904 he founded an important Socialist daily, *L'Humanité*, still of course in existence. He wrote for it forcefully if long-windedly and built up a respectable circulation of 12,000. From that time on Jaurès expressed his Socialism in three ways: on the Assembly floor, in print, and on lecture platforms, sponsored by international Socialism, in France, Germany, Belgium, the Netherlands.

Jaurès was a man at ease in his own skin and at ease with his fellows. This was the basis of his passionate love of peace, which he thought could be achieved only by Socialism. He detested chauvinism such as Delcassé's and the jingoism of the League of Patriots, which Barrès was soon to head. As early as March 1900 Jaurès wrote: 'Nothing equals the violent nationalist hatred of our chauvinists unless it be their mobility.'

Jaurès believed jingoism could be overcome in two ways. First, through arbitration of disputes. An international arbitration Tribunal had been founded at The Hague under the guiding hand of a Frenchman, Baron Paul d'Estournelles de Constant. In 1902 Estournelles prevailed on President Roosevelt to submit to the Tribunal a minor pecuniary dispute between the United States and Mexico. The award was delivered in just six weeks, and this encouraged other cases to be submitted, notably the Dogger Bank dispute over fishing rights between Britain and Russia. For his work on the Tribunal Estournelles was to share the Nobel Peace Prize in 1909.

Jaurès hoped that if major as well as minor disputes were submitted to it the Arbitration Tribunal could prevent war. At the Sixth Congress of the New International held in Stuttgart in 1907 Jaurès declared: 'In future we don't need to ask which is the Government that attacks, which the Government being attacked; the aggressor will be the Government that refuses arbitration.'

Jaurès believed the second way to beat jingoism was for French Socialists to come to an agreement with German Socialists never to make war on each other. This was Charles Andler's creed, but Jaurès made it particularly his own by proclaiming it passionately year after year up and down Europe. French Socialists, ran his argument, have forsworn capitalism, militarism, imperialism and colonialism; so have German Socialists. The future of Alsace-Lorraine should be left in abeyance, while Socialist ideals spread to a majority in each country, thus rendering war quite impossible.

On the issue of Morocco Jaurès, who like other Deputies was in the dark about Delcassé's secret treaties, was not opposed to France peacefully extending her commercial interests there. What he did forcefully oppose was France's alliance with Russia, which Delcassé since the turn of the century had been strengthening every year through state visits and attentive gestures. Jaurès opposed it first on ideological grounds. He would have known that François I had not shrunk from allying France with Muslim Turkey against her Christian rivals in Europe, but it stuck in Jaurès' gullet that Europe's foremost Republic should kowtow to an autocracy. He opposed it secondly because it was an open-ended alliance, which could one day see Russia calling on France to support her in the political quicksands of the Balkans and which gave France an unjustified feeling of strength. Jaurès would have liked to see France drop her alliance with Russia and so become free to work for détente with Germany.

In the Assembly on 19 April 1905 Jaurès attacked Government policy in Morocco:

> You ought to negotiate with Germany just as you have done with England. To do so would neither diminish nor lower nor restrict the dignity of France; what *would* harm our dignity would be to continue this policy of surreptitious advance. You are going to lead us either to imprudent commotions or to undignified withdrawals.

Those words were prophetic; it may be noted also how even Jaurès had to argue within a context of France's all-important dignity.

Jaurès was loved on the Left and respected for his integrity and courage on the Right. He was indefatigable in proclaiming his recipes for peace. But he and the Socialists were a minority. In the Assembly of 1907 there were 174 deputies on the Right, 247 Radicals, 90 Republicans and only 74 Socialists. When Jaurès offered the Government a projected law for the arbitration of major disputes, it was not even presented to the House for debate. He refused to compromise his beliefs by accepting a portfolio in a Radical Government. He declined also to court the fashionable society hostesses and writers, few of whom were Socialists. So he did not have the support from the élite that might have carried his voice across party barriers. Later, as storm clouds built up over Europe, his voice was to be heeded by an increasing number, but for the present Jaurès found himself preaching in the wilderness.

Between June 1905, when Delcassé resigned, and the opening of the international conference in Algeciras to discuss Morocco in January 1906, apart from the Socialists no one of importance in Paris raised a voice to question Delcassé's strategy towards Germany. He may have erred tactically in failing to inform the Wilhelmstrasse about French economic 'reforms', but by and large the press approved action in Morocco which would re-assert France's greatness. Particularly significant to Delcassé and his closest collaborators was the silence of the intellectual and creative élite, which was taken to mean approval.

The French delegates went into the Algeciras Conference unrepentant. In fact Delcassé, though temporarily without portfolio – he was to return to the Foreign Office in 1913 as an Ambassador – made himself stronger than ever by circulating a story that Maurice Rouvier, the Prime Minister who dismissed him, had bowed to a hint from Wilhelm about his non-desirability: 'The Kaiser,' said Delcassé, 'demanded my head on a platter.'

The Germans went into the Conference hoping for an equal opportunity with the other powers to share in Morocco's economic development – this had been guaranteed them by the 1880 Convention. France had 31% of Moroccan trade in 1903, the Germans 9% and they hoped to increase it. They hoped that Morocco would remain independent in fact as well as in theory, and they did not know of France's secret treaties with Britain and Spain. In fact they were counting on Spain to help resist French initiatives.

Algeciras is a town of white Spanish houses set among magenta bougainvillea, date palms and orange trees, looking out on the Rock of Gibraltar, a reminder to Germans of Britain's naval power. Here the Conference opened on 6 January 1906, its proceedings, as always at this period, conducted in French.

The first thorny issue was a Moroccan State Bank. Germany proposed an equal division of the bank's capital between the powers, and the bank to be subject to a mixed consular court plus one Moroccan delegate. The French took the line that 'the open door doesn't mean that those who are in the house must leave it'; they demanded 27% of the capital, against 23% for Spain, 20% each for Britain and Germany, with 10% available to smaller nations. There should be a French President, and the bank should be subject to French law.

To the German delegates' surprise Spain backed the French proposal. Unknown to the Germans, France had signed a *new* secret treaty with Spain whereby France would get the presidency of any institution and Spain a larger share, after France, than any other power. With Spain and Britain backing France the Germans were outvoted. The Moroccan State Bank was established and was to become an instrument of French financial control of the country.

The second main issue was the policing of Moroccan ports. The Germans suggested the Sultan police them – they were after all his towns – with a force under international control. The French insisted on France policing five ports, including key Tangier, and Spain controlling three. This arrangement was voted because backed by Britain, and Tattenbach, a German delegate, complained, 'The English are more French than the French.'

Finally, economic development. Here the French agreed to reassert the principle of economic liberty without any interference, for through the Bank they now had control of capital expenditure. The Conference closed on 2 April by piously upholding 'in the name of God Almighty' the sovereignty of His Majesty the Sultan and the integrity of his dominions.

The Kaiser and his Chancellor were distressed by England's support for France but they hoped Germans would profit from the declaration of economic equality. Soon Reinhard Mannesmann, eldest of six energetic brothers with a big seamless metal tube business in Düsseldorf, obtained from the Sultan a monopoly of iron mining. But this did not suit the French, who made a lot of money supplying iron ore to Germany from mines in France. Refusing to recognize the Sultan's grant, the French set up their own Union of Mines. The Mannesmanns offered to go halves with the Union. The French wouldn't agree and prevented the Mannesmanns from mining.

Second shock for Germany: a Society of Public Works was formed, France holding 50% of the stock, Germany 26% and a board including six French and four Germans. The charter specified construction and operation, but the French insisted it should be limited to construction. Whereupon the Germans proposed to build railways jointly, but the French said France must have the exclusive contract for railways because of their military importance. As a result the Society effected nothing.

In Paris the Moroccan lobby, headed by Napoléon Etienne and backed by Berthelot, who had drafted all the dispatches and texts at Algeciras, by Delcassé and by the brothers Cambon, was now cock-a-hoop. Across the Rhine, however, Wilhelm II did not like the way things were going. In June 1907 he invited Etienne to meet him informally at Kiel. In a letter to Bülow Wilhelm described Etienne as burly, strong, with a big heavy head and thick hair, intelligent eyes and a jovial manner. The two got on well and began to discuss foreign affairs. Etienne asked Wilhelm to recognize, by a speech or a gesture, France's 'preponderant' role in Morocco. Wilhelm replied that he was ready to do so, provided France concluded an alliance with Germany: 'First things first. An alliance with Germany without prejudice to your alliance with Russia: then, and only then, will the French get their "moral preponderance" in Morocco.'

Now an alliance would mean recognizing the validity of the Treaty of Frankfurt, 1871, which ceded Alsace-Lorraine. For Etienne, as for Delcassé, for Berthelot and indeed for Olivier in *Jean Christophe*, that would be 'an act of dishonour'. The meeting came to nothing.

Undeterred, Wilhelm persisted in the belief that if only he could get Jules Cambon replaced by someone less hostile he and the new Ambassador between them could achieve détente. This was partly conceit, partly idealism, partly a mistaken notion that French politics was an affair of individuals, whereas it was much more a matter of ideas and groups.

Wilhelm's choice fell on Jean Dupuy, the self-made millionaire and former Minister of Agriculture whose big-circulation *Le Petit Parisien*, while approving France's policy in Morocco, consistently worked for improved relations with Germany. Approaches were made, but after due reflection Jean Dupuy turned the offer down. Friendship in any meaningful sense, no less than a formal alliance, would entail recognizing that Alsace and Lorraine were German; that Dupuy could not bring himself to do.

Back in Morocco the French were directing their attention to the Sultan. A bright young man in his twenties, he spent extravagantly on bicycles and motorcars, elaborate fireworks and photographic equipment, while buying for his country the things the French thought it should have. The Sultan fell into debt, tribal leaders revolted and he was overthrown by his brother Mulay Hafid. To the new Sultan in 1910 the Banque Paribas, which had moved in after Algeciras, made an even larger second loan, for part of which Mulay Hafid pledged his crown jewels. He too soon began to feel the pinch, and tribal leaders again made disgruntled sounds.

Simultaneously France was enlarging her policing role. In November 1910 a French cruiser, *Du Chayla*, entered the strategic Atlantic port of Agadir and her captain went ashore ostensibly to pursue smugglers. Under the Algeciras Act Agadir was a closed port and a French ship had no right there. German newspapers headlined the incident and questions were asked in the Reichstag.

In 1911 Moroccan disquiet about the French economic stranglehold came to a head. Certain tribes rose against the Sultan in the Fez region. There were Europeans in Fez. For France the desired moment had come.

It so happened that the Ministry of Aristide Briand had fallen in February, and the Prime Minister of the day, Ernest Monis, was no more than a caretaker, while his Foreign Minister, Cruppi, had no experience in that field. Cruppi called a meeting with the War Minister, Maurice Berteaux, at which the ubiquitous Etienne was present in fierce mood. Now Berteaux wanted to be France's next President and for that needed the colonial party's forty votes. Naturally he favoured the action desired by Etienne. Cruppi and Berteaux decided jointly to send troops to Fez on 'a mission of mercy'. Thirty thousand, no less.

Jaurès roundly condemned the sending of troops and for the first time in Moroccan affairs the French non-Socialist press divided. A Catholic nationalist, Albert de Mun, wrote in the right-wing *Le Gaulois* on 22 April: 'Neither Germany nor Europe will say anything because they can say nothing.' But the more moderate *Journal des Débats* opposed the expedition: 'Once French troops are in Fez they will probably find it impossible to withdraw.' Similarly in England, while *The Times* argued that the French must protect Europeans in Fez (they numbered seventy-five and were not in fact at risk), the *Nation* strongly condemned France's failure to consult the electorate and Parliament.

On 6 May 1911 an experienced Islam-watcher, Wilfred Scawen Blunt, wrote in his diary: 'The event of the past week has been the invasion of Morocco by the French, a scandalous affair, exactly on the same lines of financial speculation and Colonial and Imperial intrigue which were followed by us in Egypt thirty years ago.'

French troops reached Fez on 21 May; in June Spanish troops occupied Tetuan, Larache and El Kasr 'to protect Spanish nationals'. Both moves broke international agreements to which Germany was a signatory.

Germany decided she must act. At the end of June her Government sent a gunboat, the *Panther*, to Agadir; on 1 July the German Ambassador informed the French Government of this move; its aim, he said, was to protect German nationals 'until Morocco returns to its former calm'.

Wilhelm's close friend, the English-born Princess of Pless, explained to Edward VII: 'It was a movement to bring things to a head and to force a Conference, so that other Powers should not go to sleep and then wake up some day to find Morocco a French colony, while England looked on all the time from the corner of her eye!'

The arrival of a German gunboat in Agadir brought cries of fury from the French press. Forgetting that France had sent a cruiser to the same port the preceding December, they branded the move *'le coup d'Agadir'*. *Coup* is a strong term, meaning 'blow', 'shock' or a combination of both, with a suggestion of trickery, as in *coup de Trafalgar*, which means 'underhand trick', though what Nelson had done that was underhand is unclear.

When the *Kölnische Zeitung* called on France to withdraw her troops and so prove she did not consider Morocco her colony, the *Journal des Débats* replied angrily, 'We have never misinterpreted or threatened interests guaranteed by the Act of Algeciras . . . In economic matters we have worked for others more than for ourselves.'

France's honour, France's grandeur were at stake. First the Kaiser had reputedly demanded Delcassé's head on a platter, now he was interfering in a country France was well on the way to making a protectorate! In Paris the political temperature rose to the point where the Government called in General Joffre and asked what chances of victory France would have if it came to hostilities; to which he replied, 'Less than seven out of ten.' The conflict of national pride over Morocco, first signalled six years before at Tangier, had now become a possible occasion for full-scale European war.

CHAPTER 16

Preparations for a Duel

The Prime Minister in 1911 was a brilliant self-made millionaire, Joseph Caillaux. Born in the Sarthe, he had followed his father into the Treasury and from there moved to politics, sitting as a Radical. Three times Minister of Finance, on each occasion he had skilfully balanced the budget. He was a man who knew his own worth. Arrogant, quick, impatient, a 'loner', he liked to do things himself in his own way, thus earning the nickname 'Self-Sufficiency'. Now aged forty-eight, he was short, slim, straight-backed, with a full moustache; he dressed elegantly, often with silk waistcoat, spats and yellow gloves. When, as often happened, he got worked up, his strong bald head became marbled with purple streaks.

His personal life had been stormy. An ardent lover of statuesque ladies, he was now in the early months of his second marriage with a grey-eyed, ash-blonde divorcee, Henriette, mother of two daughters by her first husband, Léo Claretie, an authority on toys. Joseph and Henriette Caillaux were said to be deeply in love.

Caillaux's attitude to Germany was that of a shrewd, still young businessman who had money of his own invested abroad, notably in Latin America. He saw in Germany a powerful industrial nation ahead of France in shipbuilding, heavy engineering, electrical machinery, chemicals. In the period 1900–14 Germany was to rise to be the world's second commercial power, France dropping from third to fourth, while her population

401

was growing, each marriage producing on average 4.7 children. Caillaux believed that France must live with these unpalatable truths, drop rancour, work coopera- tively and benefit therefrom. This would include investment. Caillaux had tried, unsuccessfully, to get the Paris Bourse to drop its ban on the quotation of German shares; the ban had been imposed by the Gov- ernment after France's 1870 defeat lest French savings benefit the Germans.

Caillaux, then, was under no illusions about French power and when the Agadir affair blew up, in the light of Joffre's opinion, he determined to come to a settle- ment. He happened to have a lymphatic, inexperienced Foreign Minister, Justin de Selves, so he decided to deal directly with the Germans himself.

At first the German Chancellor – Bülow had been succeeded by Bethmann-Hollweg – demanded a high price: the French Congo (half the size of Morocco) in exchange for a French protectorate in Morocco. But the Chancellor had made one blunder. He failed to inform Britain in advance of the sending of the *Panther*; with the result that Whitehall became alarmed that Germany intended to demand, or seize, an Atlantic port. A Lib- eral statesman, Chancellor of the Exchequer Lloyd George, made a speech on 21 July strongly supporting France, while contingency preparations were worked out in detail for landing up to six British divisions in North Germany.

Fortified by British support, Caillaux began to negotiate with the Germans. With a secrecy worthy of Delcassé and living up to his nickname 'Self- Sufficiency', he whittled down German demands. By the Treaty of Berlin, signed on 4 November 1911, in return for a free hand in Morocco, France ceded to Germany part only of the Congo, mainly savannah riddled with sleeping-sickness, while Germany ceded to France a small part of her Gulf of Guinea colony, Togoland.

German public opinion was deeply disappointed. At Tangier in 1905 their Emperor had guaranteed Moroccan independence – independence again endorsed at Algeciras; and now this land, rich in iron ore, was passing to France. They had been led to expect the whole Congo and in fact were to get only its dregs. But their anger was directed less against France than against England, for having supported Caillaux.

The Government-inspired *Frankfurter Zeitung* complained that Downing Street had condoned France's action in Fez, she had condoned Spain's action, by way of riposte, in seizing Larache, she had condoned Russia's interference in Northern Persia – which in 1907 had led to a division of that country into Russian and British zones of influence – and here she was making threatening signs to Germany because of a justified protest at Agadir. Touchiness began to harden into a sense of having been wronged.

It might have been expected that what Germany regarded as a humiliation would be viewed in France as a triumph. Not so. Public opinion said in effect: 'We were right all along. First the Kaiser demands Delcassé's head on a platter, then he sends the *Panther* to "our" part of the world, and now he obliges us to yield part of a French colony. Germany is indeed a warring nation.' A frontier, therefore nationalist newspaper, *Le Petit Comtois* of Besançon, complained ominously: 'In the light of present grievances those of the past reappear . . . The cession of territory in the Congo almost equal to half of France recalls to Frenchmen's hearts the loss of Alsace-Lorraine.'

When the Treaty came before the Assembly, 393 Deputies voted for it, 36 against; but no less than 141 abstained, most on the grounds that by negotiating with

Germany 'under threat' France had shown weakness and thereby encouraged German militarism.

Agadir and the Treaty of Berlin were to prove a turning-point in French attitudes, particularly in Paris. The capital had always been more nationalist than, say, Lyon, which had close commercial and banking links with Germany, Italy and Switzerland. But until the second half of 1911 nationalism had been latent: a matter less of words and gestures than of tacit approval. It had been channelled into the dazzling excitements, in so many areas, of creative achievement.

Now, however, the mood altered. Anger hung in the air, and a little fear. Many of the writers, thinkers and creators began to feel a shade or two of shame at having neglected their civic responsibilities. Among those who had been – or believed themselves to have been – soft, there appeared a noticeable stiffening of the sinews, a summoning-up of blood.

The first signs were gradual, almost oblique. André Gide, getting older and cutting down on his private pleasures, became a prominent member of the committee of a League for the Defence of French Culture. This League, founded in 1911, deplored a recent curtailment of Latin and Greek in schools – believed to be a concession to German 'scientism' – and went on to commit itself to a national revival, including the defence of traditional French values. The founder of the League, Jean Richepin, usually a bluff, joking Academician, issued its fervent if somewhat vague manifesto:

> Ours is only one manifestation of a national revival becoming evident in our young people . . . By protecting our churches they wish to safeguard religious idealism and art, and to maintain our national dignity. They are showing a taste for heroism and glory, developed

by the triumph of recent French inventions
[meaning the motor-car and aeroplane].

In and around the Sorbonne too trust was wearing
thin. Charles Andler, the expert on modern Germany
and leading exponent of détente, visited Silesia to talk
to his German Socialist friends. To his deep disappointment he found that they supported the *coup d'Agadir*,
indeed he found that they were by no means averse to
more German colonization, should land become available, to 'a place in the sun', the new catch-phrase. On
his return to Paris Andler wrote a shock warning article
criticizing the German Socialists for going back on their
declared anti-colonialism and calling on Jean Jaurès to
censure them for it.

What was Jaurès to do? Already, in *L'Humanité*, he
had thundered against the sending of troops to Fez,
then against the violation of Morocco's independence.
But Andler's call proved even more of a dilemma. At
heart Jaurès was a man committed to certain ideas
rather than an empiricist. Once a young writer submitted a book to him for his opinion; presently Jaurès
handed it back, saying he considered it a sound, fine
work. 'So you thought well of this or that argument?'
enquired the eager young author. It emerged that Jaurès
had not read the book: he had glanced at one or two
pages, liked the young man and his ideas; for him that
was sufficient.

Jaurès had committed himself for years to the proposition that German Socialists would tear up their railway lines rather than allow their German brothers
to be transported like cattle to the slaughter of war.
He believed in, and had proclaimed, their profound
non-aggressiveness. Though Andler's reporting of the
German Socialists' change of view on colonialism was
correct, Jaurès could not bring himself to believe it. He

declined to censure the Germans, whereupon he and Andler parted ways.

The Sorbonne Socialists criticized Jaurès for carrying faith in human nature too far and for underestimating the patriotism of the average German worker. They also criticized Jaurès's recent book, *The New Army*, which proposed that France should restructure its army on the lines of Switzerland's citizen-militia and concentrate on in-depth defence, not, as the High Command envisaged, on a speedy offensive.

The Left Bank thinker and writer to 'stiffen his sinews' most markedly was Charles Péguy. He had started as a convinced Socialist, committed to peace. Then he had come to distrust political solutions. In 1904 he parted company with his former friend Jaurès and began to preach individual moral renewal as the way to a more just society. But from 1906 things began to go badly for poor Péguy. The Sorbonne establishment snubbed and sneered at a renegade Socialist; his marriage became an agony; he earned less and less, sometimes went hungry; his books had only tiny sales. A note of bitterness began to creep into Péguy's writing, the bitterness of a disappointed man which had been heard before from another frustrated Catholic author, Léon Bloy.

Out of this bitterness came a new affection – for the artisans of France. These conscientious craftsmen who earn their money by manual skills, as their fathers had done, represent for Péguy the 'true values' of France. Artisans are threatened by two evils, money as idolized in a capitalist society, and science, what we now call technology.

In hard-hitting essays, *Situations*, *L'Argent* and *L'Argent Suite*, Péguy argued that these two evils were embodied in Germany. French artisans were threatened by German factories. The arch-enemy in short lay across the Rhine. But there was another, almost as sinister, enemy within. Men like Ernest Lavisse and Lucien Herr – whom Péguy termed the Socialist, anti-Christian élite at the Sorbonne (though Lavisse was a man of the Centre, not of the Left) – were secretly helping Germany. They did so by contributing articles to the German press – thereby, claimed Péguy, admitting the superiority of German newspapers to French, by encouraging Internationalism and, at the same time, weakening 'true' Catholic France through their advocacy of a wholly lay curriculum. Péguy added that these 'Socialists' had actually joined the bourgeoisie by writing money-spinning books and marrying rich wives!

What was to be done? How could France stand up to this dual insidious threat? Péguy had long been a devotee of the saint who had saved his home town from the English, and now he declared that France could be regenerated only by rediscovering patriotism in Jeanne d'Arc's sense. The French artisans, he declared, were patriots to a man. They – and the poor generally – would never have allowed it to happen. It was the doing of the rich, headed by 'that frightful little Thiers'.

> We are witnessing a profound, violent revival of France. Are we going to continue to impose on this ardour the same tired old men, the same doddering public figures who have created a situation of lassitude and decrepitude, of disarmament and denial?

Péguy called for a military structure, 'the cradle where morality, law, the arts, religion, language and race can be nurtured'. Himself a reserve infantry officer, Péguy called on the French army to fulfil a 'sacred role' by carrying French culture and the French language to her colonies and by resisting Germany's plan to use peace as a means of dominating Europe. Not so

407

much through coups such as that of Agadir, Péguy
believed, but through industrial and commercial superiority. Stripped of its rhetoric, Péguy's argument is this:
If you can't beat the Germans in production of goods,
send in the army.

Péguy was unique in taking his argument to extremes, but his fear about German technology met
with a ready response. Henri Franck from Alsace,
reckoned the most brilliant Sorbonne student of his
day, on a visit to Munich wrote home denouncing
'Teutonic Americanism' and 'Feudal Industrialism',
while the *Journal des Débats* published a warning
about possible Austro-German expansion in the
Balkans, which would increase still further Germany's
commercial lead.

> Such German hegemony ... would lead
> promptly to the invasion of our factories, of our
> shipyards, by German workmen and foremen,
> to the suppression of our merchant marine, to
> the absorption of our financial resources by
> German businesses ... M. Jaurès and his
> friends ... should realize that the essential
> mission of the French army is to protect French
> jobs and not, as they declare at their meetings,
> the rich Establishment.

On the political Right also, 'national dignity' became
a new sacred flame, tended most notably by Maurice
Barrès. As a Lorrainer, an esteemed novelist and
Deputy for the First Arrondissement of Paris, Barrès's
credentials were impeccable. Physically too he had the
advantage of resembling the Grand Condé, Louis XIV's
charismatic general. In speeches and articles Barrès
reiterated his claim that France, as the heir of Rome,
had the best right to North Africa. He did not take up
the point that Wilhelm II, successor of the Holy Roman

Emperors, might possess an equally valid claim to be 'heir of Rome'. North Africa's splendid soldiers, Barrès declared, 'a hundred thousand of them, will restore France to the rank of first-class European power'.

Barrès worked for a time with tiny, hard-of-hearing Charles Maurras, whose Action Française Party, fascist in spirit but paying lip-service to a strong Catholic Church, was already in existence. But Maurras and Action Française were to become a real force in French life only after 1918, and Barrès found support at this time chiefly from his former mistress, Anna de Noailles.

This small voluble lady, who had for years been looking round for a creed and even with Abbé Mugnier's friendly counsel had been unable to find it in Catholicism, now found it in Barrès's nationalism and, in particular, in Jeanne d'Arc. The beatification of Jeanne in 1909 had seemed to non-Catholic intellectuals irrelevant, but in the changed moral climate after Agadir it seemed very important. The nationalists' Jeanne was not, as the cause of beatification stated, a girl of heroic Christian virtue, but a Lorrainer who had stiffened her sinews, had become a heroic soldier, rallying her people at a time of danger, and finally giving her life for *la patrie*.

'I am fierce,' said Anna, 'but without a shadow of malice.' Taking leave of her flower garden and Venetian holidays, fiercely she set about reviving the spirit of Jeanne. She made friends with Dr Pierre Bucher, a Strasbourg medical practitioner who edited the *Revue alsacienne illustrée* and founded the city's Alsatian Museum. A keen patriot, Bucher demanded the creation of Alsace-Lorraine as an independent State, first stage, he hoped, on the road to reunion with France; it was he who had 'fed' Barrès material for his novels exalting the Lorraine region. Anna began to work with Pierre Bucher to promulgate the idea of an independent

Alsace-Lorraine, and she began to write a new type of poem.

Barrès loved in Lorraine the history and folklore rooted there, the past, his own forebears. Like Péguy, he spoke much of the dead, and it was this theme that Anna de Noailles elaborated in some of her new verse. The presence of the dead; how they had fought and died for France, how from their tombs they were watching the living, hoping that the living would show heroism equal to theirs. And, writing thus, Anna saw herself almost as a new Jeanne, rallying laggards.

Close in mood to the nationalism of Barrès and Anna de Noailles but even more important in their influence were two Senators, now out of office but much respected. Both had suffered from the Prussian invasion of 1870. One, Georges Clemenceau, a doctor of medicine, had been Mayor of Montmartre at the time of the Prussian shelling. A former Prime Minister, now representing the Var, he had voted against the Treaty of Berlin, denouncing it as so 'monstrously' concessive as to encourage Germany's militarism.

The other leading political nationalist, Raymond Poincaré, had been born in Lorraine, the son of a state-employed engineer. When the Prussians invaded he was a boy of ten. Evacuated by his parents to distant Dieppe, he felt deeply all the shame of such a disappointment, such a seeming defeat. But young Poincaré had a stout heart and the following year wrote a school-boy essay in which, after describing the war, he added gamely: 'To the glory of our country it has to be said . . . that the Prussians did not succeed in storming a single one of our fortresses.'

Poincaré studied law, became a successful barrister, entered the Assembly as a Republican and was now, in 1911, at the age of fifty-one, a Senator for the Meuse. He lived with a married lady, Henriette Benucci, whose

Italo-American husband had not been heard of for many years and was presumed dead; in 1912 Poincaré was to marry her.

Unlike Caillaux, unlike Jaurès, Poincaré had assiduously cultivated the Paris intelligentsia. He gave his legal services free not only to Marie Curie but to impecunious authors and actors, he presided over the Friends of the Château de Versailles and, though not a writer, was elected in 1909 to the Académie Française. He had always backed Delcassé's hard-line foreign policy and so had the support of Philippe Berthelot at the Quai d'Orsay. Poincaré was now waiting in the wings.

As public opinion became strongly suspicious of Germany after the Treaty of Berlin, the Assembly sought a scapegoat for what was regarded as that nationally humiliating document. The Quai d'Orsay in particular hated Caillaux – Berthelot described him as a 'madman' – and made their views known to the Opposition. Caillaux was accused of having handled negotiations with Germany that should, by protocol, have been left to his Foreign Minister and Ambassadors. Caillaux arrogantly, rashly denied the charge *in toto*; documents were produced to show he was not telling the whole truth and in January 1912 Caillaux had to resign. For the moment he leaves the stage but will presently reappear.

Who was to take his place? Plainly a man of strong character and proven patriotism. Though he might not be much to look at, with square head, thick nose, small close-set eyes and heavy jowls, Poincaré was known to be physically and morally very tough, hence the café song: '*Il a les poings, les poings carrés.*' 'Prudence Lorraine', as he was also called, neither smoked nor drank. As a Republican he belonged to the Centre and could call on support from Radicals and certain Socialists. As an Academician, he satisfied the conservative intelligentsia. In the eyes of a majority of Frenchmen Raymond Poincaré was the obvious choice.

The President therefore called on Poincaré to form a Ministry to replace Caillaux's. Poincaré accepted, taking office on 14 January 1912. Remembering how political divisions had weakened France in 1870–71, Poincaré gave priority to concord. He called on men mainly of the Centre to sink their domestic differences in what he called a Government of National Union. Appointing Delcassé to be Navy Minister – in view of Germany's new navy a key job – Poincaré himself took the post of Foreign Minister as well as Prime Minister.

Poincaré sent a tough general, Louis Lyautey, to be French Resident in Morocco, tightened links with Britain and with Russia, which he visited in August, and rejected an informal proposal from across the Rhine that Alsace-Lorraine should become an autonomous state within the German Empire. 'In listening to such proposals,' Poincaré told Jules Cambon, 'we would have difficulty with England and with Russia, we would lose the benefit of the policy France has followed for many years, we would secure only illusory advantages for Alsace, and we would find ourselves isolated.' This was an admission of how, since Agadir, the conflict of interests with Germany had widened beyond Morocco to involve all the great powers, and to embrace such distant affairs as the building of the Baghdad railway and the now intense naval rivalry between Britain and Germany.

By his formation of a Government of National Union Poincaré answered a deeply felt need by many in the Centre and on the Right for strong leadership. That Poincaré's thinking was close to that of Péguy in the early *Cahiers*, of Barrès, Dr Pierre Bucher and Anna de Noailles, emerges from part of a speech he made in

Nancy in 1912: 'The fatherland, like mankind,' Poincaré declared, 'is composed more of the dead than the living.' Not least the French dead lying in cemeteries now belonging to Germany. Furthermore, Poincaré counted many writers, artists and thinkers among his friends. By speaking to them he ensured currency for his beliefs, and so there now arose in Paris a new spirit. The *joie de vivre* of the past eleven years gave way to deep distrust of Germany.

Intellectuals were to play a leading part in the shift of mood by drawing attention to what they considered German failings and pinning on the Germans a series of unflattering labels. The first example is André Gide.

Gide did not cross the Rhine at this period but he did go to Zürich in January 1912 and there thought fit to record in his Journal what a Swiss named M. Simon had to say on the Germans:

> Their strength and health increase with their stupidity . . . A German who gets dead drunk Sunday evening (and this is the supreme debauch for him) is behind his desk again on Monday morning, stupefied, but not much more so than usual, just as exact and diligent as if he had drunk nothing but water the day before.

There we have the 'brutish German' label.

Another line was pursued by the gifted artist Charles Huard, who went to Berlin and there made an album of drawings. These he published with a short text. 'The ugliness shocks you,' wrote Huard of the German capital. 'It comes from the women's vulgarity and lack of elegance, their total absence of charm.' Huard went on and on about ugliness. Soon a new label was current: 'The

413

ugly German'. It affected even Romain Rolland who in 1911 complained to a friend about unprepossessing German tourists on the roads near Rapallo, describing one as 'a Siegfried Wagner, fat, proud, self-satisfied – as an Assyrian eunuch'. Since Rolland often comments on the energy of modern German music compared to French subtlety and nuance, the last word is odd, unless it be an unguarded slip, revealing of Rolland's own awareness that he was primarily a critic, not a creator.

Even Proust made use of the 'ugly German' label. In the later pages of his novel he describes the Baron de Charlus carrying perversion to the point where he prefers Germans to Frenchmen or Anglo-Saxons because they are domineering and ugly.

A third label was offered by the best-selling novelist Marcel Prévost, for whom to his annoyance Marcel Proust was sometimes, at parties, mistaken. Having already published *Monsieur et Madame Moloch*, which made a bogey of Pan-Germanists, a minority, though a vocal one, that advocated a union of Germanic peoples in Eastern Europe, and revealed its true significance under Hitler, Prévost next offered his ironically titled *The Guardian Angels*, in which German nannies in decent French homes are depicted as spies for the Fatherland. The 'German spy' charge caught on: soon there were stories of spies under the bed, spies in the bed.

If German nannies were secretly reporting French army movements, German wives, it was next rumoured, could be quite as militaristic as their Kaiser. The wife of Richard Strauss was heard to complain in a Paris drawing-room about the slowness of the stage hands in the production of *Salomé*. What Frau Strauss actually said is unclear. But she happened to be a general's daughter, and what Paris society claimed she said was, 'The only way to get the French to get a move on, is to prod them with bayonets.' Though Rolland doubted its authenticity, the story went the rounds as evidence of yet another 'militarist German', Parisians forgetting that it was a Frenchman, Talleyrand, who first said, 'You can do everything with bayonets – except sit on them.'

Another label grew out of an actual scandal. In 1907 a leading German periodical alleged that some of the Kaiser's entourage were practising homosexuals. Three elderly ADCs resigned and the Kaiser's closest friend, handsome poetry- and music-loving Philip, Prince Eulenburg, though not a homosexual, felt obliged because of the resultant hubbub to see the Kaiser no more. The 'Eulenburg affair' was a gift to Paris gossip-writers, and Octave Mirbeau, hard-hitting novelist of the realist school, played up to the gossip. In his book devoted to a tour of France by motor-car Mirbeau describes a (probably imaginary) meeting with a Frenchman in Strasbourg who has just returned from Berlin and gives him news of that city:

> When we Frenchmen go in for vice, we do so lightly, a smile on our lips . . . But the Germans, who are pedants lacking in tact and taste, practise vice – how shall I put it? – scientifically. It's not enough for them to be pederasts like other people, they have invented the science of *homosexuality* . . . They practise pederasty as they practise epigraphy . . . They have studied old stones and noted all the names of all the boyfriends of all the Pharaohs, dynasty by dynasty . . . Heavy-handed pederasts, Sodomites by the book . . . Instead of men making love we have *homosexuals*, with pedantry. Go to Berlin, I tell you . . . go and see Berlin . . . it's worth the journey.

It is true that Germans did coin the word 'homosexuality', which, incidentally, soon found its way into French, and that a Viennese Jew pioneered scientific study of the sexual impulse. But as for the insinuation that Berlin had more homosexuals than Paris, it is at the least very doubtful, for of those on both sides of the Rhine whose private lives are known from letters, diaries and confessional fiction, the French in this respect seem to have outdone the Germans. Already in 1904 Abbé Mugnier had noted, 'Charles du Bos [a promising young writer], who is twenty or twenty-one, has just told me that the young generation begin their sex life much earlier, at thirteen or fourteen. They tire earlier of women, hence the increase in pederasty. Quest for different sensations.'

The 'homosexual German' slander stuck and it too became a label. Marcel Proust, who in his novel is at pains to make his French narrator heterosexual, in the later chapters stresses the Baron de Charlus's German blood and his German sympathies, almost as concomitants of his homosexuality.

None of these labels was in itself of the first importance but cumulatively they damaged. They helped further to feed distrust and dislike of the German as such. Earlier we saw Picasso being harassed by 'boring' Germans who questioned him about the meaning of one of his paintings, and we saw him dispersing the Germans by firing off a revolver. No one else literally fired off a revolver but the systematic denigration of Germans actively fed a new belief that France alone stood for civilization, that civilization as such stood at risk, and that Frenchmen must do something about it. By sending the *Panther*, and by taking from France territory in the Congo, the Germans had, so to speak, thrown down the gauntlet. Parisians in particular, not a few of whom, as we have seen, readily fought duels as did the Germans, either with sword or pistol, considered the present situation with Germany one where honour was at stake and therefore might call for a duel. A duel on a national scale that might last two months, or, in this new age of speed as little as two weeks, but none the less a duel.

They therefore adopted the appropriate posture, flourishes and language. On 10 February 1912, when the stormy Parliamentary debate on the Treaty of Berlin ended, by order of the Government the first torchlit military parades through the city for twenty years took place.

At 8.30 p.m., on the Right Bank, the 24th infantry regimental band, in blue and red uniforms, escorted by an officer on horseback, marched along rue Lafayette, Boulevards Magenta and Rochechouart, playing *Sambre et Meuse*, *Les Allobroges* and *A la Chiffa*. On the Left Bank the 102nd infantry regimental band took a circular route from Rue de Babylone, playing *Chant du Départ* and *Mourir pour la patrie* on their bugles, horns and fifes, banging their drums. They were followed, according to the press, by children singing to the martial music, and were cheered by big crowds. Many joined in the parade, marching behind the soldiers. In case of trouble the routes had been kept secret, but this precaution soon proved unnecessary. Every Saturday thereafter one or more *retraites militaires* took place. They reminded Parisians of past victories and kept them keyed to the notion of honour.

The main trade union, the CGT, still opposed the military stance of Poincaré's Ministry, but reserved its demonstration for the morrow of the first military parade, when 100,000 attended the funeral of a soldier who had died in detention, allegedly from his superiors' brutality. They marched from the Gare de Lyon to the Père-Lachaise cemetery singing the *Internationale*. The

police intervened and in scuffles twenty-one gendarmes were injured.

If Paris was not yet fully unified, the Government
was now receiving valuable support from writers. The
most gifted of the younger political journalists, André
Tardieu, a Parisian graduate in law, had made a reputation by his vivid reporting of the Morocco crises from
Delcassé's point of view. Now at thirty-six he published
The Mystery of Agadir. The 'mystery', for Tardieu, was
that France had at last awoken from her daydream.
Forgetting that Joffre had said the army would be use-
less, Tardieu wrote:

> The country now understands what it owes to
> its Army. It has escaped from the pacifist
> dream. It has regained a sense of realities. In
> 1911 it affirmed its resoluteness and in the
> same circumstances will be found ready to
> affirm it again. The Governments of yesterday
> could believe that regard for life counselled
> weakness. This same regard will counsel
> energy to the Governments of tomorrow.

Tardieu's book was acclaimed and ensured his election, soon, as a Deputy. Another more personal book
also met with success. Ernest Psichari, aged twenty-
nine, described his life on active service in Morocco,
now a French military protectorate. In *The Call to Arms*
he praised the profession of soldiering as it had not been
praised since Napoleonic days. 'Happy the young men,'
he chanted, 'who have led the frugal, simple, chaste life
of warriors.' Jean Schlumberger decided he was not
altogether happy about the way Psichari separated the
army from the rest of society and praised its special
moral code, law and mystique, but the book appealed to
many young intellectuals, all the more since Psichari
was the grandson of the still revered Ernest Renan.

In 1900 war had been unthinkable; from the *coup d'Agadir* onward it was not only thinkable but thought by some writers to be desirable. Abel Bonnard informed *Figaro* readers: 'War refashions everything anew . . . We must embrace it in all its savage poetry', while the right-wing *Le Gaulois* went still further: 'War is of divine essence . . . God wished to be called the Lord of hosts.' Two esteemed Catholic intellectuals still in their twenties, Henri Massis and Alfred de Tarde, writing under the name Agathon, declared: 'War is a young word, quite fresh, possessing the seductive power which the eternal bellicose instinct has awakened in men's hearts.' Certainly in the hearts of undergraduates, who now swore by the philosopher Maurice Blondel's maxim: 'Thought is fulfilled only in action.' When Professor Henry of the Ecole des Sciences Politiques delivered a lecture attacking the Germans, 3000 students rose to cheer the call with which he ended: 'On your feet, Gauls! On your feet, Frenchmen! Stand up to the Barbarians!'

'The Barbarians', and Britain too, were re-arming. Poincaré's Government, in spring 1912, introduced a bill to Parliament to raise the period of military service to three years – it had been reduced in 1905 to two years. Though it was opposed by many Radicals, including Caillaux, as likely to increase still further Germany's fear of being encircled by Russia, France and Britain, itself stemming from a sense of having been wronged by those powers at Algeciras and after, the Bill met with a favourable response from a majority of the Paris newspapers and among the undergraduates. It has to be added that the mood in the provinces was less warm. In October 1912 a distinguished Lyonnais doctor of medicine and Deputy, Victor Augagneur, told readers of *Lyon républicain* that France should steer well clear of any conflict in the Balkans that might involve her ally Russia. Public opinion in Paris, he warned, was too much under the influence of the nationalists: it should be stated again and again that war was unthinkable.

Many of the good things that France had achieved since 1900 now began to be turned towards less benevolent ends. The prime example is the aeroplane. In its infancy the aeroplane had been hailed as an invention that rendered frontiers – and therefore nationalism – obsolete. We saw that for the go-ahead rich it had become a status symbol: in the *Bottin Mondain* a family who owned one had an aeroplane symbol included in its listing. But now its military potential was beginning to be considered.

In September 1910 the President had attended manœuvres in Picardy, where aeroplanes were used. The General Staff concluded that the aeroplane was excellent for reconnaissance but 'no aeroplane will ever be powerful enough to carry bombs'. By early 1912, however, experts saw that if fitted with one or more small-arms weapons the aeroplane could become of offensive value. On 11 February a meeting was held at the Sorbonne to raise money to build military aircraft. Captain Bellenger described the possibilities of what he termed the new 'Fifth Arm'; Senator Reymond said the German Emperor had drawn on his personal fortune to encourage aviation – Germany had built her first successful plane as late as 1909 – and that Frenchmen must help their Government; Clemenceau asked the crowd to give 'ten sous, three sous, even one sou', but at least to give something. A collection raised 3000 francs in ten minutes.

Twelve days later *Le Matin* organized a subscription: 'For aviation and *la patrie*'. It aimed to raise 50 million francs to buy 5000 planes (actually an aeroplane cost 20,000 francs). Sarah Bernhardt, dressed in the famous white uniform she had worn for her triumph as l'Aiglon, went round collecting and once again scored a success.

Paris's municipal council contributed 50,000 francs to the fund. Many Parisians, the well-off but also clerical workers, waiters, shop assistants, added what they could afford and by October 3,900,000 francs had been raised. Thanks partly to such voluntary efforts, by 1914 France was to have 1500 military planes; Germany 1000, plus 40 airships; Britain 82.

In the production of motor-cars also came a shift away from enjoyment. Though racing-cars continued popular – in fact competition between top French and German drivers on the circuits aroused intense excitement across the country – much new plant was producing heavy lorries to carry troops and haul artillery. Instead of being delayed by geese or sheep, the country motorist might now have to dawdle impatiently behind a long motorized convoy.

In the arts we find a similar change of direction. Parisians in 1913 were mad about the tango, and every smart party featured the Argentinian import. Anything less military than the tango's pointing, posturing positions would be hard to imagine, which is perhaps why, as we saw, Wilhelm II forbade German officers to dance it, but on 25 October 1913 Jean Richepin of the Académie Française, founder of the League for the Defence of French Culture, gave a rousing talk on the tango to the Five Academies, in which he admitted the dance's alien origin but praised France for adapting it, and went on to claim that it was basically a war-dance, like the pyrrhics or rigadoons played by the fifers of Napoleon's armies. For Richepin and the many who applauded his lecture, the tango in short represented one more aspect of France's new stance: champion of civilization, with its guard up.

The cinema, for most of the decade a purveyor of comedy of character and amiable ridiculousness, was finding that the newsreel could grip audiences in direct proportion to its emotional content. In February 1912 Madame de Caillavet's son challenged Emile Mas, drama critic of *Comœdia*, for allegedly insulting him over his successful play *Primerose*, and when the duel took place in the Parc des Princes, no less than five ciné cameras were there to record the little drama for audiences across France.

Romain Rolland's Viennese admirer, peace-loving Stefan Zweig – the two had become close friends and saw each other in Paris – visited Tours in spring 1914 and went to the cinema. Zweig was aware of nationalism in Austria and in Germany, where it took the form chiefly of anger and dread of England's navy and Russia's numbers, but here in Tours, watching a newsreel, he found a shriller mood. The newsreel depicted the Kaiser visiting Emperor Franz Josef in Vienna. When, at the station, Wilhelm stepped down from his carriage wearing a general's uniform, moustache curled stiffly upwards, a wild whistling, stamping of feet and yelling began in the dark hall.

> Men, women and children, all joined in, as if personally insulted. I was frightened to the depths of my heart. For I sensed how deeply the poison of the propaganda of hate must have advanced through the years, when even here in a small provincial city the simple citizens and soldiers had been so greatly incited against the Kaiser and against Germany that a passing picture on a screen could produce such a demonstration.

And Erik Satie had called the cinema a cure for neurasthenia!

Paris ballet still dallied in a never-never Oriental world, but Paris theatre embodied the new concerns and mood. The sublime took shape as France, the ridiculous as Germany. Among current productions Kistemaeckers' *L'Exilée* was set in an imaginary East German court. A young French doctor teaches the coarse King's sons the history of the French Revolution and to sing the *Marseillaise*. The King protests; the Frenchman defends his right to proclaim truth and liberty even abroad – and finally gets his way. In *Alsace*, by Leroux and Camille, one of the French characters says, '*Vive l'Alsace!*' '*Vive la France*,' says another, whereupon the first replies, 'It's the same thing, my child.' The German characters are heavy, ugly, common, indiscreet, with no taste or tact, who scorn and hate anything not German. As the Paris critic Henry Bidou commented, 'Even the most fervent patriotism should not caricature neighbours.'

Ironically, real-life Germans, far from 'scorning and hating anything not German', were at this very period, from 1912, becoming increasingly interested in French theatre. In 1913 the brilliant company of the Hellerau Institute of Art staged *The Tidings Given to Mary*. Claudel, then consul in Frankfurt, cooperated actively in the production. But in his letters to Lugné-Poe Claudel says nothing about why a German company should have chosen his play.

In fact, beginning with Reinhardt's production of *Everyman*, German producers and playwrights had become drawn to medieval Christendom, fervent and as yet undivided, and to the spiritual life generally. This was one form of a large, very important movement.

Expressionism, as it came to be called, had no manifesto and consisted of related personal quests. The Expressionist painter Kandinsky called people to rise from their graves of material existence and greet the coming 'Epoch of the Great Spiritual'. Believing, in the words of the poet Gottfried Benn, that 'The world has been thought to pieces,' Expressionist writers communicated visions, dreams, moments of ecstasy. This was no facile romanticism, for they focused on man's anguished condition and his need for some never clearly identified form of redemption.

With a few exceptions the Expressionists had no patience with frontier-talk or mass nationalism. Their concern was with the individual seen metaphysically. In that spirit another young Austrian, Franz Werfel, published a book of pacifist verse with the title *Friend of the World*.

Ludwig Meidner, who had studied the Fauves in Paris, and was, like Werfel, a Jew, conveys on a wider scale a kindred dread. In *Apocalyptic Landscape* (1912) he depicts houses in a state of collapse, bridges falling down, rivers overflowing their banks; over the hills hangs the moon and all around is fire; in the centre lies the figure of a man. In *Apocalyptic City* the unseen threat is particularized as war. Meidner depicts buildings shattered by shells and bombs, a devastation not seen in the past but possible soon. In *House on the Corner* he depicts a building in the split second of an explosion, still whole but about to be blown to bits. It is a painting to make one shudder.

While Charles Péguy in Paris was calling for a military structure – the enemy of individualism – German Expressionists were hymning the individual. An illuminating contrast!

An astute picture dealer and publisher, Herwarth Walden, made Berlin the centre of Expressionism, publishing new writing in his magazine *Der Sturm* and exhibiting Kandinsky and other Expressionists. For the first German Autumn Salon in 1913 Walden showed eighty-five contemporary artists from twelve countries. He had Apollinaire come from Paris to lecture at the Sturm gallery on Robert Delaunay, who was flirting with Expressionism, and a little later Apollinaire had this to say: 'In Berlin, Munich, Düsseldorf, Cologne, not a day passes without the opening of a new exhibition devoted to the work of a new French artist.'

The Expressionist movement was a potential bridge at the level of philosophy, literature and the arts between Germany and France. To change metaphor, it might have earthed and rendered safe a dangerous high-voltage jingoism. But it was not to be. Even Apollinaire, with his cosmopolitan background, saw the German Expressionist painters chiefly in stylistic terms: admirably poetic, maybe, but too immoderate, while in *Mercure de France* for February 1914 Ernest Raynaud repeated, with a nasty new sting in the tail, a familiar complaint: that German poetry was imprecise and sad, 'the anguish of a drifting heart, the cry of a soul lost in the night: in short it bears all the signs of its Semitic origins'. It can be said that from late 1913 politics and patriotism coloured almost every other mode of envisaging life.

Morocco, and France's policy of grandeur there, had had a domino effect. Italy sought compensation for French and Spanish gains in Morocco by invading Tripoli and seizing the Dodecanese islands. The Balkan peoples, encouraged by this partition of the Ottoman Empire, took the opportunity to break away from Turkey. The Habsburg and Romanov Empires, regarding themselves rather than the Balkan races as the rightful heirs to the Ottomans, pressed their claims in a rivalry that was soon to lead to Sarajevo.

In Paris Raymond Poincaré became President of the Republic in February 1913. His well-knit, sturdy figure kept fit by three-quarters of an hour's gymnastics every other day, Poincaré reassured people with the spring in his step and ready smile. That summer he had the satisfaction of seeing the Bill for three years' military service become law. Also, he replaced a soft-line diplomat as Ambassador to St Petersburg by Delcassé, whose patriotism, according to a Quai d'Orsay colleague, himself a hard-liner, was 'turning into a fixation . . . I would even say to monomania.'

'The Gnome' had again wriggled to the top. Already in 1904 he had foreseen events, declaring to his wife: 'at one blow our North African Empire is doubled and our Mediterranean presence singularly strengthened'. And now, through her alliance with Russia, France had attained a position of strength vis à vis Germany – or so it seemed.

In St Petersburg Delcassé made known that if Russia wanted a further loan – and she was almost as dependent on French loans, now totalling 17 billion francs, as the Sultan of Morocco had been earlier – she must at once begin to construct 5500 kilometres of strategic railways so that troops could be rushed if need be to the German frontier, and she must increase her army by 90,000 men, the bulk of them to be stationed on the German frontier. It was a strangely hectoring tone from an ally but Sazonov, the volatile Russian Foreign Minister, agreed to the conditions.

What of the movement for détente? With an energy even his denigrators admitted, Jaurès travelled Europe, rallying faint-hearted Socialists, still proclaiming that German workers would tear up their railway lines rather than allow their brothers to be transported like

cattle to the slaughter. But now his unswerving Socialism was being held against Jaurès, and the cause of
peace became identified in many French minds with
strikes, unrest and possible revolution.

In 1912 the texts of France's secret treaties with
Spain were leaked. D'Estournelles de Constant, the
Nobel peace laureate, condemned them in a powerful
speech in the Senate and flayed Delcassé's double-
dealing. His arguments, though sound, caused hardly a
ripple. It was eight years too late.

The chief figure now in trying to understand Germany as opposed to fearing her and in trying to put a
brake on rearmament was Joseph Caillaux. 'His Self-
Sufficiency' had become Minister of Finance in 1913.
Still a dandy in his dress, ostentatious, storming, impatient with those of slow intelligence, a 'loner', Caillaux
had quite a different style from the more guarded and
prudent Poincaré, supported by a network of carefully
chosen influential friends.

Caillaux caused a furore in the Assembly by opposing
the Bill for three years' military service and, when it
was voted, a second furore by saying it should be paid
for by the introduction of income tax. France traditionally met most of her spending needs through indirect
taxes. It is interesting to note that Caillaux, as Frenchmen so often did in this period, justified his policy by
appealing to the past: he declared that the income tax
which so alarmed the upper classes was simply the
equivalent of the *taille* of the *ancien régime*.

By early 1914 Joseph Caillaux had become a bogey to
hard-line nationalists. General Elections were due in
May and Caillaux, new president of the Radical Socialists – the largest party – was expected to do very well.

At this decisive moment in France's history Gaston
Calmette, editor of *Le Figaro*, launched an attack on
Caillaux far more virulent than the one he had made on

Nijinsky. Over a period of three months he wrote or published 138 articles, cartoons or innuendoes against 'Congo Caillaux', 'Germany's Man', 'Socialist Dupe', 'Paniquisite', 'Shady Financier' – for Caillaux was alleged to have made money on the Berlin Bourse at the volatile time of Agadir.

In March 1914 Calmette went further even than this. He published a letter written in 1901 by Caillaux to Berthe Gueydan of New Orleans, then his mistress and later his first wife. In the letter Caillaux said: 'I have had a great success. I have smashed the income tax while seeming to defend it. I got myself cheered by the Centre and the Right, and I have not displeased the Left overmuch.' Since Caillaux was currently urging the nation to accept income tax, it damaged both the Minister and the man.

Caillaux was furious with Calmette. His big bald head mottled with purple streaks, he informed his wife Henriette that he intended to smash the editor's face in. He said this, thought Henriette, as though he meant it.

Henriette knew that some of her letters to Joseph when she had been his mistress had been intercepted by his first wife, who had later burned them, but might well have taken copies and be offering them for sale. The *Figaro* having hinted that 'more letters' might be published, Henriette consulted her lawyer, only to learn that no legal action against Calmette was possible.

Henriette was a woman of character and considerable stupidity. She decided to take things into her own hands. She penned a note to Joseph, recalling his threat to smash Calmette's face in. 'France and the Republic need you,' she wrote. 'I shall do it instead.' In her chauffeur-driven official grey de Dion-Bouton, but with the rosette removed, she drove to a gunsmith's, tried out a Browning, bought it, and hiding it in her muff, arrived at the *Figaro* offices. Told that Calmette was out, she waited.

Three-quarters of an hour later, at 6.00 p.m., Calmette arrived, a burly figure with waxed moustache and pince-nez, currently in the final stages of a divorce from the wife he had married for her money. First he saw Paul Bourget, the novelist, who had been waiting some time, then was handed Madame Caillaux's card. Very surprised, after some hesitation Calmette had the lady shown in.

Henriette felt for the safety-catch on her Browning, still in her muff, and released it. 'Doubtless you know why I'm here?'

'Good heavens no, Madame. But please be seated.'

Henriette took out the Browning, fired all six shots, four of which hit their target. Fatally wounded, Calmette slumped into an armchair. Staff rushed in, seized the Browning and hustled its owner into another office. There Henriette said calmly: 'There's no more justice in France. It was the only thing to do.' Presently the police arrived and as they led his wife to the cells Joseph Caillaux tendered his resignation as Minister of Finance.

In the General Elections of May Caillaux stood in his Sarthe constituency and was re-elected. Nationwide his Radical Socialist Party – plus Independents – increased their seats from 149 to 195, thus emerging as by far the largest grouping. The Left as a whole obtained nearly an absolute majority, and this was seen by many, though not all, interpreters as a vote of no confidence in Poincaré's foreign policy. However that may be, with his wife in prison about to stand trial – she was to be acquitted in July – the shadow of murder hung over 'His Self-Sufficiency'. There was no way the President or the country could have such a man in high office, and the post of Prime Minister, on 13 June, went to René Viviani.

Born in French Algeria, which made him as fervently patriotic as any Lorrainer, Viviani had a gift for oratory – he it was who boasted of 'extinguishing the lights of religious faith' – but he suffered from poor health and intellectually did not belong in Caillaux's class. He was ready to retain the three years' service law and to acquiesce in Poincaré's foreign policy. Only Jean Jaurès now was left to speak for détente. But how many would listen? For it was known that Poincaré felt sure France could win a war in two months, and in spring 1914 no less a person than the President's wife, Henriette Poincaré, known to Parisians chiefly for her fondness for animals, was heard to say: 'What we need is a good war and the suppression of Jaurès.'

CHAPTER 17

Paris at War

In Germany meanwhile Wilhelm II and his Chancellor since 1909, Bethmann-Hollweg, were worried by a new situation in the Balkans. After breaking free from Turkey, Serbia was fomenting trouble among minority groups in Austria-Hungary, urging them to wrest independence. Austria-Hungary was Germany's one firm ally, so the Kaiser would in any case have felt threatened. But Russia was further muddying the waters. Making a show of strength to compensate for their defeat by Japan in 1905, the Russians offered strong moral backing to the Serbs and to minority groups within the Austro-Hungarian Empire. Bertie, British Ambassador in Paris, was to sum it up: 'If . . . the Emperor of Russia adhere to the absurd and obsolete claim that she is protectress of all Slav States, however bad their conduct, war is probable, Germany will be bound to support Austria, and France will have to help Russia.'

Wilhelm II was deeply uneasy at Delcassé's encouragement of Russia's ambitions. According to the Bishop of Ripon, visiting him in June 1913, 'He was quite cordial. But he spoke with a note that was new to me . . . He spoke of the dangerous position in which Germany was placed between two powers which might prove hostile.'

But of Wilhelm II it may be said that, like the Habsburgs, he had learned nothing and forgotten nothing. About international politics he continued to be the know-all. He and his fellow-monarch, Franz Josef, and Franz Josef's heir Archduke Franz Ferdinand, could handle matters. The three of them would continue loyal friends: against that friendship no alliance could prevail. England urged him to slow his naval programme: he would not do so; he had set himself to make Germany a great naval power, and if Britannia was piqued, so much the worse for Britannia.

Wilhelm continued to keep a close eye on every detail, every nuance of the international crisis. Too close an eye perhaps, given his temperament. As the situation deteriorated, his conceit suffered, his touchiness became raw, his determination grew not to suffer any further humiliation such as Algeciras and its aftermath.

In June 1914 Colonel House, President Wilson's trusted emissary, who was working behind the scenes for détente between England and Germnay, had a half-hour's talk with the Kaiser and was struck by 'an unreasoning nervousness which might at any moment result in a reckless attack'.

On 12 June 1914 Wilhelm II arrived at Konopischt Castle in Bohemia for a three-day stay with his kinsman, Archduke Franz Ferdinand, heir to Emperor Franz Josef. The Archduke was tall, well-built, energetic, with intelligent saddish eyes and a walrus moustache. He had married for love the charming Sophie Chotek, though she lacked the required noble ancestry; they had three children, the youngest thirteen. Konopischt was a happy house; Wilhelm liked being there. He shared with his host a passion for hunting and gardens; about both subjects Wilhelm was an expert and did not hide his superior knowledge.

Wilhelm and Franz Ferdinand set great store by the Austro-German alliance, which the former had described to his cousin in these terms: 'If the two best armies in the world stand side by side, determined to

accept no slight . . . this is a fact which all other diplo-
mats as well as states just have to accept, whether it
suits them or not.' We notice the word 'slight'.

At Konopischt the two men almost certainly discussed Serbia's trouble-making within the Empire,
especially in Bosnia, and Vienna's growing impatience
with her small neighbour. Wilhelm had recently
advised Vienna to restrain her pressure on Serbia, and
this view chimed in with Franz Ferdinand's belief that
Austria should extend her influence in the Balkans by
loans and trade, not force. For the Archduke had a
healthy respect for Russia and would have liked to have
made a threesome of the alliance by bringing in Tsar
Nicholas.

The meeting went well apparently and Wilhelm sent
a thank-you telegram: 'The roses in my garden are
blooming. Rhododendrons are also blooming despite
three weeks of rain. *Waldmannsheil.* Many greetings to
all. W.' As Wilhelm made ready for the Kiel Regatta,
Franz Ferdinand prepared to attend army manœuvres
in the mountains south-west of Sarajevo.

Three of his young Bosnian subjects were lying in
wait for him there. Earlier that year in the Serbian capital, Belgrade, they had met members of the 'Union or
Death' group, popularly called 'Black Hand', dedicated
to speedy union of all Serbs, and a plot had been
hatched to kill the Archduke. The plot was probably
approved, and perhaps promoted, by Dragutin
Dimitriyevich, chief of the intelligence section of the
Serbian General Staff, and a leading member of 'Black
Hand'. The background to so bold a plan lay in recent
assurances from Serbia's 'protectress'. In November
1913 the Serbian Minister had been told, 'Russia will
do everything for Serbia,' a message repeated by the
Tsar to King Peter in February.

At the end of May a member of Black Hand had

handed over to the conspirators six bombs and four Browning pistols. Having trained the youths in their use, he gave them 130 dinars, a road map of Bosnia, a note to the frontier official at Shabats and some cyanide, then sent them on their way.

On 28 June, wearing military uniform and a cocked hat, the Archduke drove with his wife through the streets of Sarajevo in an open Viennese sports car, a Graef und Stift, the third in a party of six. As the cars travelled along the Appel Quay, beside the river, a tall youth in a long black coat and a black hat drew out a bomb resembling a rectangular cake of soap. He snapped off the cap and hit the detonator against a lamp-post. He could not wait twelve seconds, as he had been taught, because the car would have passed by. He threw the bomb at the green feathers of the Archduke's hat. It fell behind him on the car's folded roof and rolled into the street, bursting under the next car and wounding a dozen people.

Consternation ensued and angry alarm. While the wounded were taken to hospital, it was decided to adhere to the programme. An official welcome took place at the town hall, after which the motor tour was resumed.

As the Archduke's car slowed at the corner of Appel Quay and Franz Josef street a short young man with long hair and deep-set blue eyes drew a revolver and fired twice. One bullet hit Sophie, the other Franz Ferdinand. Flinging his arms round his wife, the Archduke cried, 'Sophie, Sophie, don't die. Live for our children.' But Sophie was already dead and soon after reaching the Governor's residence the Archduke too succumbed.

In Paris news of the Sarajevo assassinations caused less stir than the Caillaux shooting. Only the Right showed much sympathy for Franz Josef, who had already lost his brother Maximilian, shot in Mexico, his wife Elisabeth, victim of an assassin's knife in Geneva, and his only son Rudolf, who had died in a suicide pact at Mayerling. Now, at the age of eighty-four, the Emperor had lost his nephew and heir.

Wilhelm heard the news at the Kiel Regatta; 'very depressed and angry', he cancelled further races. To the British Ambassador, Goschen, he confided 'that the assassination was a dreadful blow to him – both because it was only a fortnight ago that he had been staying with them and seen their happy family life, and because it was such an upset of everything they had planned and arranged together'. He telegraphed condolences to Franz Josef, ending 'We must bow before God's decree which once more has imposed heavy trials.'

The Austrian Foreign Minister, Berchtold, took an extremely grave view of the assassinations. He decided that the only sure way of protecting the southern part of the Empire from revolution and break-up was to take punitive military action against Serbia. This Austria could do only with the approval of her ally. So after the Archduke's funeral he put the question to Berlin.

On personal and political grounds Wilhelm was disposed to respond favourably. But also he wished to localize the dispute. He believed that the Tsar would not associate himself with 'the murderers of princes' and would stay out of the area. In this belief Wilhelm promised Berchtold support for his plan. Having got it, Berchtold set in motion the cumbersome machinery for action against Serbia.

Attention now centred on Russia. It so happened that on 20 July Raymond Poincaré, with Prime Minister Viviani, landed at Kronstadt from the battleship *France* on a long-planned three-day visit to the Tsar.

Poincaré knew from his Ambassador in Vienna that 'Growing condition of unrest in southern Slav provinces of Dual Monarchy is such that Austro-Hungarian Government are compelled either to acquiesce in separation of those provinces or make a desperate effort to retain them by reducing Serbia to impotency.'

Poincaré knew too that Austrian action against Serbia would pose no direct threat to Russia. Serbia, moreover, was not an ally of Russia, and Russia had no historic role in the Balkans. Nor would action in Serbia endanger France, Belgrade lying 900 miles from Paris.

What of Russia's attitude to the danger area? Wilhelm had assumed that Nicholas as a divine-right monarch would shrink from siding with murderers of princes, and that was true. But Wilhelm had made the blunder, like Napoleon with Tsar Alexander, of assuming that Nicholas was truly an autocrat, truly in control. In fact Nicholas was surrounded by noblemen and politicians anxious to contain domestic revolutionary pressures by a show of national strength abroad, and the Tsar was already more than half way to sharing their view.

In these dangerous circumstances it followed that if a clash in the Balkans between two great powers was to be averted, Poincaré must, with speed, urge prudence and moderation on Russia, and that he could do because he was now in direct and daily contact with the Tsar and his advisers and, moreover, could speak out of France's long friendship.

Talks between Poincaré and the Russians began on the afternoon of 20 July in the Winter Palace. Poincaré, according to the French Ambassador, spoke persuasively and with authority to the Tsar, and it was he who directed the conversation. At a state banquet Poincaré solemnly reaffirmed French obligations under the alliance – the purpose of which Delcassé had extended from 'maintenance of peace' to 'maintenance of the balance of Power' – and on 21 July told his Ambassador that '[Foreign Minister] Sazonov must be firm and we must support him.'

On that same day Poincaré was approached by the British Ambassador, Buchanan, with a proposal from Foreign Minister Grey that Austria and Russia should discuss the crisis together.. This might have been the political equivalent of a tourniquet for arterial bleeding. The French President, however, showed no interest, and Buchanan telegraphed London: 'His Excellency expressed opinion that a conversation *à deux* would be very dangerous at present moment.'

While urging firmness on Russia and checking the British plan because it would allow Russo-Austrian *pourparlers* without Poincaré present, the French President did little to try to restrain Vienna. Only three days later did Viviani instruct France's Ambassador there to give Berchtold counsels of moderation.

By then – on the previous day, 23 July – Austria had presented a note to Serbia making ten very stiff demands, the sixth that Austrian Government delegates should take part in the investigation of the murders. On 25 July Serbia agreed to all the demands save the sixth and mobilized. Poincaré and Viviani were then at sea, steaming home, while Berthelot at the Quai d'Orsay had sole charge of foreign affairs. It was on that date that Crowe of the Foreign Office wrote a minute of great importance.

The minute begins with an evident reference to Poincaré's failure to act on the British proposal: 'The moment has passed,' wrote Crowe, 'when it might have been possible to enlist French support in an effort to hold back Russia . . .

'Whatever we may think,' continued Crowe, 'of the merits of the Austrian charges against Serbia, France and Russia consider that these are a pretext, and that the bigger cause of the Triple Entente [the third member being Britain] is definitely engaged.' Poincaré in effect had chosen to see Germany's support for Austria as one more stage in the aggressive role for which Delcassé, the Quai d'Orsay and the rancorous generally had for so long cast Wilhelm's Empire and which, since Agadir, French opinion had come to endorse.

And the conclusion, for Crowe? 'I think it would be impolitic, not to say dangerous, for England to attempt to controvert [the French] opinion.' Crowe's minute, approved by the Government, became Britain's official policy.

On 28 July Austria declared war on Serbia. Two days later Russia mobilized. On the 31st Germany declared a state of war emergency, followed by an ultimatum demanding that Russia cease military preparations. When that went unheeded, next day Germany declared war on Russia.

The French press had been preparing the public for war with optimistic reports of Russia's peasant army: regiment after regiment of Nijinskys. Russia 'is becoming the strongest military power the world has ever seen', and with articles by retired generals promising that if France held out for a month, the Russian 'steamroller' would quickly crush Germany. But in the provinces at least the actual declaration of war by Germany on France, which happened on 3 August, caused anguish and alarm. A young seamstress, daughter of an arsenal worker, was doing a day's sewing for a woman who kept a small dairy in Cherbourg when a fishwife suddenly entered: 'My poor Mère Cordier, *une guerre europlane est déclarée*! What will become of our boys?' The malapropism is touching, prophetic and revealing of ordinary people's feelings.

In the capital reaction was much less sombre. Several of the Parisians we have met saw war as an occasion for new experiences. On 28 July Misia Edwards had Diaghilev round to her flat to hear Satie and Viñes play Satie's *Trois Morceaux en forme de Poire*. She had been urging the Russian to consider Satie's music for a ballet and she could see that he was now likely to say yes. Then a friend burst in: 'Austria has declared war on Serbia.' 'What luck!' thought Misia. 'Oh God, let there be a war.' Recalling her reaction later, Misia said she had wanted the adventure.

Misia's was not an isolated reaction. Another Parisian, Paul Claudel, then consul in Hamburg, had doubted there would be a war: commercial self-interest would restrain Germany. He was astonished to see the newspaper placard, '*Krieg*', and voiced what he termed the feelings of people across Europe, quite likely his own feelings too: 'Freedom from one's job, from one's wife, from one's children, from a fixed place; adventure.'

For Louis Gillet, brilliant young art historian, former pacifist, now a lieutenant in the 80th regiment safely in the Cotentin near Cherbourg, the outbreak of war was also adventure. 'Beautiful to fight with pure hands and an innocent heart, to give one's life for divine justice,' he wrote to his mentor Romain Rolland. 'We'll give a good shaking to this cloud of Germanism, this fog of vulgarity that weighs on the world.'

Ten days later: 'What a country we are, my friend, what an admirable race! In the same week as the Caillaux trial, amid all the Parliamentary scandals and in-fighting, what an awakening! The same men, the same cast of politicians suddenly become equals of the immortal men of the Revolution! . . . Today we witness France's resurrection. Always the same: victory over Otho at Bovines, Crusades, cathedrals, Revolution, always we're the world's knights, God's paladins . . . We who were saying this twenty years ago, when no one would believe us, we have a right to be pleased.'

Three days after war broke André Gide also scented adventure, of a different kind. 'The wonderful behaviour of the Government, of everyone, and of all France, as well as of all the neighbouring nations, leaves room for every hope. One foresees the beginning of a new era: the United States of Europe bound by a treaty limiting their armaments; Germany subjugated or dissolved; Trieste given back to the Italians, Schleswig to Denmark; and especially Alsace to France.' The last phrases seem to me revealing of Gide's unwritten thoughts during the period marked by tacit approval of grandeur.

It may be useful, by way of contrast, to compare another gifted novelist's comment when war broke. Like many Germans, Thomas Mann was hardly aware of France, so large loomed the shadow of Russia. 'My chief feeling is a tremendous curiosity – and, I admit it, the deepest sympathy for this execrated, indecipherable, fateful Germany which, if she has hitherto not unqualifiedly held "civilization" as the highest good, is at any rate preparing to smash the most despicable police state in the world.'

On the March evening when Madame Caillaux killed Calmette, Proust, who was in Paris, wrote of his shock to a friend, describing Calmette's press campaign as 'so disinterested and so noble', and Madame Caillaux as a 'Fury'. Although he owed his literary reputation largely to Calmette's patronage and made so much in his letters of friendship's duties, Proust did not attend the funeral.

As to the possibility of war and the need to speak out on the deepening crisis, Proust did not want to trouble himself about these matters either. According to his close friend Maurice Duplay, 'Marcel and I refused to believe there could be a war. It would be too frightful, we thought.'

On the day Germany declared hostilities, in a business letter to his stockbroker, Proust wrote: 'Millions of men are going to be massacred because it is advantageous to the Emperor of Austria to have an outlet on the Black Sea.' The remark is surprising, for among Franz Josef's motives in chastizing Serbia there was never any question of pushing on through Bulgaria to the Black Sea. Proust had failed to grasp the essentials. Moreover, he puts the blame on someone else. There is no heart-searching here about whether French policy, as countenanced by Proust and his set, had perhaps played its part in the drift to war.

Blaming someone else became widespread among creative artists. The nationalist playwright Edmond Rostand, staying at his Basque country house that summer, felt 'despair,' writes a friend, 'at the madness of his fellow-men . . . struck down by the blow disappointments inflict on highly strung temperaments'. Another shifter of blame was Claude Debussy. 'When,' he asked, 'will we cease to entrust the destiny of nations to men who consider mankind as a stepping-stone to success?'

Within days of the outbreak of war Paris became a different kind of city. Streets were deserted: no buses, a few trams with women conductors. Theatres and cinemas had closed; cafés shut at 8.00 p.m., restaurants at 9.30. As darkness fell, searchlights probed for Zeppelins. At the Louvre treasures were placed in iron crates; iron shutters went up on many a shop. One mattress-maker chalked on his shop door: 'Sleep peacefully, your mattress-maker is at the front.' Other signs promised reopening in September.

'Every day,' wrote an Englishwoman, 'sees the residents in the richer quarters closing their shutters and bidding their concierges goodbye . . . We, the bourgeoisie, have always said that the great danger to Paris was a revolution among the working-classes, the mob! We were proved wrong, the mob stood steady when the bourgeoisie did not.'

On 2 August the painter Maurice Vlaminck took a tram to the Porte Maillot. 'The governor of Paris,' he noted, 'had taken strong measures to defend the capital. A dozen or so big trees had been cut down and were laid across the Avenue de Neuilly with a view to stopping German cavalry; palisades and iron spikes set in timber were erected in the streets. As I looked at this improvised defence system I didn't know whether to laugh or cry.'

'Nearly everyone is running away,' wrote Apollinaire from Deauville, referring to the privileged, but with a poet's exaggeration. As German troops swept through Belgium, across a frontier France had neglected to fortify and up the Marne valley, on 29 August gunfire was heard in Paris, and on 2 September the Government fled to Bordeaux, Delcassé among them, now Foreign Minister. Rodin left for London with Rose, later going on to Rome to make a bust of the Pope. Debussy took his wife and Chou-chou to Angers, where the sound of bugle and drum reminded him of the 'two Richards' – Wagner and Strauss – and where the locals talked of 100,000 Cossacks about to fall on the Germans like an avalanche. Marcel Proust caught a crowded train for Cabourg – his journey lasted twenty-two hours – and found the local hospital already crowded with wounded. Anna de Noailles headed for Bayonne, where she read her poetry to wounded soldiers in hospital. She also visited Edmond Rostand. Food was scarce, refugees went hungry, but the irrepressible Anna, out on a walk and observing a fine pig, was heard to remark: 'Just fancy, in that one plump animal the contents of a Felix Potin shop [Paris's most expensive delicatessen]!'

Anna, as it happened, was completing a very fine poem. Three days before war broke a young, slightly mad nationalist named Raoul Villain had been roaming the streets of Montmartre, in his pocket a revolver. He had wanted first to kill the Kaiser but had settled now for killing the man newspaper writers – Péguy included – called 'the Kaiser's tool'. While Jean Jaurès was having a break in the Café du Croissant from composing next day's edition of *L'Humanité*, he was shot dead by Villain.

Though Jaurès had stood at the opposite pole politically, Anna de Noailles began work on a deeply-felt poem expressing her shock and grief at the murder of so brave a statesman. It begins:

> *J'ai vu ce mort puissant le soir d'un jour d'été.*
> *Un lit, un corps sans souffle, une table à côté:*
> *La force qui dormait près de la pauvreté!*[1]

It is perhaps Anna de Noailles' best poem and a threnody of permanent value about the troubled eve of war.

Gaston Gallimard, young publisher associate of André Gide, not only left Paris but in order to avoid the army feigned a series of illnesses. For twelve months from his hospital bed he mystified doctors, until finally his pretended illness induced real illness. When called up for his medical he was declared unfit.

---

[1] I saw this strongly built man lying dead one summer's evening.
A bed, a lifeless body, a table nearby:
Power sleeping next to poverty.

Romain Rolland happened to be in Switzerland with his mother in August 1914. He explained to Louis Gillet that he refused to hold the Germans as a nation responsible for the war, and he would never renounce his German friends. He intended therefore to remain in Switzerland and there work for peace. He was naturally vilified by the French press, which treated him, Rolland complained, 'as an enemy of my country because I want France to be pure, human and victorious not only on the battlefield but in matters of the heart'. In 1915 Romain Rolland was to publish a pamphlet, *Above the Mêlée*, in which he called on intellectuals on both sides to agitate for peace: it won him angry abuse.

The majority of French people, however, including a number of those we have met, rose to the occasion with sincere patriotism. Marie Curie offered her gold and silver medals to be melted down and with her second Nobel Prize bought war bonds, knowing they would soon be worthless. Henri Ghéon worked night and day at a hospital in Le Nouvion en Thiérache, dressing, cauterizing, extracting shrapnel, amputating, as wounded arrived from the Battle of the Marne, and later continued with gallantry as medical officer with the 29th artillery.

Among the painters two physically strong men, Georges Braque and André Derain, rejoined their regiments and fought bravely at the Front. Picasso, as a Spaniard, understandably felt no call to serve; though the cheap press spoke of Kubismus, because of its success in Berlin, and attacked its practitioners as pro-German, he continued to paint in this now suspect style. Henri Matisse came to Paris and tried every way he knew to get into the army. But at forty-five he was judged too old and returned home to serve, so to speak, as a painter. Marie Laurencin could have been relied on to show spirit but as it happened she had fallen in love with a second-rate painter, Otto von Wagten, married him and so acquired German nationality: she and her husband were caught by the war in Spain. Her kindred spirit, Raoul Dufy, joined up and drove a van for the military postal service. Jean Cocteau, classified unfit for army duty, quickly went to work for the Red Cross and proved an efficient ambulanceman.

Marie Laurencin's lover, Guillaume Apollinaire, grateful to France for all she had done for one of Polish-Italian origin, enlisted in the French army. From Nîmes he wrote to a friend: 'I so love art that I have joined up.' It was an implicit assertion that the achievements of the past fourteen years were worth any and every sacrifice. Yet paradoxically Apollinaire was beginning to feel that art and innovation were not in themselves enough. Like his friend Max Jacob, Apollinaire was experiencing the pull of religion, as he described in perhaps his best poem, *Zone*, set in Paris:

> *Ici même les automobiles ont l'air d'être anciennes,*
> *La religion seule est restée toute neuve, la religion*
> *Est restée simple comme les hangars de Port Aviation.*
> *Seul en Europe tu n'es pas antique ô Christianisme*
> *L'Européen le plus moderne c'est vous Pape Pie X*
> *Et toi que les fenêtres observent la honte te retient*
> *D'entrer dans une église et de t'y confesser le matin.*[1]

But it was now too late to 'enter a church'. In the 38th regiment of field artillery he saw very heavy fighting

---

[1] Here even the motor-cars seem old-fashioned,
Religion alone has remained quite new, religion
Has remained simple like aeroplane hangars.
In all Europe only you, Christianity, are not antiquated,
The most modern European is you, Pope Pius X,
While you [my soul], watched by windows, are held back by shame
From entering a church and confessing your sins.

445

and received a severe head wound from which he subsequently died.

Among the musicians, Ravel was unfit for active service and Debussy over-age. But Reynaldo Hahn, foreseeing war, had taken out French citizenship as a symbolic gesture, like Apollinaire's, that France stood for civilization against barbarism. The darling of the Paris salons, who had played and sung at so many parties, left his piano for the barracks of the 31st infantry regiment in Albi, where he begged to be sent to the front as cyclist-secretary, a move which Proust, in alarm, pulled strings to prevent.

Meanwhile, in Paris, the Germans moved up the Marne valley, threatening Paris. It became imperative to throw in reinforcements. At the suggestion of the owner of the G7 Taxi Company, André Walewski, who happened to be a grandson of Napoleon, 1100 motor taxis were requisitioned to rush 5000 men of the 7th D.I. to the sector round Nanteuil le Haudouin, 50 kilometres north-east of Paris. The little red taxis played their part in the Battle of the Marne between the 6 and 13 September, which was to halt the German advance.

Among those who fought in the run-up to the battle was Lieutenant Charles Péguy. In his later writings the architect of a Harmonious City had helped to whip up extreme nationalism, but as an exemplary reserve officer he had gone annually to camp to keep in training and to train others. On 5 September he led his company over a field of beetroot with no cover and fell with a German bullet through his head. His death was to become symbolic: Charles Péguy, the writer-patriot, who loved France in Jeanne d'Arc and had given his life as she did.

That autumn Louis Gillet's battalion saw action. 'We have had the most frightful shelling,' he wrote to

Rolland. 'Without being able to do anything about it we have been pinned down for twenty-six days; I must admit that I had no idea life could be so hellish and humiliating. In moments like this one isn't proud of oneself . . . A trench full of corpses, indeed partly composed of corpses – English, German, French – you cannot imagine what it's like. Soldiers back from the Marne and the Aisne had never seen so many.' Gillet's battalion suffered 50% casualties.

Frenchmen's bravery is well conveyed by Proust when he has Robert de Saint-Loup write from the Front: 'You should see all these fellows, mostly of humble origin, workmen, small shopkeepers, who had no idea they had heroism in them and would have died in their beds without having known it, yet here they are running under heavy fire to help a friend, to carry a wounded officer and, wounded in their turn, smiling as they die because the chief doctor tells them that the trench has been recaptured from the Germans. I assure you, my dear fellow, that that puts the French in a good light and makes me understand the epic periods of our history that seemed improbable when we studied them at school. The epic is so splendid that you would find, as I do, that words cannot describe it . . . I feel the term "*poilu*" is ripe for great poets, like the words Deluge, Christ or Barbarians which were already pervaded with greatness before Hugo, Vigny and the rest used them in their verse.'

Misia Edwards' hope of adventure found fulfilment. She obtained permission from her friend General Gallieni, Governor of Paris, to form an ambulance unit. She had fourteen dress-shop delivery vans converted into motor-ambulances, and enrolled a number of male nurses, including José Sert, Paul Iribe and Jean Cocteau, who had a special uniform made by Paul Poiret and at this stage treated it all as a lark. He spoke whimsically to Gide before leaving for the Front, telling him of the lady of the Red Cross who shouted on the stairway: 'I was promised fifty wounded men for this morning, I want my fifty wounded.'

Misia led her ambulance unit out of Paris, heading the column in her large Mercedes. When the unit found and began to collect the first wounded, at Haye les Roses, Misia burst into tears. At Meaux they passed the small red Paris 'taxis of the Marne', filled with soldiers. They reached Rheims for the first bombardment, and Cocteau described the much shelled cathedral as resembling 'a piece of old lace'.

One of Misia's difficulties was that she had orders to return to Paris after nightfall, so that the sight of the wounded should not adversely affect morale. Her private Red Cross did excellent work, as did that of another artistic Mæcenas, Comte Etienne de Beaumont. As the fighting receded from Paris, Misia handed over her motor ambulances to the Russian Government, which indeed was seriously short of such facilities.

The Paris intelligentsia began to address a new question: Were the German soldiers much like the French, a mixture of good and bad, but sharing a similar code of honour? Or were they barbarians, who had no code and committed atrocities?

Marcel Proust held the former view. So did André Gide. But Jean Richepin wrote an article speaking of four thousand French children who supposedly had had their right hands cut off by German soldiers, while Jean Cocteau contributed to a little literary review drawings of such mutilations. André Gide, who worked tirelessly for eighteen months on a committee to help Belgian refugees, carried out a personal investigation into these charges and announced that he could find no evidence for them, it was all hearsay and rumour. Gide, incidentally, went out of his way to save his friend Rilke's flat and belongings from sequestration.

The peacetime slur that the Germans practised homosexuality now predictably reappeared. *The French Soldier's Ten Commandments*, printed in Paris in 1915, had the following under the sixth commandment:

> *Luxurieux point ne seras*
> *Comme les Boches . . . inversement.*

Neither Gide nor Cocteau chose to comment on this.

A question much debated was whether the Germans, innocent perhaps of cutting off hands, had not proved themselves barbarians by shelling Rheims cathedral and burning the old town of Louvain? Rolland claimed this was barbarous and invited friends to sign a manifesto to that effect. Stravinsky for one saw the fallacy in confusing beauty and the good, and refused; he admitted the Germans' atrocious taste in such matters as public statuary but that, he said, did not make them barbarians.

Joseph Péladan, novelist and art critic, in a front page *Figaro* article on 28 September 1914 demanded an end to the teaching of German in schools and universities. 'It has been proved that we can speak to the Germans only with the sword.' Others picked up the taunt about German ugliness and extended it to their language: Richepin of the Académie Française berated the 'bespectacled gorillas spouting their Ostrogoth patois'.

Wagner rankled with the French, partly because he had said many unkind things about them. On 27 September Frédéric Masson, Academician, historian of Napoleon, writing in *Echo de Paris*, denounced *The Mastersingers* as an inept work that unjustly sniped at French conservatism. 'Wagnerism being the complete expression of German culture, Frenchmen infected

with it choose to play into the hands of Germany.'
Seventy-nine-year-old Saint-Saëns contributed his
little bit in *Le Figaro*: 'The Germans . . . have turned
back civilization to the days of extreme barbarism. . . . as
for Richard Wagner, they have used his genius in order
to infiltrate the German soul into the soul of all
nations.'

Debussy too believed that Wagner's influence might
corrupt. To Godet he deplored 'this seizure of our
thoughts, our structures, which we've accepted with a
nonchalant smile. That is our mistake – serious,
unpardonable, difficult to correct, for it is within us like
bad blood. Just fancy – one example from many – that
when musical directors swim out of their depth – what
depth! – they find nothing better to do than consult the
Wagner almanac.' This view was not shared by Proust,
who enjoyed singing aloud his favourite Good Friday
music from *Parsifal* and asked, 'If the war had been
against Russia, what would we have said about Tolstoy
and Dostoievsky?'

Debussy would have liked to contribute to the
struggle by writing a Heroic March but his health had
declined and anyway he probably did not have that
kind of music in him; what he did instead was sign the
score of his piano and cello sonata, and write under the
signature '*musicien français*'. Such gestures earned him
the name Claude de France. 'I want,' he explained, 'to
give a proof, however small, that even 30 million
Boches cannot destroy French thought.'

Paul Claudel, from the safety of a new job in Rome,
wrote the equivalent of Heroic Marches in verse, pulling out the stops of Redemptive Suffering. Following
the Marseillaise, Claudel proclaimed in one poem, with
poor agronomy and poorer taste, that the fatherland
must be fertilized with French poilus' blood. A soldier
promises his general to fight on against the Germans:

'As long as there is living French meat to march across your damned barbed wire, As long as there is a mother's son to march over your science and chemistry . . .' In another poem – later to be held against him – Claudel declared that the death of so many men in battle is not plain loss, it has a positive side, since it brings 'grief to our hearts, tears to our eyes'.

Paul Claudel was typical of many in his unquestioning self-righteousness. But in a few Parisians we have glimpses – hardly more – of soul-searching and twinges of guilt. Though a notorious womanizer in later life, in his impoverished youth Rodin had seriously thought of becoming a priest and his first bust had been of his spiritual director and hero, Pierre Julien Eymard, now a canonized saint. According to Rolland, 'Rodin in his deep sorrow accuses no one but himself. He maintains, though not in so many words, that we must all say *mea culpa*. Without knowing it he is, I think, becoming a Christian. He considers the Germans as Huns – but also as God's scourges.'

Louis Gillet began to have somewhat similar thoughts. 'I can see only one meaning in this war – even if, as we must, we win it,' he wrote from the trenches, 'and that is punishment for our sins, Europe's sins and the world's: never have I better understood the infinite value of life and our criminal wastage of such a Divine gift.' However, in the next sentence but one: 'It goes without saying, my friend, that the great criminal remains the German Emperor and his general staff.'

Max Jacob was another to whom, as he put it, 'war and meditation in sorrow were teaching the realities.' His vision of Christ in a long yellow robe had been followed by others, but he had delayed 'dying and being reborn'. Then, in January 1915, after a further apparition, he decided to delay no longer and went for instruction to the superior of the Convent of Sion in rue

Notre-Dame-des-Champs. On 18 February 1915 Max was baptized Cyprian. Picasso, who stood godfather, gave him an inscribed copy of Thomas à Kempis's *Imitation of Christ*.

The Abbé Mugnier, confessor to the Paris *literati* and the priest Proust asked to pray by his bedside half an hour *after* his death, when that day should come, was, with Romain Rolland, one of the few who actually disapproved of the war. On 18 August he wrote in his diary: 'The country is said to be transformed: patriotism and faith join hands and so on. But faith, real faith, is a matter of humanizing, of loving one's neighbour, beyond national frontiers.' He deplored the Church's lack of leadership in the pre-war years: it had organized international congresses to proclaim the real presence of Christ in the Eucharist, but had countenanced nationalism. He concluded, 'We have taken completely the wrong road.'

Elsewhere Mugnier singles out Maurice Barrès' group: 'They have led us to disaster. 1870 should have been buried and forgotten.' On 12 November he chides himself: 'There is heavy fighting in the north. And I believe that the only real fighting is within: killing the enemies inside us. You talk of heroism. That's what heroism really is. But you prefer the other, which fits in well with your personal hatreds. You fulfil your natural bent and win glory into the bargain.'

The return of the Government on 11 December signified that Paris was again deemed to be safe. But soon French, British and German armies entered on a war of attrition in barbed-wire, sandbagged trenches, long chunks of France becoming in every sense No Man's Land. Armageddon, as Churchill called it, had arrived.

This is perhaps the moment to recall and assess some

of the factors in the run-up to war. How did the desire
for peace evinced in 1900 slowly turn to suspicion, then
to fear, and finally to hate? A main reason, I believe,
was a failure by opinion-makers to get to grips with the
real twentieth-century Germany. An array of 'serious'
periodicals discussed almost exclusively Germans of
the past. They studied Germany as a concept, not as a
contemporary force. The chief political writer in the
influential *Revue de Paris*, Victor Bérard, was an
ancient geography professor, who in article after article
harked back to Frederick of Prussia or Napoleon's
Confederation of the Rhine. He never tries to assess
Wilhelm II as a person or to discover what motivates
him. The contemporary literary and artistic scene in
Germany, which could have shed light on motivation,
was ignored in favour of articles about Schiller or
about Goethe's admiration for France – 'good' Germans,
if only they had been alive now! Similarly, French
analysts shirked the technical schools and company-
sponsored research underlying Germany's commercial
success.

Did German vaunting and restlessness largely stem,
as Harold Nicolson, in a history of the period, was to
claim, from thwarted energy; their boasting from lack of
self-confidence, and their untruthfulness – for example,
over the true extent of Dreadnought building – from the
circumstance that, as with so many musical people,
they possessed fancy but no constructive imagination?
French writers did not even ask, and the failure is very
surprising from a people who, down the years, have
excelled in psychological analysis.

Norman Angell, tireless worker for peace and as editor of the Paris *Daily Mail* well placed to observe, considered nationalism in France had grown strong to fill
the vacuum caused by religious disbelief. That is true of
some, such as Barrès, but among the most vociferous

nationalists were Catholics of all parties, including Albert de Mun, much esteemed as 'the workers' Deputy'.

Some Frenchmen shrank from facing the real Germany because, like an Ibsen play, it was 'distressing' and best avoided. Some – the *Revanchards*, those who from 1871 were already advocating a war of revenge – had made up their minds on the subject. But – a vital factor – many leaders of opinion skirted the real issues because they had chosen to be Parisians in the narrowest sense, to become citizens of a closed world, a beautiful place of self-fulfilment which made them feel good. Evil, since it could not be in them, was projected outside, on to 'enemies' – non-classical art, highly mechanized factories, eventually on to the German nation.

There were of course mitigating circumstances: German naval rearmament, blustering speeches by Wilhelm, many tactless acts by the German Foreign Office, growing nationalism in Europe. Even so, Mugnier may well have been right in his diagnosis. Frenchmen should have been killing the enemies within. At another level, probably no people can successfully pursue at the same time a policy of national grandeur and a lifestyle of self-fulfilment. The former demands that one should know one's neighbour, the latter that one should know oneself.

After Agadir came fear and jingoism, which is a symptom of inadequacy in the context of too high expectations. At this point many of the Parisian intelligentsia went further down the road to emotion, announcing that France equalled Civilization, Germany Barbarism. This was not only an over-simplification, it had fatal consequences. For it implied that a conflict was built into such terms. As George Kennan has noted, the unjustified assumption of war's likelihood became the cause of its final inevitability.

Optimism arising from local achievements blinded

Frenchmen also to the nature of the war they were preparing to enter. They set high store by their air force,
but the Germans, with new machines powered by Benz
and Mercedes engines, more reliable than French
engines, were to have control of the air from Mons in
1914 to the Somme in 1916. French infantry continued
to wear blue coats and red breeches – the 'historic' colours no one yet dared change – while Germans wore
field-grey and British khaki, so the French were easy
targets, especially for German machine-guns – again a
weapon the French were slow to adopt. In so-called
expert books and articles retired generals spoke much
about morale, honour, the spirit of 1789, too little about
the relative fire-power of French and German artillery.

If we turn from her failings to the strength of the French
nation in winter 1914–15 we find patriotism of quite
remarkable magnitude. It was fed, paradoxically, by
that very historical sense that had falsified Frenchmen's view of their power status in the decade from
1900. Jeanne d'Arc, François I, Louis XIV, Turenne,
Hoche, Marceau, the armies of 1793, Napoleon and his
marshals – all live again. The felt presence of past
heroes is evoked in writings and songs, and also the
village cemeteries of Alsace-Lorraine. This patriotism
sustained the poilus – at least until the mutinies of
1917 – in their horrendous ordeal by mud, wire, shelling, rats and, later, poison gas with only short spells of
leave.

Out of the horrors came one unexpected good. In the
trenches believers and unbelievers endured extremes of
hunger and thirst, heat and cold, the lice and the rats,
side by side with Catholic army chaplains. Together,
with equal courage, laymen and priests suffered and
shed their blood, together many of them died. Such a

455

sharing bred fraternity and put an end once and for all to extreme anti-clericalism.

Among the well-educated the non-military achievements of the recent past were equally a source of strength. In the correspondence of soldiers at the Front to whom literature and the arts symbolized their inner life there are many references to the creative people of recent years, especially to Claudel, to Péguy and Péguy's young protégé, Alain-Fournier, author of *Le Grand Meaulnes*, who fell in 1914, despite a promise by Aristide Briand to Alain-Fournier's mistress, the actress Madame Simone, that the young subaltern would be pulled back to a safe posting. A wounded soldier lying in hospital in 1918 listened to a newspaper being read aloud: bulletins from the Front, then an item that Claude Debussy had died. At this the soldier broke into tears. 'A friend of yours?' he was asked, and the other replied, 'Almost a brother.' An amateur musician, he had carried the score of *Pelléas* in his knapsack and during lulls it had been his pleasure to work through the music phrase by phrase.

For the poilu in the trenches, even with its lights dimmed Paris became a symbol, a harmonious city whose long, straight, broad avenues were a visual expression of classicism, whose cafés fed the mind also, fountainhead of innovative refinement, paradigm of civilized living. In reality it had not been quite that, but by contrast with Armageddon it did indeed embody a Golden Age.

Paris as a symbol exerted an even more important influence. By late 1916 the French military effort was beginning to flag, and America was debating whether to enter the war on the side of the nation that had helped her to win her independence. Recent achievements in Paris, not least the work of painters, had won the admiration of discriminating Americans, and they added their influential voices to those of the politicians. Western civilization, they warned, stood at serious risk. In June 1917 the first United States division was to disembark at St Nazaire, none too soon for the hard-pressed French.

One last point is worth making; it stems from Paris's unique reputation in the pre-war years. Tsar Nicholas had been working fast to improve workers' conditions and social welfare. In what is termed his 'Great Experiment' he drew on pioneer work done by Arthur Fontaine, close friend of Jammes and Gide, in international labour agreements, and also on improvements in French working conditions by a series of Radical governments. Yet the war waged by Russia and France with the aim of maintaining the balance of power in Europe perforce halted that 'Great Experiment', thereby precipitating the Bolshevik Revolution of 1917, and changing twentieth-century history. It is perhaps the ultimate paradox.

SOURCES AND NOTES

Introduction

'First to follow Truth . . .'
'France: 1913' in *Rudyard Kipling's Verse* (1943), p.291.
'the way they feel about the dead . . .' G. Stein, *Paris France* (1940), p.13.

CHAPTER 1 *A Bourgeois Civilization*

The look of Paris in 1900 has been preserved in the photographs of Eugène Atget (he took 10,000 in all), who received encouragement from Georges Braque and Maurice Utrillo, and in drawings and engravings in *L'Illustration*. Though on weekdays Parisians crowded the Grands Boulevards, smaller streets, as we see from silent films shot on location, had surprisingly little traffic and few pedestrians. They were like village streets.

Paintings of women by Jean Béraud, the fashion journals, *La Gazette du bon ton* and *Journal des dames et des modes*, show what well-dressed ladies wore, while men's fashions can be studied in portraits by Boldoni and J.E. Blanche and in the caricatures of Sem. Statistics of the city, working hours and so on, are conveniently gathered in Jean Baptiste Duroselle, *La France et les Français 1900–1914* (1972).

Daisy, Princess of Pless, by Herself (1928), is a well-informed if somewhat breathless guide to the differences between social life in Paris, London and Berlin. Paul Morand's *1900* (1936) wittily recalls the lifestyle and parties.

The Danish pavilion at the Paris Exhibition. E.F. Benson, *Final Edition* (1940), p.53. The opening of the Paris Exhibition was reported fully in all newspapers; fast shoddy work to have it ready in time resulted in the collapse of a pedestrian flyover and several deaths.

'*O Claude-Achille Debussy* . . .' *Correspondance de Claude Debussy et Pierre Louÿs: 1893–1904* (1945), p.146.

Misia Natanson, later Misia Edwards. Arthur Gold and Robert Fiedale, *Misia* (1980), which supersedes Misia's own memoir with the same title (1952).

'You could say I've touched . . .'
Pierre Laborde, quoted by
Marie T. Eyquem, *Pierre de
Coubertin* (1966), pp.166–72.

Robert de Montesquiou. Poet of
bats and blue hydrangeas,
model for Huysmans' dilettante des Esseintes, who kept
a jewelled tortoise,
Montesquiou was to a much
smaller degree a part-model
for Proust's Baron de Charlus
(Montesquiou was
narcissistic, not domineering). Montesquiou's mother
was not of the *noblesse*, which
helps to explain the son's
exaggerated snobbery.

CHAPTER 2 *A New Confidence*

For the changing philosophical
background, the major books
named in the text; also L.S.
Crawford, *The Philosophy of
Emile Boutroux* (Cornell
Studies in Philosophy, No.
16, Cornell, 1924); P.
Gaultier, *Les Maîtres de la
pensée française* (1921).

Jean-Paul Lacroix, *Maurice
Blondel, sa vie, son œuvre*
(1963); Blondel et Teilhard
de Chardin, *Correspondance*
(1965).

Of Henri Bergson vignettes
appear in most memoirs by
friends and acquaintances
and he is the subject of a long
chapter in Raissa Maritain,
Les Grandes Amitiés (1962);
see also Jean Guitton, *La
Vocation de Bergson* (1960),
and Jacques Maritain, *La*

Philosophie bergsonienne, rev.
ed. (1930). Madeleine
Barthélemy-Madaule, *Bergson*
(1967) gives a good brief
account of his views.

The séance held by Elisabeth
Greffulhe: L'Abbé Mugnier,
Journal (1985), pp.169–70.

CHAPTER 3 *A New Vigour*

Christopher Andrew, *Théophile
Delcassé and the Making of the
Entente Cordiale* (1968); and
*France Overseas: the Great
War and the Climax of French
Imperial Expansion* (1981).

Delcassé's unpublished letters
to his wife from Russia in the
Archives du Ministère des
Affaires Etrangères reveal his
determination as early as
1900 to keep Germany out of
the Mediterranean and to
increase French territory in
North Africa.

'the practice of subterfuge . . .'
Sir Edmund Monson, dis-
patch of November 1900.

'league anew/With the Goth
. . .' 'The Rowers' (1902).
Rudyard Kipling's Verse
(1943), p.284.

'Although there were considerable crowds . . .' C. Hardinge,
Old Diplomacy (1947), pp.
94–5.

The Moroccan Question:
Charles-André Julien, *Le
Maroc face aux impérialismes
1415–1956* (1978); E.N.
Anderson, *The First Moroccan
Crisis 1904–1906* (Chicago,
1930); Harold Nicolson, *Sir
Arthur Nicolson, Bart., First
Lord Carnock* (1930).

459

On Wilhelm II, *The Diary of Edward Goschen 1900–1914*, edited by Christopher H.D. Howard, Camden fourth series, vol. 25 (1980); M.L.G. Balfour, *The Kaiser and His Times* (1964); Virginia Cowles, *The Kaiser* (1963).

G. Lowes Dickinson, *The International Anarchy 1904–1914* (1926).

'The Tangier incident . . .', V. Cowles, *Edward VII and His Circle* (1956), p.300.

CHAPTER 4 *A Quest for Sincerity: André Gide*

J.E. Blanche's portrait of Gide and his friends is in the Musée de Rouen.

The most important newly published source for Gide's life until the age of forty-five is André Gide et Henri Ghéon, *Correspondance 1897–1944*, two volumes (1976). Details of the journey to Touggourt in 1900–1901 emerge from these letters, and from Madeleine's letters to Gide in J. Schlumberger, *Madeleine et André Gide* (1956), pp.165–7.

'Marriage for Gide . . .' Pierre de Lanux, *Le Figaro littéraire*, 13 December 1952.

'You're in something of a hurry . . .' André Gide et Paul Valéry, *Correspondance 1890–1942* (1955), p.342.

Paul Valéry during our period was working in isolation, hammering out philosophical first principles; he would return to poetry in 1917 with *La Jeune Parque*.

'Nietzsche gambles against himself . . .' Gide-Valéry, *Correspondance*, pp.342–3.

'his tanned face . . .' Francis Jammes, *Caprices du Poète* (1923), pp.197–9.

'For two years after my own conversion . . .' A. Gide, *Journal*, 5 December 1905.

'Yes, Claudel has been of great service . . .' Francis Jammes et André Gide, *Correspondance 1899–1926* (1948), p.236.

'Suddenly I hear a voice . . .' A. Gide, *Journal*, 16 May 1908.

The founding of the *Nouvelle Revue Française* is described by Auguste Anglès, *André Gide et le premier groupe de la Nouvelle Revue Française* (1978).

Gaston Gallimard. Pierre Assouline, *Gaston Gallimard, Un demi-siècle d'édition française* (1985).

CHAPTER 5 *Redemptive Suffering: Paul Claudel*

'the relief and conformation of the earth . . .' P. Claudel, *Œuvre Poétique* (Pléiade edition, 1967), p.67.

'Suddenly my heart was touched . . .' P. Claudel, *Revue de Jeunesse* (1913).

'Monsieur Paul Claudel . . .' Francis Jammes, *Caprices du Poète* (1923), pp. 90–92.

Claudel's affair with R. is well described in H. Guillemin, *Le 'Converti' Claudel* (1968), but many relevant facts and documents still remain a secret of Claudel's heirs.

'Tu es droite . . .' *Partage de Midi*

(1906), ll., 1031 ff.

Berthelot. 'clad in pale alpaca . . .' A. Bennett, letter of 24 June 1915; his *musée secret*: A. Bennett, *Journal*, 26 May 1905. Before his death Berthelot burned his notebooks but the Berthelot archives in Paris contain many letters to him showing his network of friends among intellectuals and artists.

'*J'ai voulu l'âme . . .*' P. Claudel, *Œuvre Poétique* (Pléiade edition, 1967), p.245.

'*L'esprit de joie . . .*', *Idem*, p.250.

'A word exists . . .' *Connaissance de l'Est* (1900), in *Œuvre Poétique*, p.46.

'The Bell', *Œuvre Poétique*, pp.70–72.

'By obliging us . . .' P. Claudel, letter to *Le Temps*, 10 June 1914.

For Claudel, playwright and production adviser: *Claudel, Homme de Théâtre: Correspondance avec Lugné-Poe 1910–1929* (Cahiers Paul Claudel 5, 1964).

'In heaven's name, Gide . . .' P. Claudel et A. Gide, *Correspondance 1899–1926* (1949), p.217.

Camille Claudel's letters, mostly unpublished, are in the archives of the Hôtel Biron.

'Before that miraculous last act . . .' J. Lacouture, *François Mauriac* (1980), p.191.

CHAPTER 6 *Apotheosis through Art: Marcel Proust*

Any biographical portrait of Proust will take as its starting point George D. Painter's meticulously researched *Marcel Proust*. That book has been severely criticized by the Proust scholar Henri Bonnet for its Freudian interpretation of Proust's character, for its emphasis on Proust's feelings of guilt about being Jewish and for its claim that Proust was a practising homosexual. (*Bulletin de la Société des Amis de Marcel Proust et des Amis de Combray*, no. 17, 1967, pp.576–90.)

Furthermore, since Painter three important memoirs have appeared: Marcel Plantevignes, *Avec Marcel Proust: Causeries, souvenirs sur Cabourg et le boulevard Haussmann* (1966); Maurice Duplay, *Mon Ami Marcel Proust: Souvenirs intimes* (1972) and Céleste Albaret, *Monsieur Proust: Souvenirs recueillis par Georges Belmont* (1973). All confirm Bonnet's strictures.

The main evidence that Proust was a practising homosexual is an entry in Gide's Journal for 13 May 1921: 'He [Proust] claims never to have loved women save spiritually and never to have known love except with men.' Since this contradicts so much evidence on the other side, I believe that Gide put his own interpretation on whatever Proust may have said on that occasion: Gide had a tendency to lend his own sexual proclivities to fellow-writers. To my mind the most reliable biography is still that by André Maurois, *A la Recherche de Marcel Proust* (1949), which was written in close consultation with Proust's niece, Suzy Mante Proust. But it needs now to be supplemented by the three books mentioned above as well as by *Le Carnet de 1908* (Cahiers Marcel Proust, n.s. 8; 1976).

The scene in the Casino, summer 1908. Plantevignes, pp.16–18.

The scene in the bar. Plantevignes, pp.19–22.

The challenge to a duel. Plantevignes, pp.99–115.

'I can't possibly tell you . . .' M. Proust, *Correspondance avec sa mère 1887–1905* (1954), p.241.

'It seems to me that I think of you . . .' *Idem*, p.264.

Treatment of asthma. *Larousse Médical Illustré* (1912), pp.100–1.

'An hour is not just an hour . . .' Plantevignes, p.644; cf. p.326.

'Dinner yesterday at the Daudets . . .' Letter to R. Hahn, 15 November 1895.

'Surely, in the field of education . . .' M. Proust, *Textes Retrouvés*, ed. P. Kolb (1965), p.57.

'If the new generation . . .' *Idem*, p.61.

The novel reviewed by Proust was Saussine's *Le Nez de Cléopatre* (1893).

Proust's gallant attitude to women. Duplay, pp.123–4.

'How pretty she must look . . .' Plantevignes, pp.290–1.

'Drops of rain . . .' *Jean Santeuil* (Pléiade edition 1971), p.186.

'You see them in terms of your style of dancing . . .' Plantevignes, p. 63.

'If as you say I'm not a believing Christian . . .' Letter to L. Hauser, August 1914.

'My poor little canary . . .' Céleste Albaret, *Monsieur Proust*, Eng. trans. (1974), p.142. Young Marcel Proust was an altar-boy and devoted to the Blessed Virgin. See the highly important Esquisse LXIV in *A la Recherche du Temps Perdu*, I (new Pléiade edition, 1987), pp.868–71.

'I don't know if it's true . . .' Proust, *Correspondance* XI (1983), p.230.

'by far the most important point . . .' M. Proust, *Matinée chez la Princesse de Guermantes: Cahiers du Temps Retrouvé*, ed. Henri Bonnet (1982), p.331.

Letter to *L'Intransigeant. Lettres retrouvées* (1966), p.144.

'Apparently subjective and dilettante . . .' Letter to Jacques Rivière, cited in P. Kolb, *Choix de Lettres* (1965), p.203.

CHAPTER 7 *The Birth of Cubism: Pablo Picasso*

For Picasso's early life the great indispensable book is Josep Palau i Fabre, Picasso: *Life and Work of the Early Years 1881–1907* (Oxford, 1981), supplemeted now by *Picasso: Sketchbooks*, ed. Arnold and Marc Glimcher (1986).

The letter of Casagemas and Picasso from Paris: Palau i Fabre, *op. cit.*, p.513.

The Bateau Lavoir years: Roland Dorgelès, *Bouquet de Bohême* (1947).

Pierre Dax and Georges Boudaille, *Picasso: The Blue and Rose Periods* (1967).

Fernande Olivier, *Picasso et ses amis* (1933) is a fair, frank and revealing account of Picasso's first long love-affair.

Relations with Gertrude Stein: G. Stein, *Two: Gertrude Stein and Her Brother and Other Early Portraits (1908–1912)* (New Haven, 1951); *Everybody's Autobiography* (1938). Her homosexuality: 'Pablo and Matisse have a maleness that belongs to genius. Moi aussi, perhaps.' Notebook entry when Stein was establishing her liaison with Alice B. Toklas. M. DeKoven, *A Different Language* (Madison, Wis., 1983), p.136.

Max Jacob, *Correspondance* I, ed. François Garnier (1953). 'Artists have been urged . . .' Letter to Jacques Doucet, p.31.

Jacob's poem about Spain: *Le Laboratoire Central* (1921), p.10.

For Guillaume Apollinaire, né Wilhelm Apollinaris de Kostrowitzky, Francis Steegmuller, *Apollinaire, Poet Among the Painters* (1963).

G. Apollinaire, *Alcoöls* (1913). His poem about imprisonment, 'A la Santé', is reprinted in *Œuvres Poétiques* (Pléiade edition, 1956), pp.140–45.

Braque: Propos de l'artiste, recueillis par Dora Vallier (Cahiers d'Art, 1954); John Russell, *Georges Braque* (1959); Jean Leymarie, *Braque* (1961).

CHAPTER 8 *The Harmonious City: Charles Péguy*

The Catholic Revival. Alfred Loisy, *L'Evangile et l'Eglise* (1902) – known as the 'little red book'.

Edouard Le Roy, *Dogme et Critique* (1907).

Marc Sangnier, *Textes* (1958); Jean de Fabrèques, *Le Sillon de Marc Sangnier* (1964); Jeanne Caron, *Le Sillon et la démocratie chrétienne 1894–1910* (1966). Jean Lacouture, *François Mauriac* (1980). Jacques Maritain, *La Philosophie bergsonienne, Etudes-critiques* (1914); G. Phelan, *Jacques Maritain* (1937).

Péguy's main prose works and all his poetry are conveniently collected in the Pléiade series. A sound, if wordy, biography is Daniel Halévy, *Péguy et les Cahiers de la quinzaine* (1943), which may be supplemented by J. and J. Tharaud, *Notre Cher Péguy* (1926). The Tharaud brothers were protégés of Romain Rolland, whose letters and articles contain many references to Péguy, while Raissa Maritain devotes a chapter to her friend in *Les Grandes Amitiés* (1962).

'For the first time since the world began . . .' C. Péguy, *Œuvres en prose* I (1959), p.1068.

'Each person gets the Jews he deserves . . .' Halévy, *op. cit.* Ch. 9 describes Péguy's Jewish friends.

'The strength of Catholicism . . .' Mugnier, *Journal* (1985), p.313.

'O nuit . . .' '*Le Mystère des saints innocents*', in Péguy, *Œuvres Complètes*, vol. 6 (1919), p.111.

CHAPTER 9 *A Music of Nuance: Claude Debussy*

Edward Lockspeiser, *Debussy* (1951); James Harding, *Erik Satie* (1975); Roger Shattuck, *The Banquet Years* (1959), pp.88–145.

'From the tenor to the vendor . . .' A. Bennett, *Paris Nights* (1913), p.67.

'As I listened . . .' M. Garden and L. Biancolli, *Mary Garden's Story* (1952), pp.63–4.

'We did the first act . . .' *Idem*, pp.67–8.

Maeterlinck challenges Debussy to a duel. W.D. Halls, *Maurice Maeterlinck* (1960), pp.76–7.

Dress rehearsal of *Pelléas. Mary Garden's Story*, pp.70–71.

'Sung conversation . . .' J. Renard, *Journal* (1935), p.509.

'As the gentlemen . . .' Fernand Gregh, *L'Age d'Or* (1947), pp.311–12.

Debussy's need to open windows. *Debussy: Notes et Documents* (Revue de Musicologie 1962), p.113.

Structure of *La Mer*. Roy Howat, *Debussy in Proportion* (1983).

Debussy's workroom. Pasteur Vallery-Radot, *Lettres de Claude Debussy à sa femme* (1957), pp.34–5.

'my desire always to go further . . .' *Lettres à deux amis* (1942), p.157.

'One gives orders . . .' *Lettres inédites à André Caplet* (1957), p.38.

'Mon cher Maître . . .' C. Debussy et Gabriele d'Annunzio, *Correspondance Inédite* (1948), p.32.

Debussy's horror of having a God over him. René Peter, *Claude Debussy* (1931), p.103.

'the music makes you believe . . .' E. de Gramont, *Souvenirs du monde* (1966), p.256.

'the infinitely delicate task . . .' I. Benrubi, *Souvenirs sur Henri Bergson* (1942), pp.40–41.

Debussy, *Peter Pan* and Rackham. *Debussy: Notes et Documents* (1962) pp.105-6 (by Paul Hooreman).

CHAPTER 10 *The Russian Connection*

Russians in Paris: Cornelia Otis Skinner, *Elegant Wits and Grand Horizontals* (1963), pp.222-5.

'I kept wondering . . .' Serge Lifar, *Serge Diaghilev* (1940), p.168.

The financing of the Ballets Russes: A. Haskell, *Diaghileff* (1935). See also Richard Buckle, *In Search of Diaghilev* (1955) and *Nijinsky* (1971); Gabriel Astruc, *Le Pavillon des Fantômes* (1929).

Diaghilev's *'Fiant fontes'* at the Châtelet: A. Haskell, *op. cit.*, p.208.

Diaghilev's superstitious habits; A. Haskell, *op. cit.*, p.214.

'Paris never recovered from the fact . . .' Arnold Bennett, *Paris Nights* (1913), p.75.

'Camondo and Benac smiled . . .' A. Haskell, *op. cit.*, p.215.

Scheherazade. 'The eunuchs . pursued . . .' Arnold Bennett, *op. cit.*, pp.75-6. After the performance Bennett walked past a large department store and mentally compared with the seraglio the salesgirls slaving there for a pittance: a very unParisian line of thought.

Le Sacre du Printemps. French interest in primitive religion: for example, 'Essai sur la nature et la fonction du sacrifice', in *L'Année sociologique*, ii (1897).

'The opening bassoon melody . . .' R. Craft, *Igor Stravinsky: Memories and Commentaries* (1960), p.226.

The first night of *Le Sacre*: Pierre Monteux, in M. Lederman, *Stravinsky in the Theatre* (1951), p.129; R. Craft, *Conversations with Igor Stravinsky* (1959), p.60.

Misia Edwards as a patron of music: A. Gold and R. Fiedale, *Misia* (1980).

Auguste Renoir at the ballet: J.E. Blanche, *Propos du Peintre* I (1919), p.240; J. Renoir, *Renoir, My Father* (1964), pp.405-7.

Maurice Ravel. Autobiographical sketch in *La Revue Musicale* (December, 1938); *Ravel au miroir de ses lettres: Correspondance réunie* (1956); Henriette Fauré, *Mon maître Maurice Ravel* (1978); *Ravel Remembered*, edited by Roger Nichols (1987).

Stravinsky contended that Diaghilev commissioned Hahn's *Le Dieu Bleu* because Hahn was 'the salon idol of Paris, and salon support was very useful.' R. Craft, *Igor Stravinsky: Memories and Commentaries* (1960), p.212.

'And this was Russia! . . .' Arnold Bennett, *op. cit.*, p.70.

Cocteau's role as publicist. Francis Steegmuller, *Cocteau: a biography* (1970).

CHAPTER 11 *A World on the Move*

Eve Curie, *Madame Curie* (1938); C. and M. Capez, *Pierre et Marie Curie* (1956); Françoise Giraud, *Une Femme Honorable* (1981).
'Two minerals containing uranium . . .' Eve Curie, *op. cit.*, p.131.
'a new substance . . .' *Idem*, p.136.
Marie's notebooks. *Idem*, p.135.
Notebook entry of 28 March 1902. *Idem*, p.144.
'indicating some damage . . .' *Idem*, p.161.
The automobile. 'In our beautiful avenues . . .' Madame de Caillavet to Brandes, 24 June 1904, in *Correspondance de Georges Brandes* I (Copenhagen, 1952), p.208.
'France as far as automobilism . . .' F. Young, *The Complete Motorist* (1904), p.303.
Octave Mirbeau, *La 628-E8* (1907). 'I owe you many joys . . .' p.5.
Luigi Barzini, *Peking to Paris* (1972).
A. Rhodes, *Louis Renault* (1969).
Aviation. 'And I felt the earth . . .' P. Jullian, *Robert de Montesquiou* (English translation, 1967), p.208; Gabriel Voisin, *Mes dix mille cerfs volants* (1961).
The Duchesse de Rohan and Wilbur Wright. Ghislain de Diesbach, *La Princesse Bibesco 1886–1973* (1986), p.136, quoting Bibesco's unpublished diary.
Dick and Henry Farman, *The Aviator's Companion* (1910); Georges Salel, *Louis Blériot: Notice Biographique* (Cambrai, 1959).

CHAPTER 12 *Parisiennes*

'as soon as a woman has personality . . .' Edith Wharton, *French Ways* (1919), p.117.
'it is because American women . . .' *Idem*, pp.102–3.
'power of absorbed and intellectual attention . . .' Edith Wharton, *A Backward Glance* (1934), p.274.
Marguerite Appell. Camille Marbo (her *nom de plume*), *A Travers deux siècles: Souvenirs et rencontres 1883–1967* (1967).
Abbé Henri Huvelin, *Ecrits spirituels* (1959).
Lady Ripon. I. Stravinsky, *Memories and Commentaries* (1960), pp.36–7.
Anna de Noailles. R. Benjamin, *Sous l'œil en fleur de Madame de Noailles* (1928); C. Du Bos, *La Comtesse de Noailles et le climat du génie* (1949); Mugnier, *Journal* (1985), pp.195–200; 207–14; 323–8.
Colette. Michèle Sarde, *Colette: Free and Fettered* (1981). 'It almost seems that youth . . .', p.161. Virginia Woolf said that human nature changed in or about December 1910; she was thinking of the Bloomsbury set, which then became licentious in its sexual conduct. No one in Paris made such an extrapolation

from Colette's ways. The major change in Parisian attitudes came in the following year: see chapter 16.

'Fashion is the real thing . . .' G. Stein, *Paris France* (1940), p.29.

Paul Poiret, *En habillant l'époque* (1930); his luxury books: *Les Robes de Paul Poiret, Les Choses de Paul Poiret*.

'I am ashamed of being only a man . . .' Louis Gillet in a letter to Rolland (*Cahiers Romain Rolland* 2, 1949), p.179. In October 1902 Gillet was to make a love marriage.

Madame Cruppi. She was encouraged in her feminist crusade by Romain Rolland; I have drawn on her correspondence with him in the Fonds Romain Rolland, Bibliothèque Nationale.

CHAPTER 13 *Theatre: the Sublime and the Ridiculous*

Sarah Bernhardt: the most reliable biography is by Louis Verneuil, a playwright who became Sarah's grandson-in-law and had access to family papers: *The Fabulous Life of Sarah Bernhardt* (1942). On this I have drawn heavily and to it am much indebted. Cornelia Otis Skinner's already mentioned *Elegant Wits and Grand Horizontals* (1963) is highly diverting but accepts uncritically many of the legends that grew round the actress.

Theatre censorship had been introduced in 1398 by royal decree, abolished in 1791, reimposed in 1793, abolished in 1848, reimposed in 1871, the Minister of Education and Arts being held responsible for administering it. Zola supported censorship on moral grounds. The censor could ban a play if it threatened national security or France's international relations, if it incited to crime or if it defamed a living person. Censorship was abolished in 1906 not as a result of pressure for more freedom but merely because the Assembly declined to vote the censors' annual remuneration. From 1906 the mayor became responsible for the theatre in his city in the name of public order. In England, meanwhile, in 1909 after a governmental inquiry it was decided to retain the existing system, which had prevented the public staging of Ibsen's *Ghosts*, Brieux's *Maternité* and many more.

Tristan Bernard: biographies by R. Blum (1925) and Jean Jacques Bernard (1955). 'The first day of Creation . . .' Tristan Bernard, *Contes, répliques et bons mots*, ed. Patrice Boussel (1964), pp.10–11.

Flers and Caillavet, *Le Roi* (1908).

Georges Feydeau, *Théâtre complet*, 9 vols (1948–56).

'to use a metaphor . . .' F. W. Chandler, *The Contemporary Drama of France* (1920), p.136.

The early French cinema: Georges Sadoul, *Histoire générale du cinéma*, vol. 2 (1948); M. Bardèche and R. Basillach, *Histoire du cinéma* (1935).

G. Apollinaire, *La Bréhantine. Cinéma-drame* (Paris: Lettres Modernes, 1971).

'M. Ollinger-Jacob . . .' E. Satie, *Ecrits* (1981), p.129.

CHAPTER 14 *Celebration with Colour*

Raymond Escholier, *Matisse, ce vivant* (1956).

Gertrude Stein, *Tender Buttons* (New York, 1914).

Alfred Werner, *Raoul Dufy* (1970); Maurice Laffaille, *Raoul Dufy: catalogue raisonné de l'œuvre peinte* (1972).

André Derain, *Lettres à Vlaminck* (1955); Maurice de Vlaminck, *Tournant dangereux. Souvenirs de ma vie* (1929).

'You are the world's greatest painter . . .' Michel Georges-Michel, *From Renoir to Picasso* (1957), pp.144–5.

Flora Groult, *Marie Laurencin* (1987).

CHAPTER 15 *Attitudes to Germany*

E. Tonnelat, *Charles Andler. Sa vie et son œuvre* (Strasbourg, 1937); Charles Andler, *Vie de Lucien Herr 1864–1926* (1932).

Richard Strauss et Romain Rolland, *Correspondance, Fragments de Journal* (*Cahiers Romain Rolland* 3; Paris, 1951): 'There is too much music in Germany': p.219; 'che – veux': p.55; Strauss looked 'like . . . one of those Huns that settled in Germany': p.149.

'In the history of Europe . . .' Rolland, *Correspondance avec Louis Gillet* (*Cahiers Romain Rolland* 2, 1949), pp.111–12.

Georges Brandes, *Correspondance* I (Copenhagen, 1952): letter to Madame de Caillavet of 26 December 1903, and her reply, 18 January 1904 (pp.199–201).

On Jaurès, the biographies by M. Auclair (1959) and by John H. Jackson, *Jean Jaurès. His Life and Work* (1943).

CHAPTER 16 *Preparations for a Duel*

Joseph Caillaux, *Agadir* (1919); Jean-Claude Allain, *Caillaux, le défi victorieux 1863–1914* (1978).

'Ours is only one manifestation . . .' J. Richepin, in *Le Figaro*, 14 June 1911.

'We are witnessing . . .' C. Péguy, *L'Argent Suite*, in *Œuvres Complètes*, XIV (1932), p.183.

Revealing of values in the Barrès-Noailles-Bucher set are Henri Franck, *Lettres à quelques amis* (1926).

'In listening to such proposals . . .' R. Poincaré, *Le Lendemain d'Agadir* (1926), p.126.

'When we Frenchmen go in for vice,' O. Mirbeau, *La 628-E8* (1907), pp.409–10.

'Charles du Bos . . .' Mugnier, *Journal* (1985), p.146.

'The country now understands . . .' A. Tardieu, *Le Mystère d'Agadir* (1912), p.605.

The long title of Agathon's influential book published in 1913 sums up undergraduate aims: *Les Jeunes Gens d'aujourd'hui: Le goût de l'action – La foi patriotique. – Une renaissance catholique. – Le réalisme politique.*

'Men, women and children . . .' S. Zweig, *The World of Yesterday* (1943), p.164.

Raymond Poincaré, *The Origins of the War* (1922), but see Gordon Wright, *Raymond Poincaré and the French Presidency* (1942), who disputes Poincaré's claim that he had virtually no freedom of action.

For events of 1912-14, *Collected Diplomatic Documents relating to the outbreak of the European War* (1915).

The shooting of Gaston Calmette: newspaper reports of the trial and the verdict; René Floriot, *Deux Femmes en Cour d'Assises: Madame Steinheil et Madame Caillaux* (1966).

CHAPTER 17 *Paris at War*

Wilhelm II's activities, foreign policy statements, telegram and confidences. Virginia Cowles, *The Kaiser* (1963); *The Diary of Edward Goschen 1900-1914*, edited by Christopher H.D. Howard. Camden fourth series, vol. 25 (1980).

'If . . . the Emperor of Russia adhere . . .' Lord Bertie, *Diary*, I (1924), p. 2.

The Kaiser's nervousness. *The Intimate Papers of Colonel House*, I (1926), p.255.

'that the assassination . . .' Goschen, p.289.

'The moment has passed . . .' Crowe, in *Collected Diplomatic Documents relating to the outbreak of the European War* (1915).

'My poor Mère Cordier . . .' *Bibliothèque de Travail*, No. 960 (1984).

'Beautiful to fight . . .' Louis Gillet, *Correspondance avec Romain Rolland* (1949), p.289.

'What a country we are . . .' *Idem*, p.299.

'The wonderful behaviour of the government . . .' André Gide, *Journal*, 6 August 1914.

'My chief feeling . . .' Thomas Mann, *Letters* 1889-1955 (1970), p.70.

'Millions of men . . .' Marcel Proust to Lionel Hauser, 1 August 1914.

'Every day sees the residents . . .' M.E. Clarke, *Paris Waits* (1915), p. 50.

'*J'ai vu ce mort puissant . . .*'

Anna de Noailles, *Les Forces Eternelles* (1920), p.41.

'*Ici même les automobiles . . .*' Guillaume Apollinaire, *Œuvres poétiques* (Pléiade edition, 1956), p.39.

'We have had the most frightful shelling . . .' Gillet, *op. cit.*, p.299.

'I can see only one meaning . . .' Gillet, *op. cit.*, p.300.

Max Jacob's conversion. *Correspondance* I (1953), pp.37–9.

'As long as there is living French meat . . .' Paul Claudel, *Œuvre poétique* (Pléiade edition 1967) '*Tant que vous voudrez, mon général*', pp.533–35.

The Abbé Mugnier's comments on the war, *Journal* (1985), pp.269, 272, 276.

German restlessness largely due to thwarted energy. Harold Nicolson, *Sir Arthur Nicolson, Bart.* (1930), p.290.

Norman Angell, *The Great Illusion* (1910).

George F. Kennan, *Fateful Alliance: France, Russia and the Coming of the First World War* (Manchester, 1984), p.257. For an alternative interpretation, V.G. Berghahn, *Germany and the Approach of War in 1914* (1973): Berghahn argues that Germany's militarism was to a considerable degree a response to alarming internal pressures on the monarchy.

Nicholas II's 'Great Experiment'. Kyril FitzLyon and Tatiana Browning, *Before the Revolution: A View of Russia under the Last Tsar* (1977).

INDEX

471

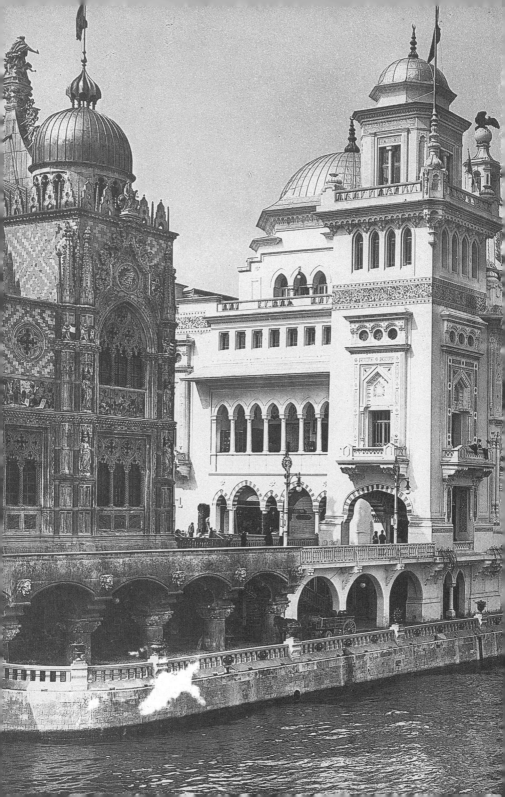